THE

Vestry Book and Register

OF

BRISTOL PARISH, VIRGINIA,

1720—1789.

TRANSCRIBED AND PUBLISHED

BY

CHURCHILL GIBSON CHAMBERLAYNE.

CLEARFIELD

Originally published
Richmond, Virginia, 1898

Reprinted for
Clearfield Company, Inc. by
Genealogical Publishing Co., Inc.
Baltimore, Maryland
1999

International Standard Book Number: 0-8063-4843-7

Made in the United States of America

LIST OF SUBSCRIBERS.

R. B. Abernethy, Gonzales, Texas.
Charles W. Alban, St. Louis, Mo.
L. D. Alexander, New York, N. Y.
Henry T. Alley, New York, N. Y.
Walter S. Alley, New York, N. Y.
Archer Anderson, Richmond, Va.
Mrs. C. Archer, Varina Grove, Va.
W. T. Armistead, Richmond, Va.
Miss Cary Atkinson, Charles Town, W. Va.
John Wilder Atkinson, Wilmington, N. C.
John W. Atkinson, Jr., Richmond, Va.
William M. Atkinson, Gonzales, Texas.
Robert Atkinson, Baltimore, Md.
Samuel P. Avery, New York, N. Y.
L. D. Aylett, Richmond, Va.
Mrs. George W. Bagby, Richmond, Va.
T. Lewis Banister, New Hartford, N. Y.
George A. Barksdale, Richmond, Va.
R. T. Barton, Winchester, Va.
W. H. Baxter, Petersburg, Va.
T. S. Beckwith, Petersburg, Va.
Bell Book and Stationery Co., Richmond, Va.
Mrs. John Eldridge Bentley, McMinnville, Tenn.
Bishop of Ohio, Cleveland, Ohio.
Charles M. Blackford, Lynchburg, Va.
William Root Bliss, Short Hills, N. J.
Miss Anna D. Bolling, Weisbaden, Germany.
William F. Boogher, Washington, D. C.
James N. Boyd, Richmond, Va.
John W. Brodnax, Manchester, Va.
Alexander Brown, Norwood, Va.
J. Wilcox Brown, Baltimore, Md.
Philip A. Bruce, Richmond, Va.
Mrs. Joseph Bryan, Richmond, Va.
Mary A Bulkley, Rye, N. Y.
Robert Mosby Burton, St. Louis, Mo.
H. H. Cabaniss, Atlanta, Ga.
J. W. Cabaniss, Macon, Ga.
G. C. Callahan, Philadelphia, Pa.
P. R. Carrington, Richmond, Va.
J. R. Cary, Richmond, Va.
Wilson Miles Cary, Baltimore, Md.
Joseph J. Casey, New York, N. Y.
Jno. Hampden Chamberlayne, Jr., Richmond, Va.
Philip E. Chappell, Kansas City, Mo.
Gracey Childers, Clarksville, Tenn.
J. H. Claiborne, New York, N. Y.
M. H. Clark, Clarksville, Tenn.
Peyton N. Clarke, Louisville, Ky.
Odin G. Clay, St Paul, Minn
Miss Mary C. Clemens, St. Louis, Mo.
H. Clement, Fort Leavenworth, Kan.
T. E. Coffin, Talley, Va.
C. W. Coleman, Williamsburg, Va.
Fulton Colville, Atlanta, Ga.
Holmes Conrad, Winchester, Va.
S. Victor Constant, New York, N. Y.
J. C. Courtney, Atlanta, Ga.
William Cox, Manchester, Va.
Isaac Craig, Alleghany, Pa.
James T. Crocker, Portsmouth, Va.
F. C. Cross, Luling, Texas.
E. R. Crutcher, Kansas City, Mo.
Holmes Cummins, Memphis, Tenn.
R. H. Dabney, University of Va.
Pascal Davie, Richmond, Va.
Benjamin Dennis, Manchester, Va.
George W. Dewey, New York, N. Y.
J A. Dibrell, Little Rock, Ark.
R. T. W. Duke, Jr , Charlottesville, Va.
Mrs. Mary E. Dunlop, Petersburg, Va.
Mrs. Medora DuVal, Fort Smith, Ark.
Jno. C. Easley, Richmond, Va.
G. G. Eaton, Washington, D C.
William H. Egle, Harrisburg, Pa.
Mrs. Richard Eppes, City Point, Va.
Merritt Eslick, Jr., Pulaski, Tenn.
Nathan Eubank, Heron, Tenn.
J. P. Fitzgerald, Farmville, Va.
S. W. Fleming, Harrisburg, Pa.
George Foy, Dublin, Ireland.
Miss Rosa Freeman, Austin, Texas.
Mrs. Theo. K Gibbs, Newport, R. I.
Miss Katherine Gibson, Baltimore, Md.
Robert A. Gibson, Richmond, Va.
W. W. Gillette, Petersburg, Va.
C. M. Gilliam, Petersburg, Va.
R. D. Gilliam, Petersburg, Va.
Robert Gilliam, Petersburg, Va.
F. P. Glass, Montgomery, Ala.
Armistead C. Gordon, Staunton, Va.
B. W. Green, Richmond, Va.
Miss Lucy F. Green, Columbia, S. C.
R. B. Green, Richmond, Va.
Daniel Grinnan, Richmond, Va.
Joseph A. Groves, Orrville, Ala.
Jno C Hagan, Richmond, Va.
Alexander Hamilton, Petersburg, Va.
R. A. Hardaway, Tuscaloosa, Ala.
W. A. Hardaway, St. Louis, Mo.
J. C. Hardeman, Macon, Ga.
Henry C. Hardy, New York, N. Y.
Jno. T. Harris, Jr., Harrisonburg, Va.
Mrs. Geo E. Harrison, Morristown, N. J.
Mrs. J. W. Harrison, Richmond, Va.
J. R. Harwell, Nashville, Tenn.
Horace Edw. Hayden, Wilkes-Barre, Pa.
John D. Horsley, Lynchburg, Va.
A. S. Hughes, Denver, Colo.
Charles J. Hughes, Jr. Denver, Colo.
Frank Hume, Washington, D. C.
Charles Hare Hutchinson, Philadelphia, Pa.
Edward Ingle, Baltimore, Md.
Richard Irby, Ashland, Va.
Edward W. James, Richmond, Va
Francis Marion Jefferson Little Rock, Ark.
George C. Jefferson, Richmond, Va.
Christopher Johnston, Baltimore, Md.
Miss Mary Johnston, Birmingham, Ala.
Wm. Jolliffe, Buchanan, Va.
Mrs. A. B. Jones, Mobile, Ala.
Geo. F. Judah, Saint Jago de la Vega, Jamaica.
R. G. H. Kean, Lynchburg, Va.
Margaret A. Kearney, Perth Amboy, N. J.
A. M. Keiley, Alexandria, Egypt.
Mrs. Aldine S. Kieffer, Dayton, Va.
Geo. W. Kirkman, Fort Russell, Wy.
Lucian L. Knight, Atlanta, Ga.
Mrs. Wm. H. Lambert, Germantown, Philadelphia, Pa.

James H. Lane, Auburn, Ala.
Chas. Trotter Lassiter, Petersburg, Va.
Mrs. Eliza W. Lay, Baltimore, Md.
James A. Leach, Richmond, Va.
Wm. J. Leake, Richmond, Va.
Edmund J. Lee, Philadelphia, Pa.
E. G. Leigh, Jr., Richmond, Va.
Libraries:
- Bronson, Waterbury, Conn.
- Cincinnati Public, Cincinnati, Ohio.
- Cossitt, Memphis, Tenn.
- East Lynnhaven Parish, Va. Beach, Va.
- Free Public, Worcester, Mass.
- General Theological Seminary, New York, N. Y.
- Harvard College, Cambridge, Mass.
- Library of Congress, Washington, D. C.
- Long Island Historical Society, Brooklyn, N. Y.
- Maine Historical Society, Portland, Me.
- Maryland Historical Society, Baltimore, Md.
- Mercantile, New York, N. Y.
- Minnesota Historical Society, St. Paul, Minn.
- New York Genealogical and Biographical Society, New York, N. Y.
- New York Historical Society, New York, N. Y.
- New York Public New York, N. Y.
- Norfolk Public, Norfolk, Va.
- Ohio State, Columbus, Ohio.
- Peabody Institute, Baltimore, Md.
- Pennsylvania Historical Society, Philadelphia, Pa.
- Pennsylvania State, Harrisburg, Pa.
- Petersburg Benevolent Mechanics Association, Petersburg, Va.
- Richmond College, Richmond, Va.
- Syracuse Central, Syracuse, N. Y.
- Virginia Historical Society, Richmond, Va.
- Virginia State, Richmond, Va.
- William and Mary College, Williamsburg, Va.
- Wisconsin Historical Society, Madiison, Wis.
- Wyoming Historical-Geological Society, Wilkes-Barre, Pa.
- Yale University, New Haven, Conn

Mrs. Mary C. Lightfoot, Opelika, Ala.
John S. Logan, St. Joseph, Mo.
Leslie Longley, St. Louis, Mo.
Heth Lorton, New York, N. Y
Mrs. William Lee Lyons, Louisville, Ky.
Geo. Norbury Mackenzie, Baltimore, Md.
James S. Mackie, Newark, N. J
Mrs. Charles Marshall, Baltimore, Md.
William Puryear Massie, City of Mexico, Mexico.
Joel Munsell's Sons, Albany, N. Y.
Hu Maxwell, Morgantown, W. Va.
P. H. Mayo, Richmond, Va.
Mrs. Eleanor Childs Meehan, Covington, Ky.
P. G. Miller, Goochland C. H., Va.
S. P. Mitchell, Petersburg, Va.
Mrs. A. R. Mixon, Mobile, Ala.
Noah Farnham Morrison, Newark, N. J.
Mrs. Portia L. Morrison, Farmville, Va.
John Morton, Richmond, Va.
Beverly B. Munford, Richmond, Va.
Miss Mattie P. Myers, Richmond, Va.
W. Gordon McCabe, Richmond, Va.
W. B. McIlwaine, Petersburg, Va
Miss Junia McKinley, Atlanta, Ga.
W. V. Nance, Elkhorn, W. Va.
Herbert M. Nash, Norfolk, Va.
Miss Annie Belle Northen, Atlanta, Ga.
William W. Old, Norfolk, Va.
D. Wilmer Orr, Petersburg, Va.
Allin Browder Owen, Evansville, Ind.
Henry T. Owen, Richmond, Va
Thomas M. Owen, Carrollton, Ala.
J. B. Pace, Richmond, Va.
Mann Page, Brandon, Va.
Mrs. John Paul, Harrisonburg, Va.
William J. Payne, Richmond, Va.
John C. Pegram, Providence, R I.
Ann Eliza Atkinson Pleasants, Galveston, Texas.
Robert Atkinson Pleasants, Cuero, Texas.
William P. Poythress, Richmond, Va.
Thomas R. Price, New York, N. Y.
Charles L. Pullen, New Orleans, La.
G. P. Putnam's Sons, New York, N. Y.
Mann S. Quarles, Richmond, Va.
Ro. W. Rainey, Petersburg, Va.
Thomas Wallis Rainey, Harrodsburg, Ky.
George H. Richmond & Co , New York, N. Y.
Flournoy Rivers, Pulaski, Tenn.
P. G. Robert, St. Louis, Mo.
Mrs. Sarah Jennie Roberts, Pulaski, Tenn.
Leigh Robinson, Washington, D. C.
Thos. L Rosser, Charlottesville, Va.
A. S. Salley, Jr , Orangeburg, S. C.
Edward W. Scott, Jr., Richmond, Va.
Mrs. O D. Smith, Auburn, Ala.
R. K. Smith, Leavenworth, Kan.
W. G. Stanard, Richmond, Va.
B F. Stevens, London, England.
Miss. A C. Stewart, Brook Hill Va.
Mrs. John Stewart, Brook Hill, Va
F. E. Stith, Mobile, Ala
W. E Stith, Washington, D. C.
Henry Stockbridge, Baltimore, Md.
Mrs. Wm. C. Stubbs, New Orleans, La.
Tazewell T. Talley, Columbia, S. C.
H. L. Taylor, Bentonia, Miss.
Jordan S. Thomas, Charlotte, N. C.
R C. Thruston Ballard, Louisville, Ky.
Miss Elizabeth Bailey Traylor, Forest Home Ga.
F. B. Traylor, Barton Heights, Va.
George Archer Traylor, Crawford, N. J.
John A. Traylor, Richmond, Va.
John H. Traylor, Dallas, Texas.
Ro: Lee Traylor, Richmond, Va.
Benj B. Valentine, Richmond, Va.
Edward P. Valentine, Richmond, Va.
Granville G. Valentine, Richmond, Va.
Mann S. Valentine, Jr., Richmond, Va.
Mrs. Sarah Bowman Van Ness, East Lexington, Mass
B. B. Vaughan, Petersburg, Va.
Fielding Vaughan, Mobile, Ala.
Selden Walke, Richmond, Va.
Legh R. Watts, Portsmouth, Va.
George M. West, Richmond, Va
J. B. White, Kansas City, Mo.
Mrs. Fielding Lewis Williams, Bristol, R. I.
T. C. Williams, Jr., Richmond, Va.
Miss Virginia Williamson, Gardiner, Me.
Edgar S. Wilson, Macon, Ga.
Woodrow Wilson, Princeton, N J
Charles E Wingo, Richmond, Va.
Barton H. Wise, Richmond, Va.
W. A. Witherspoon, Petersburg, Va.
E. A Young, Richmond, Va.
John D. Young, Louisville, Ky.

PREFACE.

Bristol Parish, Virginia, was established in the year 1643 by Act of the House of Burgesses.

The manuscript volume here reproduced, contains the earliest records of this parish known to be in existence. Copious extracts from it were taken by Dr. Slaughter and embodied in his "History of Bristol Parish." The minutes of all vestry meetings from October 30, 1720 to April 18, 1789 are complete except for the period between October 28, 1722 and November 11, 1723. Two leaves of the manuscript are here missing. The earliest recorded date in the register of births, baptisms and deaths is April 12, 1685; the latest, March 9, 1798.

For many years the book was generally supposed to be lost. During the year 1894, however, it came to light in the library of the late Reverend Churchill J. Gibson, of Petersburg, Virginia, where it had been most probably ever since 1848. (See p. 344.)

The volume is a folio eleven by fifteen inches in size and contains three hundred and twenty-four written pages. The water mark in the paper is a *fleur de lis*, surmounted by a crown, over the initials L. V. G.

In the preparation of the copy for the printer, care was taken to follow the original in every eccentricity of spelling and abbreviation and in all mistakes. With the exception of the variations noted on page 396, this is as accurate a reproduction of the manuscript as types will make. Wherever brackets occur in the work, the corresponding portion of the manuscript is either illegible or worn away by time and use. An intentional omission in the original is indicated by a blank space or a dash.

The following publications are suggested as helpful to any seeking further information respecting Bristol Parish:

The History of Virginia from its First Settlement to the Present Day. Commenced by John Burk and continued by Skelton Jones and Louis Hue Girardin. Vols. I-IV, 8vo. Petersburg, 1804-16.

The Life of the Reverend Devereux Jarratt, Rector of Bath Parish, Dinwiddie county, Virginia, written by himself in a series of letters addressed to Reverend John Coleman. 12mo. Baltimore, 1806.

The Statutes at Large; Being a Collection of All the Laws of Virginia, from the First Session of the Legislature in the Year 1619. Vol. I-XIII, 8vo. By William Waller Hening. Richmond, 1809-23.

References:

Vol. I, page 251. The parish established. Page 424. Court ordered to be held.

Vol. 4, page 95. Chapel ordered to be erected. Page 443. Dale formed from Henrico and Bristol. Page 467. Raleigh formed from Bristol and St. Andrew. Page 525. Ordered to pay back to Raleigh and Dale, tobacco levied for building Brick Church.

Vol. 5, page 212. Bath formed from Bristol. Page 261 Part of Bath re-incorporated in Bristol.

Vol. 7, page 143. Glebe in Dale ordered to be sold and one-half of the money to be paid to Bristol Page 613. Boundary between Bristol and Martin's Brandon settled.

Vol. 8, page 431. Impowered to sell Glebe.

The Bland Papers; being a Selection from the Manuscripts of Colonel Theodorick Bland, Jr., of Prince George County, Virginia. To which are prefixed an Introduction and a Memoir of Colonel Bland. Edited by Charles Campbell. Vols. I-II, 8vo. Petersburg, 1840-43.

Historical Collections of Virginia; containing a Collection of the Most Interesting Facts, Traditions, Biographical Sketches, Anecdotes, Etc., relating to its History and Antiquities. By Henry Howe. 8vo. Charleston, 1845.

A History of Bristol Parish, with a Tribute to the Memory of its Oldest Rector, and an Appendix containing the Epitaphs of Some of its Early Officers and Friends. By the Rev. Philip Slaughter, the present incumbent. Richmond, 1846.

The History of the Church of England in the Colonies and Foreign Dependencies of the British Empire. By the Rev. James S. M. Anderson. Vols. I-II, 8vo. London, 1848. 2d Ed., Vols. I-III, 12mo. London, 1856.

Old Churches, Ministers and Families of Virginia. By Bishop Meade. Vols. I-II, 8vo. Philadelphia, 1857.

History of the Colony and Ancient Dominion of Virginia. By Charles Campbell. 8vo. Philadelphia, 1860.

A History of Bristol Parish, Va., with Genealogies of Families Connected therewith and Historical Illustrations. By Rev. Philip Slaughter, D. D. 2d Ed. Richmond, 1879.

William and Mary College Quarterly Historical Magazine. Vol. V, page 230. Vol. VI, page 18. Nos. for April and July, 1897.

Inscriptions in Blandford Churchyard. (The Brick Church on Wells's Hill.)

The student of the history of this section of Virginia should consult the manuscript Land Patents which are preserved, continuous from about 1623, in the Capitol at Richmond, and such fragments of the early manuscript records of Henrico and Prince George Counties as have been preserved. The Dinwiddie County Records were destroyed by fire about 1823.

My obligations to my brother, John Hampden Chamberlayne, Jr., for material aid in compiling the index, and to Mr. Robert Lee Traylor for many helpful suggestions during the progress of the work are here acknowledged.

CHURCHILL GIBSON CHAMBERLAYNE.

Richmond, Va., August 20, 1898.

VESTRY BOOK.

Bristoll P'ish—ss: At A Vestry called At the Chappell Octob^{r} 30th—1720.

Present. Mr. Geo. Roberson Minister, Maj^{r} Robt Bolling Church-warden, Maj^{r} Robt Munford, Maj^{r} Wm. Kennon, Capt Peter Jones, Capt Hen. Randolph, Mr. Inst. Hall, Capt Rich. Kennon, Mr. Luis Green, Junr, Mr. Tho. Bott.

Whereas John Ellis son of Jno Ellis Junr by Acsident had his Legg brook his father being at the time A Trading wth Indians it was then ordrd by the Vestry that John West should take care of the fores'd Ellis & Employ a Doct^{r} to Cure the same. The father of the s'd Lad returning & refusing to pay the Doct^{rs} demands The s'd Docter refusing to do any more to the cure, but leaving him in a lame Condition & his legg perishing. Upon Complaint Tis ordrd By this Vestry That Maj^{r} Robt Bolling now being Church-warden take care of the fores'd Lad & Agree with some Docter to cure the same And his Agreem^{t} to be Allowed by the P'ish on the Account of John Ellis Junr Father of the fores'd Lad.

Test CHA. ROBERTS C^{lk} Vest^{r}.

Bristoll P'ish—ss: At A Vestry held at the Chappell Xb^{r} 7th 1720.

Present. Mr. Geo. Robertson Minist^{r}, Maj^{r} Robt Bolling, Mr. Geo. Wilson Church-wardens, Capt Peter Jones, Maj^{r} Wm. Kennon, Mr. Luis Green, Mr. Tho. Bott.

Madam Anne Bolling haveing two negroes by name Kinney & Doll both disabled from work prays they may be Acquitted from paying P'ish Levies, is granted. Tho. Andrews being Anciant & Craysey & not Able to Work is Acquitted from paying P'ish Levies.

John Moor Minor being old & not Able to Work is Acquitted from paying P'ish Levies. Andrew Crawfoot being not Able to work is Acquitted from paying P'ish Levies for the ensuing year.

Robt Glascock being upwards of 60 years old & lame is Acquitted from paying P'ish Levies. Cha. Gillam being lame of his hands & feet is Acquitted from paying P'ish Levies for ye future.

Majr Wm. Kennon is ordrd to be Church-warden for the Nort-side Bristoll P'ish. Mr. Luis Green is ordrd to be Church-warden for the sout-side Bristoll P'ish.

Margaret Micabin servt to Mr. David Crawley having a bastard Child Mr. Crawley prays the Gentlemen of this Vestry to bind out the s'd Child as they think fitt. It is ordrd by the Vestry that the Church-wardens bind out the s'd Child named John Sadler born the 26th July last 1720. The fores'd Child is by indenture bound unto Mr. David Crawley to serve according to Law.

Mr. Tho. Bott haveing an orphant boy bound to him by his mother desires the same may be confirm'd By this Vestry.

Tis ordr that ye s'd boy be bound by Indenture to Serve to ye Age of 21 years he now being three years old. the fores'd boy is Named Mark Melthon & is bound unto Mr. Tho. Bott & his Heirs by Indenture as afores'd.

Test CHA. ROBERTS Clk Vestr.

(2) Bristoll P'ish—ss: At A Vestry Held At the Chappell Xbr 17th—1720.

Pr'sent. Mr. Geo. Robertson Ministr, Majr Wm. Kennon, Mr. Luis Green Church-wardens, Majr Robt Bolling, Capt Hen. Randolph, Capt Peter Jones, Mr. Tho. Bott, Mr. Inst. Hall, Mr. Geo. Wilson.

It is ordered that the ferry be continued to Mrs. Eliz. Kennon the next Ensuing years as formerly.

It is ordered that Daniell Glidwell being an Idiot is Acquitted from paying levies. It is ordered that the Child Widow Bass now hath nursing for ye P'ish be bound out by Indenture to ye fores'd Widdow Bass by the Church-wardens.

Majr Robt Bolling is required & ordered Collector for the South-side Bristoll P'ish. Mr. Geo. Wilson is required & ordered Collector for ye north side Bristoll P'ish.

Bristoll P'ish Dr.	℔ tobb.	
To Mr. Geo. Robertson Minister,	16,000	Casq.
To Mr. Tho. Bott Readr &c.	2,100	168
To Mrs. Eliz. Kennon for keeping the ferry,	2,500	200
To Cha. Roberts Clk Vestry,	400	32
To Hen. Tatam for setting the psalms,	500	40
To Widow Bass for keeping an orphan Child,	720	58
To Majr Wm. Kennon for A Regester Book,	400	32
To John West for keeping Jno Ellis Junr his son 4 months &c.	1,000	80
To Doctr Joss Irby for Ellis his son tendance & cure,	2,000	160
To Cha. Roberts for taking down & putting up ye Chap. Wind.	50	4
To. Majr Robt Bolling for Insolvents,	549	
	26,219	774
To Cask for 9,670 at 8 ꝑ C. is	774	
To sall. at 10 ꝑ C.	2,622	
due to the P'ish,	65	
	29,680	

ꝑ Cont'r Cr.

By 848 tithables at 35 ꝑ pole is 29,680.

It is ordrd And Mr. Luis Green Church-Warden is here by Impow'red by this Vestry To Attach & seese so much of the Estate of John Ellis Junr to the Vallue of three Thousand pounds of tobb. & Casq with Cost And make return to the Vestry of the same.

The Above Account proportioned as followeth:

South side.	℔ tobb.	
To Mr. Geo. Robertson Ministr,	11,000	Cask.
To Mr. Tho. Bott Readr,	1,400	112
To Doctr Joss Irby,	2,000	160
To John West,	1,000	80
To Cha. Roberts,	450	36
To Hen. Tatam,	500	40

To Mrs. Eliz. Kennon,	1,000	80
To Maj^{r} Robt Bolling,	549	
	17,899	508
To sall,	1,789	
To Casq,	508	
	20,196	
Cont^{r} C^{r},		
By 577 tithable at 35 ℔ pole,	20,195	

It is ordered by the Vestry & Maj^{r} Robt Bolling is hereby Impow'red to Collect, receive & recover of the above 577 tithables 35^{lb} tobb. ℔ pole by distress or other-wise & to make good paym^{t} as above rend'ring Acco^{t} to ye Vestry & no arrears.

Test CHA. ROBERTS Cl^{k} Vestry.

NORTH SIDE.

To Mr. Geo. Robertson Minist^{r},	5,000	Cas.
To Mr. Tho. Bott,	700	56
To Widow Bass,	720	58
To Maj^{r} Wm. Kennon,	400	32
To Mrs. Eliz. Kennon,	1,500	120
	8,320	266
To sall,	832	
To Casq,	266	
due to this P'ish,	67	
	9,485	
Contr.		
By 271 tithables at 35 ℔ pole,	9,485	

It is ordered by the Vestry and Mr. George Wilson is hereby Impow'red to Collect, receive & recover, of the above 271 tithables 35^{lb} tobb. ℔ pole by distress or other-wise & to make good payment as above rend'ring Acco^{t} to the Vestry & no Arrears.

Test CHA. ROBERTS C^{lk} Vest^{r}.

(3) Bristoll P'ish—ss: At A Vestry Called At the Chappell Jan. 8th—17$\frac{20}{21}$.

Present. Mr. Geo. Robertson Minist^{r}, Maj^{r} Wm. Kennon Church-warden, Maj^{r} Robt Bolling, Mr. Tho. Bott, Maj^{r} Robt Munford, Mr. Geo. Wilson.

It is ordered That Maj^{r} Robt Bolling do Agree with Wm. Davis to take care [&] provide for Wm. Fisher being old Impotent & lame And what the s'd Bolling doth Agree for to be Allowed by this P'ish.

And is ordered That Maj^{r} Wm. Kennon do Agree with Hen. Vodin or whom he sh[all] think fitt to take care & provide for Wm. Dodson sen^{r} being old & Impotent, And what th[e] s'd Kennon doth Agree for to be Allowed by this P'ish.

Test CHA. ROBERTS C^{lk} Vest^{r}.

Bristoll P'ish—ss: At A Vestry Called At the Chapple June 18th—1721.

Present. Mr. Geo. Robertson Minist^{r}, Maj^{r} Wm. Kennon Church-warden, Maj^{r} Robt Bolling, Capt Rich. Kennon, Maj^{r} Robt Munford, Mr. Geo. Archer, Capt Peter Jones, Mr. Tho. Bott, Mr. Geo. Wilson.

It is ordered that John Walker being poor & Impotent, be acquitted from paying P'ish Levies. And it is further ordered that William Fisher he now being a charge to this P'ish, hath A desire to goe to England. Maj^{r} Robt Munford is by this Vestry desir'd & ord'red to Agree & pay for his passage and to [be] repay'd by the parrish at the next laying of the Levie.

Test CHA. ROBERTS C^{lk} V'str.

At A Vestry Called At ye Chappell sep^{tr} 17th—1721.

Present. Mr. Geo. Robertson Minist^{r}, Maj^{r} Wm. Kennon, Mr. Luis Green Church-wardens, Maj^{r} Robt Bolling, Capt Hen. Randolph, Maj^{r} Robt Munford, Capt Rich. Kennon, Capt Peter Jones, Mr. Tho. Bott, Mr. Ins^{t} Hall.

Upon the petition of Wm. Tucker sheweth that Robt Coleman lys at his house in a very weak, helpless condition & has been so these six months past which proves very Chargeable & troublesome to the s'd Tucker Tis ordrd That Wm. Tucker take care of the fores'd Robt Coleman & find him such necessaries as is convenient And at the laying of the next Levie, the s'd Tucker to bring his Account to the Vestry & what is thought just to be Allowed from the P'ish.

Tis further ordrd that the Church-wardens Enquire how the fores'd Robt Coleman gave his Estate [to] Robt Tucker sen^{r} & upon what terms.

Test CHA. ROBERTS C^{lk} Vest^{r}.

(4) Bristoll P'ish—ss: At A Vestry held at the Chappell Nov. 23th—1721.

Present. Mr. Geo. Robertson Minist^{r}, Maj^{r} Wm. Kennon, Mr. Luis Green Church Wardens, Maj^{r} Robt Bolling, Capt Hen. Randolph, Maj^{r} Robt Munford, Capt Rich. Kennon, Capt Peter Jones, Mr. Geo. Archer, Mr. Ins. Hall, Mr. Tho. Bott, Mr. Geo. Wilson.

It is ordered that Wm. Dodson jun^{r} be Allowed for the time he hath keep his father to this day six hundred p^{ds} of tobb. And for the future to take care of his s'd father and to bring his Acco^{t} to the next Vestry of laying the P'ish Levies. It is ordrd that Andrew Crawfoot continue Levie free untill he is able to work.

It is ordrd That A mollatto wench belonging unto Capt Peter Jones being troubled wth fitts be acquitted from paying P'ish Levies.

It is ordrd that the Church-Wardens bind a Bastard Child to Benj^{a} Dison which was born of a serv^{t} Woman of his According to Law.

It is ordrd And Capt Bullard Herbert is hereby Elected Vestry-man for this P'ish in the room of Capt Ja. Thweat he the s'd Thweat haveing for these two years past neglected Appearing At the Vestries.

The fores'd Capt Bullard Herbert this day hath take the Oath of A Vestry-man.

It is hereby ordered and Agreed By the Vestry that two Chappells be Built for the Ease & convenience of the frontire Inhabitants of ye s'd P'ish (Viz) one on Sapponey Creek near the Bridge. The other on Namosend Creek near the mouth. Both which Chappells are to be of the following dementions. Fourty foot in len'th twenty foot in breadth twelve foot pitch fram'd on good sills & underpin'd with good Blocks or rock-stones A good substantiall frame, to be weather-borded with good Clap-bords

& cover'd wth shingles Nail'd on Either to bords or saw'd laths as the work-man shall think fitt the inside to be common plain work, the seats to be single benches, Except the two upper pews, & them to be double & close with dores the floor lay'd with inch plank & Each Chappell Ceal'd with halfe-inch plank & A common plain gallary A pulpet & reading desk & communion table, with windows & Doors. And it is ordered by ye s'd Vestry that notice be given for Workmen to come in & undertake the s'd work. Maj^{r} Robt Bolling, Maj^{r} Robt Munford, Maj^{r} Wm. Kennon and Mr. Luis Green jun^{r} are Appointed to Agree with the undertakers & to take bond for their performance.

It is ordered And Capt Henry Randolph is hereby impowr'd to be Church-warden for the Ensuing year on the north-side Bristoll P'ish. It is like-wise ordered that Maj^{r} Robt Munford be Church-warden for the Ensuing year for the south-side Bristoll P'ish.

It is further ordered & Agreed upon that the Collectors of the P'ish dues be allowed 20 ℔ C. for Collection.

BRISTOLL P'ISH DR.	℔ tobb.	
To Mr. Geo. Robertson Minist^{r},	16,000	Casq.
To Mr Tho. Bott C^{lk} P'ish,	2,100	168
To Mrs. Eliz. Kennon for keeping the ferry,	2,500	200
To Cha. Roberts C^{lk} Vest^{r} 400 &. for taking down & putting up ye Chappell windows & nails 50,	450	36
To Hen. Tatam for Setting ye psalms,	500	40
To Maj^{r} Robt Mumford on Acco^{t} Wm. Fisher 8^{lb} 6^{d} in tobb. at 5^{lb} ℔ C. is	3,320	266
To Wm. Davis for keeping Fisher 7 months,	800	64
To Wm. Tucker for keeping Robt Coleman 3 months,	400	32
To Hen. Vodin for keeping Wm. Dodson 2 month,	200	16
To Maj^{r} Wm. Kennon on Acco^{t} Wm. Dodson sen^{r},	800	64
To Mr. Geo. Wilson 2 insoll,	70	
To Mr. Luis Green jun^{r} for a horse-block,	100	8

To Wm. Dodson jun^{r} for keeping his father, .	600	48
	27,840	942
Sall at 20 ꝑ C.	5,568	
Casq at 8 ꝑ C.	942	
	34,350	

ꝑ CONT'R CR.

By 619 tithables South Side
By 275 ditto North Side
is 894 At 38^{lb} tobb ꝑ pole is 33,972^{lb} tobb.

(5) The Afore Acco^{t} proportioned as followeth:

BRISTOLL P'ISH—SS: SOUTH-SIDE.	℔ tobb.	
To Mr. Geo. Robertson Minist^{r}, ...	11,000	Cas.
To Mr. Tho. Bott C^{lk}, ...	1,400	112
To Mrs. Eliz. Kennon for keeping the ferry, .	1,300	104
To Maj^{r} Robt Munford on Acco^{t} Wm. Fisher,	3,320	266
To Wm. Davis for keeping Fisher 7 Mon. .	800	64
To Cha. Roberts C^{lk} Vest^{r}, ...	450	36
To Hen. Tatam for setting the psalms, . .	500	40
To Mr Luis Green jun^{r} for A horse-block, .	100	8
Sall at 20 ꝑ C, ...	3,854	
Cask, ...	662	
	23,786	

ꝑ CONT'R CR.

	℔
By 619 tithables at 38 ꝑ pole, ...	23,5 2[2]
due to ye Coll^{r}, ...	2[6 4]
	23,7[8 6]

It is ordered by the Vestry & Maj^{r} Robt Mun[ford] is hereby Impowred to Collect, receive & recov[er] of the above 619 tithables 38^{lb} tobb ꝑ pole by distress or other wise And to make good pay[m^{t}] as above rendering Acco^{t} to the Vestry and [no] Arrears.

North Side.	℔ tobb.	
To Mr Geo. Robertson Minist^{r}, ...	5,000	Casq.
To Mr Tho. Bott C^{lk}, ...	700	56
To Mrs. Eliz. Kennon for the ferry, . . .	1,200	96
To Hen. Voden for diet Wm. Dodson 2 Mo^{s}, .	200	16
To Maj^{r} Wm. Kennon for necessaries for Wm. Dodson, ...	800	64
To Mr. Geo. Wilson for insoll, ...	70	
To Wm. Dodson jun^{r} on Acco^{t} of his father, .	600	48
Sall at 20 ℘ C, ...	1,714	
Cask, ...	280	
	10,564	

℘ Cont'r.	
By 275 tithables at 38 ℘ pole, ...	10,45 [0]
due to the Coll^{r}, ...	11 [4]
	10,56 [4]

It is ordered by the Vestry & Capt Hen. Randolph (is) hereby Impowrd to Collect, receive, & recover of the 275 tithables 38^{lb} tobb. ℘ pole by distress or other wise [and] to make good paym^{t} as above rendering Acco^{t} to [the] Vestry and no Arrears.

Test Cha. Roberts C^{lk} Ves[t^{r}].

At A Vestry Called at the Chappell March 18th, 172½.

Present. Mr. Geo. Robertson Minist^{r}, Maj^{r} Robt Munford, Capt Hen. Randolph Churchward[ens], Maj^{r} Robt Bolling, Maj^{r} Wm. Kennon, Capt Peter Jones, Capt Rich. Kennon, Mr. Tho. Bott, Mr. Geo. Wilson.

Upon the petition of John Walker that he is lame of his limbs that he is [not] able to help himselfe & hath been so Ever since octob^{r} last & can find no help.

It is ordrd by this Vestry that Maj^{r} Robt Munford do take care & Agree [with] some person to take care of the s'd Walker; And what Agreem^{t} he [shall] make his Acco^{t} to be deliver'd At the Laying of the next P'ish Levi[es] & to be allowed.

Test Cha. Roberts C^{lk} Vest^{r}.

At A Vestry Called At the Chappell June 10th, 1722.

Present. Mr. Geo. Robertson Ministr, Majr Robt Munford, Church-warden, Majr Robt Bolling, Majr Wm. Kennon, Capt Peter Jones, Capt Rich. Kennon, Mr. Tho. Bott, Mr. Geo. Wilson.

It is ordr that Nath. Parrot being lame his right hand being cut off be acquitted from paying P'ish Levies.

James Franklin senr being very old not Able to work & hath none to help h[im].

Tis' ordrd he be Acquitted from paying P'ish Levies. Wm. Temple Senr being Anciant by ordr of Prince Geo. Court is Acquitted from paying Publiq Levies it is hereby ordr that he be acquitted from pay[ing] P'ish levies.

It is ordr that David Maccullon being in A very week condition & not able [to] work be acquitted from paying P'ish Levies.

Test CHA. ROBERTS Clk Vestr.

(6) [Bris]toll [P]'ish—ss: At A Vestry Called At the Chappell 28th octobr, 1722.

Present. Mr. Geo. Robertson Ministr, Majr Robt Munford, Church-warden, Majr Robt Bolling, Majr Kennon, Capt. Peter Jones, Capt Kennon, Capt Jno Herbert, Mr. Geo. Wilson, Mr. Tho. Bott.

It is ordrd That William Snelgrove Son of Jane Matts wife of Wm. Matts Indian the s'd Snelgrove be bound unto Robt Lyon to serve sixteen years from the date of the Indenture whic is Nov. 7th, 1722.

Test CHA. ROBERTS Clk Vestr.

[Bri]stoll P'ish—ss: At A Vestry held At the Chappell, Novr 8th, 1722.

Pr'sent. Mr. Geo. Robertson Ministr, Majr Wm. Kennon, Mr. Tho. Bott, Capt Bullard Herbert, Mr. Geo. Wilson, Mr. Geo. Archer.

Upon the pettition of Eliz. Lett It is ordered that James Lett her son now being at Tho. Grigories be by the Church-wardens bound unto Daniell nance & his Wife untill the s'd James Lett come to Lawfull Age.

It is ordered & Maj^r^ Robt Munford is hereby required to Continue Church-warden for this Ensuing year.

It is ordered & Mr. Geo. Wilson is hereby Appointed Church-warden for this Ensuing year.

It is ordered that Margaret Brannum two years old the 10th this Instant be bound unto Godfry Radgsdale & his heirs to serve According to Law.

It is ordered That the Church-wardens bind out three Moll. Children their Mother a Mollatto the names of the Children Peter, Dick & Nan, To serve James Williams & his heirs According to Law.

It is ordered that the Church-wardens take care & rail in the Chappell And the Church five rails in one pannell four foot & halfe high And Eight foot in len'th.

BRISTOL P'ISH DR.	℔ tobb.	
To Mr. Geo. Robertson Minister, . .	16,000	Casq.
To Mr. Tho. Bott C[lk] P'ish, ...	2,100	168
To Mrs. Eliz. Kennon for keeping the ferry,	2,500	200
To Cha. Roberts C[lk] Vest[r] & taking down y[e] windows and putting up, ...	450	36
To Hen. Tatam for setting the psalms, .	500	40
To Mr. Tho. Eldridge for defending the sute ver. John Ellis, ...	600	48
To Mr. Geo. Wilson for two tithables over Chargd, ...	76	
To Coll. Littleberry Eps for Cap[n] Tuckers papers, ...	60	5
To Wm. Dodson jun[r] on Account of his father, ...	1,400	112
To Joseph Tucker on account Rob[t] Coleman,	1,400	112
To Maj[r] Munford on Account of John Walker, ...	600	48
	25,686	769
Cas, ...	769	
Sall, ...	5,137	
	31,592	

(11) Bristoll P'ish—ss: At A Vestry held At the Chappell Nov. 11th, 1723.

Present. Mr. Geo. Robertson Minist^{r}, Maj^{r} Robt Munford, Mr. Geo. Wilson Church-wardens, Capt Bullard Herbert, Maj^{r} Wm. Kennon, Mr. Inst. Hall, Capt Hen. Randolph, Mr. Tho. Bott, Capt Rich. Kennon, Capt Drury Bolling, Mr. Geo. Archer.

Capt Tho. Jefferson produceing an Acco^{t} for work done to ye New Church more that his Agreem^{t} to the Vallue of Six thousand pounds of tobb. tis ordrd that three thousand pounds tobb. being due to the P'ish from John Ellis Junr the s'd tobb. be pay'd unto the s'd Cap[^{t}] Tho. Jefferson in part & it is ord^{r} that there be three thousand pounds of tobb. levied o[n] the P'ish for ye s'd Jefferson.

Capt Drury Bolling is hereby Appointed Vestry-man for this P'ish.

It is ordrd that Dan. Glidewell live with Wm. Gent And that the s'd Gent be allowed one thousand p^{ds} tobb. ꝑ year at the next laying of ye P'ish levies which shall be in the year 1724.

It is ordrd that Maj^{r} Robt Munford & Capt Hen. Randolph be Church-wardens for the next Ensuing year.

Bristoll P'ish Dr.	℔ tobb.	
To Mr. Geo. Robertson Minist^{r}, ...	16,000	Casq.
To Mr. Tho. Bott C^{lk} P'ish, ...	2,100	168
To Mrs. Eliz. Kennon for keeping the ferry, .	2,500	200
To Hen. Tatum for setting the psalms, . .	500	40
To Cha. Roberts C^{lk} Vest^{r} 400 to taking down ye windows & putting up 50 to carrying ye Church book & returning each other sunday & finding a bagg 180, ...	630	51
To Wm. Davis on Acco^{t} Wm. Fisher, . .	200	16
To Wm. Bass & Jno West for railing In ye Church & Chappell, ...	4,000	320
To Capt Tho. Jefferson for work done to ye Church More than bargain, ...	3,000	240
	28,930	103(5)

To Maj[r] Wm. Kennon to posts & rails for y[e] Church & Chappell & making good what y[e] fresh carry'd away from y[e] landing and carrying the same to both places, . .	5,000	400
To ditto for books for the P'ish, . . .	1,000	80
To Maj[r] Munford for Insolvent, . . .	390	
To ditto for Marga. Moguire, . . .	522	4[2]
To John Mays for A diall-post, . . .	50	4
To Wm. Dodson for picking up y[e] rails carry'd by the fres't, ...	60	[5]
To Mary Dison for washing & Cleaning y[e] Church, ...	300	24
To Mr. Geo. Wilson for Insolvents, . .	502	
To ditto for a horse block, ...	50	4
To Hen. Vodin for keeping Marga. Moguire,	215	17
To Jn[o] Peterson jun[r] on y[e] Acco[t] Cloud Barber,	650	52
To Mr. Inst. Hall for A horse block, . .	50	4
	37,719	1,667
Sall at 15[lb] ℔ C.	5,658	
Casq, ...	1,667	
	45,044	
To Wm. Dodson 1,400 Casq & Sall 322, .	1,722	
	46,766	
℔ Cont[r] C[r] By 1,049 tithables At 45 ℔ pol. is	47,205	
	46,766	
Due to P'ish, ...	439	
Proportion Carry'd over, ...	47,205	

(12) Proportion from y[e] other side.

BRISTOLL P'ISH—SS: 1723. SOUTH SIDE DR.

To Mr. Geo. Robertson Minist[r]	11,100	Casq.
To Mr. Tho. Bott C[lk], ...	1,500	120
To Jn[o] West, ...	2,000	160
To Mrs. Eliz. Kennon, ...	1,700	136

To Capt Jefferson,	2,200	176
To Wm. Dodson sen^r,	1,000	80
To Wm. Bass,	800	64
To Maj^r Wm. Kennon,	4,500	360
To Hen. Tatum,	500	40
To Cha. Roberts,	630	51
To Wm. Davis,	200	16
To Maj^r Munford,	912	42
To John Mays,	50	4
To Jno Peterson jun^r,	650	52
To Instant Hall,	50	4
	27,792	1,305
Sall at 15 ꝑ C^t,	4,169	
Casq at 8 ꝑ C^t,	1,305	
	33,266	
Due to P'ish,	439	
	33,705	

ꝑ Con't Cr.

By 749 tithables at 45 ꝑ pole is	33,705

It is ordered by the Vestry & Maj^r Robert Munford is hereby Impow'red to Collect receive, & recover of the Above 749 tithables 45^{lb} tobb. ꝑ pole by distress or otherwise & to make good payment as above rendering Acco^t to ye Vestry & no Arrears.

Test Cha. Roberts C^{lk} V'st^r.

North side Dr.

To Mr. Geo. Robertson Minist^r,	4,900	Casq.
To Mr. Tho. Bott,	600	48
To Wm. Bass,	1,200	96
To Mary Dison,	300	24
To Geo. Wilson,	552	4
To Hen. Vodin,	215	17
To Mrs. Eliz. Kennon,	800	64
To Capt Jefferson,	800	64

To Wm. Dodson, ...	460	37
To Maj^{r} Wm. Kennon, ...	1,500	120
	11,327	474
Sall at 15 ꝑ C. is	1,699	
Casq, ...	474	
	13,500	
ꝑ CON'TR CR.		
By 300 tithables at 45 ꝑ pole is . . .	13,500	

It is ordrd by the Vestry & Capt Hen. Randolph is hereby Impow'red to Collect, receive, and recover of the above 300 tithables 45^{lb} tobb. ꝑ pole by distress or otherwise and to make good payment as above rendering Acco^{t} to the Vestry and no Arrears.

Test CHA. ROBERTS C^{lk} Ves^{tr}.

Bristoll P'ish—ss: At A Vestry Called at the Church Jan^{r} 12th $172\frac{3}{4}$.

Present. Mr. Geo. Robertson Minist^{r}, Maj^{r} Robt Bolling, Maj^{r} Wm. Kennon, Mr. Tho. Bott, Capt Rich. Kennon, Mr. Geo. Wilson, Capt Hen. Randolph Church-warden.

It is ordered that whereas Mr. James Baugh dec'd was Appointed to procession from Puckett's run down to y^{e} lower end of the P'ish Mr. Alexand^{r} Marchell is by this Vestry to officeate with Benj^{a} Loket in the room of the dec'd Baugh.

It is ordered that whereas the precinct belonging unto Mr. Tho. Bott jun^{r} is thought too large for them it is ordered that they procession up to Noon[ing] Creek on ye south side ye main road.

It is ordered that Godfry Fowler Junr & Mark Moor procession from Nooning Creek to the Extent of the P'ish.

(13) Bristoll P'ish—ss: At A Vestry called at the Chappell 24th May, 1724.

Present. Mr. Geo. Robertson Minist^{r}, Mr. Geo. Wilson Church warden, Maj^{r} Robt^{t} Bolling, Maj^{r} Wm. Kennon, Capt Peter Jones, Capt Hen. Randolph, Mr. Tho. Bott.

It is ordrd That Joseph Gill being in A weak Condition not Able to work be Acquitted from paying P'ish Levies.

Test CHA. ROBERTS C^{lk} Vest^{r}.

Bristoll P'ish—ss: At A Vestry Called at the Chappell June 7th, 1724.

Present. Mr. Geo. Robertson Minist^{r}, Maj^{r} Robt Munford Church warden, Capt Peter Jones, Maj^{r} Wm. Kennon, Capt Bullard Herbert, Capt Richd Kennon, Capt Drury Bolling, Mr. Tho. Bott.

Upon the petition of Raise Newhouse he being in a very weak Condition & for these severall years past has not been Able to labour for the support of himself & poor small small Children beggs that he may be Exempt from paying Levies for the future he is ordrd by the Vestry to be Levie free as also is Allow 600^{lb} tobb. for his support be levied at the next laying the P'ish Levies.

Abra. Overby son of Nico^{a} Overby sen^{r} being born lame & in an helpless condition.

It is ordered that the s'd Abra. Overby be Acquitted from paying levies.

Test CHA. ROBERTS C^{lk} Vest^{r}.

Bristoll P'ish—ss: At A Vestry Called at the Chappell June 21th 1724.

Mr. Geo. Robertson Minist^{r}, Maj^{r} Robt Bolling, Maj^{r} Wm. Kennon, Capt Peter Jones, Capt Bullard Herbert, Capt Drury Bolling, Mr. Ins^{t} Hall, Mr. Tho. Bott.

It is ordrd That the Gen^{tm} of the Vestry Meet at the Chappell on June 29th instant then & there Appoint men to take Account of Crops of tobb. whether they be According to the new Law.

Test CHA. ROBERTS C^{lk} Vest^{r}.

(14) Bristoll P'ish—ss: At A Vestry held at the Chappell June 29th, 1724.

Present. Mr. Geo. Robertson Minist^{r}, Maj^{r} Robt Munford, Mr. Geo. Wilson Church-wardens, Maj^{r} Robt Bolling, Capt Hen. Randolph, Capt Peter Jones, Mr. Tho. Bott, Capt Bullard Herbert, Mr. Ins^{t} Hall.

It is ordrd that Dennis Daly be Allowed four hundred pounds of tobb. for Support of himself & family to be Allowed by the P'ish to be paid him by the Church-warden And the s'd Church-warden to bring his Acco[t] to the next laying the levies.

As Also In persuance to an Act for the better & more Effectuall Improving the staple of tobb. the southside of the P'ish is divided into two precincts y[e] upper presinct bounded as followeth, Viz: to begin at Appomattox ferry, thence As Monkassaneck Road Runs to Stony Creek Bridge between Cap[t] Jon[ ] and Jos. Wynn's, thence up Stony Creek to the Upper road to Nottoway River, thence along that Roade to Nottoway River thence up between y[e] same & Appomattox River to the Extent of y[e] P'ish.

Cap[t] Peter Jones & his son Abra Jones are Appointed Counters for the s'd precinct.

All below the s'd Roads to the Extent of the P'ish & south side of Nottoway River the lower precinct, Instance Hall and John Mays are appointed Counters for the same.

Mr. Tho. Bott & his Son are Appointed by the Vestry Counters of the tobb. plants on the North side of the P'ish between old-town Creek & Appomatuk River & where the old-town Creek fails at the head between Wintopock road & the s'd river to y[e] furthermost Extent of y[e] P'ish And Wm. Rowlet & Abra. Burton are Appointed Counters as afores'd between the s'd old-town creek & Swift creek all the way from the River upwards.

Alex. Marshall & Matt. Liggon are Appointed Counters of tobb. plants between Swift creek all y[e] way to the Lower bounds of the P'ish where it bounds on Henrico P'ish.

It is ord[rd] that Jack Cook belonging to Mr. John Fizjarrell be Acquitted from paying P'ish levies till he mends he now being Ailing.

Test CHA. ROBERTS C[lk] Vest[r].

Bristoll P'ish—ss: At A Vestry Call'd At the Chapple July 5th, 1724.

Present. Mr. Geo. Robertson Minist[r], Maj[r] Rob[t] Munford, Mr. Geo. Wilson Church Wardens, Maj[r] Rob[t] Bolling, Maj[r] Wm. Kennon, Cap[t] Peter Jones, Cap[t] Hen. Randolph, Cap[t] Bullard Herbert, Mr. Tho. Bott, Mr. Ins[t] Hall.

Cap[t] Peter Jones & his son Abra Jones was ord[rd] to Count the tobb. plants in the upper precincts on ye south side this P'ish the fores'd Abra desiring he may be Acquitted & his bro. Wm. Jones be put in his place is granted.

As also It is ordered that the Vestry meet at the Chapple on Saturday the 18th Instant to Appoint and Agree with workmen to make and put up Sash Windows to the Chapple.

Test CHA. ROBERTS, C^{lk} Vest^{r}.

Bristoll P'ish—ss: At A Vestry held at the Chappell July 18th, 1724.

Present. Mr. Geo. Robertson Minist^{r}, Maj^{r} Robt Munford Church warden, Capt Bullard Herbert, Maj^{r} Wm. Kennon, Mr. Geo. Archer, Capt Richd Kennon, Mr. Geo. Wilson.

It is ordered & Agreed upon by the Vestry And Richard James to & with ye same Agree to make five Sash windows to the Chapple the s'd windows to be made up with Sash Glass the same to be the breadth of the old windows & about one foot or more longer & to do them well & workman like with what Expedition he can he finding all things necessary for the same at his own proper cost & Charge.

And the fores'd Vestry when the work so finished as afores'd doth promise & Agree to levie at the next laying of the P'ish levies two thousand pounds of tobb. & Casq. to pay unto the said Richd James for his s'd work as also the s'd James to have all the Glass belonging unto the old windows, And the s'd James doth Agree to make A Casement to the little window next the pulpett into the fores'd bargain.

(15) Bristoll P'ish—ss: At A Vestry held at the Chappell 9th Octob^{r} 1724.

Present. Mr. Geo. Robertson Minist^{r}, Maj^{r} Robt Munford, Mr. Geo. Wilson Church wardens, Maj^{r} Robt Bolling, Maj^{r} Wm. Kennon, Capt Peter Jones, Capt Rich. Kennon, Capt Drury Bolling, Mr. Tho. Bott.

It is ordered that John Tilman have the keeping of Dan. Glidewell this next ensuing year & to be allowed by ye P'ish one thousand ℔ tobb.

Hen. Royall pettitioneth that he hath two Moll. Children born in his house by Name Wm. & hannah may be bound to him & his heirs according to Law his pett. is granted.

Capt Hen. Randolph pett. that he hath a Moll. girl born in his house named Annakin Jenkins may be bound to him & his heirs according to Law his pett. is granted.

Ordered that Pegg a negro woman belonging to Capt Stith Bolling be levie free.

Mary Lain pett. for reliefe Tis ordered that the Churchwarden take care for the s'd Lain & she is allowed for this year 400^{lb} tobb.

It is ordered & Agreed upon that. Rich James ridge the Chapple in lew of the Exchainge of the glass. Rich. Deardin is Acquitted from paying Levies. It is ordered that Maj^{r} Robt munford & Capt Hen. Randolph are Churchwardens the next Ensuing year.

Bristoll P'ish Dr.	℔ tobb.	
To Mr. Geo. Robertson Minist^{r},	16,000	Casq.
To Mr. Tho. Bott Clark,	2,100	168
To Mrs. Eliz. Kennon for the ferry,	2,500	200
To Cha. Roberts C^{lk} Vestry,	450	36
To Hen. Tatam for setting the psalms,	500	40
To Mary dison for washing ye Church,	300	24
To Rich. James for sash windows,	2,000	160
To Raise Newhouse for support,	600	48
To Wm. Gent for keeping Dan Glidwell,	1,000	80
To Maj^{r} Wm. Kennon ℘ Acco^{t},	1,133	91
To Maj^{r} Robt Bolling for Insoll,	455	
To ditto for Dennis Daly,	400	32
To ditto for A copy of ye tobb. Law,	40	
To Maj^{r} Robt Munford for Insoll. & other Charges (Casq 271),	841	22
To the Church warden on the south side on Acco^{t} of Mary Lain,	400	32
To Capt Hen. Randolph for Insoll,	495	
	29,214	
Sall at 15 ℘ C.	4,382	
Casq,	933	
	34,529	

℔ Cont'r Cr.	℔ tobb.
By 1,108 tithable at 31[lb] tobb. ℔ pole is . .	34,348
due to ball.	181
	34,529

North side proportioned. South side proportioned. And Carried over.

(16) Bristoll P'ish Dr. 1724 South Side Proportion.

	℔ tobb.	
To Mr. Geo. Robertson Minist[r], ...	11,400	Casq.
To Mr. Tho. Bott reader, ...	1,500	120
To Mrs. Eliz. Kennon for y[e] ferry, . .	1,634	131
To Cha. Roberts C[lk] Vestry, ...	450	36
To Hen. Tatam for setting ye psalms, . .	500	40
To Mary Dison for cleaning y[e] Church, . .	300	24
To Rich. James for y[e] window, ...	1,600	128
To Wm. Gent, ...	1,000	80
To Raise newhouse, ...	600	48
To Maj[r] Rob[t] Bolling for Insoll, ...	455	
To ditto for Dennis Daly, ...	400	32
To ditto for a cop[a] tobb. Law, ...	40	
To Maj[r] Rob[t] Munford, ...	841	22
To ditto for y[e] use of Mary Lain, ...	400	32
Sall at 15 ℔ C.	3,168	——
Casq, ...	693	693
	24,981	

℔ Cont'r Cr.	℔ tobb.
1724 By 800 tithables at 31 ℔ pole is, . .	24,800
due to y[e] Col[r], ...	181
	24,981

It is ordered by y[e] Vestry & Maj[r] Rob[t] Munford is hereby Impowr'd to Collect, receive, & recover of y[e] above 800 tithables 31[lb] tobb. ℔ pole by distress or otherwise & to make good payment as afores'd rendering Acco[t] to the Vestry & no Arrears.

Test Cha. Roberts C[lk] Ves[tr].

1724 NORTH SIDE BRISTOL P'ISH PROPORTION.

	lb tobb.	
To Mr. Geo. Robertson Minist^{r}, ...	4,600	Casq.
To Mr. Tho. Bott reader, ...	600	48
To Maj^{r} Wm. Kennon for book &c., . .	1,133	91
To Capt Hen. Randolph for Insoll, . .	495	
To Rich. James for window &c., . . .	400	32
To Mrs. Eliz. Kennon for ye ferry, . .	866	69
Sall at 15 ℔ C., ...	1,214	——
Casq, ...	240	240
	9,548	

℔ CON'TR CR. lb tobb.

1724 By 308 tithable at 31 ℔ pole is, . .	9,548

It is ordrd by ye Vestry & Capt Hen. Randolph is hereby Impow'red to Collect, receive, & recover of ye above 308 tithables, 31^{lb} tobb. ℔ pole by distress or otherwise & to make good payment as afores'd, rendering Acco^{t} to ye vestry & no Arrears.

Test CHA. ROBERTS C^{lk} Test^{r}.

Bristoll P'ish—ss: At a Vestry called decem. 25th, 1724 at the Chapple.

Present. Mr. Geo. Robertson Minist^{r}, Maj^{r} Robt Munford Church warden, Maj^{r} Robt Bolling, Maj^{r} Wm. Kennon, Capt Peter Jones, Mr. Geo. Wilson, Capt Bullard Herbert.

It is ordered that whereas Joseph Sergant being Ailing in body & limbs the s'd to be bound unto James Thompson to serve him 3 years for his Cure & the Church warden is hereby Impow'red to see & take Care of y^{e} s'd Joseph.

Test CHA. ROBERTS C^{lk} Vest.

Bristoll P'ish—ss: At A Vestry called at y^{e} Chapple March 14th, 172$\frac{4}{5}$.

Present. Mr. Geo. Robertson Minist'r, Maj^{r} Robt Munford Church warden, Maj^{r} Robt Bolling, Maj^{r} Wm. Kennon, Capt Drury Bolling, Capt Rich. Kennon, Capt Bullard Herbert, Mr. Geo. Wilson, Mr. Tho. Bott.

It is ordrd that Poll an Indian Girl daughter to Sara an Indian woman y^e s'd Girll being born in the house of Mr. Peter Rowlet the s'd Girl be bound unto the s'd peter Rowlett to serve him & his heirs as ye Law directs in such Cases.

Test CHA. ROBERTS C^lk Ves^tr.

(17) Bristoll P'ish—ss: At A Vestry Called at ye Chappell 4th Aprill, 1725.

Present. Mr. Geo. Robertson Minist^r, Maj^r Robt Munford, Capt Hen. Randolph Church wardens, Maj^r Robt Bolling, Maj^r Wm. Kennon, Capt Peter Jones, Capt Rich. Kennon, Capt Bullard Herbert, Mr. Tho. Bott, Capt. Drury Bolling, Mr. Geo. Wilson.

It is ordered by ye Vestry by & with the Consent of Hugh Lee that the s'd Hugh Lee take care of Mary Lain & find her diet, washing & lodging for the time of six months and he to be Allowed at the rate of one hundred ℔ tobb. ℘ month, she being in a very lame condition.

It is further ordered that John Lee being in A very Low Condition & not Able to help himself John Mays is or'ered to take care of the s'd John Lee & the s'd John Mays for his trouble is Allowed one hundred ℔ tobb. ℘ month.

Bristoll P'ish—ss: At A Vestry called At ye Chapple May 16th, 1725.

Present. Mr. Geo. Robertson Minist^r, Maj^r Robt Munford, Capt Hen. Randolph Church Vardens, Maj^r Robt Bolling, Maj^r Wm. Kennon, Capt Drury Bolling, Mr. Geo. Wilson, Capt Peter Jones, Mr. Tho. Bott.

Charles Hill being upwards of sixty years of Age & being very much Ailing that he cannot work to support him self prays he may be sett levie free this Vestry that for ye future orders he ye s'd Cha. Hill be levie free.

As also Charles Gillam being lame & not able to work the Vestry orders that the s'd Cha. Gillam for the future be leavie free.

Bristoll P'ish—ss: At A Vestry called at the Chappell May 30th 1725.

Mr. Geo. Robertson Minist^r, Maj^r Robt Munford Church warden, Maj^r Robt Bolling, Maj^r Wm. Kennon, Capt Drury Bolling,

Capt Rich. Kennon, Capt Peter Jones, Mr. Geo. Wilson, Capt Bullard Herbert, Mr. Tho. Bott.

Upon the complaint of John Vaughan sen^r He having been long sick & is now not Able to work as Also being Aged prays he may be leavie free Tis ordered by this Vestry that the s'd Vaughan be leavie free.

(18) Bristoll P'ish—ss: At A Vestry held at the Chapple June 28th 1725.

Present. Mr. Geo. Robertson Minist^r, Maj^r Robt Munford, Capt Hen. Randolph Church Wardens, Maj^r Robt Bolling, Maj^r Wm. Kennon, Capt Bullard Herbert, Capt Rich. Kennon, Mr. Geo. Wilson, Mr. Geo. Archer.

It is ordered that two Chapples be built for the convenience of the Frontire of this P'ish one upon or near the plant'acon of Mr. John Stith upon Sapponey Creek convenient to ye upper Nottoway river road & Maj^r Robt Bolling & Maj^r Robt Munford to Appoint the place.

The other on the upper side of Numanseen Creek as near ye river as it can conveniently be placed to be directed by Maj^r Wm. Kennon & Maj^r Robt Bolling. And it is further ordrd that Notice be given for workmen to come & make proposals for undertaking ye Same. And that Maj^r Robt Bolling, Maj^r Robt Munford & Maj^r Wm. Kennon Attend at ye Chapple on ye Second Munday in August next to Agree with the Undertakers. And it is ordered and Agreed upon that Each Chapple are to be of ye following dementions, forty foot in lenth, twenty foot in bredth, twelve foot pitch, fraim'd on good Sils under pin'd with good blocks or rock-stones, A good Substantiall frame to be weather-borded with good Clap-bords & covered with shingles nail'd on Either to bords or saw'd laths as the workman shall think fitt the in side to be comon plain work the seats to be single benches, Except the two upper pews & them to be double & close with dores, the floors lay'd with inch-plank & Each Chapple ceal'd with halfe inch-plank & A comon plain gallary & pulpett & A reading-desk & a comunion-table with windows & doors.

And it is further ordrd that Whereas the P'ish being divided into precincts for counting tobb. plants the South-side of the s'd

P'ish being divided into two precincts, the upper precinct bounded as followeth to begin at Appamattuck ferry, thence as Monkassaneck road runs to stony-creek bridge between Capt Rich. Jones, & Capt Joss Wynns, thence up stony-creek to ye upper Road to Nottoway river, thence along the road to Nottoway river, thence up between the same & Appamattuck river to ye Extent of ye P'ish. Capt Peter Jones & his Son Peter Jones are Appointed Counters for ye s'd precinct.

All below ye s'd roads to ye Extent of ye P'ish & South-side Nottoway river being ye lower precinct Instance Hall & John Mays are appointed counters for the same.

Mr. Geo. Archer sen^{r} & Mr. Robt Bevell are Appointed counters of ye tobb. plants on ye north-side ye P'ish between Old-town-creek & Appamattuck river & where ye old town creek fails at ye head between Wontapock road & ye s'd river to ye further most Extent of the P'ish. Mr. Wm. Rowlett & Wm. Chambers are Appointed Counters as afores'd between ye s'd old-town creek & swift creek all ye way from ye river upwards.

Mr. Alex. Marchell & Matt Ligon are Appointed counters of tobb. plants between swift creek all the way to the lower bounds of ye P'ish where it bounds on Henrico P'ish.

And it is ordered that all ye fores'd Counters of tobb. plants Make return of their proceedings at or upon the 10th day of August next.

Godfry Radgsdale doth pettition that he hath A Moll. girll born in his house prays the same Moll. by name   may be bound to him & his heirs as the law directs in such cases his pettition is granted.

Mrs. Fran. Wynn haveing A Moll. boy by name Ned son of Eliz. Stuard born in ye house of Mrs. Wynns prays ye s'd Moll. be bound to her & her heirs as ye law directs in such cases tis granted.

Wm. Eaton prays a Moll. Boy by name Wm. who formerly lived with Wm. Standback be bound unto ye s'd Eaton to serve According to law ye s'd Eaton & his heirs. tis granted.

Test CHA. ROBERTS C^{lk} Vest^{r}.

Aug[t] 9th, 1725.

Bristol Parish—ss: At a Meeting at the Chapple by order of Vestry made June 28th, 1725.

Maj[r] Robert Bolling, Maj[r] Rob[t] Munford & Maj[r] Wm. Kennon to agree with workmen to build two Chapples in y[e] Parish.

It is agreed upon with the Gent[n] aforenamed to and wth Rich[d] James that the s[d] Rich[d] James build a Chapple at Namisseen Creek & the s[d] James give good Security to perform y[e] s[d] well & workman like according to bond, & Security given from under hand. The afores[d] Gent[n] doth agree to pay unto the s[d] James 135[l] Curr[t] Money to be paid at two paym[ts] in tob[o] at the price Curr[t] at 3 Standing dealers doth allow, y[e] s[d] Chapple to be finisht at or upon Christmas come twelve Month Maj[r] Wm. Ken- & Wm. Bass Security for the Said James.

It is further agreed upon wth the Gent[n] afores[d] to and with Edw. Colwell the s[d] Colwell build a Chapple at Sappony Creek where Maj[r] Bolling & Maj[r] Munford shall appoint the s[d] Colwell to give Security for the performance of the Same to be well & workman like according to y[e] dementions in bond mentioned the s[d] Colwell to have 140 £ Cur[t] money to be paid at two payments in Tob[o] at the Price Curr[t] as 3 Standing dealers doth allow; y[e] said Chapple to to be finished at or upon Christmas come twelve Month Maj[r] Rob[t] Munford Security for the said Colwell.

It is agreed that the Price Curr[t] of Tob[o] be as Col[o] Harrison, Maj[r] John Bolling, Maj[r] Rob[t] Bolling, Maj[r] Rob[t] Munford & Maj[r] Wm. Kennon doth allow or any three of them.

Test CHA. ROBERTS C'lk Vestry.

Copy'd from y[e] Rough. JOHN WOOBANK.

(19) Bristoll P'ish—ss: At A Vestry called at the Chapple octob[r] 3d 1725.

Present. Mr. Geo. Robertson Minist[r], Maj[r] Rob[t] Munford Church-warden, Maj[r] Rob[t] Bolling, Maj[r] Wm. Kennon, Cap[t] Drury Bolling, Mr. Geo. Archer, Cap[t] Bullard Herbert, Mr. Tho. Bott, Mr. Geo. Wilson.

Upon the pett. of Margarett Butler And she appearing to this Vestry declaring that she being disabled by Sickness is not Able to help her selfe; Tis ordrd by this Vestry that ye s'd Marg^{a} Butler live with Rich. Butler untill The Vestry can Agree with A Docter to cure her if possible he can the fores'd Rich. Butler to be allow by ye P'ish for the time she lives with him at ye rate of Eight P^{ds} of tobb. ℔ Month, & he to find her diet, lodging, & washing for the time.

Test CHA. ROBERTS C^{lk} Vest^{r}.

Bristoll P'ish—ss: At A Vestry Called at the Chappel Octob^{r} 3d 1725.

present. Mr. George Robertson Minist'r, Maj^{r} Robt Munford, Cap. henry Randolph Church Wardens, Maj^{r} Robt bolling, Maj^{r} Wm. Kennon, Capt Drury bolling, Mr. George Archier, Capt Buller herbert, Mr. thom. Bott, Mr. George Willson.

It is ordrd that Ann Gill be allow'd by ye Vestry five yards blew plains from Maj^{r} Munford he to be payd at the next laying ye leavyss as also Capt Randolph to let ye s'd Gill to have linnin to make two shirts he to be allow'd for It at the laying the next levies. It Is ord'red that Maj^{r} Munford Continue Churchwarden for the next Insuing year. Mr. George Wilson is Elected Church Warden for the next Ensuing y^{r} & Collector.

It is ord^{r} y^{t} Doc^{t} Jos^{p} Irby take Cath. bell and to discharge ye P'ish.

GEO. ROBERTSON Minister.

Bristoll P'ish—ss: At A Vestry held at ye Chappel No^{vr} ye 14th 1725.

present. Mr. George Robertson Minister, Maj^{r} Robt Munford, Mr. George Wilson Church Wardens, Coll. Robt bolling, Maj^{r} Wm. Kennon, Capt peter Jones, Capt Rich. Kennon, Capt buller herbert, Mr. tho. bott.

It is ord'red y^{t} Cath. Arthur being Destitute of an habitation & not Able to to work James W'ms Is heare by ord'red by Consent to take the s^{d} Cath^{r} Into his house and to find her diet washing and lodging Convenient and he to be Allowed by the parish at ye next laying the parish leavy at ye rates of five pound per year.

CHA'S ROBERDS Clerk Vest^{r}.

Bristoll P'ish—ss: At A Vestry held at the Chapple Sunday ye 20th 1725 feb^{r}.

pr'sent. Mr. George Robterson Minister, Maj^{r} Robt Munford, Mr. Geo. Wilson Church Wardens, Coll. Robt bolling, Maj^{r} Wm. Kennon, Capt buller herbert, Capt Richd Kennon, Capt peter Jones, Mr. thom. bott.

It is Ord'red y^{t} John Mayes be Clerk of the Vestr. for this p'ish and to be allow'd four hundred pound of tob^{co} ꝑ^{r} year by ye p'ish. It is ord'red y^{t} y^{e} Church Wardens Provide nesssaries for an Orphand Child now under the Care of susan Parham that she be allow'd for the same at the laying the next p'ish leavy.

Test JNO. MAYES Clerk Vest.

(20) Bristoll P'ish—ss: At A Vestry held at y^{e} Chapple Sunday y^{e} 6th march 172$\frac{5}{6}$.

prisant. Mr. George Robertson Minister &c.

It Is ord'red y^{t} ye Church Weardens Provide necesisary Cloathin for John Eaginton. And they to be allow'd for the same at y^{e} Laying the next parrish leavy.

Capt buller herbert Having A mollatto boy by name Ned son of Elizabeth stuard born In his house prayes ye s^{d} boy be bound to him and his heirs as ye law Directs In such Cases. Tis Granted.

Test JNO. MAYES Clerk Vest^{r}.

Bristoll P'ish—ss: At A Vestry held At ye Chapple Sunday ye 15th may 1726 may.

present. Mr. George Robertson Minister, Maj^{r} Robt Munford, Capt Henry Randolph, Maj^{r} Wm. Kennon, Capt Richd Kennon, Capt peter Jones, Mr. th^{o} bott.

James bank being an oald man Veary poor and not able to work as Useual prayes he may be Acquitted from paying leavy tis granted.

Testis JNO. MAYES Clerk Vestr$_{y}$.

Bristoll P'ish—ss: At A Vestry held at y^{e} Chapple Sunday y^{e} 29th may 1726.

present. Mr. George Roberson Minister, Coll. Robt bolling, Maj. Wm. Kennon, Maj^{r} Robt Munford, Capt Richard Kennon, Capt peter Jones, Mr. thomas bott.

Samuel sental being an oald Man and Veary Much afflicted with pains In his feet So y^{t} he Is not able to work for his living as Useal humbly Seweth to this Vestry y^t he May be Acquitted from paying Leavy tis granted.

Testis JNO. MAYES Clerk Vestry.

Bristoll P'ish—ss: At A Vestry held At ye Chaple Sunday ye 12th June 1726.

presant. Mr. Georg Robertson Ministor, Coll. Robt bolling, Maj^r Wm. Kennon, Maj^r Robt Munford, Capt Henry Randolph, Capt buller Herbert, Capt Richard Kennon, Capt peter Jones, Mr. thomas bott.

John Trap being an oald Man Veary poor and not Able to Work As Useal humbly prayeth to this Vestry y^t he may be Acquitted from paying leavy tis granted.

John Dillihay Servant to Susannah Grig being A poor Craisey Sickley lad and not Able to Work Sufficiant for his maintinance She humbly prayeth to this Vestry y^t She may be Acquitted from paying leavy for him tis Granted.

It is ord'red y^t Maj^r Wm. Kennon Send for books Suitable for two Chapples and likewise three basons for the Use of baptism and he to be allowed for the Same by the p'ish.

Testis JNO. MAYES Clerk Vestry.

(21) Bristol p'ish—ss: At A Vestry held at ye Chapple June ye 29 1726.

present. Mr. George Robertson Minister, Coll. Robt bolling, Maj^r Wm. Kennon, Maj^r Robt Munford, Capt Richard Kennon, Capt peter Jones, Mr. George Wilson, In^s hall, Mr. George Archer, Mr. Tho. bott.

It Is ord'red y^t ye South Side bristol p'ish be Devided Into two prescints for Counting tob^{co} plants growing on Each Severill plantation bounded as followeth Viz^t beginning At appamattucks fearry thence Along the road to Stoney Creak bridge then up the Creak to the upper nottaway Road then along the s^d Road to the Extent of the p'ish.

peter Jones minor and his brother Wm. Jones are Appointed Counters for the upper prescinct. And Jno Mayes and Instance Hall Are Appoynted Counters for the lower precinct. And It is further ord'red y^t Wm. Davis be allowed seven hundred pounds of tob^{co} by ye p'ish for his trouble in Looking after and Buriing Eliz. Crooker.

Test JNO. MAYES Clerk Vestry.

Bristol p'ish—ss: At A Vestry held at the Chapple Sunday ye 16th oct^{r} 1726.

present. Mr. George Robertson Minister, Col. Robt bolling, Maj. Wm. Kennon, Maj^{r} Robt Munford, Capt peter Jones, Capt bullir herbert, Mr. george Wilson, Mr. th^{o} botte.

Upon A petition of Catherine Arthur their was Leavid for her Support fourty shillings ℘^{r} annum Dureing her necessity She being Aged and Weak and not Able to support her Self.

Test JNO. MAYES Clerk Vestry.

(22) Bristol parrish—ss: At A Vestry Held at the Chapple Nov^{br} 10th 1726.

present. Mr. George Robertson Minister, Maj^{r} Robt Munford, Mr. George Wilson Church Wardens, Coll. Robt Bolling, Maj^{r} Wm. Kennon, Capt peter Jon, Mr. tho^{s} bott, Capt buller Herbert.

It Is ord'red y^{t} John Ellis s^{r} be Acquitted from paying leavy for the futer and likewise for this present year.

It Is further ord'red y^{t} Nathaniel parrot be Clerk for ye Chapple at Sapponey and he to be Allow^{d} two thousand pounds of tobc^{o} ℘^{r} annom by the parrish. It Is Likewise ord'red y^{t} Mr. tho^{s} bott be Clerk for the Chapple at Nemursssens and he to be pay'd two thousand pound of tob^{co} ℘^{r} annum by the parrish.

It Is ord'red that henry tatam be Clerk for the ferry Church and Chapell and y^{t} he be Allow'd two thousand pounds of tob^{co} by the parrish ℘^{r} annum. It Is ord'red y^{t} Robt fellows be Acquitted from paying leavis for the futer.

It Is ord'red that Wm. poythris and Richard herbert be Sworn Vestry Men.

It Is ord'red that Richard price be Bound to Drury Oliver as the law Directs. The list of tithebles not being brought It Is ord'red y^{t} Coll. bolling, Maj^{r} Munford, Capt buller herbert proportion the leavys this Year. It Is further ord'red that Mr. George Robertson Minister preach once A month at Each Church or Chappl In the parrish and he to be allow'd twenty thousand pounds of tob^{co} ℘^{r} annum.

It Is likewise ordr'd y[t] Maj[r] Rob[t] Munford and Mr. Georeg Wilson Continue Church Wardens y[e] next year.

BRISTOL PARRISH DR. 1726.	tob'co	
To Mr. George Robertson Minister,	16,000	Cask.
To Mr. thomas Bott Clerk,	02,100	168
To Mrs. Eliz[a] Kennon for the fearry,	02,500	200
To henry tatam for setting the p'lams,	00,500	040
To Mary Dison for washing y[e] Church,	00,300	024
To Mr. Rich[d] Jones for bur'ing David peoples,	00,300	024
To Cap[t] beavil for bur'ing Indian George,	00,300	024
To Jn[o] tilman for keeping Glydewell,	01,000	080
To James W'ms for Cat[r] arthur 5[al],	01,000	080
To Catherine Arthur 40.	00,400	032
To Sam[l] birch for Cath[ar] Irvin,	00,400	032
To Wm. Stiles for Ditto,	00,400	032
To loflain flin for Ditto,	00,375	030
To John Garrat for Ditto,	00,075	006
To John brierly for Ditto,	00,125	010
To fillis liles for Eliz[a] Dodson,	00,200	016
To Mary Stiles for Ditto,	00,020	002
To Maj[r] Wm. Kennon for y[e] Chappel,	12,000	960
To Maj[r] Rob[t] Munford for Colwell,	12,000	960
To Maj[r] Wm. Kennon for books,	04,000	320
To Essix beavil for Jos. Sergan,	00,075	006
To Jane hill for Richard price,	01,000	080
To Mr. George Willson for y[e] Church yard,	00,060	005
To Ditto for Insolvants,	00,046	
To Maj[r] Munford 5. 11. 2,	01,112	081
To Ditto for Insolvants,	00,920	
To John Mayes for Clerk,	00,400	032
To Ditto for Clearing y[e] yard and for blocks for Doar steps,	00,150	012
	57,758	3,256
Cask,	3,256	
Salry at 10 ℔[r] ct.	5,775	
	66,789	

℘R. CONTRA CREDIT.

by 1,236 tithebles at 54 ℘^{r} pole is	66,789
Diew to ye parrish, ...	45

(23) 1726 SOUTH SIDE BRISTOL PARRISH DR.

To Mr. Ge^{o} Robertson Minister, ...	12,000	Cask.
To Mr. tho^{o} bott Reader, ...	01,500	120
To henry tatam, ...	00,500	40
To Richard Jones, ...	00,300	24
To John tilman, ...	01,000	80
To James W'ms, ...	01,000	80
To Cath^{a} Arthur, ...	00,400	32
To Samuel birch, ...	00,400	32
To Jame hill, ...	01,000	80
To Maj^{r} Munford 5^{lb} 11^{s} 2^{d}, ...	01,112	81
To Ditto for Insolvants, ...	00,920	
To John Mayes, ...	00,550	44
To Maj^{r} Munford for Colwell, ...	12,000	960
To Maj^{r} Wm. Kennon, ...	10,600	848
	43,283	2,421
Salry at 10 ℘ ct.	4,328	
Cask, ...	2,421	
	50,031	

℘R. CONTRA CR.

by 926 tithebles at 54 ℘^{r} pole is	50,004
Due to ye Colec^{tr}, ...	27
	50,031

1726.

Test JNO. MAYES Clerk Vestry.

1726 NORTH SIDE BRISTOL PARRISH DR.

To Mr. George Robertson, ...	4,000	Cask.
To Mr. Thomas Bott, ...	0,600	48
To Mary Dison, ...	0,300	24
To Capt John Bevil, ...	0,300	24
To Wm. Stiles, ...	0,420	34

To laughlin flyn,	0,375	30
To John Garret,	0,075	06
To phillis liles,	0,200	16
To Mr. George Wilson,	0,106	05
To Essex bevil,	0,075	06
To Maj^{r} Wm. Kennon,	4,000	320
To Ditto for Richard James,	1,400	112
To Mrs. Eliz^{a} Kennon,	2,500	200
To John Bryarly,	0,125	010
	14,476	835
Sall. at 10 ꝑ^{r} Ct.	1,447	
Cask,	835	
	16,758	

Test JNO. MAYES Clerk Vestry.

ꝑ CONTRA CR.

ꝑ^{r} 310 Tythables at 54 ꝑ^{r} pole is	16,740
Due to ye Col^{r},	18
	16,758

Test JNO. MAYES Clerk Vestry.

Bristol parrish—ss: At A Vestry held at the Chapple Jan^{r} ye 22d 1726.

present. Mr. George Robertson Minister, Coll^{d} Robt bolling, Maj^{r} Wm. Kennon, Maj^{r} Robt Munford, Mr. George Willson, Capt buller herbert.

It Is order'd y^{t} henry Mayes be allowed one thousand pounds of tob^{co} for the support of Jno Eagington at the laying the next parrish leavy.

Test JOHN MAYES Clerk Vestry.

(24) Bristol parrish—ss: At A Vestry held at the Chapple feb^{r} ye 19th 1726.

present. Mr. George Robertson Minister, Maj^{r} Robt Munford, Maj^{r} Wm. Kennon, Coll. Robt bolling, Capt Richd Kennon, Mr. Wm. poythris, Mr. george Wilson.

It Is ord'red that Maj[r] Rob[t] Munford Church Warden provide Necessary Suport for John Trap he being in A poor low Condition And to bring In his Accomp[t] at the laying the next p'ish leavy.

Test JNO. MAYES Clerk Vestry.

Bristol parrish—ss: At A Vestry held at y[e] Chapple May 2d 1727.

Present. Mr. George Robertson Minister, Coll. Rob[t] Bolling, Maj[r] Wm. Kennon, Maj[r] Rob[t] Munford, Mr. Geo. Wilson, Cap[t] Buller Herbert, Mr. George Archer, Mr. thomas bott.

It Is ord'red that Wm. traylor Keep and Attend the ferry at nemursens Chapple and he to be allow'd six hundred and thirty pounds of tob[co] ℘[r] Annom. it is likewise ord'red that Maj[r] Wm. Kennon send for Church ornaments for the two new Chapples at nemursens and Sapponey.

it is further ord'red that Rob[t] Aburtnartha be leavy free.

Ditto Chachaster Sturdivant.

Ditto th[o] totty.

It is ord'red that Edward Colwell be allow'd one thousand pound of tob[co] for building the little house at Sapponey Chapp'l to be pay'd out of the tob[co] now Leavi'd. the same for Rich[d] James for window shutters at nemurssens Chapple. Ditto Wm. Davis seven hundred for bur'ing Eliz[a] Crooker.

It is ord'red that Catherine Irvin is Discharg'd from the parrish and she is to have the blanket George Wilson bought for her and a waistcoat of plains of the parish. Mr. Rich[d] herbert hath taken the oath of a Vestryman.

Test JOHN MAYES Clerk Vestry.

Bristol p'ish—ss: At A Vestry held at the Chapple July the 4th 1727.

present. Mr. George Robertson Minister, Maj[r] Wm. Kennon, Cap[t] buller herberd, Cap[t] Richard herbert, Mr. Instance Hall, Cap[t] Richard Kennon, Mr. George Willson.

It is ordered that the South Side bristol parrish be Devided into two precincts for Counting tob[oo] plants Growing on Each Severial plantation bounded as follo[weth] Viz[t] beginning at appomattox ferry thence along that Roade to Stony Creek Bridge thence up the Creek to the upper notaway Road thence along the s[d] Road to the Extent of the parrish Abraham Jones and Wm. Jones are Appointed Counters for the upper precinct. Miles thweat and John Mayes for the lower precinct.

Alexander Mershal and John Epes for the North Side of the parrish Counters.

Test JOHN MAYES Clerk Vestry.

(25) Bristoll p'ish—ss: At A Vestry held at the ferry Chapple July y[e] 24th 1727.

Present. Mr. George Robertson Minister, Coll. Rob[t] bolling, Maj[r] Wm. Kennon, Maj[r] Rob[t] Munford, Mr. George Willson, Cap[t] buller herbert, Mr. George Archer, Mr. Wm. Poytheris.

By Order of Henrico County Court Dated y[e] 3d July 1727 for procssioning

Ord'red That peter baugh and Benj[a] locket procession from puckets Run to y[e] lower End of the parrish. henry Wallton and John pride procession between puckets Run and Swift Creek. Peter Rowlet and Wm. Worsham procession between Swift Creek Oald town Creek and Yewls branch. Cap[t] John beavel and henry Royall procession betw[een] the oald town Creek and Appomatox River as high as Mr. Botts. Thomas botte and Godfery fowler procession from Mr. Botts to the Extent of the parrish between the River and the Road henry Voaden and Webster Gill procession from Yewls branch to The Extent of the parrish on the North Side of the Road.

And further it Is ord'red By Vertue of an order of prince George County Court bareing Date 11th July 1727 and In obediance to the s[d] order to procession lands on the South Side Bristoll parrish Ord'red that John Liewes and henry tatam procession all the land from puddled Dock Run to the lower End of the parrish between the River and Ma[d] bollings Road. Ord'red that Daniel Sturdifant and procession from puddle Dock Run to the Nottoway Road as far out as blackwater.

It is likewise ord'red that Tho. hardiway and Abraham Alley procession from Nottoway Road up as far as Moncosneck Road. Ord'red that Wm. parsons and John Mayes procession from puddle Dock Run to leu[t] Run between the River and the Great

Swamp and moncosneck Road. Ord'red that peter Jones and Abr[a] Jones procession from Lev[ta] Run to the Indiantown Run Including Rhohoick. Ord'red that Nicholas Overberry and Rich[d] Smith procession from the Indian town Run to Wallisses Run. Ordr'd that Matthew Mayes and bath[o] Crowder procession from Wallissis to Mohipponock Creek. Ordr'd that John Ellington and William Spain procession from Mohipponock Creek to Nemurssens Creek. ord'red that Rob[t] Tucker and John Tally procession from Nemurssens Creek up the River and Deep Creek to the mouth of the Swett house. ord'red that Wm. Coalman and thos. hobby procession from the mouth of the Swett house branch up Deep Creek and the River to the Extent. ord'red that hugh lee and James baugh procession from the land of Second Swamp. ord'red that Johhn ledbetter and Sam[l] lee procession the land of Warrick Swamp. ord'red that Wm. Epes and Rich[d] Curlile procession the land of Joseps Swamp. ord'red That Rich[d] Raines and John hill proc'ssion the land of Jones hole Swamp. Ord'red that George Tillman proc'ssion with Wm. butler from moncosneck bridge Down the Creek to the Extent. Ord'red that James Williams and George W[ms] procession from Moncosneck Road to the New Road on hatchers Run. ordr'd that Nicolas Vaughan and James hudson procession from the fors[d] Road up hatchers Run to the Extent. ord'red that George Smith and Charles W[ms] proc'ssion from the Moncosneck Road up Gravillie Run and the Cattail. Ord-'red that George Stel and James Grigg procession the land of White oak and Bares swamp. Ord'red that francis Coalman and Matthew Anderson proc'ssion the land of butter Wood Swamp and the Rockey Run. Ord'red that Cap[t] John Evans and Joseph Tucker procession the land of Stoney Creek. Ord'red that Cap[t] Drury Stith and David W[ms] procession the land for Sapponey. Ord'red that David Walker and Samuel harwell procession from the County line to lickingplace branch on nottoway River Including buck skin. Ord'red that Wm. Davis and Th[o] Jones son of peter Jones proc'ssion from lickingplace branch up nottoway to the Extent.

It is further ord'red that the Church Wearthen for the North Side build a house of Sixteen foot and twelve and an inside Chimney on the best terms he Can.

It is ord'red that the S[d] Church Wearden supply Th[o] Watkins with Such Necessaries he thinks Convenient and also to imploy a Docter to Cure him of the desease he now labours under. Ord'red that the Church Wearthens bind out to Godfery Ragsdail two Mullatto Children by name Dol and bidde as the law directs. It is that a Child be bound to Wm. Matt as the law Directs by name Mary bibby.

Mr. Wm. poythris hath taken the oath of a Vestry Man.

Test JOHN MAYES Clerk Vestry.

(26) Bristoll P'ish—ss: at A Vestry held at the ferry Chapple Nove[m] y[e] 16th, 1727.

p'esent. Mr. George Robertson Minister, Maj[r] Rob[t] Munford, Mr. Geo. Wilson Church Warthens, Coll. Rob[t] bolling, Maj[r] Wm. Kennon, Maj[r] Rob[t] Munford, Mr. Th[o] bott, Cap[t] buller herbert, Mr. Rich[d] herbert, Mr. Wm. poythris.

It is ord'red that John Brown be Exempted from paying leavy Ditto John bethell Ditto Rich[d] Westmoreland.

It is ord'red that Maj[r] Wm. Kennon Send for four Surplieces to officiate in at Div'ne Service.

Ord'red that the Church Warthens take Security of Th[o] Jones for the keeping Wm. Mote from y[e] Charg of the Parrish.

It is ord'red that Maj[r] Wm. Kennon find Catherine Urvin with Cloathes and to bring in his ac[mt] at the laying the next p'ish levy. It is ord'red that the Church Wearthens be allow'd what they are out for making The Illconvenient tob[co] Convenient at the laying the next levy. ord'red That betty Gill a bastard Child of Mary Gill be bound to Cap[t] buller herbert as the law Directs.

It is ord'red that Maj[r] Rob[t] Munford and Mr. George Willson Continue Churchwarthens and Collectors for the Ensuing year.

BRISTOLL P'ISH DR.

To Mr. Geo. Robertson Minister, . . .	20,000	Cask.
To Mr. Tho. bott, Clerk Nemussens Church,	02,000	160
To Nathaniel parrot Clerk Sapponey Church,	02,000	160
To henry tatam Clerk of the Mother Church and ferry Chapple, ...	02,000	160
To Mrs. Eliz[a] Kennon for ferry, . . .	02,500	200

To Mary Dison for Cleaning the Church, .	00,300	024
To John Mayes for Clerk Vestry, . . .	00,400	032
To Wm. Traylor for Nemurssens ferry, .	00,630	050
To Catherine Arthur 40, ...	00,400	032
To henry Mayes for Eaginton, . . .	01,000	080
To Majr Wm. Kennon Church orniments, .	08,000	640
To Mr. George Willson for the parish house,	01,000	080
To Ditto for Insolvants, ...	00,086	
To Geor. Wms for buriing Glidewell, . .	00,370	030
To John tillman for keeping Glidewill 9 months,	00,750	060
To Wm. Worsham for Cureing Tho Watkins,	00,490	039
To George Willson for keeping Catherine Urvin and one pair shoes, ...	00,440	035
To James long for keeping of Ditto, . .	00,100	008
To Mr. Tho Eldridge for Sarah Vaughan, .	00,150	012
To Majr Robt Munford, ...	00,315	025
To Natha parrot for the Church yard & hors block, ...	00,300	024
	43,231	1,851
Sall, ...	4,323	
Cask, ...	1,851	
	49,405	

Ꝑr CONTRA CREDIT.

by 1,334 tithebles at 37 Ꝑr pole is 49,405.
Due to ye p'ish 47.

(27) Bristoll p'ish—ss: at A Vestry Call'd at the ferry Chapple febu ye 18th 172$\frac{8}{7}$.

present. Mr. George Robertson Minister, Majr Robt Munford, Majr Wm. Kennon, Capt buller herbert, Mr. George Willson, Mr. Wm. poythris, Mr. Richard herbert.

Peter plantine being Much Burnt by an acsident and he being poor and aged Not able to pay for his Cure Mary hall is ord'red to Take Care of the Sd plantine and to Do her Endeavour to Cure him and She to bring in her acmt att the laying The Next parrish leavy.

Test JOHN MAYES Clerk Vestry.

Bristol p'ish—ss: at A Vestry held at the ferry Chapple Sunday y[e] 14th aprill 1728.

present. Mr. George Robertson Minister, Maj[r] Rob[t] Munford Church Warthen, Coll. Rob[t] Bolling, Maj[r] Wm. Kennon, Cap[t] buller Herbert, Mr. Rich[d] Herbert.

Rob[t] Glidewell Being affincted With a Cancur in his face which hath Made him unable to labour for his livelihood it is ord'red that the Church Warthen find him necessary Cloathin and likewise that John Browder find him necessary board and he to be allow'd one hundred pounds of tob[o] ℘[r] month.

Test JOHN MAYES Clerk Vestry.

Bristoll Parrish—ss: At a Vestry Held at The Ferry Chapple Octb[r] 15th, 1728.

Mr. George Robertson Minister, Mr. William poythris, Mr. George Willson Church Warthens, Coll[d] Rob[t] Bolling, Maj[r] Wm. Kennon, Maj[r] Rob[t] Munford, Cap[t] Richard Kennon, Cap[t] Buller Herbert, Mr. James Munford, Mr. James Munford, Mr. Instance Hall, Mr. Th[o] Bott.

Mr. James Munford admitted and Sworn a Vestry Man.

on the Motion of Edward Colwell that peter a mulatt Boy Should be Bound to him it is ord'red that the Churchwarthens Bind him to the s[d] Colwell to serve according to law.

Francis Bracy haveing Signified to this Vestry that he is willing to Provide for peter Plantine for the Useal allowance ord'red that the S[d] Plantine Immediately repair to y[e] s[d] bracy.

It is Further ord'red that frances Eliz[a] thompson Be Removed into the Next parrish Through Which She Came By y[e] Church Warthens of this Parrish So Soon as they think her in a condition to Remove to be provided for at the Charge of the parrish Dureing her Inability.

Ord'red That Mr. William Poythris and Mr. George Willson Be Church Warthens and Collectors for the Ensuing year.

It is ord'red that an ad'tion of twenty foot Squair Be Built to Each of the New Chapples.

Test JNO. MAYES Clerk Vestry.

(28) BRISTOLL PARRISH DR. Octb^{r} 1728.

		Cask.
To Mr. George Robertson Minister,	20,000	1,600
To Mr. Th^{o} Bott Clerk,	02,000	0,160
To Henry Tatam Clerk,	02,000	0,160
To Nath^{a} parrot Clerk,	02,000	0,160
To Mrs. Eliz^{a} Kennon for ye ferry,	02,500	0,200
To Mary Dison for Cleaning ye Church	00,300	0,024
To John Mayes for Clerk,	00,400	0,032
To Cath^{a} Arthur 40,	00,400	0,032
To Henry Mayes for Eaginton,	01,000	0,080
To John Browder for Glidewell,	00,700	0,056
To William Traylor for ye ferry,	00,630	0,050
To Mary Hall for peter Plantine,	00,800	0,064
To Maj^{r} Kennon for Church orniments,	08,000	0,640
To Maj^{r} Munford for ye Illconvenient tob^{o},	02,613	0,128
To George Willson for the Illconvenient tob^{o},	00,100	0,008
To George Willson for Watkins & Wine,	00,176	0,008
To Edward Collwell for plantine,	00,400	0,032
To Wm. Butler for his Care of newhous,	00,500	0,040
To Eliz^{a} Dodson for Charity,	00,250	0,020
To Titus Crutcher for Eliz^{a} thompson,	00,200	0,016
To Godfrey Rags Dail for Ditt^{o},	00,200	0,016
	45,169	3,526
Sall,	4,517	
Cask,	3,526	
	53,212	

By 1,543 Tithables at 34 ½ ℔^{r} Pole is 53,212.
Diew to ye Parrish 21.

1728 NORTH SIDE BRISTOL PARRISH DR.

		Cask.
To Mr. Robertson,	4,650	370
To Mr Tho. Bott,	0,550	044
To Mary Dison,	0,300	024
To Mrs. Eliz^{a} Kennon,	2,500	200
To Wm. Traylor,	0,630	050
To Eliz. Dodson,	0,250	020

To Godfery Ragsdail, ...	0,200	016
To Titus Crutcher, ...	0,200	016
To George Willson, ...	0,276	016
To John Mayes, ...	0,235	019
To Mary Hall, ...	0,800	064
	10,591	839
Sall, ...	1,059	
	11,650	
Cask, ...	839	
	12,489	

By 362 Tithables at 34 ½ ℘r Pole is 12,489.

It is ord'red By ye Vestry and Mr. George Willson is hereby Impowered To Collect Receive and Recover of the above 362 Tithables 34½lb tobo ℘r pole By Distress or otherwise and to Make Good payments as above Rend'ring accomt to ye Vestry and no Errors.

Test JNO. MAYES Clerk Vestry.

1728 SOUTH SIDE BRISTOL PARRISH DR.

		Cask.
To Mr. George Robertson, ...	15,350	1,230
To Mr. Tho. Bott, ...	01,450	0,116
To nathaniel parrot, ...	02,000	0,160
To henry Tatam, ...	02,000	0,160
To John Mayes, ...	00,165	0,015
To Catharine Arthur, ...	00,400	0,032
To henry Mayes, ...	01,000	0,080
To John Browder, ...	00,700	0,056
To Majr Kennon, ...	08,000	0,640
.To Majr Munford, ...	02,613	0,128
To Edward Colwell, ...	00,400	0,032
To Wm. Butler, ...	00,500	0,040
	34,578	2,689
Sall, ...	3,458	
Cask, ...	2,689	
	40,725	

By 1,181 Tithables at 34½ ℔r Pole is 40,744½.

it is ord'red By ye Vestry and Mr. Wm. Poythris is here By Impowered To Collect Receive and Recover of the above 1,181 Tithebles 34½lb tobo ℔r pole By distress or otherwise and to make good payment as above Rend'ring accmt to the Vestry and no Errors.

Test JNO. MAYES Clerk Vestry.

(29) Bristoll parrish—ss: at A Vestry held at ye ferry Chapple June ye 15th 1728.

present. Mr. George Robertson Minister, Coll. Robt Bolling, Coll. Wm. Kennon, Majr Robt Munford, Capt Richard Kennon, Capt Buller Herbert, Mr. Ric'ard Herbert, Mr. Wm. poythris, Mr. George Willson, Mr. Instance Hall.

In obedience to an act of assembly for the better Improveing the Staple of tobo it is ord'red that the parrish be Devided into precints for Counting tobo plants as followeth Vizt the South Side to begin at the parrish ferry thence along the moncosneck Road to Stoney Creek bridge thence up the Sd Creek to the Upper Nottoway Road thence along the Sd Road to Nottoway River the Extent of the parrish all above ye Sd bound James pittillo and henry Wyatt are appointed and ord'red Counter for yt precinct: and John Mayes and David Werren for the lower precinct: the North Side of the Sd parrish Allexande White and Wm. Chambers are appointed Counters of tobo plants.

It is likewise ord'red that John Grace be acquitted from paying parrish leavy.

Test JOHN MAYES Clerk Vestry.

Bristoll Parrish—ss: At a Vestry Call'd at ye ferry Chapple febr ye 16th, 172$\frac{8}{9}$.

Present. Mr. George Robertson Minister, Coll Robt Bolling, Majr Wm. Kennon, Majr Robt Munford, Mr. Wm. poythris, Capt Buller Herbert, Capt James Munford.

Upon The Motion of Daniel Jackson That John Pucket is Run away and left one of his Children With him By name Eliza pucket prayes that the Sd Child Be bound to him and his heirs as the law directs Tis Granted.

It is Likewyse ordred that agnis waller Smithis Bastard Child of Charity Smithis Be Bound to Wm. Gates and his wife Susan as the law Directs.

It is Further ordred that John Gilliam orphan of John Gilliam Decs[d] Be Bound to Joseph Grainger and his heirs as the Law Directs.

Test JOHN MAYES Clerk Vestry.

Bristoll Parrish—ss: at A Vestry Held at y[e] Ferry Chapple June 8th, 1729.

Present. Mr. Geo. Robertson Minister, Coll Robert Bolling, Coll Wm. Kennon, Coll Robert Munford, Mr. Richard herbert, Cap[t] Buller herbert, Mr. Instance hall, Cap[t] James Munford, Mr. George Willson, Mr. Wm. Poythris, Church Warthens.

Jacob Butler Being in the Parrish afflicted with Soares and sickness So that he is not able to Support himself in this his Necessity the Church Warthens are hereby ordred to agree With Doct[r] James Thompson for his Cure on the Best terms They Can and to Bring in his acc[mt] at the laying the nex p'ish leavy.

Test JOHN MAYES Clerk Vestry.

(30) Bristoll Parrish—ss: at A Vestry held at the ferry Chapple Jully 24th, 1727, for procssioning.

Present. M[r] George Robertson Minister, Coll Robert Bolling, Maj[r] William Kennon, Maj[r] Robert Munford, Mr. George Willson, Cap[t] Buller herbert, Mr. George Archer, Mr. Wm. Poythris.

By Vertue of an order of Prince George County Court Dated July 11th 1727 for processioning Every Perticuler persons land in their parrish in obedience to the S[d] order the S[d] parrish is Devided into precincts for Proc'ssioning and Returns made as followeth Viz[t] the bounds of John liewes and henry tatam Proc'ssioned the persons concern'd Being present. The Bounds of Daniel Sturdifant and Instance hall Proc'ssioned Except a line Between Batty and henry Willson the S[d] Batty Refuseing to procession. the lines Between Maj[r] Jno. Bolling and Wm. Batt & Coll. Bolling and Charles hudson, Wm. More and Charles hudson: Wm. More and Jno. Sturdifant Wm. Batt and Rob[t] Poythris: Duglas Irby and Rob[t] poythris y[e] parties Concerned not appearing: a line Between Wm. poythris and Wm.

Crawley Not Processioned y[e] S[d] Crawley Not appearing. The Bounds of Tho. hardiway and abraham alley no Return. The Bound of Wm. Parsons and Jno. Mayes processioned the Parties Concerned Being present. The Bound of peter Jones and Abraham Jones Processioned Except a line Between Coll. Bolling and Jno. Wall they not appearing in presence of James Munford, Rich[d] Jones, Peter Jones: Wm. Jones and henry Baley. the Bounds of Nicholas Overberry and Richard Smith Processioned the parties Concerned Being Present. The Bound of Matthew Mayes and Bath[o] Crowder processioned Except the land of Joseph Woodlif he not appearing the parties Concerned Being Present. The Bounds of Jno. Ellington & Wm. Spain Processioned the parties Concerned Being Present. The Bounds of Robert Tucker and Jno. Tally Processioned the parties Concern'd Being present. the Bounds of Tho. hobby and Wm. Coalman Processioned the parties Concern'd Being present. The Bounds of James Baugh and hug lee no return. The Bounds of Jno. ledbetter and Samuell lee processioned the parties Concerned Being present Except Thomas adison: Jno. Chamnis: Jno. Golikely hugh golikely Jno. Mitchell Rich[d] flewelling. The Bounds of Wm. Epes and Richard Curlile No Return. The Bound of Richard Raines and Jno. hill No Return. The Bounds of George Tillman and Wm. Butler No Return. The Bound of James W[ms] and George Williams Processioned the parties Concerned Being present Except Ralf Jackson and Gabrill harrison they not appearing. The Bounds of Nicholas Vaughan and James hudson no Return. The Bounds of George Smith and Charles W[ms] no Return. The Bounds of George Stell and James Gregg No Return. The Bounds of Matthew anderson and francis Coalman Processioned the parties Concerned Being present. The Bounds of Cap[t] Jno. Evans and Joseph Tucker No Return. The Bounds of Cap. Drury Stith and Mr. David Williams No Return. The Bounds of Mr. David Walker and Sam[l] harwell Processioned Except John Raybors and Charles Rabors. The Bounds of Wm. Davis and Th[o] Jones processioned the parties Concerned Being present.

and further it is ord'red By Vertue of an order of henrico County Court Baring Date 3d July 1727 for processioning lands on the North Side the p'ish and in obedience to y[e] S[d] order the persons appointed Make Return as followeth Viz^{t} The Bounds of peter Baugh and Benj^{a} locket no Return. The Bounds of Jno pride and henry Walthall processioned the parties Concerned Being all present. The Bounds of Webster Gill and henry Vodin processioned Except a line Betwen Wm. poythris and James Thomson: & Wm. poythris and Ja^{s} franklin: James Thomson and Maj^{r} Kannon: Eliz^{a} Randolph and Richd Willson Maj^{r} Kennon and tho^{m} totty they not appearing.

(31) Returns Made for Processioning land on the North Side Bristoll Parrish for the year 1727.

The Bounds of peter Baugh and Benj^{a} locket no Return.

The Bound of John Pride and henry Wallthall processioned the parties Concern^{d} Being all Presint. The Bound of Webster Gill and henry Vodin procss^{d} Excep a line Between Wm. Poythris and James Thompson and Wm. poythris aand Jas: franklin: and a line Between Maj^{r} Kennon and Jas: Thompson a line Between Eliz^{a} Randolpt and Richd Willson a line Between Maj^{r} Kennon and Th^{om} Totty They Not Giveing their attendance When such Processioning Was to have Been perfourmd. The Bound of peter Rowlet and Wm. Worsham Processioned the parties Concerned Being all Present. The Bound of Jno Beavil and henry Royall No Return. The Bound of Th^{o} Bott and Godfrie fowler No Return Made.

Test JNO. MAYES Clerk Vestry.

Bristoll Parrish—ss: at a Vestry Held at the ferry Chappell June 14th 1729 for Counting tob^{o} plants.

Present. Mr. George Robertson Minister, Coll Robert Bolling, Coll Wm. Kennon, Coll Robert Munford, Mr. George Willson, Capt Buller herbert, Mr. Richard herbert, Capt James Munford, Capt Richard Kennon, Mr. Instance Hall.

It is ordred that the Parrish Be Devided into precincts for Counting Tob^{o} plants as followeth Viz^{t}: The South Side to Begin at the Liv^{t} Run thence up the S^{d} Run to moncosneck Road thence along the S^{d} Road to stonie Creek thence up the S^{d} Creek to the upper nottoway Road thence along the S^{d} Road to ye Extent of the parrish all above the S^{d} Bounds James pittillo and John Butler are appointed Counters for that precinct and all Below the S[d] Bound John Mayes and Miles Thweat are to Count To the Extent of the parrish—and allexander White White and Wm. Chambers are to Count all on the North Side with in the parrish and to Make Return as the Law directs.

It is further ordred that two Mulotto Children By name peter & tom Be Bound to Henry Royall as the law Directs.

It is ordred that Liewellin Sturdifant Be Exempted from paying parrish leavy.

It is further ordred that the Church Warthens agree With Doct[r] thompson for the Cure of Jacob Butler and to Bring in their accm[t] at the laying the nex parrish leavy.

Test JOHN MAYES Clerk Vestry.

(32) Bristoll P'ish—ss: at a Vestry held at the ferry Chapple august 3d 1729.

Present. Mr. George Robertson Minister, Coll. Rob[t] Bolling, Maj[r] Wm. Kennon, Coll Rob[t] Munford, Cap[t] Rich[d] Kennon, Mr. Instance hall, Mr. George Willson, Cap Jas. Munford.

Upon the petition of Eliz[a] Glidewell that She is a poor Widow and Not able to Take Care of her Children Desires that her son Rob[t] Glidewell Be Bound to Th[o] Clemmon as the law Directs tis Granted.

Test JOHN MAYES Clerk Vestry.

Bristol Parrish—ss: At A Vestry Held at y[e] Ferry Chapple Octob[r] 15th 1729 for laying y[e] Parrish Levy Viz[t]:

Present. Mr. George Robertson Minister, Col[o] Rob[t] Bolling, Maj[r] Wm. Kennon, Col[o] Rob[t] Munford, Cap[t] Rich[d] Kennon, Cap[t] Wm. Poythris, Mr. Th[o] Bott, Mr. Ins. Hall, Mr. George Willson.

1729. Mr. Theop[l] Field took y[e] oath of allegiance &c: & the oath of a Vestryman.

To Mr. Robertson Minister,	20,000	1,600
To Mr. Th[o] Bott,	2,000	160
To Nath[a] Parrot,	2,150	172
To Henry Tatam,	1,900	152
To Eliz[a] Kennon,	2,500	200
To Mary Dison,	300	24
To Jn[o] Mayes,	400	32

To Th° Fowler, ...	1,000	80
To Wm. Traylor ℔r ferry, ...	630	50
To francis Brasie for plantine, ...	1,000	80
To Eliz[a] Dodson, ...	600	48
To Mr. James Thompson, ...	1,260	100
To Micael Hill, ...	1,000	80
To Xp[r] Martin ℔r Mrs. Thompson, . .	400	32
To Col° Rob[t] Munford, ...	712	
To Mr. George Willson, ...	231	
To Cap[t] Wm. Poythris fo Inconvenient tob°,	2,233	
To Ditto for Insolvants, ...	680	
To Ditto for Bread and Wine, ...	350	28
To Jn° Walker, ...	600	48
To Jn° Bethel, ...	600	48
To Cath[a] arthur, ...	400	32
	40,946	2,966
Cask, ...	2,966	
	43,912	
salry at 10 ℔ Ct, ...	4,094	
	48,006	

℔r Credit.

By 1,641 tith[a] at 29 ℔r Pole is	47,589
Due to y[e] Collectors, ...	417
	48,006

It is ordred that y[e] Collectors Collect and Receive from Every Tithable person 29 pound of tob° for their Parrish leavy for this Present year in Case of Refusal or nonpayment to Leavy the same by Distress.

Test Jno. Mayes Clerk Vestry.

(33) Mr. Peter Jones Jn[r] took y[e] oath of allegiance &c and the oath of a Vestryman and their upon is admitted a Vestryman.

Cap[t] Wm. Poythris and Mr. George Willson is appointed Church-warthens and Collec[rs] for y[e] Ensuing year.

Upon the Petition of Sam[l] Harwell Jun[r] it is ord'red that Betty and Jn[o] Mullattoes Be Bound to him By y[e] Churchwarthens according to Law.

Test JNO. MAYES Clerk Vestry.

1729 NORTH SIDE BRISTOL PARRISH DR.

To Mr. Robertson Minister,	5,000	400
To Mary Dison,	300	24
To Th[o] Fowler,	1,000	80
To Wm. Traylor,	630	50
To Doct[r] Thompson,	1,260	100
To Xp[r] Martin,	400	32
To George Willson,	231	
To Mr. Th[o] Bott,	541	44
	9,362	730
Sall[r],	936	
Cask,	730	
	11,028	

℘[r] CONTRA CREDIT.

By 377 tithables at 29 ℘[r] pole is	10,933	lb tob[o]
Due to y[e] Collector,	95	
	11,028	

It is ord'red By the Vestry and Mr. George Willson is here By Impowered to Collect Receive and Recover of the above 377 tithables 29 pounds of tob[o] ℘[r] pole By Distraint or otherwise and to Make Good payment as above Rendring acc[mt] to the Vestry and no Errours.

Test JNO. MAYES Clerk Vestry.

1729 SOUTH SIDE BRISTOL PARRISH DR.

To Mr. George Robertson,	15,000	1,200
To Mr. Bott,	1,459	116
To Nath[a] Parrot,	2,150	172
To Henry Tatam,	1,900	152
To Mrs. Eliz[a] Kennon,	2,500	200

To Jn° Mayes,	400	32
To francis Brasie,	1,000	80
To Eliz^a Dodson,	600	48
To Coll. Munford,	712	
To Capt Wm. poythris,	2,233	
To D°,	680	
To D°,	350	28
To Jn° Walker,	600	48
To Jn. Bethel,	600	48
To Cath^a arthur,	400	32
To Micael Hill,	1,000	80
	31,584	2,236
Sal,	3,158	
Cask,	2,236	
	36,978	

℘^r CONTRA CREDIT.

By 1,264 tithables at 29 ℘^r pole is,	36,656
Due to ye Collector,	322
	36,978

It is ord'red By the Vestry and Capt Wm. Poythris is hereby Impow'red to Collect Receive and Recover of the above 1,264 tithables 29 pound of tob° ℘^r pole By Distraint or otherwise and to Make Good Payment as above Rend'ring accm^t to the Vestry and no Errours.

Test JNO. MAYES Clerk Vestry.

(34) Bristol Parrish—ss: At A Vestry Held at The ferry Chapple Decem^br 26th 1729.

Present. Mr. George Robertson Minister, Coll° Robert Bolling, Maj^r Wm. Kennon, Coll° Robert Munford, Capt Richard Kennon, Capt Wm. Poythris, Mr. George Willson, Mr. Instance Hall, Capt Jam^s Munford, Mr. Peter Jones.

John Obanck is appointed Clerk of the ferry Chapple for which He is to be Paid Sixteen Hundred pounds of tobacco anually. samuel Pitchford is appointed Clerk of the Church for which he is to Be payd Sixtee hundred pounds of tobacco anually.

Test JNO. MAYES Clerk Vestry.

Bristol Parrish—ss: At A Vestry Held at the ferry Chapple Jan^{r} 12th 172$\frac{9}{30}$.

present. Mr. George Robertson Minister, Coll^{o} Robt Bolling, Maj^{r} Wm. Kennon, Coll^{o} Robt Munford, Capt Richd Kennon, Mr. The^{o} field, Mr. George Willson.

It is ordred that an addition of twenty foot be Built to the East End of the two outward Chapples With Doubles Pews &c:

Henry Baley agrees to Make the addition to Sapponey Chappel and to finish The Same by the 25th day december next for which he is to be payd Seventy pounds in tob^{o} at the price the Standing london Stores then Give and Coll Robt Munford is desired and appointed to take Bond for the trew performance of the S^{d} work.

Maj^{r} Wm. Kennon Likewise agrees to make the addition to the Chapple at Nemussens and to finish the Same by the 25th day of december next for which He is to be payd Seventy pound in tob^{o} at the price the Standing London Stores then Give and Coll^{o} Robt Munford is desired and appointed to take Bond for the trew performance of the S^{d} work.

it is ordered that Paul seers Be acquitted from paying parrish Leavy.

Test JNO. MAYES Clerk Vestry.

(35) Bristol Parrish—ss: at A Vestry Held at ye ferry Chapple June 7th 1730.

present. Mr. George Robertson minister, Coll^{o} Robt Munford, Maj^{r} Wm. Kennon, Capt Wm. Poythris, Capt Richard Kennon, Mr. George Willson.

Upon the Petition of Eliz^{a} Ellis that She Haveine an Indian Slave afflicted with Sickness and not able to labour it is ordred y^{t} he be Exemted from paying parrish Leavy.

Saml more is also acquitted from paying parrish Leavy. Richd Cook is likewise acquitted from paying parrish Leavy.

Test JNO. MAYES Clerk Vestry.

Bristoll Parriss—ss: at A Vestry Held at the Ferry Chapple July 9th 1730.

Present. Mr. George Robertson minister, Coll° Robᵗ Munford, Majʳ Wm. Kennon, Capᵗ Wm. Poythris, Capᵗ Richᵈ Kennon, Mr. George Willson.

Upon the Petition of Thompson Staple that He Being aged and a Cripple it is ordred That he Be acquitted from paying Parrish Leavy.

It is Likewise ordred that a Mulatto Child By name Ned Born In the yᵉ house of Godfrey Rags Dail Be Bound to Him and His Heirs as the Law Directs.

Upon the petition of Nathaniel Parrott that the House he now Lives in neer Sapponey Chappel Standing in an Inconvenient part it is agree'd on By the Vestry that the Sᵈ house Be Removed to Sum more Convenient place for the good of the parrish.

Test JNO. MAYES Clerk Vestry.

Bristol Parrish—ss: At a Vestry Call'd at the Ferry Chappel febr 14th 1730. To make Choice of a Clerk at the nemussens Chappel.

Present. Mr. George Robertson minister, Coll° Robert Bolling, Majʳ Wm. Kennon, Coll° Robert Munford, Capᵗ James Munford, Mr. Thofilus Field, Capᵗ Richard Kennon, Mr. Peter Jones, Mr. George Willson.

Mr. George Robertson minister is ordred and appointed to Make Choice of a Clerk for the Sᵈ Nemussens Chappel in the Sted of Mr. Thomas Bott Decsᵈ who makes Choice of Mr. Thomas Spain and the Sᵈ Spain is ordred and Impowered to be Clerk of the nemussens Chapple and to Resceive of the parrish 1,600 pound of Tobᶜᵒ anually.

Test JNO. MAYES Clerk Vestry.

(36) Bristol P'ish—ss: at a Vestry held at the ferry Chapple Octber 15th 1730. For laying the Parrish Leavy.

Present. Mr. George Robertson minister, Coll° Robert Bolling, Majʳ Wm. Kennon, Coll° Robert Munford, Mr. George Willson, Capᵗ Wm. poythris, Capᵗ Richard Kennon, Capᵗ James Munford, Mr. Peter Jones.

To Mr. George Robertson minister,	20,000	1,600
To Mr. Thomas Bott for Clerk,	2,000	160
To Nathaniel Parrott for Clerk,	2,000	160
To John Wobank for Clerk,	1,600	128
To Samuel Pitchford for Clerk,	1,600	128
To Eliz[a] Kennon for y[e] ferry,	2,500	200
To Mary Dison for Cleening y[e] Church,	300	24
To John Mayes for Clerk to y[e] vestry,	400	32
To William Traylor for the ferry,	630	52
To Ditto for 3 setts of hors Blocks,	100	8
To Eliz[a] Dodson for Cleening y[e] Church,	600	48
To John Crowder for Keeping Eaginton,	1,000	80
To James Hudson for Keeping plantine,	1,000	80
To Mr. Brasie for Cloathing plantine,	300	24
To Matthew Tolbert for Reeding,	150	12
To John Liewess for Reeding,	100	8
To John Mayes for Buriing Jn[o] Johnson,	300	24
To Jn[o] Powell for Cleening y[e] Church yard,	200	16
To Coll. Bolling for nessisaries to King,	695	56
To Jn[o] Walker for Charity,	600	48
To Maj[r] William Kennon for the Chapil,	14,000	1,120
To Henry Baley the same,	14,000	1,120
To Sam[l] Burch for Charity,	600	48
To Mr. George Willson for Insolvants To Ditto for Bread and Wine	769	14
To Cap[t] William Poythris for Insolvants,	1,140	
To Ditto makeing tob[o] Convenient with Bread and Wine,	2,022	162
	68,606	5,352
Sall,	6,860	
Cask,	5,352	
	80,818	

By 1709 Tithables at 47 ℔[r] pole is,	80,323
Due to the Collectors,	495
	80,818

Upon the Petition of the Remote Inhabitance of this Parrish for a Chaplil to Be Built Between Smacks and Knibs Creek it is Thought Necessary that a Chapil Be Built of the following Dem'tions Viz[t] fourty foot long twenty foot wide By the Directions of Coll. Rob[t] Bolling Maj[r] William Kennon Cap[t] Ja[s] Munford & Mr. George Willson Who are Impowered and Desired By this Vestry to agree with Workmen to Do the same on the Best terms They Can and to appoint the place Where it Shall Be Satt.

Cap[t] James Munford and Mr. George Willson is ord'red and appointed Church Warthens and Collectors for the Insuing year.

Test JNO. MAYES Clerk Vest[r].

(37) 1730 NORTH SIDE BRISTOL PARRISH DR.

To Mr. Robertson,	4,350	348
To Mr. Bott,	600	48
To Mrs. Kennon,	2,500	200
To Mary Dison,	300	24
To Sam[l] pitchford,	1,600	128
To Wm. Traylor,	730	60
To George Willson,	769	64
To Maj[r] Kennon,	4,000	320
Sall,	1,448	
Cask,	1,142	
	17,475	

CR.

℔ 371 tithables at 47 ℔ pole is,	17,437
Due to y[e] Collector,	38
	17,475

1730 SOUTH SIDE BRISTOL PARRISH DR.

To Mr. Robertson,	15,650	1,252
To Mr. Th[os] Bott,	1,400	112
To Nath[a] Parrott,	2,000	160
To John Wobank,	1,600	128
To John Mayes,	700	56
To Eliz[a] Dodson,	600	48

To John Browder,	1,000	80
To James Hudson,	1,000	80
To Francis Bracie,	300	24
To Mat Tolbert,	150	12
To John Lewis,	100	8
To John Powell,	200	16
To Collo Bolling,	695	56
To John Walker,	600	48
To Majr Kennon,	10,000	800
To Hen' Baly,	14,000	1,120
To Collo Bolling,	600	48
To Capt Poythris,	3,162	162
	53,757	4,210
Sall:	5,376	
Cask,	4,210	
	63,343	

CR.

℔ 1,338 tithables at 47 ℔ Pole is,	62,886
Due to the Collector,	00,457
	63,343

It is ord'red By the Vestry and Capt James Munford is Hereby Impowered to Collect Receive and Recover of the above 1,338 Tithables 47 pounds of tobo ℔ Pole By Distraint or otherwise and to make good Payment as above Rend'ring account to ye Vestry and no arreers.

Test JNO. MAYES Clerk Vestry.

Bristol P'ish—ss: Aat a vestry held at the fery Chapple May 30th, 1731.

pr'sent. Collo Robt Bolling, Majr Wm. Kennon, Collo Robt Munford, Capt Richd Kennon, Capt Wm. poythris, Mr. George Willson, Capt James Munford, Mr. peter Jones.

Upon the petition of Richard Cook Francis Merrymoon & Lenord Dison That They Being antient and not able to labour it is ordred By the Vestry yt They be acquitted from paying parish Leavy. Jno Kemp Being afflicted with Long sickness and not able to helpe himself It is ordred By the Vestry that the Church Warthens take Care and provide for the S^d^ Jn° Kemp and to bring in their accm^t^ at the laying the next parrish Leavy.

Test JNO. MAYES Clerk Vestry.

(38) Bristol p'ish—ss: Aat a Vestry Held at the ferry Chapple august 3d 1731. For appointing Processioners of land.

present. Mr. George Robertson Minister, Coll° Robt Munford, Maj^r^ Wm. Kennon, Mr. The° Field, Capt Richd Kennon, Capt Wm. poythris, Mr. George Willson, Capt James Munford, Coll° Robt Bolling, Mr. peter Jones.

By Vertue of an order of Henrico County Court Dated in obedience to the Said order to procession lands on the north Side Bristol p'ish to Be divided into precincts is as followeth vizt.

It is ordred That Henry Batt and peter Baugh procession from puckets Run to the lower End of the parrish: Richard Walthal & Jn° pride procession Between puckets Run and Swift Creek: George Willson Jn^r^ & Wm. Worsham procession Between Swift Creek oald town Creek & youls Branch Robert Beavil & Henry Royall proc'ssion Between oald town Creek & appomatox River as hig up as Mr. Botts: Thomas Bott & Godfrey Fowler procssion from Mr. Botts: to ye Extent of the parrish Between the River and the Road. Henry Vodin & Webster Gill procssion from youls Branch to ye Extent of the parrish on the North Side of the Road.

and Further it is ordred By Vertue of an order of prince George County Court Bareing Date and in obedience to the S^d^ order to procssion lands on ye South Side Bristol p'ish to Be Devided into precincts is as followeth Viz^t^:

It is ordred that Jn° Liewess & James Sturdivant procession from pudledock Run to the Lower End of the p'ish Between the River & madam bollings Road: Saml Jordain & Wm. Batt Procession from puddle Dock Run to the nottoway Road as far out as Blackwater. Thomas Hardiway & abr^a^ alle procssion from nottoway Road up as far as moncosneck Road. William Parsons & Jno° Mayes procession from puddle dock to Leu^t^ Run ween the River & the Great Swamp & moncosneck Road.

Peter Jones & abr^a^ Jones procession from Leut^n^ Run to the Indiantown Run Including Rohowick. Nicolas overberry &

Richd Smith from the Indiantown Run to Wallaces Creek Matthew Mayes & Bath^{o} Crowder procssion from Wallisses Creek to mohiponock out to hatchers Run. Jno Ellington & Wm. spain procssion from mohiponock to nemussens out as far as Bollings lower line. Robert Tucker & Jno Tally procession from nemussens up the River and winticomack. Walthur Childes & Robert Tucker Jn^{r} from winticomake up the River to Deep Creek so up Deep Creek to the sweathouse so up the south side the sweat house and winticomake to ye Extent. William Green and abr^{a} Green procession from the mouth of the sweat hous up the north side the sweathouse and the south side the main Deep Creek to the Extent. ord^{r} y^{t} Henry anderson & Richard Booker procssion from deep Creek up to Bever pond Creek and flatt Creek. Abr^{a} Burton & Jno fergrasson up the River & flat Creek to ye Extent. ordred y^{t} Jonathan Mote & Wm. Mershal procssion from Beaver pond Creek up the north side Deep Creek Includeing the Branchis: Ordred That James Baugh and andrew Beck Procession Between Blackwater Swamp & Second Swamp from ye p'ish Line to ye moncosneck Road. Ordred Thomas & Saml Lee procession Between Second Swamp and Warwick Swamp from ye parrish Line To ye moncosneck Road. Ordred y^{t} William Epes & Richard Carlile procession ye land Below Jones holes Road Between The parrish line and warwick Swamp: Ordred y^{t} Richard Raines & John hill procession from warwick Swamp to ye p'ish: Line: Between Jones hole Road and Rhowanty Road. Ordred y^{t} Wm. & James Butler procession from moncosneck Bridge to Rowanty Bridge Between moncosneck Road & Rowanty Road. Ordred that George Smith & George tilman s^{r} procession from moncosneck Crek to Stonie Creek Between the moncosneck Road and ye parrish Line. Ordred y^{t} Joseph Tucker & William Jones procession from stonie Creek to sapponie Creek Between the parrish Line and ye Chapple Road. (39) Ordred y^{t} Israil Robertson & David Williams Procession from Sapponey Creek To nottoway River Between the County Line and ye Road that Leeds to ye Cut banks from the Chapple. Ordred that Williams Jones & Robert Williams procession from the Cutt Bank Road up Nottoway River to the Great Creek. Ordred y^{t} Thomas Jones & John Jones procession from ye mouth of the Great Creek up Nottoway River to ye Extent of ye parrish. Ordred that George Williams & William Vaughan procession from ye Moncosneck Road up ye North Side moncosneck & hatchers Runs to the Whiteoak Road & as far in as Rohowick. Ordred that John Smith & Robert Winn procession from Moncosneck to Stoney Creek Between the Moncosneck Road and ye Chapple Road. Ordred that Henry Thweat & francis Bracy procession from ye Chapple Road to ye Butterwod Road Between hatchers Run & Stoney Creek. Ordred y^t John Coalman ^ procession from ^ & Thomas nunally Between ye Chapple Road & Butterwood Road from Stoney Creek to ye Extent. Ordred y^t Edward Mitchel & James Thweat procession Between ye Butter-Wood & Whiteoak To the Extent. Ordred that George Stel & Roger More procssion from the Butterwood Road up the North Side Whiteoak to ye Extent as far in as nemussens and hed of Whipponock.

Ord'red that arthur Macklain Continue at Doct^r Jo^s Thompsons and he to Be allowed 1,200 pounds of tobc^o ꝑ annum: for his accomendation & takeing Care of his soare Legg.

Test JNO. MAYES Clerk Vestry.

Returns of Processioning for the year 1731.

Abraham Jones S^r & J^r Processioned all the Lands in their Precinct but Coll^o Robt Bollings Rohowich land & Henry Balys. Thos & Saml Lee processioned all the lands in their Precinct. William Jones & Robert Williams the same. Walter Chiles & George Tucker the same. George Williams & Wm. Vaughan the same. Thos & Jno Jones the same. Willm & Abraham Green Processioned all the land the could find some people failing to meet them. Richd Raines & Jno Hill Processioned all the lands in their Precinct. Wm. Epes & Richd Carlile the same. Geo. Tilman & Geo. Smith the same. Abra. Burton & Jno Ferguson the same. Robert Tucker & Jno Tally the same. Edward Mitchell & Ja^s Thweat the same. Hen^y Thweat & Fra^s Bracey the same. James Baugh & Andrew Beck Processioned the Land in there Pres^t save the Line of Moses Beck Edw^a Statten, Jno Poythress Abra. Jones, Richd Bland, Sam Jordan, Jno Curiton, Thos Grigory, Dav^d Crawly, Jno Butler, Bath^o Crouder, Abra. Ally, Jno Fitzgerrall & Robt Poythress none attending but Jno Butler. Joseph Tucker & Will. Jones Processioned all the lands in there prec^{t}. John Elington & Will Spain the same. Jno Smith & Robt Wynn the same. Geo. Stell & Roger Moor the same. (40) Saml Jordan & Wm. Batt Processioned all the lands in there Precinct. David Williams & Israel Robertson processioned all Except Richd Blands and Willm Stark they not attending. Nich^{o} Overby S^{r} & Richd Smith Processioned all but Thos Booths wch he refused. Hen^{y} Batt & Peter Baugh Processioned all but Alex^{r} Marshall with Wm. Legan & Jno Puckett shoemaker wth Jno Puckett Turner they refusing. Jno Pride & Richd Walthall processioned all the Lands in there Precinct the partys all present. Jno Mayes & Will Parsons Processioned all the Lands save a Line between Buller Herbert dec'd & Ins^{t} Hall the Adm^{r} of Herbert Refuseing.

(41) Bristol parrish—ss: At a Vestry held at the Ferry Chaple October the 21st 1731 for Settling the Parish Levey.

Present. Mr. Geo. Robertson Min^{r}, Coll^{o} Robt Bolling, Mr. Peter Jones, Coll^{o} Robt Munford, Mr. The^{o} Field, Capt Willm Poythress, Maj^{r} Wm. Kennon, Capt Jas. Munford, Mr. Geo. Willson, Mr. Ins^{t} Hall, Capt Richd Kennon.

		Cask.
To Mr. Geo. Robertson Min^{r}, ...	20,000	800
To Thos Spain C'lk, ...	1,600	64
To Nath. Parrott Cl'k & Cleaning ye Church,	1,600	64
To Jno Woobank Cl'k, ...	1,600	64
To Saml Pitchford Cl'k, ...	1,600	64
To Mrs. Eliz^{a} Kennon for the Ferry, . .	2,500	100
To Mary Dison for Cleaning ye Church, .	300	12
To John Mayes Cl'k ye Vestry, ...	400	16
To Wm. Trayler for the Ferry, ...	630	25
To Eliz^{a} Dodson for Cleaning the Church, .	600	24
To John Crouder for Egington, ...	1,000	40
To Will. Mayes for Plantain, ...	1,000	40
To Coll^{o} Bolling for d^{o}, ...	200	8
To Coll^{o} Munford for M^{c}lain &c., ...	925	37
To D^{o} for Bethell omitted last year, . .	600	24
To Jno High for Farrell, ...	800	32
To Capt Munford Last years ball^{a}, . . .	457	
To D^{o} for Insolvents, ...	705	

To Persons twice listed,	1,222	
To 10 ꝑ Ct. on 1,565 & Sundrys,	1,934	77
To Thos Frost for Service,	100	4
To John Tally for Service,	400	16
To Nath. Parrott for Cleaning ye Church	200	
To D^o for a Chest,	150	23
To D^o for Cleaning round ye Church,	230	
To Eliz^a Womack for Nursing a Child,	1,000	40
To Martha Willson for keep^g Jno Thackers Child,	800	32
To Sus^a Bly for attending Phillis Thacker,	100	
To Capt Poythress for Insolvents,	145	
To Geo. Willson for D^o,	223	
To Doct^r Thompson for M^{c}lain,	700	28
To D^o for Kemp & Thacker,	2,000	80
To Danl Vaughan for Maintainance,	600	24
To Eliz^a Bevell for keep^g Shorys Child,	250	10
To Kath^a Arther,	400	16
To Nath. Parrott for Bolts & Staples,	70	3
To Washing the Curplis,	50	
To a Horse Block,	50	6
To Enlarging ye Churchyard,	50	
To Dav^d Barrett & Wife,	1,000	40
To Capt Fitzgerrall for Barretts Wife,	700	28
To 4 ꝑ Ct. on 50,591,	2,024	
To Olive Poxon for Jno Kemp,	600	24
To Jno Bethell,	600	24
To Jno Walker,	600	24
To Geo. Willson, Last years Ball^a,	38	

(42) Order'd that John Tally Keep the Ferry at Namosend Church. Order'd that the Church Wardens bind out John Thacker. Order'd that Two Melettos be bound to Capt Peter Wynn as the Law directs by Name Tom & Will. Order'd that Thos Williams Shorey be bound to Saml Pitchford. Order'd that Sarah Bly be bound to John Derby till she be Eighteen years of Age or Married and that she be taught to read. Order'd that Lewis Brian be bound to Thos Whood as the Law Directs aged Twelve years Last July. Order'd that Eliz^a Brown

be bound to Hen^y Voden as the Law directs. Order'd that Neptune Money be bound to James Thompson as the Law directs born the 16th of August 1730. Order'd that Willm Mote be Exempted from paying Parish Levey. James Cole the same. Order'd that Capt Charles Fisher, Capt Willm Stark and Robert Bevell be Vestry men. Order'd that a Ferry be keept at the Point and that it be attended when the sermon is at the Mother Church and that the Min^r pass when he hath Occation. Order'd that Coll^o Robt Bolling & Mr. George Willson agree with any man to attend the same. Order'd that Mathew Talbott be Clerk of the Chaple that is to be built at or near Flatt Creek. Order'd that a Maletto Child Named Tom be bound to Eliz^a Ragsdale as the Law directs.

Test

Bristoll Parish—ss: Att a Vestry held at the Ferry Chaple Feby 6th 1731.

Present. Mr. Geo. Robertson Min^r, Coll^o Robt Munford, Capt Richd Kennon, Capt James Munford, Mr. George Willson, Maj^r Willm Kennon, Mr. Robt Bevell.

Order'd that Willm Bleik (Alias Pride) be bound to Willm Pride supposed to be his Father. Order'd that the Children of William Stow dece'd be bound out by the Vestry as the Law Directs. Order'd that George Tucker be Prosessioner in the Stead of Robert Tucker jun^r who is Lame and cannott Officiate as prosessioner.

Test

Bristoll Parish—ss: Att a Vestry held at the Ferry Chaple the 5th of March 1731.

Present. Mr. Geo. Robertson Min^r, Mr. Theophelous Field, Coll^o Robt Bolling, Capt Charles Fisher, Coll^o Robt Munford, Mr. Peter Jones, Maj^r Willm Kennon, Mr. Robert Bevell.

Order'd that Mary Blys Child be bound to Peter Gill Born the 17th feb^y 1729 Named Joshua Irby. Order'd that Will Lofftis be Levey Free.

Test

(43) 1731 SOUTH SIDE BRISTOLL PARISH DR.

To Mr. Robertson,	16,000	640
To Thos Spain,	1,600	64
To Nath. Parratt,	1,600	64
To Jno Woobank,	1,600	64
To Mrs. Kennon,	500	20
To Jno Mayes,	400	16
To Eliza Dodson,	600	24
To Jno Crouder ℘ Eaginton,	1,000	40
To Wm. Mayes ℘ Plantine,	1,000	40
To Collo Bolling ℘ do,	200	8
To Collo Munford ℘ Mclain,	925	37
To Do ℘ Bethell last year,	600	24
To Jno High ℘ Farrell,	800	32
To Capt Munford last yrs balla,	457	
To do ℘ Insolvents,	705	
To do ℘ Persons twice listed,	1,222	
To do ℘ 10 ℘ Ct. on 1,565 & Acct,	1,934	77
To Jno Tally,	400	16
To Nath. Parratt,	580	23
To Capt Poythress Insolvts,	145	
To Doctr Thompson,	2,000	80
To Danl Vaughan,	600	24
To Kath. Arther,	400	16
To Nath. Parratt,	220	9
To Davd Barratt & Wife,	1,000	40
To Capt Fitz Gerrall ℘ Barrett,	700	28
To Olive Poxon ℘ Kemp,	600	24
To Jno Bethell,	600	24
To Jno Willson,	600	24
	38,988	
To 4 ℘ Ct. on do,	1,575	
To Sallery 20 ℘ Ct.	7,797	
To ye Cask,	1,456	
	49,816	
due to ye Parish,	296	
	50,112	

CR.

By 1,392 Pole at 36 ℔ pole,	50,112	

NORTH SIDE BRISTOL PARISH DR.

To Mr. Robertson,	4,000	160
To Saml Pitchford,	1,600	64
To Mrs. Kennon,	2,000	80
To Mary Dison,	300	12
To Thos Frost,	100	4
To Eliz^a Womack,	100	4
To Martha Willson,	800	32
To Eliz^a Bly,	100	4
To Doct^r Thompson,	700	28
To Geo. Willson,	161	
To Wm. Trayler,	630	25
To Eliz^a Bevell,	250	10
Sallary 14 ℔ Ct.	1,505	
Cask,	423	
4 ℔ Cent. on 10,741,	429	
	13,098	

CR.

By 372 Pole at 34 ℔ pole,	12,648
due to ye Collecter,	450
	13,098

Bristoll Parish—ss: Att a Vestry held at the Ferry Chaple April the 30th 1732.

Present. Mr. Geo. Robertson Min^r, Capt Charles Fisher, Coll^o Robt Munford, Maj^r Wm. Kennon, Mr. Theoph^l Field, Mr. Geo. Willson, Capt Ja^s Munford, Mr. Robt Bevell.

Order'd that a Causway be Built from the Ferry Landing to the Chanell on the South side.

Test JOHN MAYES Clerk Vestry.

(44) At a Vestry held at the Ferry Chaple June the 25th 1732.

Present. Mr. George Robertson Min^r, Capt Willm Poythress,

Coll^{o} Robert Munford, Mr. George Willson, Maj^{r} Willm Kennon, Capt Richd Kennon, Mr. Theophelous Field, Capt Charles Fisher.

Order'd that Godfry Fowler be acquitted from paying Parish Levey. Peter Rowlett Junr the same. John Stroud the same. John Davis the same. that William Willson son of Richd Willson be bound by the Church Wardens as the Law directs.

Test

At a Vestry held at the Ferry Chaple Feby 6th 1731.

Present. Mr. Geo. Robertson Min^{r}, Capt Richd Kennon, Coll^{o} Robert Munford, Mr. Geo. Willson, Capt James Munford, Mr. Robt Bevell, Maj^{r} Wm. Kennon.

Order'd that Wm. Bleik als. Pride be bound to Wm. Pride supposed to be his Father. Order'd that the Children of Wm. Stow dece'd be bound out as ye Law directs. Order'd that Geo. Tucker be Prosetioner in the stead of Robt Tucker jun^{r} who is lame & cannot Officiate as processioner.

(45) 1732 Bristoll parish—ss: At a Vestry held at ye Ferry Chaple for Settling ye Parish Leavey October 30th 1732.

Present. Mr. Geo. Robertson Min^{r}, Capt James Munford, Coll^{o} Robt Bolling, Mr. Peter Jones, Coll^{o} Robt Munford, Capt Cha. Fisher.

To Mr. Geo. Robertson Min^{r}, ...	20,000	800
To Thos Spain Cl'k, ...	1,600	64
To Nath. Parratt Cl'k & Sexton, ...	2,000	80
To Jno Woobank Cl'k, ...	1,600	64
To Mary Dison ꝑ Cleaning ye Church, . .	300	12
To Wm. Trayler for Cask omited last year, .	30	
To Maj^{r} Kennon for Saml Pitchford, . .	1,600	64
To Ditto for Wid^{o} Womack last year, . .	900	36
To Ditto for D^{o} this year, ...	1,000	40
To Ditto for Martha Willson, ...	1,200	48
To Jno Crouder ꝑ Eaginton, ...	1,000	40
To Wm. Mayes for Plantine, ...	1,000	40
To Abra. Jones ꝑ Hinson, ...	300	12
To Jno Bethell, ...	600	24
To Jno Tally for Ferry & Sexton, ...	1,000	40

To Danl Vaughan,	600	24
To Kath. Arther,	400	16
To David Barrett,	1,000	40
To D^{o} for his Wife,	1,000	40
To Olive Poxon for Kemp,.	600	24
To Jno Mayes,	400	16
To Mrs. Kennon ℘ Ferry,	2,500	100
To Capt Munford ℘ Insolvents,	1,337	
To Coll^{o} Munford ℘ Banks,	1,112	45
To Mathew Talbott ℘ Reading,	400	16
To Marg'ett McWire,	200	8
To Jane Sentall Cleaning ye Church,	250	10
To Jos. Patterson last year Levey,	36	
To Coll^{o} Bolling ℘ Plantine,	77	3
To Thos Bevell ℘ Tinson,	250	10
To Geo. Willson last year ball^{e},	450	18
To Capt Bolling for Ferry,	400	16
To Corn^{s} Fox ℘ Arnall,	200	8

Ord'red that Capt Wm. Poythress & Geo. Willson be Church-wardens ye Ensueing year. that Ruth Mathews be bound to Robt Downing as ye Law directs. that two Mellattos Named Patt aged three year Griffen aged Nine Months be bound to Phillip Morgan as ye Law directs. that Thos Whood be Levey free. that John Reams be the same. that Mrs. Eliz^{a} Kennon Receive Twelve hundred pound of Tobacco for keeping the Ferry the Ensueing year.

Test JNO. MAYES Clerk Vestry.

(46) 1732 SOUTH SIDE BRISTOLL PARRISH DR.

To Mr. Robertson Min^{r},	18,000	720
To Thos Spain,	1,600	64
To Nath. Parratt,	2,000	80
To Jno Woobank,	1,600	64
To Jno Crouder ℘ Eaginton,	1,000	40
To Wm. Mayes ℘ Plantin,	1,000	40
To Ab. Jones ℘ Hinson,	300	12
To Jno Bethell,	600	24

To Jn° Tally,	1,000	40
To Dan[l] Vaughan,	600	24
To Kath. Arther,	400	16
To Dav[d] Barratt,	1,000	40
To D° Wife,	1,000	40
To Olive Poxon ℔ Kemp,	600	24
To Jn° Mayes,	400	16
To Mrs. Kennon,	900	36
To Ja[s] Munford Insolv[ts] 1,337, disc[s] last y[rs] ball[a] 296,	1,041	
To Coll° Munford,	1,112	45
To Math. Talbott,	400	16
To Marg[t] M[c]Wire,	200	8
To James Sentall,	250	10
To Jos. Patterson last y[r],	36	
To Coll° Bolling ℔ plantine,	77	3
To Corn[s] Fox ℔ Arnall,	200	8
	35,316	
Sall[y] 25 ℔ Ct.,	9,524	
Cask,	1,370	
4 ℔ Ct,	1,412	
	47,622	
due to y[e] Parish,	654	
	48,276	

CR.

By 1,414 Pole @ 34 ℔ pole,	48,276

NORTH SIDE BRISTOLL PARRISH DR.

To Mr. Robertson,	2,000	80
To Sam[l] Pitchford,	1,600	64
To Mrs. Kennon,	1,600	64
To Mary Dison,	300	12
To Wm. Trayler,	30	
To Eliz[a] Womack last y[r],	900	36
To D° this year,	1,000	40
To Martha Willson,	1,200	48

To Geo. Willson, ...	450	18
To Thos Bevell ℘ Tinson, ...	250	10
To Jno Bolling, ...	400	16
	9,730	
Sallary 14 ℘ Ct., ...	1,666	
Cask, ...	388	
4 ℘ Cent, ...	389	
	12,173	
due to ye Parish, ...	79	
	12,252	

CR.

By 377 Pole at 32½ ℘ pole, ...	12,252	

(47) At a Vestry held Feb 6th 1732.

Present. Mr. Robertson Minister, Mr. George Willson, Coll^{o} Bolling, Cap^{tn} Munford, Mr. Robert Bevell, Cap^{tn} Fisher, Mr. Field, Cap^{tn} Poythress, Mr. Pr Jones.

Order'd that Doct^{r} Thompson be p^{d} 425 Tob^{o} for his care and Buriall of Arther M^{c}clain and that the Collector charge the Same in his accompt. Ord. that James Sturdivant be p^{d} 30 Tob^{o} for a Levy overcharged last year. Ord. that John Barret an Orphan Boy be bound to Cap^{tn} James Munford as the law directs.

It is agreed by the Vestry that the Chappel order'd for the convenience of the upper Inhabitants of this Parish be built on or near Mr. Samuel Cobbs land on flat Creek. And that the persons appointed by the order of Vestry the 15th day of October 1730 meet at Nummisseen Chappel on Saturday the 17th Instant to agree with workmen for building the Same in Current Money and report their proceedings to the next Vestry.

Order'd that James Gallimore an orphan be bound to Robert Tucker Ju^{r} as the Law directs. Order'd that Ann Gallimore be bound to John Bradshaw as the Law directs or married. Order'd that Samuel Gallimore be bound to Robert Coleman as the Law directs. Order'd that Elisabeth Gallimore be bound to John Tucker. Order'd that Elionar Gallimore be bound to. David Ellington. Order'd that Wm. Gallimore be bound to Cap^{tn} John

Bevell. Order'd Isham Cleaton be bound to Charles Clay. Order'd that Wm. Burgess be bound to Cap^tn John Coleman. Order'd that Esther Floyd be bound to George Tucker.

Test JNO. MAYES Clerk Vestry.

At a Vestry held Feb 26 1732.

present. Mr. George Robertson Minister, Coll^o Bolling, Cap^tn Fisher, Maj^r Kennon, Cap^tn Kennon, Coll^o Munford, Cap^tn Munford, Mr. Jones, Mr. Willson.

It is Order'd and agreed that a Chapple be built on Mr. Cobbs Land near Flat Creek for the conveniency of the upper inhabitants of this Parish of the Same dementions and workmanship with the first Chapple Built at Nummisseen. And it is farther agreed between the Vestry and Richard Booker Gent. that the said Booker doth undertake to beginn and finish the S^d Chapple in manner above s^d for the Sum of Ninty four pounds ten Shillings current money of Virginia which Sum the Vestry agree to pay the S^d Booker upon finishing the s^d work the s^d Booker farther agrees to Tarr the s^d Chapple the value of the Tarr being paid by the Vestry. Maj^r Wm. Kennon and Mr. George Willson are desired by Vestry from time to time to Inspect the workmanship. upon the motion of Mr. Richard Booker leave is given him to build a Pew for his familys conveniency at his own charge on one Side of the communion Table leaving room for the communicants to kneel between the same and the communion Table.

Upon the petition of John Bently it is agreed by the vestry that he officiate as Sexton for the flat Creek Chapple when finished. Ord'red That James Bently be acquitted from paying Parish Leavy.

Test JNO. MAYES Clerk Vestry.

(48) Bristoll Parish—ss: At a Vestry held at the ferry Chapple Novb^r 12th 1733.

Pressent. Mr. George Robertson Minister, Mr. Theo. Feild, Coll. Robert Bolling, Maj^r Wm. Kennon, Coll. Robert Munford, Captn Richard Kennon, Maj^r James Munford, Mr. Peter Jones, Captn Charles Fisher. Mr. George Wilson, Captn Wm. Poythress Church Wardens.

	lbs Tobbo.
To Mr. George Robertson Minsr,	16,000
To Do for Extrodinary Services Done,	4,000
To Thomas Spain for Clerk Service,	1,600
To Nathaniell Parrott Do & finding Wine,	2,136
To John Woobank Do,	1,600
To Samuell Pitchford Do,	1,600
To Mary Dison for Cleaning ye Church,	300
To Jno Crowder for Eaginton,	1,000
To Jno Talley for ferry & Sexton,	1,000
To Jno Beathell Parishoner,	0,600
To Daniell Vaughan Do,	600
To Jno Mayes Clerk of ye Vestry,	400
To Mrs. Kennon for ye ferry,	1,200
To Jane Scentall for Cleaning ye Church,	250
To Richard Muns Parishoner,	600
To Math. Talbot for Reading,	1,600
To Jno Evans for Edward Dunn,	316
To Charles Anderson for Amy Cross,	150
To Majr Wm. Kennon for keeping Slinson two Months & Burying him,	400
To Jno Floyd for keeping Ann Newhouse 6 Months,	600
To Eliz. Wamock for keeping a Child Do & Burying ye Same,	600
To Martha Worsham for keeping a Child one year,	1,200
To Mr. Wm. Batts for Burying Jacob Butler,	200
To Henry Bailey for work Done to Sappony Chapple,	218
To Robt Bolling Esqr for Peter Plantin,	174
To Jno Darby in full for Jno Slinson D D.,	200
Carried to ye Other Side,	39,744
(49) Brought from ye Other Side,	39,744
To Captn Jno Bolling,	400
To Coll. Robt Munford,	48
To Mr. George Wilson,	459
To Captn Wm. Poythress for Ball. of Insolvts in 1732,	500
To Henry Wilson for Glaising ye Church windows,	200
To Francis Epes a tithable twice listed,	32

Ordered That 10,000^{lb} of Tobacco be Leveyed Towards Defraying ye Charges of a Chapple Ordered to be Built at Flatt Creek, . . .	10,000
To Cask & Sallary at 8 ℘^{r} Cent, ...	4,118
	55,501

Ordered That Jno Williams be Levey free being Troubled with fitts till he recover[s]. Ordered that Neptune Jackson be bound to Wm. Taylor as ye Law Directs. Ordered that Robt Winfeild be parish levy free. Ordered that Cap^{tn} Wm. Poythress be paid at ye laying of ye Next Parish Levey 1,000^{lb} pd^{s} of Tobacco for his maintain'g Mary Barrot & Child ye Ensueing Year. Ordered That Mrs. Eliz. Kennon keep & maintain ye ferry The Ensueing Year for 1,200 pd^{s} of Tobacco. Ordered That Cap^{tn} Wm. Poythress & Mr. George wilson Continue Church wardens. Ordered That two Children Joseph & Sarah franks be Bound to Charles Anderson as the Law Directs.

Ordered that the Church wardens Employ a fitt person to Examine into the Condition of ye Chapple at ye ferry & if they find it Capable of being well Repaired That then they Imploy workmen to D^{o} ye Same to be paid at ye Laying the Next Levey According to ye Just Valuation of ye Service or if they find it Otherways that They Make a Report of ye Condition thereof to ye Vestry.

Ordered That Nathaniell Parrott is Discontinued as Clerk of Sapponie Chapple and That there be publick Notice given for persons to appear at ye ferry Chapple To Try for ye Same on Monday ye 19th of this Instant.

Ordered That Captn Wm. Stark be a Vestry Man he haveing Takeing the Oath.

Ordered That Captn Walker be pay'd 800 pd^{s} of Tobacco by ye Church wardens for keeping a Child Named Jno Williams & that ye Said Child be bound to ye Said walker as ye Law Directs.

Ordered That Mr. Rob^{rt} Whitehall be appointed Clerk of Sapponie Chapple In ye Stead of Nathaniell parrott & to Receive Annuall 1,600 pd^{s} of Tobacco from ye parish for his Said Service.

Test JNO. MAYES Clerk Vestry.

(50) Bristoll Parrish—ss: North Side Dr.

To Mr. Geo^{r} Robertson Minister,	2,000
To Samuel Pitchford,	1,600
To Mrs. Kennon,	1,200
To Mary Dison,	300
To Maj^{r} William Kennon,	400
To Eliz^{a} Wamack,	600
To Martha Worsham,	1,200
To John Derby,	200
To Capt John Bolling,	400
To Mr. George Willson,	459
To Capt Richard Booker,	2,065
	10,424
To Cask & Sall^{r} at 8 ꝑ C^{t},	833
	11,257

Cr.

By 388 tithables at 29 ꝑ pole is,	11,252
Due to the Collector 5^{lb} tob^{o}.	

(51) Bristoll Parrish—ss: At A Vestry Held at the ferry Chapple 11th March 1733.

Present. Mr. George Roberson, minister, Robt. Bolling, Robert Munford, William Starke, Charles Fisher, Theofilus Field, Richard Kennon, William Poythriss, James Munford, Peter Jones, Gentlemen Vestrymen.

Upon The Petition of Wm. Jones that he Being antient & Infirm Ordred that He be Exempted from Paying Parish Levy for the futer. Ordred that Jno field be Exempted from Paying Parrish Leavy. Ordred that Sarah plantine be Bound to Thomas more as the law directs. Ordred that Wm. puckit be Exempted from paying parish levy for ye futor. Ordred that the Church warthens find John Walker with such nessisaries as They shall see Convenient for his support and that they bring in their account at the laying the next parish leavy.

Ordred That a new Church be Built of Brick on Wellses Hill for the Conveniency of this Parrish Sixty foot long and twenty five foot Wide in The Clear Eighteen foot Pitch with Compass Sealing and Compass windows the Isle Eight foot wide Laid with portland stone or Bristol marble Sash Glass Covered first with Inch Plank Ciphir'd and a Coat of hart Cipruss or pine Shingles ¾ of an Inch thick at ye lower End naild on foalding Shuttors of windscut for the windows.

Ordred That advertisement be set up by the Clerk of the Vestry For workmen to meet This Vestry at Thomas Hardiways on Saturday The fourth Day of May next to agree for the Building the S^d^ Church.

Test JNO. MAYES Clerk Vestry.

Bristoll Parrish—ss: A a vestry held at The ferry Chapple 20th June 1724.

Present. Mr. George Robertson Minester, Robert Bolling, Robert Munford, William Poythriss, George Willson, Charles fisher, Richard Kennon, Gentlemen Vestry men.

Ordred that the Church Warthins take up twenty three pounds five shilling upon Intrest to pay Richard Booker undertaker of The Church Built at flatt Creek it Being the Balance Due to him for the S^d^ work.

Test JNO. MAYES Clerk Vestry.

(52) Bristol Parish—ss: At a Vestry held at the Ferry Chapple November 11th 1734.

Present. Robert Bolling, James Munford, Robert Munford, Peter Jones, Theo. Field, Richard Kennon, Charles Fisher, William Stark. William Poythress Church Warden.

To Mr. George Robertson Minister,	16,000
To Ditto for extraordinary Services,	4,000
To Thomas Spain Clerk att Nemosend Chapple,	1,600
To Robert Whitehall for Ditto att Sapponey,	1,600
To John Woobank for Ditto att the ferry Chapple,	1,600
To Phillip Prescott for Ditto at the moth^r^ Church,	1,600
To Matthew Talbott for Ditto at flatt Creek,	1,600
To Mary Dison for Cleaning the Church,	300
To John Crowder for Eaginton,	850
To John Tally for Ferry and Sexton,	1,000
To John Bethell Parishoner,	600

To John Mayes for Clerk of the Vestry, . . .	400
To Elizabeth Kennon for keeping the Ferry, . .	1,200
To Jane Sental for Cleaning the Church, . . .	250
To Richard Munns Parishoner, ...	600
To Capt John Bolling for Ferry at ye Point, . .	400
To Elizabeth Cook for ye care of George Brown, .	300
To Richard Whitmore, ...	200
To Matthew Talbott for services done & a pewt^{r} bas^{n},	221
To Mr. William Eppes for Services done for ye parish,	75
To Capt Charles Fisher for Glass & Lead &c. . .	270
To Richard Booker for the Ball. due for the building the Chappel at Flatt Creek to be sold by the Church warden for that purpose and to Acco^{t} with ye Vestry for such Sale, ...	4,000
To Charles Anderson for being Sexton and other Services done att Sapponey Chapple, ...	300
To be Leaved towards the Building of a new Church pursuant to an Order of Vestry ye 11th of March 1733, ...	25,000
To John Bentley Sexton for 6 months to this time, .	125
Carried Over, ...	64,091

(53) Order'd that Rebecca Chaves be bound to John West as ye Law directs; that Benjamin Burges be bound to Wm. Gates as ye Law directs; that Elizabeth Hudson Smithes be bound to Richard Tally as ye Law directs; that John Epperson be bound to Humphrey Price as ye Law directs; that the Church wardens employ a Doct^{r} for the cure of George Brown and to agree for his maintenance; that the Church Wardens provide a place for the Support of John Ingles and Mary Barrett; that the Church wardens bind out John Thacker as ye Law directs; that John Woobank Cl'k of ye Church & Vestry has 2,000^{l} Tob^{o} annually; that Robert Whitehall have for his being Cl'k 1,600^{l} D^{o} D^{o}; that Samuel Tatam be Levey free; that John West be ye Same; that Robert West be exempted from paying parish Levey dureing his Inabillity; that Sarah Chaves be bound to William Mackewen as ye Law Directs; that Col^{o} Robert Bolling, Capt William Stark and Maj^{r} William Poythres agree with workmen for Build-

ing a new Church according to the former Order made March ye 11th 1733; that Maj^r William Poythress & Mr. George Willson be Church warden[s] the Ensueing Year.

Test JOHN WOOBANK Cl'k Vestrey.

	l.	Cask.
(54) Brought Over, ...	64,091	800
To Maj. William Kennon for keeping Mary Haines, ...	300	
To John Floyd for keeping Ann New House,	600	
To William Worsham for keeping John Thacker, ...	800	
To Mr. George Wilson for Services done to ye Parish, ...	64	
To Mr. James Vaughan for a Tithable too much, ...	29	
To Maj^r William Poythress for keeping Mary Barrett and her Lame Child, . . .	1,000	
Cask, ...	800	
To Sallery for Collecting and paying in Inspector's Notes 67,655 @ 4 p Cent. . .	2,706	
	70,390	

Test. JOHN WOOBANK, Cl'k Vestrey.

Order'd that a Church be built of Brick on Wellses Hill to be 60 foot by 25 foot in the Clear and 15 foot to the spring of the Arch from the floor which is to be at least 18 Inches above the highest part of the ground 3 Bricks thick to the water Table and 2½ afterwards to the plate, the roof to be fram'd according to a Scheme now before us, the Isle to be 6 foot wide Lay'd with white Bristol Stone, galerey at the west end as long as the peer will admitt a window in the same as big as the pitch will admitt. 7 windows in the body of the Church of Suitable dimentions glaz'd with sash glass the floors to be well lay'd with good Inch & ¼ plank the Pews to be fram'd the fronts rais'd pannil & ¼ round with a decent pulpit and Type a decent rail and Ballister round the altar place and a table suitable thereto as usual, the roof to be first cover'd with plank and shingled on that with good Cypruss Hart Shingles Cornice Eves large board eves and Suitable doors as usual the whole to be done Strong and workman like in the best plain manner to be finished by the last of July 1737. Stone Steps to each door Suitable.

Col° Thomas Ravenscroft has agreed to build the above Church for 485£ Curr't Money to be paid at three Several payments. May y[e] 4th 1734.

Test. JOHN WOOBANK Cl'k Vestry.

(55) 1734 SOUTH SIDE OF BRISTOL PARISH DR.

To Mr. Robertson Minist[r],	16,000	640
To Thomas Spain,	1,600	
To Robert Whitehall,	1,600	
To John Woobank,	1,600	
To Matthew Talbott,	1,821	
To John Crowder,	850	
To John Talley,	1,000	
To John Bethell,	600	
To John Mayse,	400	
To Jane Sentall,	250	
To Richard Muns,	600	
To Elizabeth Cook,	300	
To Richard Whitmore,	200	
To William Eppes,	75	
To Cap[t] Charles Fisher,	270	
To Maj[r] William Poythress,	1,000	
To John Floyd,	600	
To John Bentley,	125	
To Charles Anderson,	300	
To Cap[t] Booker,	3,263	
To be Levy'd toward building the new Church,	22,058	
To Sallery and Cask @ 8 p C[t],	2,852	
To Ball: due to y[e] parish,	436	
L[s]	57,800	

CR.

By 1,700 Pole @ 34[l] p pole,	57,800

Order'd that Maj^r Wm. Poythress Church warthen do receive of every Tithable in this Parrish thirty four pounds of Neat Tob^o in Inspectors Notes for their Parish Levy for this present Year and in case of refusal or nonpayment to Levey the same by distress and pay the Several Sums to the Creditors for whome the Same was proportion'd.

Test JOHN WOOBANK Clk: Vest^y.

NORTH SIDE OF BRISTOL PARISH DR.

To Mr. Robertson Minist^r,	4,000	160
To Phillip Prescott,	1,600	
To Mary Dison,	300	
To Elizabeth Kennon,	1,200	
To John Bolling,	400	
To William Worsham,	800	
To Maj^r William Kennon,	300	
To George Willson,	64	
To James Vaughan,	29	
To Capt Booker,	737	
To be Levy'd toward building the New Church,	2,942	
To Sallery and Cask @ 8 p C^t,	654	
To Ball. due to the Parish,	30	
L^s	13,056	

CR.

By 384 Pole @ 34^l p Pole,	13,056

Order'd that Mr. Geo. Willson Church warden doe receive of every Tithable in This Parish Thirty four Pounds of Neatt Tob^o in Inspectors Notes for their Parish Levey for this present Year; and in case of refusal or non payment to Levey the same by distress and pay the Severall Sums to the Creditors for whome the same was proportioned.

Test JOHN WOOBANK Clk Vestry.

(56) At a Vestry held at the Ferry Chaple the 27th March 1735.

Present. Mr. Geo. Robertson, Maj^r Wm. Poythress, Mr. Geo. Willson C. W., Mr. Theo. Field, Col^o Robert Bolling,

Capt Charles Fisher, Col^{o} Wm. Kennon, Maj^{r} Ja^{s} Munford, Capt Peter Jones.

Order'd, that Mr Robert Munford be a Vestryman he haveing taken the Oaths as the Law directs; that Mary Hall have 100^{l} Tob^{o} p Month for Keeping Wm. West from the 20th of Feb^{ry} Last to ye 30th Ap^{l} then dy'd; that Col^{o} Robert Bolling do Support of the Order of the Vestry dated Novr ye 11th 1734.

Test JOHN WOOBANK Clk Vestry.

At a Vestry held at the Ferry Chapple May ye 27th 1735.

Present. Mr. Geo. Robertson, Maj^{r} Wm. Poythress, Mr. Geo. Willson C. W., Col^{o} Robt Bolling, Mr. Theo. Field, Col^{o} William Kennon, Capt Charles Fisher, Capt William Stark, Capt Peter Jones, Maj^{r} James Munford, Mr. Robert Munford.

Order'd that Henry Voden assigne Eliz. Brown an Orphan Girl over to Wm. Pirkason.

Test JOHN WOOBANK Clk Vestry.

(57) At a Vestry held at the Ferry Chapple June 14th 1735.

Present. Maj^{r} William Poythress Church warden, Col^{o} Robt Bolling, Capt Charles Fisher, Maj^{r} James Munford, Capt Peter Jones, Mr. Theo. Feild, Mr. Robert Munford.

Order'd that David Walker and Capt Fran^{s} Poythress be Vestrymen they haveing taken the Oaths as the Law directs.

Test JOHN WOOBANK Clk Vestry.

At a Vestry held at the Ferry Chapple August 12th 1735.

Present. Col^{o} Robt Bolling, Mr. Theo. Field, Maj^{r} James Munford, Maj^{r} Wm. Poythress, Mr. Robert Munford, Capt Wm. Stark, Capt Fran^{s} Poythress, Capt Charles Fisher, Capt David Walker.

Order'd that Capt John Banister be a Vestryman he haveing taken the Oaths as the law directs.

In Obedience to the Governors order that the Church warden do desire the workman to delay going forward with the building the Church on Well's Hill till the Governors pleasure is further known.

that Maj^r James Munford is appointed Church warden with Maj^r William Poythress.

Test JOHN WOOBANK Clk Vestry.

(58) Bristol Parish—ss: At a Vestry held at the Ferry Chapple Septemb^r 15th 1735.

Present. Maj^r Wm. Poythress, Maj^r James Munford C. W., Col^o Robert Bolling, Capt Fran^s Poythress, Capt Peter Jones, Capt William Stark, Capt John Banister, Mr. Robert Munford, Capt Charles Fisher.

Order'd That the Church wardens pay Mr. Richard Booker the Sum of Twenty three pounds five Shillings Currant Money of Virginia wth Lawfull Interest thereon from the last payment in full for Building a Chapple on flatt Creek.

That the Church wardens pay John Low Fifty Shillings out of the Parish money in their hands for one Acre Land to build a Church on Wells's Hill and that the said Low do make and Execute deeds for the Same to the use of this Parish upon payment of the Sum abovesaid.

That the Church wardens pay the remaining part of the Parish Money in their hands to Col^o Thomas Ravenscroft upon his giving bond to compleat the Church upon Wells's Hill pursuant to agreem^t made May 4th 1735 Between himself and members of this Vestry appointed for that purpose.

That Col^o Robert Bolling, Capt William Stark and Maj^r William Poythress from time to time inspect the Building of the Church on Wells's Hill and to give such directions as is most agreeable to the agreement.

That Mr. George Robertson be admitted Minister of this Parish and give his Attendance accordingly and his Ferriges at his own charge and that he does not insist upon purchaseing a glibe untill the Vestry hath discharg'd their presents Ingagements.

That John Bugg be bound to Instance Hall j^r as the law directs.

By Virtue of an Order of Prince George County Court Bareing date the 12th of August 1735 and In Obedience to the said Order do Procession the lands belonging to the aboves^d Parish and are divided into precincts as followeth Viz^t:

That John Lewis and James Sturdivant Procession from Puddle dock run to the lower end of ye Parish Between the River &

Madam Bollings Road. (59) Samuel Jordan & William Batte Procession from Puddle dock Run to the Nottoway Road as far out as Blackwater. Thomas Hardaway and Abraham Alley Procession from Nottoway Road up as far as Monkersneck Road. William Parsons and John Mayse Procession from Puddle dock to Lieu[t] Run Between the River and the great Swamp and Monkersneck Road. Abraham Jones S[r] & Abraham Jones j[r] Procession from Lieu[t] Run to the Indian Town Run Including Rohowick. Nicholas Overby and Richard Smith Procession from the Indian Town Run to Wallaces Creek. Matthew Mayse and Bartho. Crowder Procession from Wallaces Creek Cross to the white oak Road down Hatchers Run to the Extent. John Ellington and William Spaine Procession from whiponock to Namosend out as far as Bollings lower line. James Baugh and Andrew Beck Procession Between Blackwater Swamp and Second Swamp from the Parish line to the Monkersneck Road. Thomas Lee and Samuel Lee Procession Between Second Swamp and warwick Swamp from the Parish line to the Monkersneck Road. William Eppes and Richard Carlile Procession the land below Jones Hole Road Between the Parish line and warwick Swamp. Richard Raines and John Hill Procession from warwick Swamp to the Parish line Between Jones hole Road and Rowanty Road. William Butler and James Butler Procession from Monkersneck Bridge to Rowanty Bridge. George Smith and George Tillman S[r] Procession from Monkersneck Creek to Stony Creek Between the Monkersneck Road and the Parish line. Joseph Tucker S[r] and William Jones Procession from Stony Creek to Sappony Creek Between the Parish line and the Chapple Road. Israel Robinson and David Williams Procession from Sappony Creek to Nottoway River Between the County line and the Road that leads to the Cutt Banks from the Chapple. Wm. Jones and Edward Colwell Procession from the Cutt Banks Road up Nottoway River to the great Creek. Wm. Davis and John Jones Procession from the mouth of the great Creek up Nottoway River to the extent of the Parish. George Williams and William Vaughan Procession from the Monkersneck Road up the North side Monkersneck and Hatchers Run to the white Oak Road and as far in as Rohowick. Carried Over.

(60) George Tillman j[r] and Robert Wynne Procession from

Monkersneck to Stony Creek Between the Monkersneck Road and the Chapple Road. Henry Thweatt & Francis Bracey Procession from the Chapple Road to the Butterwood Road Between Hatchers Run and Stony Creek. Thomas Nunnally and Jos. Pritchett Procession Between the Chapple Road and Butterwood Road from Stony Creek to the extent. Edward Mitchell S[r] and James Thweatt Procession Between Butterwood and white Oak. George Still and Roger Moore Procession from Butterwood Road up the North side white Oak to the extent as far in as Namos. and head of Whiponock. Hugh Reese and John West Procession Between white Oake and Namos. to the extent of the County. John Poythress and John Hill Procession Between Butterwood and Nottaway River as low as the head of Beaver Pond Creek.

Test JOHN WOOBANK Cl. Vestry.

Bristol Parish—ss: At a Vestry held at the Ferry Chapple November y[e] 10th 1735.

Present. Mr. George Robertson Minist[r], Maj[r] William Poythress, Maj[r] James Munford C. W., Cap[t] William Stark, Cap[t] Peter Jones, Mr. Robert Munford, Cap[t] Francis Poythress, Cap[t] Charles Fisher, Mr. David Walker.

To Mr. George Robertson Minister,	11,666
To Thomas Spain Clerk Namos[d],	933
To Robert Whitehall D[o] at Sappony,	933
To John Woobank D[o] at Ferry Chapple,	933
To D[o] for D[o] Vestry,	233
To Phillip Prescott D[o] Moth[r] Church,	933
To Matthew Talbott D[o] Flatt Creek,	933
To Mary Dyson for Cleaning the Church,	175
To John Tally for ferry and Sexton,	583
To Elizabeth Kennon for keeping the Ferry,	700
To Jane Sentall for Cleaning the Church,	145
To Richard Munns Parishoner,	350
To James Vaughan for ferry at the point,	233
To Elizabeth Cook for the care of George Brown 5 Months & Burial,	550
Carried Over, L[s]	19,300

(61) Brought over,	Ls	19,300
To John Bently for Sexton,		145
To John Floyd for keeping Ann Newhouse,		583
To Wm. Worsham for keeping John Thacker,		466
To Majr Wm. Poythress for keeping Mary Barrett & Child,		583
To Benjamin Cook,		34
To Samuel Sental jr for Keeping Peter Plantine,		1,583
To Mary Hall for Keeping Wm. West and Burial,		425
To Henry Wilson for Repairing the Church Windows,		80
To Charles Couzens for Keeping Eliz. Gill,		200
To James Sturdivant for Keeping John Ingles,		500
To John Cuirton for Keeping Ditto,		200
To David Williams for Grubing ye Church yard etc.,		290
To Mr. George Willson for Insolvants,		359
To Majr William Poythress for Do,		1,633
		26,381
To Cask and Sallery @ 8 p Ct,		1,537
	Ls	27,918
To Mr. Geo Robertson for one & ½ months Sallery,		2,000
To Robert Whitehall Clerk at Sappony,		667
To John Woobank Ditto Ferry Chapple,		667
To Ditto Ditto Vestry,		167
To John Floyd for keeping Ann Newhouse,		417
To Majr William Poythress for keeping Mary Barrett,		417
To Samuel Sentall for keeping Plantine,		417
To David Williams for Sexton,		110
To Majr William Poythress,		135
To William Parsons for John Ingles,		360
To John Peterson for Ditto,		50
To Charles Gilliam for Support,		400
To Colo Robert Bolling,		200
To be Levy'd toward Building the New Church,		30,000
		36,007
To Cask and Sallery @ 8 p Ct,		1,528
	Ls	37,535

Test, JNO. WOOBANK Clk Vestry.

(62) 1735 Novr 10th. Dr.

North & South Side of Bristol Parrish for 7 Months.

To Mr. George Robertson,	11,666
To Thomas Spaine,	933
To Robert Whitehall,	933
To John Woobank,	933
To Ditto,	233
To Phillip Prescott,	933
To Matthew Talbott,	933
To Mary Dison,	175
To John Tally,	583
To Eliz. Kennon,	700
To Jane Sentall,	145
To Richard Munns,	350
To James Vaughan,	233
To Elizabeth Cook,	550
To John Bentley,	145
To John Floyd,	583
To William Worsham,	466
To Maj^{r} William Poythress,	583
To Benjamin Cook,	34
To Samuel Sentall,	1,583
To Mary Hall,	425
To Henry Willson,	80
To Charles Couzens,	200
To James Sturdivant,	500
To John Cuirton,	200
To David Williams,	290
To Mr. George Willson for Insolvents,	359
To Maj^{r} William Poythress for D^{o},	1,633
	26,381
To Cask & Sallery @ 8 p. C^{t},	1,537
L^{s}	27,918

1735 Nov. 10th. Cr.

By 368 Tyths in Dale Parrish @ 12¼ p. Pole,	4,508

By 588 Tiths in Rawligh Parrish @ 12¼ p. Pole,		7,203
By 1,349 Tiths in Bristol Par. @ 40¼ p. Pole,		54,297
	Ls	66,008

Order'd that Majr Wm. Poythress and Majr Jas Munford Church wardens do receive of the Collectors of Dale Parrish Four thousand five Hundred and Eight Pounds of Ntt Tobo in Inspectors Notes for their Parrish Levey.

Test. JOHN WOOBANK Clk Vestry.

Order'd that Majr Wm. Poythress and Majr Jas Munford Church wardens do receive of the Collectors of Rawleigh Parr. Seven thousand two Hundred and three Pounds of Ntt Tobo in Inspectors Notes for their Parrish Levey.

Test. JOHN WOOBANK Clk Vestry.

BRISTOL PARRISH FOR 5 MONTHS DR.

To Mr. George Robertson,		2,000
To Robert Whitehall,		667
To John Woobank,		667
To Do,		167
To John Floyd,		417
To Majr William Poythress,		417
To Samuel Sentall jr,		417
To David Williams,		110
To Majr Poythress,		135
To William Parsons,		360
To John Peterson,		50
To Charles Gilliam,		400
To Colo Robert Bolling,		200
To be Levy'd toward Building the New Church,		30,000
		36,007
To Cask & Sallery @ 8 p. Ct,		1,528
	Ls	37,535
Brought down,		27,918
		65,453
Ballance due to ye Parrish,		555
	Ls	66,008

Order'd that Maj[r] Wm. Poythress and Maj[r] James Munford Church wardens do receive of every Tithable in this Parrish Forty and a quarter Pounds of N[tt] Tob[o] in Inspectors Notes for their Parrish Levy for this present Year and in case of refusal or nonpayment to Levy the Same by distress and pay the Severall Sums to the Creditors for whome the Same was proportioned.

Test JOHN WOOBANK Clk Vestry.

(63) Bristol Parrish—ss: At a Vestry held at the Ferry Chapple Feb[r] 9th 1735.

Present. Mr. George Robertson Minister, Maj[r] Wm. Poythress Church warden, Col[o] Robert Bolling, Cap[t] Charles Fisher, Cap[t] William Stark, Cap[t] Peter Jones, Mr. Theo. Field, Mr. Robert Munford.

Order'd that James Sturdivant and John Lewis Procession from the mouth of Citty Creek to the Head thence down the Branch to the great Swamp Bridge down the Swamp to Puddle dock Run Includeing all y[e] Lands within the said Bounds to the River. That John Moore and William Gibbs Procession all Below y[e] Citty Creek to the Parrish line from the River to the County Road. That Daniel Jones Procession with Joseph Tucker S[r] in the room of William Jones Dec[d].

That Olive Poxon be exempted from paying Parrish Levey.

Test. JOHN WOOBANK Clk Vestry.

(64) RETURNS OF PROCESSIONING FOR YE YEAR 1735.

Abraham Alley & Thomas Hardaway Procession'd on the lands in their Precinct. Hugh Reese and John West the Same. William Jones and Edward Colwell the Same. John Ellington and William Spaine the Same. John Poythres and John Hill the Same. Richard Raines and John Hill the Same. George Tillman j[r] and Robert Wynne the Same. William Batte and Sam[l] Jordan processioned all the lands in their Precinct except the land of Wm. Batte and Wm. Anderson Crawleys land Robert Poythress land Wm. Batte & Sam[l] Jordain lines & the lines of Henry Willson and Wm. Parsons not appearing. Matthew Mayse and Bartho. Crowder Procession'd all the lands in their Precinct except a piece of a line between Cap[t] Banister & Wm.

Martin & another line Between Cap[t] Banister & John Peterson not appearing. William Davis and John Jones Procession'd all the lands in their Precinct except Thomas Throar Wm. Parram Joseph Matthews land they not attending. David Williams and Israel Robinson Procession'd all the Lands in their Precinct except Col[o] Drury Stiths Wm. Butler and a Tract belon[g] to one of the Sturdivants they not appearing. James Baugh and Andrew Beck Procession'd all the lands in their Precinct. Abraham Jones S[r] and Abraham Jones jun[r] the Same. George Smith and George Tillman S[r] Procession'd all the lands in their Precinct except Wm. Pettypoole & Wm. Parram they not attending.

(65) Bristol Parish—ss: At a Vestry held at the Ferry Chapple April 18th 1736.

Present. Mr. George Robertson Minist[r], Col[o] Robert Bolling, Cap[t] Charles Fisher, Cap[t] William Stark, Cap[t] Peter Jones, Mr. Theo. Field. Maj[r] William Poythress C. W.

Order'd That Thomas Reese be exempted from paying Parrish Levy until Such time he shall be able & not any longer.

Test JOHN WOOBANK Clk. Vestry.

Bristol Parish—ss: At a Vestry held at the Ferry Chapple Nov[r] 15th, 1736.

Present. Maj[r] Wm. Poythress C. W., Col[o] Robert Bolling, Cap[t] Peter Jones, Capt. Fran[s] Poythress, Mr. Theop. Feild, Cap[t] Wm. Stark, Cap[t] Charles Fisher, Cap[t] Robert Munford.

	L[s]
To Mr. George Robertson, ...	16,000
To Robert Whitehall, ...	1,600
To John Woobank, ...	1,600
To D[o] Vestry, ...	400
To David Williams for Cleaning Sappony Chapple, .	400
To Sam[l] Sental S[r] for keeping Peter Plantine, . .	1,000
To Jane Sentall for Cleaning the Church, . .	250
To D[o] due last Year, ...	105
To Maj[r] Will[m] Poythress for keeping Mary Barrett, .	1,000
To John Floy'd for keeping Ann Newhouse to the 10th of January last, ...	250

To John Brown for keeping D° from ye 11th Jan^ry^ 1735–6 to the 26th October,		635
To Mary Eaton for burying Bramble,		100
To Wm. Bobbitt S^r^ for burying John Dalahny,		100
To William Parsons for keeping John Ingles,		1,200
To Charles Gilliam S^r^ for Support,		400
To Capt Peter Jones for a Tyth over paid,		40¼
To Maj^r^ William Poythress for Insolvents,		1,005
To Mary Eaton for keeping a Bast. Child of Barnabas Moore Suppos'd to be ye Reputed father,.		800
Carried Over,	L^s^	26,885
(66) Bro^t^ Over,	L^s^	26,885
To the Church Wardens to buy Cloathes for Tanner and his Wife as they shall think fitt,		400
To Ball Suppos'd to be due to Rawleigh & Dale Parish by Virtue of an Act of the Last Assembly,		11,000
To be Levy'd toward building the New Church,		18,000
To 4 p C^t^ on 16,000 for Cask,		640
To 6 p C^t^ on 56,925 for Collecting,		3,415
To Maj^r^ Wm. Poythress for paying Wm. Parsons more than what was lev'y for him,		104
	L^s^	60,444

1736 Novr 15th Bristol Parish Dr.

To Mr. Geo. Robertson,	16,000
To Robert Whitehall,	1,600
To John Woobank,	1,600
To Ditto,	400
To David Williams,	400
To Saml Sentall,	1,000
To Jane Sentall,	250
To Ditto,	105
To Maj^r^ Wm. Poythress,	1,000
To John Floy'd,	250
To John Brown,	635
To Mary Eaton,	100
To William Bobbitt S^r^,	100
To William Parsons,	1,200

To Charles Gilliam S^r^, ...	400
To Capt Peter Jones, ...	40¼
To Maj^r^ Wm. Poythress for Insol., . . .	1,005
To Mary Eaton, ...	800
To the Church Wardens for Taner &c. . . .	400
To Ballance Suppos'd to be due to Rawleigh and Dale, ...	11,000
To be levy'd toward building the New Church, .	18,000
To 4 p C^t^ for Cask, ...	640
To 6 p C^t^ for Collecting, ...	3,415
To Maj^r^ Wm. Poythress, ...	104
	60,444

1736 Novr 15th. Cr.

By 1,394 Tiths @ 43^l^ p. Pole, ...	59,942
Due to the Collectors, ...	502
	60,444

Order'd that Maj^r^ Wm. Poythress and Maj^r^ James Munford Church Wardens do receive of every Tithable in this Parrish forty three Pounds of N^t^ Tob^o^ in Inspectors Notes for there Parish Levey for this present Year and in case of refusal or non payment to Levey the Same by distress & pay ye Severall Sums to the Creditors for whome the Same was proportioned.

Test: John Woobank Clk Vestry.

(67) At a Vestry held at the Brick Church on Wells's Hill August ye 13th 1737.

Present. Maj^r^ William Poythress C. W., Col^o^ Robert Bolling, Capt Fran^s^ Poythress, Capt William Stark, Capt David Walker, Capt Robert Munford, Capt John Banister.

Order'd that the Petition for Building a Chapple be refer'd till after the Next Assembly to be consider'd. Also the Motion for one other Chapple be refer'd for Consideration. that Capt Wm. Hamlin be added to the Vestry. that the Vestry referr the Value of two Windows the difference between a plain Cornice and Mundillion to George Todd.

Test. John Woobank Clk Vestry.

Bristol Parrish—ss: At a Vestry held at the Brick Church on Wells's Hill Nov[r] 14th 1737.

Present. Mr. Geo[r] Robertson, Maj[r] James Munford, Maj[r] William Poythress C. W., Col. Robert Bolling, Cap[t] Peter Jones, Cap[t] William Stark, Mr. Theo. Field, Cap[t] Charles Fisher, Cap[t] Fra[s] Poythress.

Mr. Wm. Hamlin haveing taken the Oaths as Usual and Subscribing the Test is appointed to be a Vestryman.

	Cask.	L[s]
To Mr. Geo. Robertson,	640	16,000
To Robert Whitehall,		1,600
To John Woobank,		1,600
To Ditto for Vestry,		400
To David Williams,		400
To Sam[l] Sentall S[r] for Plantine,		900
To Ditto for Cleaning y[e] Church,		250
To Maj[r] Poythress for Mary Barrett,		1,000
To John Brown for Ann Newhouse,		800
To William Parsons for John Ingles 7 Months,		750
To Ditto for Ditto funerall,		115
To y[e] Church Wardens for Tanner & his Wife,		400
Carried Over,		24,215

(68) Bro[t] Over, . . . L[s]	24,215
To Mary Eaton for Sarah Burgess @ 800[l] p. Annum,	693
To Col[o] Robert Bolling for Fra. Deshain & Others,	332
To John Sturdivant for 2 Setts Horse Blocks and Moveing Edward Facey out of y[e] Parish,	48
To Fra[s] Bracey for Setting Horse Blocks & Seats,	150
To John Floy'd for Edward Facey,	60
To Robert Munford for Tho[s] Jacobs,	756
To ley'd toward Build[g] a New Chapple,	10,000
To Thomas Hardaway,	480
To 4 p C[t] for Cask on 16,000,	640
To Sallery at 6 p C[t],	2,242
	39,616

Order'd that Maj[r] Poythress & Cap[t] Stark be Church wardens for the ensuing Year.

that the Church Wardens consult Mr. Stephen Dewey for recovery of 480[l] Tob[o] pd Mr. Tho[s] Hardaway for the trouble and Expenses of a Commodating Mary Perry Wife of Tho[s] Perry and to take out such Process and against such person as he shall judge ought to reimburse the Same to the Parrish.

		£.	s.
Ball. due to y[e] Parrish from Maj[r] James Munford in Cash,		3.	10
Ditto from Maj[r] Wm. Poythress in Cash,		12.	1
Ditto in Tob[o],	7,000[l]		

that the Church Wardens do receive or recover of Southwark Parrish in Surry County 70[l] Tob[o] for the removeing of Edward Facey from this to that parish the place of his Legial residence.

Test JOHN WOOBANK, Clk Vestry.

(69) 1737 Nov[r] 14th BRISTOL PARRISH DR.

	L[s].
To Mr. Geo. Robertson,	16,000
To Robert Whitehall,	1,600
To John Woobank,	1,600
To Ditto,	400
To David Williams,	400
To Sam[l] Sentall S[r],	900
To Ditto,	250
To Maj[r] Wm. Poythress,	1,000
To John Brown,	800
To Wm. Parsons,	750
To Ditto,	115
To the Church Wardens,	400
To Mary Eaton,	693
To Col[o] Robert Bolling,	332
To John Sturdivant,	48
To Fra[s] Bracey,	150
To John Floy'd,	60
To Robert Munford,	756
Toward Build[g] New Chapple,	10,000
To Tho[s] Hardaway,	480

To 4 p C^t on 16,000,		640
To Sallery @ 6 p C^t,		2,242
		39,616
Ball Due to ye Parrish,		1,593
	L^s	41,209

1737 Novr 14th Cr.

By 1,425 Tith @ 24^l p Pole,		34,200
By due from the Church Wardens,		7,009
	L^s	41,209

Test. John Woobank Clk Vestry.

(70) Bristol Parrish—ss: At a Vestry held at the Brick Church on Wells's Hill May 20th 1738.

Present. Mr. George Robertson Minister, Maj^r William Poythress C. W., Col^o Robert Bolling, Capt $Fran^s$ Poythress, Capt William Stark, Capt Charles Fisher, Mr. Theo. Field, Maj^r James Munford, Capt Peter Jones.

Order'd that Maj^r James Munford Capt Fra^s Poythress John Banister Esqr and William Hamlin Gent: do view and agree upon a proper place for Building a Chapple on Hatchers Run for the Conveniency of the upper Inhabitants of this Parish and to report the proceedings to a Vestry to be held the first Saturday in July next and that the Church Wardens do Advertize for Workmen to come in to undertake the Same.

On the Pettion of Matthew Ford he is exempted from paying Parish Levy for the future.

Test: John Woobank Clk Vestry.

Bristol Parish—ss: At a Vestry held at the Brick Church on Wells's Hill July 1st 1738.

Present. Col^o Robert Bolling, Capt Peter Jones, Capt William Stark, Capt William Hamlin, Mr. Theo. Feild, Maj^r William Poythress, Capt Fra^s Poythress, Maj^r James Munford, Capt Charles Fisher, Capt Robert Munford.

Order'd that a Church be built on the North side of Hatchers

Run on the Land of Allen Tye fifty by Twenty Two fourteen foot pitch in the Clear, Ceald with ¾ Plank Cypherd, the Height of the Pews; Naild on with 8d Nailes or Brads and above that with ½ Inch plank naild with 6d Nailes or Brads Close Pews plain Winscott within and Shass ¼ Rounds without, 2 Windows on the front side and 3 on the Back 2 Windows at the East end and one at the west for light to the Gallery. weather Boarded wth feather edge Plank with a Bead Rough from the pitt 9 Inches wide rise 6 Inches Inch on the thick edge and ¼ on the Thin Cover'd with Clear Inch plank Cypher'd Inch and ½ on each edge and Cover'd on that with good hart pine or Cyprus Shingles ¾ thick on the lower and 22 Inches long (71) and Seven Rise Substantial fram'd doors plaine Cornice eves Communion Table, Gallery and Stares to be raild with Banisters Hung with rising Joints as also the pew doors a decent Pulpit & Type & desk wth Gallery Suteable to the Building, the Isle to be 5 foot the pews 4½ wide Shash windows proportion'd to the Building Glaz'd with diamond Glass the whole House to be well Tarr'd the doors windows and Cornice to be prim'd and twice painted with white lead and under pin'd Close with Rock stones 15 Inches high from the Ground. the whole plank work with Clear plank and free from Knotts good locks Bolts and Barrs for the doors outside doors for the defence of the Inn doors & Sells, Hung wth Cross garnets and hooks to Keep them open and Bolts to fasten them and every thing Nessesary to make the work Compleate the floor to be laid with Inch & ¼ Clear hart plank plain'd Naild down with 20d Nailes or Brads to be finished by the last of October in the Year 1740.

Mr. Isham Eppes undertakes to Build the above Chapple according to the dementions above mentioned for £119: 15s: od. Current Money to be paid at three Several payments.

Test. JOHN WOOBANK Clk Vestry.

At a Vestry held at the Brick Church on Wells's Hill November 13th 1738.

Present. Mr. George Robertson Minister, Capt William Stark, Majr William Poythress C. W., Colo Robert Bolling, Capt Peter Jones, Mr. Theo. Field, Capt William Hamlin.

	Cask.	Ls
To Mr. George Robertson, ...	640	16,000
To Mr. Robert Whitehall, ...		1,600
To John Woobank, ...		1,600
To Ditto Vestry, ...		400
To Saml Sentall jr for Plantine, . . .		900
To Saml Sentall Sr for Cleaning the Church, .		250
To John Brown for Ann Newhouse, . .		800
To John Hall for Studstill, ...		600
To John Fitz Gerrald for Mary Barrett, . .		1,000
To John Blackman for Cummings, . . .		300
To Sarah Williams relect of David Williams for Sappony Chapple, ...		250
To Peter Mitchell for one Levey, . . .		43
To Colo Robert Bolling for Sundrys as p Acct 0£ 17s. 3d.		
To Thomas Spain for Reading at Namesd, .		400
(72) Brought Over, ...		24,143
To James Pittillo for Cath: Arthur, . .		466
To Capt William Stark as p Accot £10: 18: 5.		
To Thomas Hardaway Sr, ...		250
To Stephen Dewey 0: 15: 0.		
To be levy'd toward Building a Chapple, .		12,000
To Mr. George Robertson for ferriages allow'd to this day 2: 6: 8¾.		
To Samuel Sentall Sr, ...		24
To Cask, ...		640
To 6 p Ct on 37,523, ...		2,250
		39,773

Orderd that Thompson Stapley be exempted from paying his Parish Levey. that the Church wardens pay to Isham Eppes what money they have he giving Bond and Security for the Same. that the Church wardens take care to provide for Samuel Tatum if he is not able. that Thomas Mitchell be Levy free.

1738 Novr 13th. BRISTOL PARRISH DR.

	L^s
To Mr. George Robertson,	16,000
To Robert Whitehall,	1,600
To John Woobank,	1,600
To Ditto,	400
To Samuel Sentall, j^r,	900
To Samuel Sentall S^r,	250
To John Brown,	800
To John Hall,	600
To John Fitz Gerrald,	1,000
To John Blackman,	300
To Sarah Williams,	250
To Peter Mitchell,	43
To Col^o Robt Bolling 0: 17: 3.	
To Thomas Spain,	400
To James Pittillo,	466
To Capt Wm. Stark 10: 18: 5.	
To Thos Hardaway S^r,	250
To Stephen Dewey 0: 15: 0.	
To be levyd toward Building a Chapple,	12,000
To Mr. Geo. Robertson for ferriages 2: 6: 8¾.	
To Samuel Sentall S^r,	24
To Cask,	640
To 6 p C^t,	2,250
Ball. due to the parrish,	263
L^s	40,036

L 14: 17: 4¾ Cash.

1738 Novr 13th. CR.

By 1,502 Tyths @ 26 p Pole,	39,052
By due from Church wardens,	984
L^s	40,036

Ordered that the Church wardens do receive of every Tithable in this Parish Twenty Six Pounds of N^t Tob^o for their Parish Levey for this Present Year and in case of Refusal or Nonpayment to levy the Same by distress.

Test JOHN WOOBANK Clk: Vestry.

(73) At a Vestry held at the Brick Church on Wells's Hill August 20th 1739.

Present. Cap[t] Wm. Stark, Maj[r] Wm. Poythress C. W., Col[o] Robert Bolling, Cap[t] Francis Poythress, Mr. Theo. Feild, Cap[t] Charles Fisher, Maj[r] James Munford, Cap[t] Peter Jones.

Order'd That John Lewis and John Gilliam j[r] Procession from Puddle dock Run to the lower end of y[e] Parish Between the River and Madam Bolkings Road. That Miles Thweatt and William Batte Procession from Puddle dock Run to the Nottoway Road as far out as Blackwater. That Thomas Hardaway and Abraham Alley Procession from Nottoway Road up as far as Monkersneck Road. That William Parsons and John Mayse Procession from Puddle dock to Lieu[t] Run Between the River and the great Swamp and Monkersneck Road. That Abraham Jones S[r] and Abraham Jones j[r] Procession from Lieut. Run to the Indian Town Run Includeing Rohowick. That Nicholas Overbey and John May j[r] Procession from the Indian Town Run to Wallaces Creek. That Matthew Mayse and Bartho: Crowder Procession from Wallaces Creek Cross to the white Oak Road down Hatchers Run to the Extent. That John Ellington and William Spaine Procession from whiponock to Namosend out as far as Bollings lower line. That James Baugh and Andrew Beck Procession Between Blackwater Swamp and Second Swamp from the Parish line to the Monkersneck Road. That Thomas Lee and Samuel Lee Procession Between Second Swamp and warwick Swamp from the Parish line to the Monkersneck Road. That William Cotten and Peter Tatum Procession the land below Jones Hole Road Between the Parish line and warwick Swamp. That Richard Raines and Cuth: Williamson Procession from warwick Swamp to the Parish line Between Jones Hole Road and Rowanty Road. That William Butler and James Butler Procession from Monkersneck Bridge to Rowanty Bridge. That George Smith and Edward Winfield Procession from Monkersneck Creek to Stoney Creek Between the Monkersneck Road and the Parish line. Carried Over.

(74) Order'd That Joseph Tucker S[r] and Joseph Tucker j[r] Procession from Stoney Creek to Sapponey Creek Between the Parish line and the Chapple Road. That Israel Robinson and John Robinson Procession from Sappony Creek to Nottoway

River Between the County line and the Road that leads from the Cutt Banks to the Chapple. That William Jones and Henry Baley Procession from the Cutt Banks Road up Nottoway River to the great Creek. That William Jones and John Jones Procession from the Mouth of the great Creek up Nottoway River to the Extent of the Parish. That George Williams and William Vaughan Procession from the Monkersneck Road up the North side Monkersneck and Hatchers Run to the white Oak Road and as far in as Rohowick. That Robert Wynne and Joshua Wynne Procession from Monkersneck to Stoney Creek Between the Monkersneck Road and the Chapple Road. That Francis Bressie and John Mansion Procession from the Chapple Road to the Butterwood Road Between Hatchers Run and Stony Creek. That Jos: Pritchett j^r^ and Caleb Pritchett Procession Between the Chapple Road and Butterwood Road from Stony Creek to the extent. That Edward Mitchell S^r^ and James Thweatt Procession Between Butterwood and white Oak. That George Still and Roger Moore Procession from Butterwood Road up the North side white Oak to the extent as far in as Namos. and head of Whiponock. That Hugh Reese and Robert West Procession Between white Oak and Namos: to the extent of the County. That John Poythress and Thomas Twittey Procession Between Butterwood and Nottoway River as low as the head of Beaver-pond Creek. That Richard Nance and Thomas Gent j^r^ Procession Between the South fork of the Cattale Run and Gravely Run from the Chapple Road up.

That the above said Persons Procession the lands in their Several precints and make returns of all lands they Procession with the Names of the persons present when Processioned and to make returns of all Lands not Processioned.

Test. JOHN WOOBANK, Clk Vestry.

(75) At a Vestry held at the Brick Church on Wells's Hill October 23d 1739.

Present. Mr. George Robertson Minister, Col^o^ Robert Bolling, Capt Fra^s^ Poythress, Capt Peter Jones, Capt Charles Fisher, Mr. Theo. Feild, Capt William Stark, Maj^r^ James Munford, Maj^r^ William Poythress.

	Cask.	L^s
To Mr. George Robertson Minist^r, . .	640	16,000
To Robert Whitehall, ...		1,600
To John Woobank, ...		1,600
To Ditto for Vestry, ...		400
To John Brown for Ann Newhouse, . .		800
To Samuel Sentall S^r for Cleaning the Church,		250
To John Hall for Studstill, ...		800
To John Fitz Gerrald for Mary Barrett, . .		1,000
To Sarah Williams relect of David Williams for Sappony Chapple, ...		250
To Ditto for Sundry Services as a reward, .		100
To Thomas Spaine for Read^g at Namos^d, .		400
To James Pittillo for Cath. Arthur, . .		700
To Mary Hall for Keeping an Orphan Child,		250
To Col^o Robert Bolling by Order of Joseph Mayse for Keeping Peter Plantine, . .		900
To Col^o Robert Bolling for Sundrys as p his Acc^t, ... £1: 19s. 5½d.		
To Capt William Stark for the Ball of his Acco^t, ... 4: 15. 6½.		
To Mr. George Robertson for ferriages to this day, ... 2: 4: 4.		
To be levy'd toward Building a New Chapple & paying of the old ingagements, . .		10,000
To 6 p C^t Sallery for Collecting on 35,690, .		2,141
		37,831

Order'd That the Church wardens demand of the Administ^s of Matthew Lee the Estate of Frances Lee Daughter of the said Matthew Lee a poor Orphan to be disposed of for reimbursing the present and futer experience in maintaining the s^d Orphan. That William Russell j^r be exempted from paying his Parish Levey for the future.

		L^s
Tob^o due from Maj^r William Poythress, ...		4,730
From ditto in Cash, ...	21: 12: 3¾.	

(76) Order'd That a Chapple be built for the Convenience of the lower parts of this Parish be fifty by Twenty Two.

That Cap[t] William Stark and Maj[r] James Munford be Church wardens for the ensuing year.

Test JOHN WOOBANK Clk Vestry.

1739 October 23d. BRISTOL PARISH DR.

To Mr. George Robertson,				16,000
To Robert Whitehall,				1,600
To John Woobank,				1,600
To Ditto,				400
To John Brown,				800
To Samuel Sentall S[r],				250
To John Hall,				800
To John Fitz Gerrald,				1,000
To Sarah Williams,				250
To Ditto,				100
To Thomas Spaine,				400
To James Pittillo,				700
To Mary Hall,				250
To Col[o] Robert Bolling,				900
	£	s.	d.	
To Ditto,	1	19	5½	
To Cap[t] Wm. Stark,	4	15	6½	
To Mr. Geo. Robertson,	2	4	4	
	8	19	4	
To be levy'd toward building a New Chapple &c.				10,000
To Cask,				640
To 6 p C[t] Collecting,				2,141
			L[s]	37,831

1739 Octo. 23d. CR.

By 1,504 Tyths at 25[l] Tob[o] p Pole,		37,600
due to the Collectors,		231
	L[s]	37,831

Order'd That the Church wardens do receive of every Tithable in this Parish Twenty five pounds of N^{t} Tob^{o} for their Parish levy for this present Year and in case of refusal or nonpayment to levy the Same by distress.

Test. JOHN WOOBANK Clk Vestry.

(77) At a Vestry held at the Brick Church on Well's Hill Decr 10th 1739.

Present. Mr. George Robertson, Minister, Capt Peter Jones, Capt Fra^{s} Poythress, Capt Charles Fisher, Maj^{r} William Poythress, Mr. Theo: Feild, Capt Wm. Stark, Capt Wm. Hamlin.

Order'd that Col^{o} Robert Bolling, Maj^{r} Wm. Poythress & Capt Wm. Eppes do appoint a place for Building the new Chapple & that Mr. John Ravenscroft undertakes to build the Same for £134: 10s: to be paid at three Several payments to be finished by the last of December 1741. to be done in the Same manner & Same dementions as the former. That Instance Hall & John Sturdivant Procession all the Land Between the Nottoway Road Puddle Dock Run Mrs. Bollings Road to the Extent of the Parish. That John May j^{r} be appointed Reader at some convenient place where the Church is to be built & to be allowed 1600^{l}: Tob^{o} p. Annum. That Col^{o} Robert Bolling, Capt Peter Jones & Mr. Theo: Feild are appointed to view & to see that the work of the new Chapple to be built be compleat & done workmanlike.

Test: JOHN WOOBANK Clk Vestry.

At a Vestry held at the Brick Church on Wells's Hill Feb^{ry} 5th 1739.

Present. Mr. George Robertson Minister, Col^{o} Robert Bolling, Capt Peter Jones, Maj^{r} Wm. Poythress, Maj^{r} James Munford, Capt Wm. Stark, Mr. Theo: Feild, Capt Wm. Hamlin.

Order'd That George Browder be Sexton of Hatchers Run Chapple. That the aforesaid Chapple be built on Thos Bonners land Between Thos Bonners plantation & John Whitmores on the great Branch of Joans Hole convenient to the Spring. That Mr. Theo^{k} Bland be appointed a Vestryman. That Joshua Pritchett S^{r} be exempted from paying his Parish Levy for the future.

(78) That Mr. John Ravenscroft Letter be entered on Record & the Original be preserved.

Copy. Feb[ry] 4th, 1739.

Gentlemen: My business obliging me to go home I cant possibly wait on you to Morrow but to prevent any further misunderstandings about this Church, I declare it never was my Intention to perform the work in any other than a substantial and workman like manner that I shall take a perticular care that, that part of the plank & framing w[ch] is expos'd to the weather be of a good Hart Stuff, I mean Sills sleepers, door posts, windows frames, & weather boarding in perticular, & in every other part so well as to do the Parish Justice & preserve my own Character. I am willing to enter into bond wth security for performance of the work, & that any body may view it whilst tis carrying on. I hope this may prevent any further suspicion of fraud from

Your Humb: Serv[t]

JOHN RAVENSCROFT.

Test JOHN WOOBANK Clk Vestry.

At a Vestry held at the Brick Church on Wells's Hill Feb[ry] 23d 1739.

Present. Col[o] Robert Bolling, Cap[t] Robert Munford, Mr. Theo. Feild, Cap[t] Wm. Stark, Cap[t] Peter Jones, Cap[t] Charles Fisher, Maj[r] Wm. Poythress.

Order'd That the former order made the 5th Instant be vacated & that the Chapple then order'd to be built on Tho[s] Bonners Land be built on Titmashes Land the Vestry being well convinced it will be most convenient to a Majority of this Parish than Bonners beside the Conveniency of a good Spring convenient thereto which cannot be had at any Intermediate Place & it is further Order'd that Mr. John Ravenscroft Undertaker thereof have forthwith a Copy of this order.

That Col[o] Rob[t] Bolling Cap[t] Peter Jones & Mr. Theo. Feild are appointed to view & to see that the work of the new Chapple to be built be compleat & done workman like.

Test JOHN WOOBANK Clk Vestry.

(79) At a Vestry held at the Brick Church on Wells's Hill May 26th 1740.

Present. Col[o] Robert Bolling, Cap[t] Wm. Stark, Cap[t] Peter

Jones, Mr. John Banister, Maj[r] Wm. Poythress, Cap[t] Will[m] Hamlin, Mr. Theo. Feild, Mr. Theo[k] Bland, Cap[t] Charles Fisher.

Order'd That Mr. Richard Heartswel be received Minister of this Parish dureing the approbation of the Vestry he haveing agreed to accept thereof on these Terms.

That the Chapple appointed to be built on Titmass's Land the 5th of Feb[y] last be Instead thereof built at the most convenient place to water nearest to one Mile & half distance East from the said Titmass's and that Col[o] Rob[t] Bolling Cap[t] Wm. Stark Cap[t] Peter Jones & Mr. Theo[k] Bland view & assertain the Place & report the Same to the next Vestry and that as soon as may be thereafter the Undertaker have Notice thereof.

Test JOHN WOOBANK Clk Vestry.

At a Vestry held at the Brick Church on Wells's Hill May 27th 1740.

Present. Col[o] Rob[t] Bolling, Cap[t] Wm. Stark, Mr. Theo. Feild, Cap[t] Charles Fisher, Maj[r] Wm. Poythress, Mr. Theo[k] Bland, Cap[t] Peter Jones.

Mr. Richard Heartswel haveing in company with Several of the Vestry yesterday Evening declared that he did not understand the order of Vestry that day made for receiveing him as Minister of this Parish on the Terms therein mentioned altho entered in his presence & with his approbation & now insisting on Twenty Pounds p Ann in lieu of a Glebe which he with some warmth, said he thought he merrited; & without such Allowance would not stay, thereupon the Church wardens conviend this Vestry who upon the representation of this matter by several of their own Members, Orders that the said Richard Heartswel be discharged as Minister of this Parish on the Terms by him & the Vestry agreed to on the 26th Instant or on any other whatsoever.

Test JOHN WOOBANK Clk Vestry.

(80) RETURNS OF PROCESSIONING FOR THE YEAR 1739.

Thomas Hardaway and Abraham Alley Processioned all the Lands in their Precinct. Samuel Lee and Thomas Lee the Same. James Baugh and Andrew Beck the Same. Instance Hall and John Sturdivant the Same. Joseph Turner and William Turner the Same. John Mayse and William Parsons the Same. James Williams and William Butler the Same. John Jones and William Jones the Same. John Lewis S^{r} and John Gilliam the Same. Miles Whweatt and William Batt the Same excepting two lines of Batte & Jordan they disagreeing & another peice belonging to the heir of Arther Browder the Heir being an Infant. Nicholas Overbey S^{r} and John May the Same excepting Charles Fishers John Fitz Gerrald and Wm. Overbeys nobody appearing. Richard Raines and Cuthbert Williamson the Same excepting Thos Carklons and James Harrisons nobody appearing. George Williams and William Vaughan the Same excepting Isham Eppes's & Thomas Williams's nobody appearing. Abraham Jones S^{r} and Abraham Jones j^{r} the same excepting Part of a Line of John Ravenscroft & a Line of Wm. Eatons the Lines not to be found. Robert Wynne and Joshua Wynne the Same excepting Israel Peterson & Mary Smith Lands nobody appearing. John Roberson and Israel Roberson the Same excepting Henry Dicksons, Thomas Dicksons they having an Order of Council to go round their old Lines & Wm. Butlers nobody appearing. John Mansion and Fra^{s} Bressie the Same excepting Joseph Mayse and James Butler nobody appearing. Wm. Jones and Henry Baley the Same excepting John Watkins & John Merritts Lands nobody appearing.

(81) At a Vestry held for Bristol Parish Octo^{r} 22d, 1740.

Present. Robert Bolling, Peter Jones, William Poythress, Robert Munford, Theo: Feild, William Stark, Charles Fisher.

To the Executors of Mr. George Robertson dec^{d},	4,000
To Cask for Ditto,	160
To Robert Whitehall Clk Sappony,	1,600
To John Woobank,	2,000
To John Brown for keeping Ann Newhouse,	800
To Samuel Sentall Sexton of the Brick Church,	250
To Thomas Spaine Clk at Hatchers Run,	1,600
To Sarah Williams Sexton at Sappony,	250
To Thos Spaine for Arrears Last year,	1,200
To James Pittillo for keeping Kat. Arther,	700
To William Stark for Mary Barrett,	800

To D° for Ledbetters Keeping Tudstal,	700
To D° for Dentons Keeping M. Delahay,	600
To D° for Mary Halls Keeping Fra Lee,	800
To D° for Ball due last year,	231
To D° for Ball this year for delinquents.	350
To John May Clerk Warwick for 7 Months,	921
To the Reverend Mr. Stith for Preaching,	2,560
To Mr. Heartswell,	960
To Tho[s] Hardaway for Jane Anderson,	200
To Wm. Tanner & his Wife,	400
To the building of New Chapple,	15,000
To Mary Allen,	200
To George Browder,	75
To the Sallery for Collecting,	2,181
To Wm. Stark for Sundry goods to Sundry poor persons, £8. 11s. 0½d.	•
	38,538

Order'd that Thomas Gent. be exempted from paying the Parish Levy. the Church at Hatchers Run be rebuilt. that Cap[t] William Stark & Theo: Feild be Church wardens for the present year. that the Church wardens Collect of every Tithable person L25 Tob° their parish Levy for this present year & in case of refusal or nonpayment to levy the Same by distress. that the Southern Chapple be built at the Harrican nearest to the best water.

Test JOHN WOOBANK Clk Vestry.

[82] 1740, Octb[r] 23d. BRISTOL PARISH DR.

To Eex: of Geo: Robertson,	4,000
To Cask for Ditto,	160
To Robert Whitehall,	1,600
To John Woobank,	2,000
To John Brown,	800
To Sam[l] Sentall,	250
To Sarah Williams,	250
To Tho[s] Spain,	1,600
To Ditto,	1,200
To James Pittillo,	700

To Wm. Stark,	800
To Ditto,	700
To Ditto,	600
To Ditto,	800
To Ditto,	231
To Ditto,	350
To John May,	921
To Mr. Stith,	2,560
To Mr. Heartswell,	960
To Thos Hardaway,	200
To Wm. Tanner & wife,	400
To Building of New Chapple,	15,000
To Mary Allen,	200
To George Browder,	75
To Sallery,	2,181
To Wm. Stark, £8: 11s: 0½d.	
	38,538
To Ball due to the parish,	262
	38,800

1740, Octr 23d. Cr.

By 1552 Tyths at 25l Tobo p pole,	38,800

Ball due to the parish.

Orderd that the Church wardens do receive of every Tithable in this Parish Twenty five pounds Neat Tobo for their parish levy for this present yr and in case of refusal or nonpayment to levy the Same by distress.

Test John Woobank Clk Vestry.

[83] At a Vestry held at the Brick Church December ye 2d 1740.

Present. Capt Wm. Stark, Robert Bolling, Theo. Feild, Peter Jones, William Poythress, Theok Bland, James Munford, Charles Fisher.

Orderd that a Chapple be Built on Hatchers Run at the most Convenient Place to be agreed on by James Munford Capt Peter Jones John Banister Esqr & Capt William Hamlin or the majority of them and of the Same dimentions and manner wth that on Hatchers Run lately burnt & that other now Building on Jones Hole to be underpin'd with Stone or Brick which is undertaken by Mr. James Clark for one hundred & Eighteen pounds Currant Money of Virginia & to be finished in two years and to be paid for in two years from the fifteenth of October next at two payments the said Clark entring into bond wth good Security to the Church wardens or Vestry for this performance of the worke in the manner & time Ofer'd before any payment made him.

Test JOHN WOOBANK Clk Vestry.

At a Court held for Prince Geo. County the 9th day of December 1740.

Ordered that Moll Daughter of Elizabeth Bird a mulatto woman, be bound by the Churchwardens of Bristoll Parish, to Some proper person, in the manner the Law directs.

Test JOHN MAY Clk Vestry.

[84] At a Vestry held for Bristoll Parish March 6th 1740.

Presant. Robert Bolling, Charles Fisher, Wm. Poythress, David Walker, Ja[s] Munford, Theodorick Bland, Peter Jones.

It is ordered and agreed that Mr. Robert Ferguson be receiv[d] into this Parish as Minister thereof for Twelve months from the fifteenth of January last as a Probationer and to be paid at the usual rate of Sixteen Thousand Pounds of Tobacco with the allowance also of four thousand Pounds of Tobacco for his board instead of a Glebe.

Orderd that John May j[r] be Clerk of the Brick Church in the roome of John Wobank and that John Wobank be Clerk of the Church in the roome of John May j[r] and it is further orderd that John Wobank Deliver the parish records to the Church wardens and be discontinued Clerk of the Vestry.

Test JOHN MAY Clk Vestry.

We of the Jurors being Summoned & Sworn persuant to a venire facias Issued out of Prince George County Court bearing date the Twenty Second day of Decem[br] 1740. We upon our Oaths do find that Samuel Jordan & William Batte in our presence did agree that the old Lines in dispute should be, and at all times hereafter, is and shall be Lines & bounds of their Lands forever: persuant to Such agreement between the parties aforsaid, We went to the beginning of one of the Lines aforsaid, in the presence of the Sheriff, the Surveyor being absent which beginning Tree (being a poplar) is, and Stands on a Branch of Bailies Creek, and from thence to a Small pine; from thence Wee went to the other line in Dispute, and beginning at a Pine Stump, run the said Line in the presants of the Sheriff, by the agreement of the parties aforsaid, which was by the Said parties Amicably admitted to be true Lines as now by us Settled.

[85] Witness our hands and Seals, all of which doing in persuance of the Writt aforesaid: I have hereunto Set my hand, and Seal, so answer.

William Stark Sher^{f} [Seal],	Fran^{s} Epes forem^{n} [Seal],
John Woodleif [Seal],	Charles Fisher [Seal],
William Standback [Seal],	Theo^{k} Bland [Seal],
Drury Thweatt [Seal],	John Buttler [Seal],
John Sturdivant [Seal],	Thos Poythress [Seal],
John Cureton [Seal],	John Epes [Seal],
Edwd Mitchell [Seal].	

At a Court held at Fitzgerralds, for Prince George County on Wednesday the Eleventh day of March 1740 William Stark Sheriff of this County return^{d} the above written Report of the Jury ordered to lay out, and procession, the Land of William Batte & Saml Jordan by order of the Court is truly Recorded.

Test JOHN MAY Clk Vestry.

Test WM. HAMLIN Cl Crt.

At a Court held for Prince George County the 14th day of April 1741.

Ordered that Wm. Lewis Son of William Lewis late of this County deced: be bound by the Churchwardens of Bristoll Parish, to Richard Meanly in the Manner the Law directs for poor Orphans.

Test JOHN MAY Clk Vestry.

[86] At a Vestry held at the Brick Church on Well's hill Octo^{r} 12th 1741.

Present. Mr. Robert Fergusson Minister, Col^{o} Robt Bolling,

Capt Peter Jones, Capt Willm Stark, Mr. Theo: Feild, Maj^{r} Willm Poythress, Capt Theo^{k} Bland.

	L^{s}
To the Rever^{d} Robt Fergusson, ...	12,000
To Cask for Ditto at 4 ꝑ C^{t}, ...	480
To Ditto in Lew of a Gleab, ...	3,000
To John Woobank for 3 months, ...	533
To Robt Whitehall Cl^{k} of Sapp^{y} Chap^{le}, . . .	1,600
To Thom^{s} Spain, ...	1,600
To John May Ju^{r}, ...	1,600
To Ditto for Cl^{k} of the Vestry, ...	100
To John Brown for keeping Ann Newhose, . .	800
To Geo: Williams Ju^{r} Cl^{k} of Jones Hole, . . .	1,067
To Saml Sentull Sexton of the Church, . . .	250
To Sarah Williams Ditto of Sapponey Church, .	250
To Jam^{s} Pittello for keeping Cath^{r} Arther, . .	700
To Capt Willm Stark for Mary Barrut, . . .	800
To Ditto for Fraces Lee, ...	800
To Capt Willm Eppes for Marg^{ry} Delawayhay, . .	600
To John Ledbetter for Tedstal, ...	800
To William Tanner & his wife, ...	400
To Mary Alley, ...	200
To Ball Due to the Col^{r} for Delenquents, . . .	450
To Capt Theo^{k} Bland for one tith Over Lis^{d}, . .	25
To Mr. Theo: Feild for Sundrys, . £1: 14: 0.	
To Ditto for Sundrys to Fra^{s} Deasonne's, . .	205
To the Ball^{ce} due in the hands of the Churchwarth^{ns},	262
Towards paying for the Church & Chappel and Purchasing a gliebe, ...	41,431
To 6 ꝑ C^{t} for Collecting, ...	4,079
	73,508

[87] 1741 Octo^{r} 12. BRISTOL PARISH DR.

To the reve^{d} Robt Fergusson, ...	15,480
To John Woobank, ...	533
To Robert Whitehall, ...	1,600
To Thom^{s} Spain, ...	1,600
To John May Ju^{r}, ...	1,700
To John Brown, ...	800

To Geo: Williams Ju^{r},		1,067
To Saml Sentull,		250
To Sarah Williams,		250
To Jam^{s} Pettillo,		700
To Capt Willm Stark,		1,600
To Capt Willm Eppes,		600
To John Ledbetter,		800
To Willm Tanner,		400
To Mary Alley,		200
To Ball due to ye Collec^{r} Dq^{ts},		450
To Capt Theo^{k} Bland,		25
To Mr. Theo: Feild,	£1. 14s. 0d.	
To Ditto,		205
To ye Ball^{e} due in ye hands of ye Chur's,		262
To paying for ye church & Chapel and purchaceing a Glebe,		41,431
To 6 ℔ C^{t} for Collecting,		4,079
		73,508

1741 Octo^{r} 12th. CRED'R

By 1598 Tyths at 46^{l} Tob^{o} p: pole,	73,508

Order'd that the Church wardens do receive of every Tithable in this parish forty-Six pounds of Neet Tob^{o} for their Parish Levy for this prese^{t} year and in Case of Refusal or Non payment to Levy the Same by Distress.

Test JOHN MAY Clk Vestry.

Order'd that the Revd Mr Robt Fergusson be receivd as Minister of this parish.

Order'd that Capt Willm Stark & Mr. Theo: Field be Continued Church-wardens for the Insuing year.

Order'd that John May Ju^{r} be Appointed Clk of the Vestry.

Order'd that Geo: Williams Ju^{r} be Appointed Clk of the Jones Hole Chapple.

Order'd that William Delawayhay be Levy free.

Order'd that Thom^{s} Clemons be Appointed Sexton of the Chapple at Jones Hole.

Test JOHN MAY Clk Vestry.

[88] In Obedience to an order of Prince George County Court we the Subscribers met to possession the Lines between Wm. Crawley and Cap: Robt Munford and did Possession the said Lines by the consent of each partie, they being present, begining at the mouth of the Ridge Bottome, And runing up the said Bottom along the old Lines between the said parties to the Extent thereof. Given under our Hands & Seals this 29th day of Sep^{tbr} 1741.

Isham Epes Sher: [Seal],
Charles Hamlin [Seal],
George Lewis [Seal],
John Sturdivant [Seal],
Signum.
John H Hall [Seal],
John Mayse [Seal],
Wm. Parsons [Seal],

Thos Williams forem^{n} [Seal],
John Lewis Junr [Seal],
John Buttler [Seal],
James Sturdivant [Seal],
Thos Hardaway [Seal],
John Fitzgarrald [Seal].

Cop^{a} Test JOHN MAY Clk Vestry.

Att a Vestry held at the Brick Church on Wells's Hill The 22d day of December 1741.

Present. The rev^{t} Robert Fergusson Minister, Coll^{o} Robt Bolling, Mr. Theo^{s} Field, Maj^{r} Wm. Poythress, Capt Wm. Stark, Capt Peter Jones, Capt Theodrick Bland.

It is this day agreed on between this Vestry & Thos Williams that the said Williams will finish the dwelling House he is now Building Vitz: the Chimney Plaistring and underpining & compleat the said House at his own Proper Expence, and allso saw and deliver so much Inch Plank from the Pitt as will be Sufficient to Lay an upper Floare of a House twelve by Sixteen when the Same is season^{d} & Joynted: and will for the Consideration of Two hundred Pounds Currant money of Virginia to be paid in manner following, Vitz: all the money that shall Arise from the sale of the Tob^{o} already Leavey^{d} for Building of Chapells & Towards Buying a Glibe after the presant Engagements for the Chapells are discharged and the Overpluss when that is assertaind to be then paid allso in Curr^{t} money and the said Williams doth agree to Convey two hundred Acres of Land wth the plantation [89] and Buildings compleated as above mention^{d} to this parish by

Such Deeds And Conveyances as shall think fitt or advise for a Glebe for the use of this Parrish.

Coppy. Test JOHN MAY Clk Vestry.

At a Vestry held at the Brick-Church on Wells's Hill Octob[r] 14th 1742.

Present. The Rev[d] Mr. Robert Fergusson Minister, Col[o] Robert Bolling, Cap[t] Peter Jones, Major William Poythress, Cap[t] Theodorick Bland, Cap[t] William Stark, Cap[t] Charles Fisher, Mr. Theophilus Field, Mr. Thomas Short.

BRISTOL PARISH AS IT STOOD UNDIVIDED TILL SEP'TR 1ST 1742 DR.

	L.
To the Rev[d] Mr. Robert Fergusson for 10½ Months,	14,001
To 4 ℔ C[t] on Ditto for Cask, ...	560
To Rob[t] Whitehall Clk of Sapponie for 10½ Months,	1,400
To John May Jun[r] Clk of the Vestry & Brick Church for D[o] Time, ...	1,750
To George Williams Jun[r] Clk of Jones Hole D[o] Time,	1,400
To Thomas Spain Clk of Hatcher's Run D[o] Time, .	1,400
To Samuel Sentall Sexton of Brick Church D[o] Time,	218¾
To Sarah Williams Sexton of Sapponie for D[o] Time,	218¾
To Thomas Clemons Sexton of Jones Hole, . .	167
To Ditto for Clearing, Grubbing the Church Yard & other Services, ...	81
To John Brown for keeping Anne Newhose for 10½ Months, ...	700
To James Petillo for keeping Cath. Arther 10½ Months, ...	612½
To Cap[t] Will[m] Stark for Mary Barret 10½ Months, .	700
To D[o] for Francis Lee 10½ Moneths, . . .	700
To D[o] for Mary Delawayhay kept by Ilonour Whitmore 10½ Months, ...	525
To John Leadbetter for Tedstall 10½ Months, . .	700
To Wm. Tanner and his Wife for 10½ Months, .	350
To Mary Allen for 10½ Months, ...	175
To Mr. Theophilus Field for sundries, . . .	277
To Mary Hall for keeping Richard Sentall 10 Weeks before the Division of the Parish, . . .	400

To John Hall for 2 Titheables overlisted in 1740,			50
	£ sh. d.		
To Mr. Theophilus Field for Sacramentary Elements, ...	3: 19: 10½		
Cr By Sundry Fines, ...	3: 15:		
To a Ballance due to Do, ...	4: 10½		
To Capt Willm Stark, ...	1: 3: . 4		
To 6 p Ct for Collecting, ...			1,584
To a Depositum in the Hands of the Collector, .			386
			28,356

CR.

By 1,668 Titheables at 17 p Pole, ...	28,356

Order'd That a Coppy of these Debts of Bristol Parish as it stood undivided till the first of September last be laid before the Vestry of the Parish of Bath at their next Meeting.

[90] BRISTOL PARISH AS IT NOW STANDS DR.

	Lb.
To the Revd Mr. Robert Fergusson, ...	1,999
To 4 p Ct on Do for Cask, ...	80
To Do in lieu of a Glebe, ...	1,000
To John May Junr Clk of Vestry & Brick Church, .	250
To George Williams Clk of Jones Hole, ...	200
To John Brown for keeping Anne Newhose, . .	100¼
To Samuel Sentall Sexton of the Brick Church, .	31¼
To Thomas Clemons Sexton of Jones Hole, . .	31
To James Petillo for keeping Cathr Arther, . .	87½
To Capt Wm. Stark for Mary Barret, ...	100
To Do for Mary Delawayhay, ...	75
To Do for Francis Lee, ...	100
To John Leadbetter for Tedstall, ...	100
To Mary Allen, ...	25
To Mr. Theos Field to be repaid by Brandon Parish it being on Acct of Jos. Barry, ...	70
To Drury Whweet for moving Barry's Wife & Children to Brandon Parish, ...	100

To Tob^{o} towards paying the former 17 p Pole, . .	13,107
To D^{o} for Paying 15 p Pole 771 Titheables, . .	11,565
To D^{o} Besides the 6 p C on the 17 p Pole towards Paying for the Glebe, ...	7,328
To 6 p C^{t} for Collecting, ...	2,180
To a Ballance in the Hands of the Coll^{r}, . . .	21
	38,550

	£	sh	d
To Ja^{s} Harrison for one Acre of Land where Jones Hole Church is built, ...	1:		
To Mr. Theo^{s} Field, ...	1:	14:	
To Mr. John Ravenscroft for some extraordinary services at Jones Hole Church, ...	8:		
To James Clark for building the Chappel on Hatchers Run, ...	118:		
To Dr. James Thompson for Jo^{s} Barry, . .	12:		
To D^{o} for Mary Allen, ...		17:	11
	141:	11:	11

CR.

By 771 Titheables @ 50 p Pole, ...	38,550

Order'd That the Church Wardens receive of every Titheable Person in this Parish 50$^{lbs.}$ of Neat Tobacco for this present Year, and in case of Refusal or Non Payment to Levy the Same by Distress.

ROB'T FERGUSSON Min^{r}.

Capt Peter Jones & Capt Theo^{k} Bland are appointed Church Wardens for the ensuing Year.

Mr. Stephen Dewey is elected a Vestry-man in the Room of Capt Robt Munford, who personally appeared and resigned.

Samuel Sentall is discharged from being Sexton of the Brick Church and Abram Allen is appointed Sexton in his Place.

ROB'T FERGUSSON Min^{r}.

[91] At a Vestry Held at the Brick Church Jan^{ry} the 31st 1742.

Present. The Rev^{d} Mr. Robt Fergusson Minister, Col^{o} Robert

Bolling, Capt Willm Stark, Maj^{r} Willm Poythress, Capt Theo^{k} Bland, Mr. Theop^{s} Feild, Mr. Step^{n} Dewey.

We whose names are under written Being Members of the Vestrey of Bath parish being Appointed by the Said vestry to Receive the Church built on Hatchers Run by Mr. James Clark, have in pursuance of an Order Made in that behalf Met and Vewed the said church and do finde it performed According to Bargain.

JOHN BANISTER,
Jan^{ry} 21st, 1742. MATHEW MAYES.

James Clark under taker and Builder of the Chappel on Hatchers Run Haveing Compleated the said work according to Agreement, and produced a Certificate under the hands of John Banister Esqr and Capt Mathew Mayes the Persons Appointed by the Vestry of Bath Parish to View and Receive the same wch Appears by the said Certificate they have Accordingly done; it is therefore Ordered that the Church Wardens of this parish take up a sum of Money upon Intrest Sufficient to Discharge and pay The Remaining Ballance Due to the said Clark for the Service aforesaid.

Jan^{ry} 31st 1742. Test JOHN MAY Clk Vestry.

Then Receiv'd of Tho^{k} Bland one of the Church wardens of Bristol Parish Sixty one pounds Eighteen Shillings and Four pence Currant Money on Acco^{t} of the said parish.

℘ JAMES CLARK.

Feb^{ry} the 9th 1743.

Receiv'd of Mr. Robert Poythress the Sum of Twenty two pounds Fourteen shillings and two pence.

Receiv'd ℘ me JAMES CLARK.

[92] At a Vestry held at the Brick Church Feb^{ry} 28th 1742.

Present. The Rev'd Mr. Robert Fergusson Minister, Col^{o} Robt Bolling, Mr. Theo^{s} Feild, Maj^{r} Willm Poythress, Capt Peter Jones, Capt Chas Fisher, Capt Theo^{k} Bland, Mr. Stephen Dewey, Mr. Thomas Short.

Ordered that the following Building and additions be made on the Glebe of this parish as Followeth—

The present Kitching set upon sills and Moved and fited up For a stable with Rack and Manger; The House Called Perryes set in the same place and turned into a Kitching with a Brick Chimney Eight feet in the Clear under pined and Floored with brick With a shed on the Back side, Shingled with Heart shingles upon the Present Board Cover, and Floor above is to be Lade with plank and to filled in with Morter or Brick plaster'd and Sealed with Dressers and Necessary Shelves.

A Barn framed 32 feet by 20 Tenn feet pitch in the Clear, Floared flush with plank full Inch and half thick Cover'd all with Heart Shingles, upon Clapboards or Sawed Lathes the doar to be Hung without and to fall into a Rabit, and to Come below the sill for its Defence against Bad weather under pined with good Brick pillers Laid in good Morter.

A milk house 12 feet Square Plastered upon Brick filled in between the Sealing; Sealed under pined and Floared with Brick Lettis windows on the South and North sides, Dooer Made to fall in a Rabit and Long enough to Defend the Sills, with proper Shelves for Milk Shingled with Heart shingles.

A Hen house 12 feet by 8 Fraimed and inclosed with thick saped Boards; Also a Brick Oven 6 feet by 5 Covered.

Two poarches to the Dwelling house Six feet Squar Closed on Each side the Doar 18 Inches, Hiped under the Eve, and Covered with Heart shingles Under pined and Floared with well Burnt Brick and wooden steps to the same from without; Allso a Covered way without into the Seller with a Broad Step Ladder and a private Doar under the stares Within; with doar Ladder, three Window frames to the Dwelling Seller and Shetters to take in or put out Occationelly to fall in a Rabit to fastened with Wooden Boalts or Battons.

Under taken by James Clark for Sixty pounds Currant Money of Virginia to be Compleated by the Last day of November Next at wch time if the above worke is finnished and Compleated then this Vestry Agrees to pay the said Clark the sum of Sixty pounds [93] pounds Currant Money as aforesaid and in Default thereof to pay Lawfull Interest untill the said sum is paid the said Clark for the Service above said.

On the Motion of Robert Bolling William Stark Theo^{k} Bland and Stephen Dewey Leave is given them to Builde for Each of there Familyes a Seperate pew in the Galery of the Brick Church at there one Expence.

Test JOHN MAY JU'R Clk Vestry.

At a Vestry held at the Brick Church for Bristoll Parish The 23d of May 1743.

Presant. Mr. Robert Ferguson Minister, Theo^{k} Bland, Peter Jones Churchwardens, Wm. Stark, Theo^{s} Feild, Chas Fisher, Thos Short, Robt Bolling.

David Walker Vestry man & Churchwarden for the Parish of Bath having by the directions of the Vestry of the s^{d} Parish Made a demand of fiftee[n] Pounds of Tob^{o} for Every Tithable person of this Parish persuant to an act of ye Last Session of Assembly: but forasmuch as we conceive a greater sum is due from ye s^{d} Parish of Bath for thier proportion of the Parocial charge from Laying the Levey the 12th October 1741 to the divitions taking place persuant to the Said act and having understood from Several of the Members of the House of Burgises that it was not only thier oppinion, but the general Sence of that worshipfull House as most reasonable the said Parish should beare their proportion of that charge to the divition,

It^{s} Thierfore order^{d} that the Church wardens of this Parish Make a demand and Settle the differance in the most amicable & Just Manner wth the Vestry or Church wardens of the said Parish, and report their proceedings to the Next Vestry.

ROBT. FERGUSSON Min^{r}.

At a Vestry held at the Brick Church for Bristoll Parish the 6th day of August 1744.

Present. Coll. Robert Bolling, Capt Theodorick Bland, Capt Charles Fisher, Mr. Thomas Short, Capt Peter Jones, Capt William Eppes, Mr. Theophilus Feild, Mr. George Smith.

Ordered that the severall Returns of the Processioners be Recorded In a Book to be provided by the Church Wardens for that purpose.

[94] At a Vestry held at the Brick Church for the Parish of Bristoll July ye 18th 1743.

Present. The Rev^{t} Robt Fergusson Minister, Capt Theo^{k}

Bland, Capt Peter Jones, C. W., Coll^{o} Robt Bolling, Maj^{r} Wm. Poythress, Capt Wm. Stark, Mr. Steph^{n} Dewey.

The Church warthens of this parish having reported that in persuance of an order made at a vestry for this Parish dated 23d may 1743 they had made application to the Church wardens of the Parish of Bath: & made a demand of the Tob^{o} supposed to be due to the Parish of Bristoll: & to Settle the differances between the s^{d} Parishes in the most amicable & Just manner as the said order directed: and as the said Church warthens of Bath insisted on the Tob^{o} directed by the Act for devision of the Parishes of that & Bristoll, without making any allowance for what the said Parish of Bristoll conceived the s^{d} Parish of Bath was chargable with as thier Proportion of the Publick Charge before the devision of the s^{d} Parishes took place, they propos^{d} to the s^{d} Church wardens of Bath to refer the differances between them to the determination of the next assembly concerning the Intention of the Legislators at the making the Act for the division of the s^{d} Parishes, which the said Church wardens refus^{d} to do, without the Vestry of the Parish of Bristol would oblige themselves to lay before the House all the accounts of the said Parish of Bristoll; which this Vestry conceive to be needless; as the accounts of the s^{d} Parish were laid before the House at the time of the making that Act, & no opposition was made by the Parish of Bristoll or any Body for them upon the petion of ye Said Parish of Bath for the said division: And thierfore are for Submitting the whole affair to the determination of the next Assembly without any Limitation.

ROB'T FERGUSSON, Min^{r}.

[95] At a Vestry held at the Brick Church for the Parish of Bristoll the 22d of Augst 1743.

Presant. Capt Theo^{k} Bland, Capt Peter Jones, C. W., Coll^{o} Robt Bolling, Capt Chas Fisher, Maj^{r} Wm. Poythress, Capt Wm. Epes, Capt Wm. Stark, Mr. Geo^{r} Smith, Mr. Theo^{s} Feild, Mr. Thos. Short.

Ordered, that James Sturdivant & John Gilliam (with the freeholders of thier Presinct) Possession from Puddle dock Run to the lower end of the Parish, between the River & the main

Road. That Miles Thweatt & Saml Jordan (with the freeholders of thier perscient) Procession from Puddle Dock Run to the Notaway Road, and as far out as Blackwater. That Wm. Parsons & John Buttler (wth the freeholders of thier Persinct) Procession from Puddle dock Run to Lieutenants Run between the River & the great swamp and monksneck Road. That Thos Jones & Wm. Eaton Junr Procession from Lieutenants Run to the Indian Town Run Including Rohowick. That James Munford & John May (with the freeholders of thier Persinct) Procession from the Indian Town Run to the parish Line. That Edwd Burchett & Thos Chieves (with the freeholders of thier Persinct) Procession between Blackwater Swamp & the Second Swamp from Ja^{s} Baugh's path down to the Parish Line between the Said Swamps. That Chas Gee & Peter Tatam (with the freeholders of thier Persinct) Procession the Land between Joans hole Road between the County & Parish Lines & Warwick Swamp. That Richd Rains & Cuth^{d} Williamson (with the free holders of thier Presinct) Procession the Lands from Warwick swamp to the Parish Line between Jones hole Road & Notaway Road. That James Butler & Ja^{s} Pittillo (with the freeholders of thier Persinct) Procession the Lands from Monksneck Bridg, to Rowanty Brig. That Wm. Archer & Sal^{l} Vaughan with the freeholders of thier Presinct, Procession from the Monksneck Road up the north side of Monsneck & Hatchers Run to the Parish Line. [96] That Thos Hardaway & Ab^{m} Ally (wth the freeholders of thier Presinct) Procession from the Notaway Road up as far as Monksneck Road. That Jo^{s} Rives & Danl Sturdivant wth the freeholders of thier Presinct Procession from Ja^{s} Baugh's Path between Black water and Second Swamp to Monksneck Road. That John Chambless & Chris^{r} Golightly (wth the freeholders of thier Persinct) Procession from the Parish Line up to the great branch of Warwick. That Peter Leeth & Richd Gary (wth the freeholders of thier Prescinct) Procession from the great Branch of Warwick between Warwick and Second Swamp; to Monksneck Road. That Edwd Winfield & Joseph Tucker (wth the freeholders of thier Perscinct) Procession from the County Line between Stony Creek & the Fox Branch; up to the Parish Line. That Geo. Smith & Roger Daniel (wth the freeholders of thier Prescinct)

Procession between the Fox Branch & Monksneck up to the Parish Line.

Order[d] that the Several Persons above Mention[d] do appoint and avertize the time for Processioning the Several Lands within thier Several Perscincts between the Last day of Sep[t] and the Last day of March; and make return of thier Proceedings as the Law directs.

Order[d] that Sam[l] Gordon be appointed a Vestryman of this Parish in the room of Step[n] Dewey.

Order[d] that the Churchwardens pay Coll[o] Rob[t] Bolling Nine hundred & fifty Pounds of Tob[o] (out of the Parish Tob[o] in thier hands) for runing the Line between This Parish & Bath.

ROBT. BOLLING.

[97] BRISTOL PARISH DR.

At a vestry held at the Brick Church the 13th of October 1743.

Present. The Reverend Robert Fergusson Minister, Cap[t] William Starke, Cap[t] Theodorick Bland, Major William Poythress, Cap[t] Peter Jones, Mr. Theophilus Feild, Mr. Thomas Short, Cap[t] Charles Fisher, Mr. George Smith, Mr. Sam[l] Gordon.

	L
To the Reverend Robert Fergusson minister, . .	16,000
To 4 p c[t] on Ditto for cask, ...	640
To John May Clerke of the Vestry & Brick church,	1,400
To George Williams clerk, ...	1,000
To Thomas Clemmonds Sexton, ...	0,250
To Abraham Alley Sexton, ...	0,250
To Ann Newhouse for John Brown, ...	600
To James Pittillo, ...	400
To Mary Barret For Cap[t] Stark, ...	600
To Mary Delawayhay for Honour Whitmore, . .	600
To Francis Lee for mary Hall, ...	600
To Thomas Tedstill for John Ledbetter, . . .	600
To Mary Alley, ...	400
To Mary Hall Richard for Sintale, ...	350
D[o] for Charles Leath, ...	150

To Samuel Jordan	pattrolers.		50
To Instance Hall			50
To Drury Thweat,			32
To Capt William Stark,		£1: 8: 10.	
To Samuel Gordon,		1: 12: 0.	
To Capt Theodorick Bland,		1: 14: 0.	
To James Thompson,		4: 13: 10.	
		9: 8: 8.	
To Drury Thweat for carrying Barry and his wife to Brandon Parish,			70
To Tobacco toward discharging ye Parish debts,			12,090
To Collection,			2,168
			38,300

BRISTOLL PARRISH CR.

By 766 Tithables @ 50. ℔ Pole,	38,300

Order'd that Peter Jones and Theodorick Bland be continued Church Wardens ye Ensueing Yeare.

Ordered that ye Church wardens Receive of Every Titheable person fifty pounds of neet Tobaco for there parish Leavy and on Refussal or Nonpayment to Leavy the same by distress.

ROBERT FERGUSSON Minister.

[98] at a vestry held at the Brick Church for Bristol Parish the 6th day of August 1744.

Present. Coll. Robert Bolling, Capt Theodorick Bland, Capt Charles Fisher, Mr. Thomas Short, Capt Peter Jones, Capt Wm. Eppes, Mr. Theophilus Feild, Mr. Geo. Smith.

Ordered that the Several Returns of the processioners Be Recorded in a book to be provided by the Church Wardens for that Purpose.

Ordered that the Church Wardens Agree with some Person on the best terms they can to carry Richd Sentale a poor person to the Spring on New River for the Recovery of his health.

Ordered that Representation of the unequal Division of Bristol Parish be drawn up by the church Wardens of the Said Parish Ready to be Signed and Certified at the next court to be held for Receiving and Certifieing all propositions and Greviances to the next assembly and that Coll. Rob[t] Bolling, Cap[t] William Starke & Mr. Theodorick Bland attend the house in behalf of this parish when the Subject matter of the Said Representation shall be ordered by the house to be taken into Consideration.

ROBERT BOLLING.

[99] Bristol Parish—at a Vestry held at the Brick Church y[e] 9th September 1744.

Present. The Reverend Mr. Robert Fergusson min[r], Coll. Robert Bolling, Mr. Theophilus Feild, Maj[r] William Poythress, Mr. Samuel Gordon, Cap[t] William Stark, Mr. Thomas Short, Cap[t] Theodorick Bland, Cap[t] Peter Jones, Mr. George Smith.

Ordered that Coll. Robert Bolling Mr. William Stark and Mr. Theodorick Bland or any of them attend the worshipful the house of Burgeses in behalf of this parish upon the Subject matter of A Representation Signed and Certified to the present Gen[l] assembly now Sitting at the time the house will please to take the Same into Consideration and that the Said Gentlemen Lay before the house an Extract of the Vestrys minutes Concerning the publick Charges of this parish as it Stood undivided from a meeting of the Vestry the 14th October 1741 for Laying the Levy till y[e] first of September 1742 when the act for dividing the Said parish of Bristol took Place & to obtain y[e] Sense of the house wheither the parish of bath were not to pay their proportion of the publick Charg till that time as they had Equal advantages in all Respects which Severall worthy members of the house informed us was their Sense & beleaved it to be the Gen[l] Sense of the house and that y[e] 15 L of tobacco Levied by the Said act upon the inhabitants of this parish for y[e] parish of Bath, was only in Consideration of publick Buildings and Purchasing a Glebe and therupon this Vestry derected their church-wardens to apply to the Said parish of bath for their proportional part of the charge till ye Said Division took place, which the Vestry of Bath absolutely Refused to pay pretending they were Exempted by the Said act for Division which is humbly Submitted for Determination to the assembly.

And that the Gentlemen above Said petition the assembly in behalf of this parish that a bill may be Brought into the house for Selling a Glebe now in the parish of Dale Purchased by ye parish of Bristol as it Stood undivided From ye Said parish and that Bristol parish be paid their Proportion of the monney arising from Such Sale [100] according to the number of Titheables at the Division and also that the church ornaments of Velvet fringed with Gold and Silk having Bristol parish in a Cypher imbrodered with Gold and Silk and such plate as have the name of ye Said Parish Engraved thereon now in possession of ye parish of dale be Returned to the Said parish of Bristol.

ROBERT FERGUSSON.

At a Vestry held at the Brick Church October the 12th 1744.

Present. the Reverend Mr. Robert Fergusson Min^r^, Capt Wm. Stark, Maj^r^ Wm. Poythress, Capt Peter Jones, Mr. Samuel Gordon, Charles Fisher, Capt Wm. Eppes, Mr. Theophilus Feild, Mr. Theodorick Bland.

BRISTOL PARIS. DR.

To the Reverend Mr. Robert Fergusson,	16,640
To George Smith clk of the Vestry and Brick Church,	1,050
To George Williams clk Jones hole,	1,000
To Abraham ally Sexton,	0,250
To Thos Clemmonds Sexton,	0,250
To John Brown for keeping ann Newhouse,	0,600
To Mary hall For Francess Lee,	0,600
To D^o^ for Richard Sintale,	1,000
To Richard Ally for his mother,	0,400
To Capt Wm. Eppes for delawahay,	150
To Edward Birchit for Tudstil,	642
To Instance Hall for Olive Poxen,	1,000
To Mr. Samuel Gordon for cloaths for poor people,	670
To Capt Wm. Stark for an Account,	391
To Samuel Tatam,	500
To Colo. Bolling for an account,	488
To John Williams for his Sister,	600
To Francis Degern,	400
to John Floyde for mary Banks,	83
To Burwell Green for his Levy Being a patroler,	50
	26,764

[101] To Peter Jones for collecting 400 for more Leys than was Listed, ...	24
To John may for serving two Sundays not formaly accounted for, ...	53
To Capt Isham Eppes for paying Chain Carriers & attending the surveyer at running the parish Line,	100
To Wm. Stark for Mary Barret, ...	600
To tobacco towards Discharging the parish Debts, .	5,360
To 6 ꝑ C^{t} for Collecting, ...	1,974
	34,875
By 775 Tithables at 45 ꝑ^{r} pole, ...	34,875

Ordered that the Church wardens of this parish receive of Each tithable 45L of Neet tobaco for their parish Levy for the insuing Year and in case of Refusial or nonpayment to Levy the Same by Distress and pay the Same to the Seve^{l} Creditors to whome they are proportioned.

ordered that Capt Peter Jones and theodorick Bland pay the monney in their hands to Maj^{r} wm. poythress.

Ordered that the parish Ceditors be paid in tobaco which for the Insewing year is to be computed at 14^{s} Currancy ꝑ hundred.

Ordered that Mathias Howard be set Levy free.

Ordered that cap^{t} Charles Fisher and Mr. Samuel Gordon Be Church wardens for the insewing Year.

Ordered that the several parish accounts Be filed.

Ordered that Wm. Butler Senr be set Levy free.

ROBERT FERGUSSON min^{r}.

[102] At a Vestry held at the Brick Church February y^{e} 27: 174$\frac{4}{5}$.

Present. The Reverend Mr. Robert Fergusson Minister, Colo. Robert Bolling, Mr. Theophilus Feild, Maj^{r} William Poythress, Mr. Thomas Short, Capt Peter Jones, Mr. George Smith.

Whereas the Vestry of Bath parish have caused the Vestry of this to be Summoned to appear before the honourable the General Court on the First day thereof on the penalty of 100^{l} Each Vestryman to answer their bill in Chancery Exhibited by William Jones and John Jones Church-wardens for the said parish, it is therfore Ordered that Mr. Wm. Stark Mr. Theophilus Feild and Mr. Samuel Gordon attend the honourable the Ge[l] Court on the first day thereof in behalf of this parish Pursuant to their Order dated the Second November 1744. that they employ such Councel as they think fit for the defence of this parish and take such Transcripts from the Records of the Vestry as they think Necessary for that Purpose.

ROBERT FERGUSSON Min[r].

At a Vestry held at the Brick Church October 11th 1745.

Present. The Reverend Mr. Robert Fergusson minister, Mr. Samuel Gordon, Capt Charles Fisher, C. W., Colò. Robert Bolling, Mr. Theophilus Feild, Capt Peter Jones, Mr. Geo. Smith, Capt William Eppes.

BRISTOLL PARISH DR.

To the Reverend Mr. Robert Fergusson,	16,640
To Geo. Smith Clk Vestry and Brick church,	1,400
To Arares For Last year,	205
To Geo. Williams Clk Joneshole,	1,000
To Abraham Ally Sexton,	250
To Thomas Clemmonds Sexton,	250
To John Brown for Ann Newhouse,	600
To Richd Alley for his mother,	600
To Edward Birchet for Tudstill,	700
To Mary hall for olive poxen,	800
	22,445
[103] Brought over,	22,445
To Samuel Tatum,	500
To John Williams for his Sister,	150
To Daniell Vaughan for keeping Margret w[ms],	561
To Frances Disshon,	400
To Mary Barret,	600
Tò Frances haddon for keeping Richd Sental,	571
To Tho[s] Clemmonds for Burning Round Joneshole Chapple two years Past,	100
To Colo. Bolling for Running the parish Line,	1,375
To Mr. Theophilus Feild for Summondsing five Markers and attending three days,	190

To William hardaway three days, ...	90
To John Birtchet three days, ...	90
To Wm. wells Junier three days, ...	90
To Solomon Crook three days, ...	90
To Joseph Crook two days, ...	60
To Drury Thweat according to a following Order of vestry, ...	50
To Capt William Stark for Sundries to Olive poxen Amounting to S10. 10d, ...	78
To Tobaco towards discharging the parish debts, .	9,805
To 6 ℔ Ct for Collection, ...	2,241
	39,886

BRISTOL PARISH CR.

By 880 Tithables at 45 ℔ pole, ...	39,600
By a Ballance due by Capt Fisher, ...	286
	39,886

Ordered that the Church wardens of this parish Receive of Every Titheable person 45l of neet Tobaco as their parish Leavy and in Case of Refusial or nonpayment to levy the Same by distress and to pay the Several Sums to the parish Crediters to whome they proportioned.

[104] BRISTOL PARISH CR.

By 6,035l Tobaco sold at, ...	35.	0.	1½
By one fine, ...	2.	10.	
	£37.	10.	1½

BRISTOL PARISH DR.

To Colo. William Poythress for Ballance due to him, ...	7.	14.	6
To Francess haddon for carrying Richd Sental to the Spring on new River and Bringing him back again, ...	21.		
To Mr. Theophilus Feild to Give to a Lawor to be employed in the Disbute Betwixt Bath parish and this, ...	5.		

To D° for his trouble in going to Williamsburg in behalf of this parish, . .	1. 17. 6
Ballance due from Cap[t] fisher, . . .	1. 18. 1½
	37. 10. 1½

It is ordered that Drury Thweat Constable be paid by the Churchwardens of this parish 50[l] of Tobaco for his trouble in Removing John holmes a Vagrant from this parish to the Next Constable two difrant times in order to be carried into westopher parish in Charles Citty County pursuant to a warrant Directed to him for that purpose und[r] the hand of Theodorick Bland Gent. one of his majesties Justices of the peace for the County of Prince George and that the wardons apply to the Churchwardens of westopher parish to Reimburse the Said 50[l] of Tobaco to this parish.

it is ordered that John Brown a weak and infurm Person be Set Levy Fre.

ROBERT FERGUSSON min[t].

[105] At a Vestry held at the Brick Church august 25th 1746.

Present. The Rever[d] Mr. Robert Fergusson, Colo. Rob[t] Bolling, Mr. Samuel Gordon, Maj[r] Peter Jones, Cap[t] Charles Fisher, Mr. Theophilus Feild, Cap[t] William Stark.

This Day Mr. James Boiseau Mr. Hugh Miller & Mr. James Murray were Chosen and Appointed Vestrymen For this parish in the room of Cap[t] Thomas Short Deceas[d] of Maj[r] Theodorick Bland & Maj[r] James Munford who have moved out of this Parish.

ROBERT FERGUSSON.

At a Vestry held for Bristol parish March the 23d 174$\frac{6}{7}$.

Presant. The reverend Mr. Robert Fergusson Minister, Robert Bolling, James Murray, William Poythress, Samuel Gordon, William Starke, Hugh Miller, Charles Fisher, James Boisseau.

This day Maj[r] Theoderick Bland was chosen & Appointed Vestryman for this Parish in the room of Maj[r] Peter Jones who is Moved out of the parish.

Test RICHARD TAYLOR Clk Vestry.

At a Vestry held for Bristol parish April 5th 1747.

Present. The Reverend Mr. Robert Fergusson, Minister, Robert Bolling, Theoph[s] Feild, William Poythress, Samuel Gordon, Charles Fisher, Hugh Miller, William Starke, James Boisseau.

Ordered That Charles Fisher and Will[m] Eppes Churchwardens agree with workmen to Cover, Lath, fill in, and Loft the Quarter on the Glebe, and to make windows in the Ends of the Dwelling house, two at Each End sasht, to slide up, to give Air to the Rooms.

Test RICHARD TAYLOR Clk Vestry.

[106] At a Vestry held for Bristol parish September 29th 1746.

Present. The Reverend Mr. Robert Fergusson Minister, Coll[n] Robert Bolling, Mr. James Murray, Cap[t] William Starke, Mr. James Boisseau, Cap[t] Charles Fisher, Mr. Hugh Miller, Cap[t] William Eppes, Mr. Theophilus Field, Coll[n] William Poythress, Mr. George Smith.

BRISTOL PARISH DR.

To Mr. Robert Fergusson, ...	16,640
To George Smith Clk Vestry and Brick Church, .	1,400
To George Williams Clk Jones hole, . . .	1,000
To Abraham Alley Sexton, ...	250
To Tho[s] Clemonds Ditto, ...	250
To John Brown for Ann Newhouse, . . .	600
To Richard Alley for his Mother, ...	600
To Edward Birchett for Tudstill, ...	700
To Dan[l] Nance for Olive poxon, ...	800
To Samuel Tatum, ...	500
To Dan[l] Vaughan for Marg[t] Williams, . . .	1,000
To Francis Dison, ...	400
To Mary Barrett, ...	600
To Mary Hall for Rich[d] Sental, ...	900
To Elizabeth Hill, ...	400
To Rossanna Saunders, ...	400
To Samuel Lee for two Coffins for Hudsons wife and son, ...	140

To William Vaughan for keeping George Williams Child 18 Mo[s], ...	1,150
To Sam[l] Lee Jun[r] for takeing Hudsons son Robert,	200
To Old Church Wardens for secretaries and sherrifs fees, ...	147
To Mary Hall for keeping Hudsons Girl Ann, . .	400
To Tobb[o] to be Levied for Buying Books & Ornaments for the Churches, ...	4,504
To 6 ℔ C[t] for Collecting, ...	1,979
	34,960

CONTRA CR.

By Ballance due from Cap[t] Fisher ℔ Acc[t], . . .	511½
By 920 Tythables at 38[l] Tobb[a] ℔ pole, . . .	34,960

BRISTOL PARISH IN CASH DR.

	£	s.	d.
To Mr. Fields Acc[t] Chargis Attending the Suit, .	3.	17.	5
To Cap[t] Starks Acc[t], ...	2.	18.	1

CONTRA CR.

	£	s.	d.
By Ball[a] due from Cap[t] Fisher, ...	9.	14.	11

[107] Ordered that Cap[t] Charles Fisher pay the Ballances due to Mr. Field and Cap[t] Starke as here Stated out of the parish money in his hands.

As Also that he pay of Immediately James Sturdivants Bond of £40 with the Interest due thereon.

Ordered that Cap[t] Charles Fisher and Cap[t] William Eppes be Church Wardens for the Ensueing Year.

Ordered that the Church Wardens of this parish receive of Every Tythable person thirty Eight pounds of neat Tobbacco as their parish Levy for the Ensueing Year and to pay the several Sums to the parish Creditors as they are above proportioned, and in Case of refusal or Nonpayment to Levy the Same by Distress.

Mr. James Boisseau has Assumed to pay to the Vestry the 1,150[l] Tobbacco levied for William Vaughan for keeping George Williams Child at the next Laying of the Levy.

Test RICHARD TAYLOR Clk Vestry.

At a Vestry held at the Brick Church for Bristol parish the 31st of July 1747.

Present. The reverend Mr. Robert Fergusson Minister, Coll[n] Robert Bolling, Mr. Samuel Gordon, Coll[n] William Poythress, Mr. James Murray, Mr. Theophilus Field, Mr. Hugh Miller.

Ordered that the following persons be Appointed to procession the Lands in this parish in their several prescincts as followeth—

That Richard Taylor and John Vaughan with the freeholders of their prescinct procession from the Nottoway road up as far as Monks Neck Road from the Head of Black Water to the River. That William Parsons Sen[r] and John Lewis Jun[r] with the freeholders of their presinct procession from Puddle Dock to Lievetenants runn between the River the Great Swamp and Monks Neck road. That Thomas Jones and William Eaton with the freeholders of their presinct procession from Lieveten-ants run to the Indian town runn, Includeing Rohowick. [108] That John Edwards and John May Jun[r] with the freeholders of their prescinct procession from the Indian town runn to the par-ish line. That Robert Birchett and Thomas Cheeves with the freeholders of their prescinct procession between Black Water Swamp and Second Swamp from James Baughs path down to the parish line between the said Swamps. That Charles Gee and Peter Tatum with the freeholders of their prescinct proces-sion the Lands below Jones Hole Road, between the County and parish lines and Warwick Swamp. That Richard Rains and John Burge with the freeholders of their prescinct procession the Lands from Warwick Swamp to the parish line between Jones Hole Road and the Nottaway Road. That James Butler and James Pettillo with the freeholders of their prescinct procession the Lands from Monks Neck Bridge to Rowanty Bridge. That William Archer and selathiel Vaughan with the freeholders of their prescinct procession from the Monks Neck Road up the North side of Monks Neck and Hatchers Runn, to the parish line. That Joseph Reeves and Dan[l] Sturdivant with the free-holders of their prescinct procession from James Baughs path between Black Water and second Swamp to Monks Neck Road. That John Chamless and Christopher Golightly with the free-holders of their prescinct procession from the parish Line up to the Great Branch of Warwick. That Peter Leath and Richard

Gary with the freeholders of their prescinct procession from the Great Branch of Warwick between Warwick and Second Swamp to monks Neck Road. That John Peterson and Samuel Jordan with the freeholders of their prescinct procession from Puddle Dock Runn, to the Road that goes by Samuel Jordans plantation and from the parish Line to the Nottaway Road. [109] That William Batte Junr and Drury Thweatt with the freeholders of their prescinct procession from the parish line to the Nottaway Road and from the Road Leading by Saml Jourdans to Blackwater. That Edward Winfield and Joseph Tucker with the freeholders of their prescinct procession from the County Line between Stony Creek and the fox Branch up to the parish Line. That George Smith Junr and Roger Daniel with the freeholders of their prescinct procession Between the fox Branch and Monks Neck up to the parish Line. That James Sturdivant and John Gilliam with the freeholders of their prescinct procession from Puddle Dock Run, to Citty Creek and from the main Road to the river. That Burwell Green and John Sturdivant Junr with the freeholders of their prescinct procession from the Citty Creek to the parish Line betwixt the main Road and the river. That William pride and Thomas Jones procession the Lotts in the Towns of Petersburg and Blandford. That John Whitmore and John Bonner with the freeholders of their prescinct procession from the road over warwick Bridge to the Monks Neck road betwixt the two swamps.

Ordered that the Several persons above mentioned do Appoint and advertize the time for Processioning the Several Lands within their Several prescincts between the the Last Day of September and the Last day of March next, and make return of their proceeding as the Law Directs, and that they take Care to Date their several returns.

Test RICHARD TAYLOR Clk Vestry.

[110] At a Vestry held for Bristol parish the 23d of August 1747.

Present. The Reverend Mr. Robert Fergusson Minister, Coll^{n} Robert Bolling, Mr. Theop^{s} Field, Coll^{n} William Poythress, Mr. Hugh Millar, Capt William Starke, Mr. James Murray, Maj^{r} Theod^{k} Bland.

Ordered That Maj^{r} Theoderick Bland be Appointed to Collect the Parish Levies that are not Already Received in the room of Capt Charles Fisher Deceased and to Act as Church Warden in his Stead.

Test RICHARD TAYLOR Clk Vestry.

At a Vestry held at the Brick Church for Bristol parish the Sixteenth Day of October 1747.

Present. The Rever^{d} Mr. Robert Fergusson Minister, Coll^{n} Robert Bolling, Mr. James Murray, Coll^{n} Willm Poythress, Mr. Samuel Gordon, Capt William Starke, Mr. James Boisseau, Mr. Theoph^{s} Field, Capt William Eppes, Maj^{r} Theod^{k} Bland.

Ordered That the Reverend Mr. Fergusson agree with workmen to Cover Lath fill in and Loft the Quarter on the Glebe and bring in his Charge to the Vestry.

That Richard Taylor, Tarr the houses on the Glebe and bring in his Acco^{t} to the Vestry.

That the Church wardens pay of Immediately to the Exec^{rs} of Mr. Robert Poythress a Bond for Twenty pounds due from this parish with the Interest due thereon.

That Capt William Starke Mr. Theoph^{s} Field and Maj^{r} Theod^{k} Bland Settle the parish Accounts with the Administra^{r} of Capt Charles Fisher Deceased.

That Capt William Eppes and Maj^{r} Theod^{k} Bland be Appointed Church Wardens for the Ensueing Year.

And that the Vestry be adjourned to Saturday the 31st Day of October Instant.

ROB'T. FERGUSSON Minister.

Test RICHARD TAYLOR Clk Vestry.

[111] At a Vestry held at the Brick Church for Bristol parish the Sixteenth Day of October, Instant and then adjourned to this day being Saturday the 31st October 1747.

Present. Coll^{n} Robert Bolling, Mr. James Murray, Coll^{n} William Poythress, Mr. Saml Gordon, Mr. Theoph^{s} Field, Mr. James Boisseau, Maj^{r} Theoder^{k} Bland.

BRISTOL PARISH DR.

To the reverend Mr. Fergusson Minister, . . .	16,640
To Richard Taylor Clerk Brick Church and Vestry,	1,800

To George Williams Clk Jones Hole Church,				1,000
To Abraham Alley Sexton,				250
To Thos Clemonds Ditto, at Jones Hole,				250
To John Brown for Ann Newhouse,				600
To Richard Alley for his Mother,				700
To Edward Birchett for Tudstill,				700
To Daniell Nance for Olive Poxen,				800
To Samuell Tatum,				500
To Daniel Vaughan for Margaret Williams,				1,000
To francis Degern,				400
To James Moore for Mary Barrett,				600
To Elizabeth Hill,				400
To John Lenard Keeping Hudsons Child,				380
To Capt William Starke Balla his Accot,	£0.	11.	8	
To James Hardaway puttying Church windows,	0.	15.	0	
To Theophs Field Expensis Attending Suit,	1.	7.	6	
To Messrs Murray & Gordon,	0.	12.	9	
To Richard Taylor for seats, Horse-block, Taring the Church and finding Tarr etc,	3.	13.	9	
To Colln Poythress Horse Blocks and Clearing,	0.	12.	0	
To Richard Taylor, Taring Dwelling house and Dairy on the Glebe and finding Tarr,	0.	18.	6	
	£8.	11.	2	
To Thomas Clemonds.				81
To Edward Birchett finding Tudstill Cloths,				300
To Tobbacco to buy books and ornaments for the Churches and to pay of the parish Debts,				8,167
To 6 ℔ Ct for Collecting,				2,064
				36,632

Cr.

By 964 Tithables at 38l Tobba ℔ pole,	36,632

[112] Maj[r] Theoderick Bland Appointed Churchwarden in the room of Cap[t] Fisher Deceased haveing returned his Acco[t] to the Vestry. Ordered it be recorded.

Ordered that Maj[r] Theodorick Bland settle the parish Acco[ts] with the Administratrix of Cap[t] Fisher and that the former order made to settle the said Acc[t] be reversed.

Ordered That the Church wardens of this parish receive of Every Tithable person in this parish Thirty Eight pounds of Neat Tobbacco as their parish Levy for the Ensueing Year and to pay the Several sums to the parish Creditors as they are proportioned and in Case of Refusal or non payment to levy the Same by Distress.

ROBERT BOLLING.

Test RICHARD TAYLOR Clk Vestry.

BRISTOL PARISH TO THEODERICK BLAND DR.

To Thomas Clements,				76
To George Smith,				40
To Francis Degern,				400
To Elizabeth Hill,				400
To John Brown,				178
To Hugh Miller,				76
To William Eppes,				380
To Theop[s] Field,				190
To Wm. Vaughan,				1,150
To Commiss[n] on 5,577[l] at 6 ℔ C[t],				334½
To Tobbacco on Maycox sold at 9 | 6 ℔ C[t],	£ 3.	17.	0½	811
To Ditto Cabbin point sold at 10 | 2 ℔ C[t].	5.	11.	3¾	1,095
To Ditto on Jordans sold at 10 | 7 ℔ C[t],	11.	7.	9	2,152
To Ditto on Bollings point sold at 12 | ℔ C[t],	10.	15.	8	1,797½
	£ 31.	11.	9¼	9,080

Cr.

By Tobb^{a} rec^{d} of Capt Fishers Administratrix, . .	3,503
By D^{o} rec^{d} of Sundry persons, ...	5,577
	9,080

October the 25th 1747.

Errors Excepted ꝑ Theo^{k} Bland.

February the 29th 174$\frac{7}{8}$.

William Eppes and Theoderick Bland Church-wardens of this parish put Instance Hall (son of John Hall Deceased) an Apprentice to William Sturdivant to serve as the Law directs, to learn the trade of Shoemaking.

Test Richard Taylor Clk Vestry.

[113] At a Vestry held at the Brick Church for Bristol parish the 13th day of August 1748.

Present. The Rever^{d} Mr. Robt Fergusson Minister, Coll^{n} Robert Bolling, Mr. James Murray, Coll^{n} Wm. Poythress, Mr. Hugh Miller, Maj^{r} Theo^{k} Bland, Mr. James Boisseau.

Theoderick Bland Church Warden in the presence of the Vestry Examined the records of the processioners Returns and find the returns Truly recorded.

Anthony Walke Gent^{m} is chosen and Appointed a Vestry man of this parish in the room of Capt Charles Fisher Deceased, and that the Clerk of the Vestry give him Notice thereof.

Ordered That Maj^{r} Theoderick Bland Mr. Hugh Miller and Richard Taylor, Settle the parrish Acco^{ts} of Capt Charles Fisher Deceased, betwixt this time and the Laying the parish Levie, And that Maj^{r} Bland pay what Tobb^{a} Appears to be due to Capt Fishers Estate to his Administratrix.

That the Church Wardens pay to Mr. Augustine Claiborn Seven Shillings and Six pence for a fee against Edwd Birchett Junr.

Rob't Fergusson Min^{r}.

Test Richard Taylor Clk Vestry.

[114] At a Vestry held at the Brick Church for Bristol parish the Tenth Day of November 1748.

Present. The reverend Mr. Robert Fergusson Minister, Coll^{n} William Poythress, Mr. Hugh Miller, Capt William Starke, Mr. James Murray, Maj^{r} Theo^{d} Bland, Mr. James Boisseau, Mr. Samuell Gordon.

BRISTOL PARISH DR.

To the reverend Mr. Fergusson Minister,				16,640
To Richard Taylor Clk Brick Church & Vestry,				2,000
To George Williams Clk Jones Hole Church,				1,000
To Abr^{a} Alley Sexton,				250
To Thos Clemonds Ditto,				250
To John Brown for Ann Newhouse,				600
To Richard Alley for his mother,				700
To Edward Birchet for Tudstill,				1,000
To Danl Nance for Olive Poxen,				800
To Samuel Tatum,				500
To Daniel Vaughan for Marg^{t} Williams,				1,000
To Francis Degern,				400
To Mary Barrett,				600
To Eliz^{a} Hill,				400
To John Lenard keeping Hudsons Child,				380
To Danl Nance keeping Poxen Ten Days,				22
To Tobbacco to be sold to buy Ornaments &c.,				840
To Commission on Collecting 6 ℔ C^{t},				1,647
To Coll^{n} Willm Poythress repairing the Glebe,	£ 2.	10.	0	
To Capt Willm Starke ℔ Acc^{t},	1.	10.	3	
To Richard Taylor Taring, Seats &c ℔ Acc^{t},	2.	8.	0	
To Mary Hall for Cureing Poxen, Cloths &c.,	2.	0.	0	
	£8.	8.	3	29,029

CR.

By 1,001 Tythables at 29^{l} Tobb^{a} ℔ pole,	29,029

Ordered That Mr. James Murray and Maj[r] Theod[k] Bland be Church Wardens for the Ensueing year.

That the Church Wardens Enter into Bond to the Vestry for Collecting the parish Levies.

That the Church Wardens Acc[ts] for the year past be Recorded.

[115] That the Church Wardens provide two surplices a pulpit Cloth and Communion Cloth for the Church at Jones Hole, and a Communion Cloth for the Brick Church to be purple.

That the Church Wardens receive from Every Tythable person in this parish Twenty Nine pounds of Tobbacco as their parish Levies for the Ensueing Year, and to pay the Several Sums to the Parish Creditors as they are proportioned, and in Case of Refusal or Nonpayment to levy the same by Distress, and to pay the several sums of money as they are proportioned out of the parish money now in their hands.

ROBERT FERGUSSON Min[r].

Test RICHARD TAYLOR Clk Vestry.

BRISTOL PARISH TO THEODERICK BLAND DR.

To paid the rev[d] Mr. Fergusson,	16,640
To D[o] to Richard Taylor,	1,800
To D[o] to George Williams Jun[r],	1,000
To D[o] to Abram Alley,	250
To Tho[s] Clemonds,	331
To John Brown,	600
To Richard Alley,	700
To Edward Birchett,	1,000
To Dan[l] Nance,	800
To Samuel Tatum,	500
To Dan[l] Vaughan,	1,000
To Francis Degern,	400
To James Moore,	600
To Elizabeth Hill,	400
To John Lenard,	380
To 21 Insolvents at 38[l] Tobb[a] ℔ pole,	798
To 6 ℔ C[t] on 37,620 for Collecting,	2,257
To Tobb[a] sold at 13 | 2½,	8,210
	37,666

CR.

By 964 Tythes at 38[l] Tobb[a] ℔ pole, ...	36,632
By 26 D[o] not Listed at D[o], ...	988
By 6 ℔ C[t] on Insolvents am[o] to 798[l], . . .	46
	37,666

Nov[r] 10th 1748. Errors Excepted ℔ THEO'K BLAND.

Copy Test RICHARD TAYLOR Clk Vestry.

[116] BRISTOL PARISH TO THEODORICK BLAND DR.

To Cash paid to Rob[t] Poythress Ex[rs], .	£ 22.	14.	2
To Intrest from the 9th February 1742 to the 9th Feb[ry] 1747, ...	5.	13.	6½
To paid Cap[t] Wm. Starke, . . .	0.	11.	8
To James Hardaway, ...	0.	15.	0
To Mr. Theo[s] Field, ...	1.	7.	6
To Mess[rs] Murray & Gordon, . . .	0.	12.	7
To Coll Poythress, ...	0.	12.	0
To Cap[t] Taylor, ...	4.	12.	3
To John Lantrop by Cap[t] Taylors order,	1.	6.	0
To Elements for the Sacrament & sending them to the Churches &c, . . .	2.	0.	0
	£ 40.	4.	8½
Ball[a] due to the parish, ...	52.	19.	4¾
	93.	4.	1¼

CR.

By Ball[a] of Tobb[a] sold last year, . .	£ 31.	11.	9¼
By Benj[a] Fernando for a fine, . . .	4.	18.	
By Martha Ellis for a fine, . . .	2.	10.	
By 8210[l] Tobb[a] at 13 | 2½, . . .	54.	4.	4
	£ 93.	4.	1¼

Novem[r] 10th 1748. Errors Excepted ℔ THEO'K BLAND.

Copy Test RICHARD TAYLOR Clk Vest[r].

By an order of the Court of Prince George County dated the 15th day of February 1748 Theoderick Bland and James Murray Church Wardens of Bristol Parish have this day put Apprentice to the reverend Mr. Robert Ferguson two Mulotto Children, Named Phillip and Betty son and Daughter to Ann Evans Deceased to Serve as the Law Directs.

May the 10th 1749. Test RICHARD TAYLOR Clk Vestry.

[117] At a Vestry held at the Brick Church for Bristol Parish the 29th day of July 1749.

Present. The Reverend Mr. Robert Fergusson Minister, Maj^{r} Theod^{k} Bland, Mr. James Murray, Church Wardens, Coll^{n} Robert Bolling, Mr. Samuel Gordon, Coll^{n} William Poythress, Mr. Anth^{o} Walke, Mr. Hugh Miller.

The Vestry Judging it Necessary that an Addition be made to the Brick Church, have Appointed the Church Wardens to consult with skilfull workmen about the most Convenient way, the said Addition is to be made, and to Report it to the next Vestry.

Ordered That the fringe upon the Ornaments, ordered to be provided, be of purple and Gold.

ROBT. FERGUSSON Min^{r}.

Test RICHARD TAYLOR Clk Vestry.

BRISTOL PARISH DR.

To the rever^{d} Robt. Fergusson,	16,640
To Richard Taylor Clk brick Chur^{h},	2,000
To Geo. Williams Clk Jones Hole D^{o},	1,000
To Abram Alley Sexton,	250
To Thos Clemonds D^{o},	250
To John Brown for Ann Newhouse,	600
To Richd Alley for his Mother,	700
To Edwd Birchet for Tudstil,	1,000
To Danl Nance for Poxen,	822
To Saml Tatum,	500
To Danl Vaughan for Marg^{t} Williams,	1,000
To Fran^{s} Degern,	400
To Mary Barrett,	600
To Eliz^{a} Hill,	400

To Jno Lenard keeping Hudsons Child, . . .	380
To Tobb^{a} paid Mrs. Fisher, ...	840
To Commiss^{n} for Collecting, ...	1,647
To Insolvents ꝑ list Amoun^{t} to, ...	899
	29,928
Ball^{a} due, ...	29
	29,957
Cr.	1 Tobb^{a}
By 1,001 Tyths at 29^{1} Tobb^{a} ꝑ po., ...	29,029
By 32 D^{o} not listed, ...	928
	29,957

November 4th 1749. Errors Excepted.

Theo. Bland, Jam^{s} Murray, C Wardens.

Coppy Test Richard Taylor Clk Vestry.

[118] At a Vestry held at the Brick Church for Bristol Parish the 6th November 1749.

Present. Mr. James Murray, Coll. Theo^{d} Bland, C Wardens, Coll^{n} William Poythress, Mr. James Boisseau, Capt William Starke, Mr. George Smith, Mr. Hugh Miller, Mr. Anth^{o} Walke, Capt William Eppes.

John Crawford having almost lost his Eye sight, Ordered that he be Acquitted from paying parish levies for the future.

George Williams Senr haveing listed himself last year and this and being Constable, Ordered that the Collector do Acquit him from two levies.

Major Cotten being very poor and not able to work, ordered that he be Acquitted from paying parish levie for the future.

That the Church Wardens petition the Court to bind out Ann the Daughter of Robert Hudson.

This Day Alexander Bolling Gen^{t} was Chosen a Vestryman in the Room of Robert Bolling Esqr Deceased, and the Clerk of the Vestry is ordered to Acquaint him therewith.

Ordered That Coll^{n} William poythress and Mr. James Murray be Church Wardens for the Ensueing Year.

That the Church wardens Acco^{ts} for the year past be Recorded.

That the Church Wardens receive from Every Tythable person in this parish, Thirty three pounds of Neat Tobbacco, as their parish levie for this present year and in case of Refusal or Nonpayment to levie the same by Distress. And that the Churchwardens Enter into bond with security for Collecting the levies.

[119] 1747 BRISTOL PARISH DR.

To the Estate of the Reverend Mr. Fergusson deceased,	14,982
To Richard Taylor Clk Vestry and Brick Church,	2,000
To George Williams Clk Jones Hole Church.	1,000
To Abram Alley Sexton,	250
To Thomas Clemonds Ditto,	250
To John Brown for Ann Newhouse,	600
To Richard Alley for his Mother,	700
To Edward Birchet for Tudstill,	1,000
To Barn[a] Moore for Olive poxen and Clothing him,	1,000
To Cap[t] William Eppes for Sam[l] Tatem and his wife,	1,000
To Daniel Vaughan for Margret Williams,	1,000
To Francis Degern,	400
To Mary Barrett,	600
To Elizabeth Hill,	400
To John Lenard for Hudsons Child,	380
To Cap[t] Wm. Epps, seats & horse Blocks at the outward Church and Grubing about the Church,	200
To Mr. George Currie Keeping Cyrus Steward,	400
To the Reverend Mr. William procter,	1,000
To Tobbacco to be disposed of at the Discretion of y[e] Vestry,	5,658
To 6 ℔ C[t] for Collecting,	2,094
	34,914

CR.

By 1058 Tyths at 38[l] Tobb[a] ℔ pole,	34,914

WM. POYTHRESS, Ch. warden,
JAMES MURRAY C. W.

Test RICHARD TAYLOR, Clk Vestry.

[120] 1749 | 50 At a Vestry held at the Court house for Bristol parish the Thirteenth day of March 1749 | 50.

Present. Coll^{n} William Poythress, Mr. James Murray, C. W., Capt William Starke, Mr. Theop^{s} Field, Mr. Hugh Miller, Mr. Anth^{o} Walke, Capt Alex^{r} Bolling, Mr. James Bossieau.

Mr. Eleazer Robinson is Appointed Minister of this parish for Twelve Months on Tryal, from the 30th of October Last and it is Ordered that he have possession of the Glebe this year.

On a Complaint of William Batte Junr that Mary Barret is very Infirm, Ordered that Two hundred pounds of Tobbacco more be allowed the said Mary Barret.

Ordered that the Church Wardens Apply to the Adm^{rs} of the Rev^{d} Mr. Fergusson Deceased to put the Glebe in Repair as the Law directs.

WM. POYTHRESS, JAMES MURRAY, Ch. Wardens.

Test RICHARD TAYLOR, Clk Vestry.

[121] At a Vestry held at the Brick Church for Bristol parish the Eleventh day of October 1750.

Present. Mr. James Murray C. Warden, Coll^{n} Theod^{k} Bland, Capt William Starke, Mr. Anth^{o} Walke, Mr. Theop^{s} Field, Capt Alex^{r} Bolling, Mr. Samuel Gordon.

BRISTOL PARISH DR.

To the reverend Mr. Eleazer Robinson,	10,982
To Richard Taylor Clk Vestry & Brick Church,	2,000
To George Williams Clk Jones hole Church,	1,000
To Abram Alley Sexton,	250
To Thomas Clemonds ditto,	250
To John Brown for Ann Newhouse,	600
To Richard Alley for his Mother,	700
To Edward Birchet for Tudstill,	1,000
To Barnabas Moore for Olive poxen,	1,000
To Samuel Tatum and his Wife,	1,000
To Daniel Vaughan for Margaret Williams,	1,000
To Francis Dezearn,	400
To Mary Barrett,	800

To Elizabeth Hill, ...	400
To George Currie for Cyrus Stewart, ...	400
To 6 ℔ C^{t} Collecting 32,430, ...	1,946
To Tobb^{a} to be disposed of at the Discretion of the Vestry, ...	8,702
	32,430

CR.

By 1081 Tythables at 30^{l} Tobbacco ℔ pole, . .	32,430

Ordered That the present Church Wardens be Continued in their office till the meeting of the next Vestry. That the Church wardens Receive from Every Tythable person in this parish, Thirty pounds of Neat Tobbacco as their parish Levie for this present Year, and in Case of Refusal or Nonpayment to Levie the same by Distress and pay to the parish Creditors as they are proportioned And that they Enter in to Bond with security for Collecting and paying the same.

JAMES MURRAY.

Test RICHARD TAYLOR Clk Vestry.

[122] At a Vestry held at the Brick Church for Bristol parish the first day of March 1750 | 1.

Present. Coll^{n} William Poythress, Mr. James Murray C. W., Capt William Starke, Mr. Saml Gordon, Capt William Epes, Mr. Anth^{o} Walke, Coll^{n} Theo^{d} Bland, Mr. James Boisseau, Mr. Hugh Miller, Mr. George Smith, Mr. Theop^{s} Field.

Ordered That Coll^{n} William Poythress and Capt Alexander Bolling be Church Wardens for the Ensueing Year.

That the Church wardens pay Edward Winfield One Thousand pounds of Tobbacco for keeping Elizabeth Davies Last year, Out of the Tobbacco levied at Laying the last levie.

That Coll^{n} Theod^{k} Bland pay out of the money in his hands

To Mr. James Murray ℔ his Acco^{t}, . .	£ 2.	6.	
To Doct^{r} Robert Goldie for Poxen, . .	4.	6.	8
To Richard Taylor for stools, ...		4.	
	£6.	16.	8

That the Reverend Mr. Eleazer Robertson be Received as Minister of this Parish.

Collonel Theoderick Bland haveing proposed to build three pews in the Gallery in this Church, at his Own Expence it is Agreed by the Vestry that he shall have One of the said pews for the use of his family.

WM. POYTHRESS, JAMES MURRAY.

Test RICHARD TAYLOR Clk Vestry.

[123] BRISTOL PARISH FOR THE YEAR 1749 DR.

To the Estate of the Rev[d] Mr. Ferguson, . . .	14,982
To Rich[d] Taylor Clerk Vestry & Church, . .	2,000
To George Williams Clk Jones hole d°, . . .	1,000
To Abram Alley Sexton, ...	250
To Tho[s] Clemonds d°, ...	250
To John Brown for Ann Newhouse, ...	600
To Richard Alley for his Mother, ...	700
To Edward Birchet for Tudstill, ...	1,000
To Barn[a] Moore for Olive poxen, ...	1,000
To Cap[t] Wm. Epes for Tatum & Wife, . . .	1,000
To Dan[l] Vaughan for Marg[t] Williams, . . .	1,000
To Mary Barret & Fra[s] DeGarn, ...	1,000
To Eliz[a] Hill 400 Jn° Lenard for Hudsons Child 380,	780
To Cap[t] Wm. Epes Seats &c.,.	200
To George Currie for Cyrus Steward, . . .	400
To the Rever[d] Mr. Procter, ...	1,000
To paid the Rever[d] Mr. Robertson, . . .	5,658
To Insolvents as ℔ List, ...	627
To Commissions for Collecting, ...	2,094
	35,541
To 4 Insolvents not allowed to be Deducted out of the 490, ...	132

CR.

By 1,058 Tyths at 33 ℔ pole, ...	34,914
By 6 ℔ C[t] on 627 Insolvents, ...	37
	34,951

Amount brought forward, ...	34,951
By Ballance due, ...	590
	35,541

Errors Excepted. FRANS. EPES JUNR., for
James Murray & Wm. Poythress.

Test RICHARD TAYLOR Clk Vestry.

At a Vestry held at the Brick Church for Bristol parish the Seventeenth day of August 1751.

Present. The Reverend Eleazer Robertson Minister, William Poythress C. W., James Murray, Theoderick Bland, Samuell Gordon, Theophilus Field, James Boisseau, George Smith, Anthony Walke, William Eppes.

Ordered That William Poythress, Theophilus Field and Anth° Walke be Appointed to Settle the parish Accounts with the Administratrix of Charles Fisher, and that they make their Return before the Laying the Next levie, and it is Agreed by Augustine Clairborne in behalf of the Administratrix of Charles Fisher that their Award be a final Determination and that the Clerk of the Vestry Attend them with the parish Books.

That the persons following be Appointed to procession the the Lands in this parish in their several precincts as followeth.

That Richard Taylor and John Vaughan with the freeholders of their precinct procession from the Nottaway Road up as far as Monks Neck Road from the head of Black Water to the River. [124] That William Parsons Junr and Thomas Wilson with the freeholders of their precinct procession from Puddle Dock to Livetenants Runn between the River the Great Swamp and Monks Neck Road. That William Eaton and William pride with the freeholders of their precinct procession from Livetenants Runn to the Indian town Runn includeing Rohowick. That John Edwards and John May Junr with the freeholders of their precinct procession from the Indian town Runn to the parish Line. That Robert Birchett and Thomas Cheves with the freeholders of their precinct procession between Black Water Swamp and Second Swamp from James Baughs path down to the parish Line Between the Said Swamps. That Charles Gee and Peter Tatum with the freeholders of their precinct procession the Lands below Jones

Hole Road between the County and parish Lines and Warwick Swamp. That John Rains and John Burge with the freeholders of their precinct procession the Lands from Warwick Swamp to the parish Line Between Jones Hole Road and the Nottaway Road. That James Butler and James pittillo Senr with the freeholders of their precinct procession the Lands from Monks Neck Bridge to Rowanty Bridge. That George Williams Junr and Morriss Vaughan with the freeholders of their precinct procession from the Monks Neck Road up the North side of Monks Neck and Hatchers Runn to the parish Line. That Thomas Davenport and Daniel Sturdivant with the freeholders of their precinct procession from James Baughs path, Between Black Water and Second Swamp to Monks Neck Road. That John Chamless and Christopher Golightly with the freeholders of their precinct procession from the parish Line up to the Great Branch of Warwick. That Peter Leath and Richard Gary with the freeholders of their precinct procession from the Great Branch of Warwick Between Warwick and Second Swamp to Monks Neck Road. That John Peterson and Robert Batte with the freeholders of their precinct procession from puddle Dock Runn to the Road that goes by Samuel Jordans plantation, and from the parish Line to the Nottaway Road. That William Batte Junr and Miles Thweat Junr with the freeholders of their precinct procession from the parish Line to the Nottaway Road, and from the Road Leading by Samuel Jordans plantation to Black Water. [125] That Edward Winfield and Joseph Tucker with the freeholders of their precinct procession from the County Line Between Stony Creek and the fox Branch up to the parish Line. That George Smith Junr and Henry Daniell with the freeholders of their precinct procession between the fox Branch and Monks Neck up to the parish Line. That James Sturdivant and John Gilliam with the freeholders of their precinct procession from puddle Dock Runn to Citty Creek and from the main Road to the River. That Burwell Green and John Sturdivant Junr with the freeholders of their precinct procession from the Citty Creek to the parish Line Betwixt the Main Road and the River. That John Whitmore and Thomas Bonner with the freeholders of their precinct procession from the Road over Warwick Bridge to the Monks Neck Road Betwixt the two Swamps. That

Thomas Jones and Thomas Egleton with the freeholders procession the Lotts in the Towns of petersburg and Blandford.

That the Several persons Above mentioned do appoint and advertise the time for processioning the several Lands, within their several precincts, between the last day of September and the Last day of March next, and make Return of their proceeding as the Law Directs, and that they take care to Date their several Returns.

WM. POYTHRESS Church Warden.

Test RICHARD TAYLOR, Clk Vestry.

At a Vestry held at the Brick Church for Bristol parish the 14th day of October 1751.

Present. The Reverend Eleazer Robertson Minister, William Poythress, Alexander Bolling, Churchwardens, Theod[k] Bland, James Murray, Anth[o] Walke, James Boisseau.

On William Baughs produceing a Certificate from the Collector of the parish levies for the year 1749 and it Appearing he was overcharged it is Ordered that the Church Wardens Account with him for so much as Appears to them to be Overcharged.

Ordered That Alexander Bolling and James Boisseau be Church Wardens for the Ensueing year.

[126] 1751 BRISTOL PARISH. DR.

To the Rever[d] Eleazer Robertson Minister,	17,150
To Rich[d] Taylor Clk Vestry & Brick Church,	2,000
To George Williams Clerk Jones Hole Church,	1,000
To Abram Alley Sexton,	250
To Thomas Clemonds ditto,	250
To John Brown for Ann Newhouse,	600
To the Widdow Alley for her Mother,	1,000
To Edward Birchett for Tudstill,	1,000
To Barnabas Moore for Olave poxen,	1,000
To Henry Spier for the Widdow Tatum,	600
To Dan[l] Vaughan for Margaret Williams,	1,000
To Francis Dezearn,	400
To Mary Barrett,	800
To George Currie for Cyrus Stewart,	400
To Edward Wingfield for Eliz[a] Davis,	667

To Geo. Williams Constable Moveing Rich[d] Moore to the parish of S[t] Andrew in Brunswick, . .	150
To Alexander Bolling keeping Rich[d] Moore 55 days,	166
To William Gibbs Sen[r] Keeping Henry Reeveland three Months and Moveing him to Dale parish,	270
To George Williams Sen[r] two levies he paid in 1748 and 1749 being Constable, ...	62
To Mary Alley Washing and Carrying Surplice &c.,	150
To be disposed of at the Discretion of the Vestry, .	6,588
To 6 ℔ C[t] Collecting, ...	2,262
	37,765
By 1079 Tyths at 35[l] Tobb[a] ℔ pole, ...	37,765

Ordered That the Church wardens receive of Every Tythable person in this parish Thirty five pounds of Tobbacco as their parish Levie for the Year 1751 and in Case of Refusal or Non-payment to levie the same by Distress and pay the same to the parish Creditors as they are proportioned, and that they Enter into Bond, as the Law Orders.

WM. POYTHRESS, ALEX'R BOLLING, Ch. Wardens.

Test RICHARD TAYLOR Clk Vestry.

[127] BRISTOL PARISH FOR THE YEAR 1750 DR.

To the Reverend Mr. Robertson, ...	10,982
To Rich[d] Taylor Clk Vestry & church, ...	2,000
To Geo. Williams Clk Jones Hole, ...	1,000
To Abram Alley Sextone, ...	250
To Tho[s] Clemonds ditto, ...	250
To John Brown for Ann Newhouse, ...	600
To Rich[d] Alley for his mother, ...	700
To Edw[d] Birchett for Tudstill, ...	1,000
To Barnabas Moore for Olive poxen, ...	1,000
To Sam[l] Tatem and his wife, ...	1,000
To Dan[l] Vaughan for Marg[t] Williams, ...	1,000
To Francis Dezearn, ...	400
To Mary Barrett, ...	800
To Geo. Currie for Cyrus Steward, ...	400

To Edwd Wingfield for Eliz^{a} Davis, ...				1,000
To 6 ꝑ C^{t} for Collecting 32,430, ...				1,946
To Tobbacco Sold at 17 | ꝑ C^{t}, .	22.	4.	10½	2,617
To ditto at 16 |	12.	16.		1,600
	£ 35.	0.	10½	
To 8 patrolers, ...				240
				29,265
To Ball^{a} due to the parish, ...				3,165
				32,430

Cr.

By 1081 Tyths at 30^{l} Tobb^{a} ꝑ, ...	32,430

Bristol parish in Cash for the Year 1750 Dr.

To Thomas Wells Work at the Glebe house,	4.	12.	3
To James Murray sacramentary Elements &c.,	4.	0.	0
To John Woobank Carrying them to the Churchis, .		15.	0
	£ 9.	7.	3
Ball^{a} due to the parish, ...	25.	13.	7½
	£ 35.	0.	10½

Cr.

By Tobbacco sold ꝑ Acco^{t}, ...	35.	0.	10½

Errors Excepted this 14th October 1751.

ꝑ Wm. Poythress Ch Warden.

Test Richard Taylor Clk Vestry.

At a Vestry held at the Brick Church for Bristol parish the Second day of March 1752.

Present. The Reverend Mr. Eleazer Robertson, James Boisseau Church Warden, William Starke, Theophilus Field, Theod^{k} Bland, James Murray, Anth^{o} Walke.

Ordered That Thomas Evans and James Harrison with the freeholders of their precinct procession the Lands on the South Side Stony Creek in this parish, which was taken out of Bath parish to the parish Lines, and make Return as the Law Directs.

Test Richard Taylor, Clk Vestry.

[128] BRISTOL PARISH TO THEO'D BLAND. DR.

To paid the Ballance due from the parish to Jn° Ravenscroft,	4.	7.	7½
To 23 Ells Holland for Surplices at 9 | 1 ℔ Ell,	10.	8.	11
To 2 Ouncis thread @ 5 |	0.	10.	0
To makeing 2 Surplices 25 |	2.	10.	0
To James Murray,	2.	6.	0
To Robert Goldie,	4.	6.	8
To Richard Taylor,	0.	4.	0
	24.	13.	2½
To Ball^a due to the parish,	40.	16.	2¼
	65.	9.	4¾

CR.

By Ball^a Last Acco^t Setled,	52.	19.	4¾
By Margaret Berrys Fine,	2.	10.	
By a Fine of Benj^a Moody,	5.	0.	0
By d° Rece^d of the Sheriff for Jn° Chennlis Jun^rs fine,	5.	0.	0
Octr 14th 1751.	£ 65.	9.	4¾

At a Vestry held at the Brick Church for Bristol parish the Twenty Second day of June 1752.

Present. The Reverend Mr. Eleazer Robertson, Alex^r Bolling, James Boisseau, C. Wardens, William Eppes, Theod^k Bland, Theop^s Field, Hugh Miller, James Murray, Samuel Jordon, Anthony Walke, George Smith.

Mr. Thomas Williams is Appointed a Vestryman in the Room of Coll^n William poythress who is moved out of the parish.

Ordered That an Addition be made on the South Side the Brick Church, Thirty Feet by Twenty five in the Clear and fifteen feet from the Spring of the Arch to the Floor which is to be the same height with the present Church three Bricks thick to the Water Table and two and a half thick to the plate, the Roofe to be Framed as the present Roofe, The Isle Six Feet wide laid with white Bristol Stone. Two windows of the Same dimentions as the present on Each Side of the Addition, and Glazed with

Sash Glass, the Floor to be laid with Inch and Quarter heart plank, the pews to be Framed as those now in the Church, the Roofe to be first Covered with plank and Shingled on that with Good Cypress heart Shingles, a Cornish the Same as the present, Square Ceiling, a Door in the South End of the Addition, the present South Door to be shut up, and another Window and a pew Added in its place. The whole to be done Strong, and workmanlike in the Best plain manner, to be finished by the First day of July 1754. Also the Church to be walled in with a Brick Wall of one and a half Brick thick Five Foot from the highest part of the Ground to the Top of the Copeing, Length from East to West One hundred and Sixty Feet, from North to South One hundred and Forty Feet in the Clear, One Gate at the West End and One on the South Side the Church and the Church Wardens are to give publick Notice when it is to be Let.

That the Church Wardens Agree with some Capt of a Ship to Carry Henry Warne a poor person, on his Request to England on the Best Terms they can.

[129] James Murray, Alexander Bolling and Theodorick Bland are permitted to Build a Gallery, in the South End of the Addition to be made to the Church at their Own Expence, for the use of themselves and Families and their Heirs and successors.

ALEX'R BOLLING, JAMES BOISSEAU, C. Wardens.

Test RICHARD TAYLOR, Clk Vestry.

At a Vestry held at the Brick Church for Bristol parish the Twentieth day of November 1752.

Present. The Reverend Ele^r^ Robertson Minister, Capt William Starke, Coll^n^ Theo^d^ Bland, Mr. James Murray, Mr. Saml Gordon, James Boisseau, Alex^r^ Bolling, Anth^o^ Walke, George Smith.

1752 BRISTOL PARISH. DR.

To the Reverend Eleazer Robertson Minister, . .	17,150
To Richard Taylor Clk Vestry and Brick Church, .	2,000
To George Williams Clk Jones Hole Church, . .	1,000
To Abram Alley Sexton, ...	400
To Thomas Bonner Sexton at Jones hole, . .	400
To John Brown for Ann Newhouse, . . .	600

To the Widdow Alley for her mother, . . .	1,000
To Edward Birchett for Tudstill, and Burying him, .	415
To Barnabas Moore for Olive poxen, . . .	1,000
To Henry Spire for the Widdow Tatem, . . .	600
To Dan[l] Vaughan for Margaret Williams, . .	1,000
To Francis Dezern, ...	400
To Mary Barret, ...	800
To George Currie for Cyrus Stewart, . . .	400
To John Crew for Eliz[a] Davis, ...	1,000
To Wm. Browder for Henry Warne from 1st April,	500
To Daniel Vaughan Sen[r], ...	300
To David McCullow One levie over paid last Year, .	35
To Francis Leadbetter for his Mother five months, .	400
To Clerks fees against sprowle paid by Coll. poythress, ...	44
To Commission on Collecting 38,848 at 6 ℔ C[t], .	2,331
To Tobb[a] to be sold for Cash, ...	7,073
	38,848

Ditto. Cr.

By 1,214 Tyths at 32 ℔ pole, ...	38,848

Ordered That the Church Wardens Apply to Drury Alley for Winifred Alleys fine and on his Refuseing to bring Suit against him. Turn Over.

[130] That Mr. James Boisseau and Mr. George Smith be Church Wardens for the Ensueing Year and that they Enter into bond for payment of the parish Creditors. That the Church Wardens Receive from Every Tythable person in this parish Thirty two pounds of Tobb[a] as their parish levie for this present Year, and in Case of Refusal or Nonpayment to levie the same by Distress, and pay the same to the parish Creditors as they are proportioned.

Alex'r Bolling, James Boisseau.

Test Richard Taylor Clk Vestry.

At a Vestry held at the Brick Church for Bristol parish the 30th day of November 1752.

Present. The Reverend Eleazer Robertson Minister, George

Smith, James Boisseau C. Wardens, William Stark, Alex[r] Bolling, Theoderick Bland, Thomas Williams, Sam[l] Gordon, Theop[s] Field, James Murray.

Ordered that the Addition to the Church be built on the North side thereof. This day being the day Advertized in the Virginia Gazette for Letting the Addition to the Church, and Walling it in, Coll[n] Richard Bland being the Lowest Bidder agrees to do it for four hundred pounds Current money.

JAMES BOISSEAU, GEORGE SMITH, C. Wardens.

Test RICHARD TAYLOR, Clk Vestry.

Memorandum. That the Bricks of the Addition and wall of the Church Yard be of the Statute Size, that the present Church is to be new painted, and the new Addition to be Once primed and twice painted.

[131] BRISTOL PARISH FOR 1751. DR.

To the Rev[d] Mr. Robertson,	17,150
To Rich[d] Taylor,	2,000
To George Williams,	1,000
Abram Alley,	250
Tho[s] Clemonds,	250
To John Brown,	600
Widdow Alley,	1,000
Edward Birchett,	1,000
Barnabas Moore,	1,000
Henry Spire,	600
Dan[l] Vaughan,	1,000
Fra[s] Dezearn,	400
Mary Barrett,	800
George Currie,	400
Edward Wingfield,	667
George Williams Sen[r],	212
Alex[r] Bolling,	166
Wm. Gibbs Sen[r],	270
Mary Alley,	150
William Baugh,	99
Sallary Collecting,	2,307

Insolvents ℔ List,	1,050
Tobbacco Sold,	6,157
	38,528

CR.

By 1,079 Tyths @ 35 ℔ pole,	37,765
By 20 ditto not Listed,	700
By Commission 1,050[l] the Insolvents,	63
	38,528

Errors Excepted. FRANS. EPES Jun[r], for
Alexand[r] Bolling & James Boisseau.

Test RICHARD TAYLOR Clk Vestry.

BRISTOL PARISH FOR 1751 DR.

To paid Advertizeing the Addition to the Church,	0.	5.	0
To Sacramentary Elements,	2.	0.	0
To John Woobank carrying them,		15.	0
	3.	0.	0
Ball[a] to the parish,	42.		
	45.	0.	0

CR.

By 6,157[l] Tobb[a] sold 14 | 2 ℔ C[t],	43.	12.	2
By Fran[s] Eppes part a fine,	1.	7.	10
	45.	0.	0

Errors Excepted. ℔ ALEX'R BOLLING.

[132] BRISTOL PARISH FOR 1752 DR.

To the Rev[d] Mr. Robertson,	17,150
To Richard Taylor Clk,	2,000
To George Williams,	1,000
To Abram Alley,	400
To Thomas Bonner,	400
To John Brown,	600
To the Widdow Alley,	1,000
To Edward Birchett,	415

To Barnabas Moore,	1,000
To Henry Spire,	600
To Daniel Vaughan,	1,000
To Fran^{s} Dezearn,	400
To Mary Barret,	800
To George Currie,	400
To John Crews,	1,000
To William Browder,	500
To Danl Vaughan sen^{r},	300
To David McCullow,	35
To Fran^{s} Leadbetter,	400
To Coll^{n} poythress,	44
To Commission on 36,800,	2,208
To Insolvents ꝑ List,	896
To Tobb^{a} Sold,	5,148
	37,696

Cr.

By 1,164 Tyths at 32^{l} ꝑ,	37,152
By 17 Levies not Listed,	544
	37,696

Errors Excepted for James Boisseau & George Smith.

ꝑ Richard Taylor.

Bristol parish for 1752 Dr.

To paid Will'm Nusum Glass,	1.	2.	6
To Thos Wells putting in d^{o},	0.	5.	4
To Sundries to Judy Harris,	0.	14.	4
To Robert Hobs for 2 Bolts,	0.	14.	0
To paid for a Lock and putting on,	0.	3.	0
To James Murray Sacramentary Elements,	2.	0.	0
To John Woobank carrying them,	0,	15.	0
To 1 Gnomen for the Dyal,	—	—	—
	5.	14.	2
To Ballance due to the parish,	32.	5.	10½
	£38.	0.	0½

CR.

By Tobb[a] sold

2,120	at Boll[s] 15 | 4	16.	5.	0½
1,230	Jordans 15 |	9.	4.	6
750	Maycox 14 |	5.	5.	
1,048	Cab point 14 | 1	7.	5.	6
5,148		38.	0.	0½

Errors Excepted for James Boisseau and George Smith.

℘ RICHARD TAYLOR.

[133] At a Vestry held at the Brick Church for Bristol parish on Saturday the 17th day of November 1753.

Present. James Boisseau, George Smith Church Wardens, William Starke, Hugh Miller, Theo[s] Field, William Eppes, Theo[d] Bland, Thomas Williams, James Murray, Sam[l] Gordon, Alex[r] Bolling.

BRISTOL PARISH FOR 1753 DR.

To the Reverend Eleazer Robertson,	17,150
To Richard Taylor Clk Vestry and Church,	2,000
To George Williams Clk Jones Hole,	1,000
To Abram Alley Sexton,	400
To Thomas Bonner ditto,	400
To John Brown for Ann Newhouse,	600
To the Widdow Alley for her Mother,	1,000
To Barnabas Moore for Olave poxen,	1,000
To Henry Spire for the Widdow Tatem,	600
To Dan[l] Vaughan for Marg[t] Williams,	1,000
To Francis Dezearn,	400
To Mary Barret,	800
To George Currie for Cyrus Stewart,	400
To John Crews for Eliz[a] Davies,	1,000
To John Edwards for Henry Warne,	917
To Dan[l] Vaughan Sen[r],	500
To Fran[s] Leadbetter for his Mother,	1,000
To 6 ℘ C[t] Collecting,	2,900
To Tobbacco to be Sold for Cash,	15,293
	48,360

CR.

By 1,209 Tyths at 40 ℔ pole, ...	48,360

Ordered that the Church Wardens pay the money now in their hands to Coll^n Richard Bland towards the Addition to the Church.

That Mr. George Smith and Mr. Thomas Williams be Church wardens the Ensueing Year.

That Mr. Stephen Dewey be Appointed a Vestryman of this parish in the Room of Anth^o Walke who is moved out of the parish.

That the Church wardens pay to Mary Cotten Six hundred pounds Tobb^a to Maintain her son Major Cotten. Turn Over.

[134] That the Church Wardens Collect from Every Tythable in this parish Forty pounds of Tobbacco for their parish Levies for this Year and in Case of Nonpayment to levie the same by Distress, and to pay the parish Creditors as they are proportioned.

JAMES BOISSEAU, GEO. SMITH C. W.

Test RICHARD TAYLOR Clk Vestry.

At a Vestry held at the Brick Church for Bristol parish on Sunday the 18th day of November 1753.

Present. Theop^s Field, Alexander Bolling, William Starke, James Boisseau, Theod^k Bland, George Smith, William Eppes, Thomas Williams, James Murray.

Mr. Thomas Wilkinson is Appointed Minister of This parish for Twelve months, on tryal and that he have the Usual sallary and possession of the Glebe.

JAMES BOISSEAU, GEORGE SMITH.

Test RICHARD TAYLOR Clk Vestry.

At a Vestry held at the Brick Church for Bristol parish the Sixth day of June 1754.

Present. The Reverend Mr. Thos Wilkinson, Thomas Williams Church Warden, William Starke, James Boisseau, William Eppes, Theoph^s Field, Theod^k Bland, James Murray.

The Vestry being Satisfied with the Tryal they have had of the

Reverend Mr. Thomas Wilkinson it is Ordered that he be Received as Minister of this parish.

THOMAS WILLIAMS Church Warden.

Test RICHARD TAYLOR Clk Vestry.

[135] BRISTOL PARISH TO JAMES BOISSEAU DR.

To Clark and Sherifs fees 76[l] Tob.	0	12	0
To 1 Blanket for Warne,	0	10	0
To p[d] Coll Bland,	5	15	0
	6	17	0
due to the parish,	6	13	0
£	13	10	0

CR.

By Jane Black 1 fine,	2	10	0
By Winifrid Alley 1 d°,	2	10	0
By Eliz[a] Vaughan 1 d°,	2	10	
By phill Edwards 1 d°,	0	5	0
By Ab[r] Bywater 1 d°,	5	15	0
	13	10	

November 17th 1753. Errors Excepted. JAMES BOISSEAU.

Test RICHARD TAYLOR Clk Vestry.

1753. BRISTOL PARISH. DR.

To the Rev[d] Mr. Ele Robertson,	17,150
To Richard Taylor Clk Vestry &c,	2,000
To George Williams Clk,	1,000
To Abram Alley Sexton,	400
To Thomas Bonner Sexton,	400
To John Brown for Ann Newhouse,	600
To Barnabas Moore for poxen,	1,000
To the Widdow Alley for her mother,	1,000
To Henry Spire for the widdow Tatem,	600
To Dan[l] Vaughan for Marg[t] Williams,	1,000
To Francis Dezearn,	400
To Mary Barrot,	800

To George Currie for Cyrus Stewart, ...	400
To John Crews for Eliz[a] Davis, ...	1,000
To Henry Warne by John Edwards, . . .	917
To Daniel Vaughan Sen[r], ...	500
Ty Francis Leadbetter for his moth[r], . . .	1,000
To 6 ℔ C[t] for Collecting, ...	2,900
	33,067
To Tobb[a] for the use of the parish, ...	15,293
	48,360

1753. CONTRA. CR.

By 1,209 Tyths at 40 ℔ pole, ...	48,360

Ditto. DR.

To Mary Cotten ℔ Order Vestry, 600						
To Mr. Tho[s] Williams,	465	@ 12	8	2.	18.	10½
To d[o] Williams, . .	357	@ 12	3	2.	3.	8¾
To Mr. Sam[l] Gordon, .	1,792	@ 12	1	10.	16.	5¾
To Mr. William Newsum,	1,157½	@ 12	4	7.	2.	8½
To Mr. Charles Turnbull,	3,000	@ 12	6	18.	15.	0
To Jerry White, . .	290	@ 9	3	1.	6.	10
To Mr. John Butler, .	847	@ 8	4	3.	10.	7
To Mr. Theoph[s] Field, .	1,556	@ 9	11	7.	14.	3
To Drury Thweat, .	5,228½	@ 12	8	33.	2.	3
	15,293			£ 87.	10.	8½

1753 By Tobb[a] for the use of the parish 15,293.

1753 BRISTOL PARISH DR.

To Cash paid Coll[n] R[d] Bland, ...	84.	2.	8½
To James Murray ℔ Ord[r] Vestry, ...	3.	8.	0
	87.	10.	8½

1753 CONTRA CR.

By Tobb[a] Sold Sundrys, ...	87.	10.	8½

[136] At a Vestry held at the Glebe for Bristol Parish the Fifteenth day of November 1754.

Present. The Reverend Thomas Wilkinson, Theo[d] Bland,

Stephen Dewey, James Boisseau, Theop[s] Field, James Murray, Thomas Williams, George Smith.

BRISTOL PARISH FOR THE YEAR 1754 DR.

To the Reverend Thomas Wilkinson,	17,280
To Richard Taylor Clk Vestry and Church,	2,000
To George Williams Clk Jones Hole Church,	1,000
To Abram Alley Sexton,	400
To Thomas Bonner Ditto,	400
To John Brown for Ann Newhouse,	600
To the Widdow Alley for her mother,	1,000
To John Kemp for Olave poxen,	1,000
To Henry Spire for the Widdow Tatem,	800
To Dan[l] Vaughan for Marg[t] Williams,	1,000
To Francis Dezearn,	400
To Mary Barret,	800
To George Currie for Cyrus Steward,	400
To John Crews for Eliz[a] Davis,	1,000
To John Edwards for Henry Warne,	655
To Dan[l] Vaughan Sen[r],	500
To Francis Leadbetter for his Mother,	1,000
To William perkins One Levie over paid last Year,	40
To John Davis One D[o],	40
To Steph[n] Dewey drawing a Deed for poxens Estate,	100
To Coll[n] poythress Insolvents Last Year,	1,061
To 6 ℔ C[t] Collecting,	3,375
To Tobbacco to be sold for the use of the parish,	21,399
	56,250
By 1,250 Tyths at 45 ℔ pole,	56,250

Ordered that the Churchwardens pay to James Murray three pounds Eight Shillings for Sacramentary Elements & Carrying them last year.

That Coll[n] William poythress have leave to Inclose a piece of Ground for a Burying place for his Family tho' the Same should be within the Walls of the Church Yard, provided that he inlarge the same so as that the Yard Includes the Same Superficial Measure (Exclusive of the said piece of Ground) as the present Yard to be Walled is to Include.

[137] Ordered That the surveyor of the County be Applyed to, to Lay of the Glebe land, and that Mr. Lewis parham be Acquainted with the time, and the Church Wardens to Attend the Laying of the Same.

That Mr. Thomas Williams and Mr. Stephen Dewey be Appointed Churchwardens for the Ensueing Year.

That the Church wardens recieve from Every Tythable person in this parish Forty Five pounds of Tobbacco for their parish Levie for this present Year, and in Case of Nonpayment to levie the same by Distress, and to pay the parish Creditors as they proportioned.

That Theoderick Bland, Theop[s] Field, Alex[r] Bolling, and James Boisseau or any three of them do view the Several houses on the Glebe, and to agree with undertakers to make Such Repairs and Additions as they shall think Necessary.

THOS. WILKINSON Min[r].
GEO SMITH, THOMAS WILLIAMS Church Wardens.

Test RICHARD TAYLOR Clk Vestry.

In Obedence to an Order of the Vestry of Bristol parish we the Subscribers met on the Glebe of the Said parish and viewed the mantion house of the said Glebe which we find to be much out of Repair, the Sills much decay'd and the workmanship of the whole house so badly performed in Every Respect, that we offer it to the Vestry as our Opinions that the most Frugal way will be to make only such repairs as will make the house habitable until the Vestry shall think proper to build a new house, which we think Absolutely necessary, to be done.

Given under our hands this 4th day of December 1754.

T. FEILD, THEO'K BLAND,
JAMES BOISSEAU, ALEX'R BOLLING.

Test RICHARD TAYLOR Clk Vestry.

[138] At a Vestry held at the Glebe for Bristol parish the Second day of August 1755.

Present. The Reverend Thomas Wilkinson Minister, Thomas

Williams Church Warden, Theophilus Field, Samuell Gordon, Theoderick Bland, James Boisseau, James Murray, George Smith.

Ordered that the persons following be Appointed to procession the Lands in this parish in their Several precincts as Followeth.

That Richard Taylor and John Vaughan with the Freeholders of their precinct procession from the Nottaway Road to Livetenants Runn, and up the Said Runn to the head of Ravenscrofts Land Includeing the Glebe, and from the head of Black Water to the Main Road. That William parsons Jun[r] and Thomas Willson with the Freeholders of their precinct procession from puddle Dock to Livetenants Runn between the River the Great Swamp and Monks neck Road. That William Eaton and Halcott pride with the Freeholders of their precinct procession from Livetenants Runn to the Indian town Runn Includeing Rohowick. That John Edwards and John May Jun[r] with the Freeholders of their precinct procession from the Indian town Runn to the parish line. That Robert Birchett and Edward Birchet Jun[r] with the Freeholders of their precinct procession Between Black Water swamp and Second Swamp from James Baughs path down to the parish Line Betwixt the Said Swamps. That Charles Gee and William Chamliss with the Freeholders of their precinct procession the Lands Below Jones Hole Road between the County and parish Lines and Warwick Swamp. That John Rains and John Burge with the Freeholders of their precinct procession the Lands from Warwick Swamp to the parish Lines between Jones Hole Road and the Nottaway Road. That Francis Haddon and William perkins with the Freeholders of their precinct procession the Lands from Monks Neck Bridge to Rowanty Bridge. [139] That George Williams and Morriss Vaughan with the Freeholders of their precinct procession from the monks neck Road up the North Side of Monks neck and Hatchers Runn to the parish line. That Thomas Davenport and Dan[l] Sturdivant with the Freeholders of their precinct procession from James Baughs path Between Black Water and Second Swamp to monks neck Road. That John Chamliss and Christopher Golightly with the Freeholders of their precinct procession from the parish Line up the Great Branch of Warwick. That peter Leath and Richard Geary with the Freeholders of their precinct procession from the Great Branch of Warwick between Warwick and Second Swamp to monks Neck Road. That John peterson and Robert Batte with the Freeholders of their precinct procession from puddle Dock Runn to the Road that goes by Sam[l] Jordans plantation, and from the parish Line to the Nottaway Road. That William Batte and Miles Thweat Jun[r] with the Freeholders of their precinct procession from the parish Line to the Nottaway Road and from the Road leading by Sam[l] Jordans to Black Water. That Francis Moreland Sen[r] and Joseph Tucker Jun[r] with the freeholders of their precinct procession from the County Line between Stony Creek and the Fox Branch up to the parish line. That David Abernathy and Bennet Kerby with the Freeholders of their precinct procession Between the Fox Branch and Monks Neck up to the parish Line. That James Sturdivant and John Gilliam with the Freeholders of their precinct procession from puddle Dock Runn to Citty Creek and from the main road to the River. That Burwell Green and John Sturdivant Jun[r] with the Freeholders of their precinct procession from the Citty Creek to the parish line Between the main Road and the River. That John Whitmore and James Cole with the Freeholders of their precinct procession from the Road Over Warwick Bridge to the Monks Neck Road Betwixt the two Swamps. That Thomas Evans and James Harrison with the Freeholders of their precinct procession the Lands on the South Side Stony Creek in this parish, which was taken out of Bath parish, to the parish Lines.

[140] Ordered that Thomas Jones and Thomas Egleton with the Freeholders procession the Lotts in the towns of petersburg and Blandford.

That the several persons before mentioned to Appoint and Advertize the time for processioning the Lands within their several precincts between the Last day of September and the Last day of March next, and make return of their proceeding as the Law Directs, and that they take Care to Date their Several Returns.

That a stable Twenty feet Long and Sixteen feet wide, and Seven feet pitch be Built on the Glebe by Mr. William Eaton, and a Shed at One End of the Barn now Built, the Width of the Barn and Eight feet out, both the Stable and Shed to be shingled with heart Shingles, and a Gate to be made to the Glebe house as Mr. Wilkinson shall Direct, to be paid at the same time that he is paid for the Other Repairs.

THOMAS WILLIAMS Church Warden.

Test RICHARD TAYLOR Clk Vestry.

At a Vestry held at the Glebe for Bristol parish the Twenty Fifth day of November 1755.

Present. The Reverend Thomas Wilkinson, Stephen Dewey, Tho[s] Williams Church Wardens, Theophilus Field, Samuel Gordon, James Murray, James Boisseau, Hugh Miller, George Smith, William Eppes.

Ordered That Thomas Williams pay the money now in his hands due to the parish to William Eaton towards the work he has done on the Glebe, he Allowing 5 ℘ C[t] Discount.

The Vestry have Adjourned to Thursday next to meet at the Brick Church at Eleven O Clock.

THOMAS WILLIAMS, Church Warden.
STEPHEN DEWEY Church Warden.

Test RICHARD TAYLOR Clk Vestry.

[141] The Vestry According to Adjournment have met at the Brick Church this 27th November, 1755.

Present. The same Vestry as on Tuesday and Theod[k] Bland.

BRISTOL PARISH FOR 1755 DR.

To the Reverend Thomas Wilkinson Minister, .	17,280
To Richard Taylor Clk Vestry and Brick Church, .	2,000
To George Williams Clk Jones Hole, . . .	1,000
To Abram Alley Sexton, ...	400
To Thomas Bonner ditto, ...	400
To John Brown for Ann Newhouse, ...	300
To the Widdow Alley for her Mother, . . .	1,000
To John Kemp for Olave poxen, ...	1,000
To Henry Spire for the Widdow Tatem, . . .	800
To Dan[l] Vaughan for Margaret Williams, . .	1,000
To Francis Dezearn to be paid Geo. Smith, . .	125

To Mary Barret, ...	800
To George Currie for Cyrus Stewart, ...	400
To John Crews for Eliz^{a} Davis, ...	1,000
To John May for Henry Warne, ...	1,000
To Daniel Vaughan Senr, ...	500
To Francis Leadbetter for his Mother, ...	1,000
To Major Cotten, ...	600
To John Watkins for Ann Newhouse 6 Months, .	300
To Francis Dezearn, ...	275
To Thomas Willson for Judith Nance 5 Months, .	500
To Stephen Dewey for Ditto 4 Months, ...	400
To David Smith for Insolvents, ...	630
To Benj^{a} Watkins Surveying the Glebe, . . .	450
To Tobbacco to be Sold, , ...	9,130
To 6 ℔ C^{t} Collecting, ...	2,700
	44,990

CR.

By 1,343 Tyths at 33½^{l} Tobb^{a} ℔ pole, ...	44,990

Ordered That the Church Wardens Apply to the Vestrys of Martins Brandon and Bath parish to Know, if they will Join with this parish towards Building a workhouse, to keep the poor of the three parishes in, pursuant to an Act of the General Assembly.

That the Collector pay the parish of Bath Sixty pounds Tobb^{a} for moveing a poor person into this parish.

William Eaton is Appointed a Vestryman of this parish in the Room of William Starke Deceased. Turn Over.

[142] That Stephen Dewey and William Eaton are Appointed Church Wardens for the Ensueing Year.

That the Church Wardens Receive from Every Tythable person in this parish, Thirty three pounds and a half of Tobbacco for their parish Levies for this Year, and in Case of Nonpayment to levie the Same by Distress, and pay the parish Creditors as they are proportioned.

THOMAS WILLIAMS, STEPHEN DEWEY, Church Wardens.

Test RICHARD TAYLOR Clk Vestry.

BRISTOL PARISH FOR 1754 DR.

To paid James Seavern Attending Maurice Hawks 30 days,	3	15	0
To Wm. parsons a Coffin for d°,	0	10	0
To Gordon & Boyd for Warne,	1	5	4
To Cash paid Richard Bland,	54	17	6
To Natt Raines Burying Fox,	1	17	3
To Robert Ravenscroft a Coffin,	0	10	0
To Thomas Bonner Sundries at the Outward Church	1	13	
To paid for two Locks,	0	6	0
To Ja[s] Murray Sacramentary Elements & sending to Churches,	3	8	0
To John May attending Warns suit,	0	17	9
To Doct[r] Hunter for Maurice Hawks,	5	0	0
To Maj[r] Cotten for 600[l] Tobb[a] Last y[r],	3	11	0
To William Eaton toward work done As ℔ Order Vestry,	49	19	3
	£127	10	1

CR.

By 21,399[l] Tobb[a] Sold at 11 | 10,	126	10	1
By 3 fines for not going to Church,		15	
By 1 Fine from Fra[s] Haddon,		5	
	£127	10	1

Errors Excepted. November 25th 1755.

℔ THOMAS WILLIAMS Church Ward[n].

Test RICHARD TAYLOR Clk Vestry.

WILLIAM EATON TO BRISTOL PARISH DR.

To Recovered Ag[t] Black,	2	0	4½
To 417[l] Tobb[a] Costs 11 | 10,	2	9	4
To Lawyers Fee,	0	15	
To Cash from Tho[s] Williams,	49	19	3
To Discount allowed 5 ℔ C[t],	2	9	11½
To an Order on Mr. Dewey for the Ball.,	10	19	3
	68	13	2

CR.

By his Acc^{t} for work done at the Glebe . .	68 13 2

[143] At a Vestry held at the Brick Church for Bristol Parish June 23d 1756.

Present. The Rev^{d} Mr. Thomas Wilkenson, Stephen Dewey, William Eaton C. W., Theo^{s} Field, Samuel Gordon, Theo^{k} Bland, James Murray, William Eppes, James Boisseau, George Smith, Alex^{r} Bolling, Hugh Miller.

Ordered That Henry Williams be Appointed Clerk of the Brick Church. That John Woobank be Appointed Clerk of the Vestry.

STEPHEN DEWEY, WILLIAM EATON Church Wardens.

Test JOHN WOOBANK Clk Vestry.

At a Vestry held at the Brick Church for Bristol Parish the 19th Novr 1756.

Present. The Reverend Mr. Thomas Wilkinson, Stephen Dewey, William Eaton C. W., Theophilus Field, Theo^{k} Bland, Hugh Miller, George Smith, William Eppes, James Boisseau, Samuel Gordon, James Murray, Alexander Bolling.

BRISTOL PARISH FOR 1756 DR.

	l Tob^{o}.
To the Reverend Thomas Wilkerson, ...	17,280
To Richard Taylor late Clk of the Church & Vestry,	664
To George Williams Clk Jones Hole, . . .	1,000
To Abraham Alley Sexton, ...	400
To Thomas Bonner Ditto, ...	400
To John Brown For keeping Ann Newhouse 5 Months	250
To the Widdow Ally For her Mother, . . .	1,000
To John Kemp For keeping Olive Poxon, . .	1,000
To Henry Spire For keeping the Widdow Tatum, .	800
To Daniel Vaughan For Margaret Williams, . .	1,000
To George Smith For Francis Dezearn, . . .	600
To Mary Barret, ...	800
To George Currie For Cyruss Stewart. . . .	400
To John Crews For Elizabeth Davis, . . .	1,000

To Sam[l] Vaughan For Henry Warne, ...	1,000
To Daniel Vaughan Sen[r], ...	500
To Francis Ledbetter For keeping his Mother 5 Months, ...	417
To Stephen Dewey For Judith Nance, ...	1,200
To Major Cotton, ...	600
To John Watkins For Ann Newhouse 7 Months, .	350
To Henry Williams Clk Church For 5 Months, .	417
To John Woobank Clk Vestry For 5 Months, . .	205
To James Newsum recording Processionings, . .	200
To Theo[k] Bland Clk Prince George Court For his Tickett, ...	207
To George Nicholas D[o] of Dinwiddie D[o] Ditto, .	48
Carried Over, ...	31,738

[144] BRISTOL PARISH DR. Brought Forward, . 31,738

To William Davis his Acco[t], ...	31
To Daniel Vaughan For Horse Blocks &c. . .	100
To David Smith, ...	36
To Tobacco to be sold For the use of the Parish, .	6,588
To 6 p Cent for Collecting, ...	2,457
	40,950

DITTO CR.

By 1,365 Tithables @ 30[l] Tob[o] p Pole, ...	40,950

Ordered That William Smith Son of Patrick Smith be exempted from paying his Parish Levey.

That Stephen Dewey pay William Eaton the Sum of Ten Pounds Nineteen Shillings & Three Pence being the Ballance of his Acco[t].

That Theoderick Bland & William Eaton be Church Wardens for the Ensuing Year.

That the Church Wardens give Bond and Security for performance of their Office.

That Stephen Dewey pay to the Church Wardens the Ballance due in his hands.

That Stephen Dewey Commence process against Mary Hall

for not Complying with her Husbands Will in keeping Judith Nance.

That a House be built on the Glebe Thirty Two Feet by Sixteen with Two Rooms a Brick Chimney in the middle to be underpinn'd with Brick & Flowered with Brick weather Boarded with Clap boards and Shingled with hart of pine or Cypruss Shingles, the loft to be laid with Plank, also a Corn Crib Eight Feet by Fourteen and the Church Wardens to agree with Workmen to perform the same.

That Theodorick Bland apply to the Vestry of Brandon Parish to join this Parish in Building a Workhouse for the Poor of each Parish.

That the Church Wardens Receive from every Tithable person in this Parish Thirty Pounds Tob° for their Parish Levy for this Year and in case of refusal or non payment to Levey the same by distress and pay the Parish Creditors as they are Proportioned.

Abraham Alley agrees to keep Judith Nance for Eight Hundred pounds Tob° p Annum.

STEPHEN DEWEY, WILLIAM EATON, C. W.

Test, JOHN WOOBANK, Clk Vestry.

[145] At a Vestry held at the Brick Church for Bristol Parish Decr 12th, 1756.

Present. The Reverend Mr. Thomas Wilkinson, William Eaton, Theodorick Bland, C. W., Theophilus Field, Thomas Williams, James Murray, Stephen Dewey, James Boisseau, Hugh Miller.

Ordered That Stephen Dewey, Alexander Bolling, Theodorick Bland, Willm Eaton do meet the persons appointed by the Vestry's of Brandon & Bath Parishes to agree in settleing the Terms of the Poors House.

That Stephen Dewey pay Sterling Thornton One Parish Levey, being Overcharged him in the Year 1755.

This day Theodorick Bland and William Eaton Churchwardens Enter into Bond, &c., according to the former Order made, & dated 19th November Last.

STEPHEN DEWEY, WILLIAM EATON, Church Wardens.

Test. JOHN WOOBANK Clk Vestry.

At a Vestry held at the Brick Church For Bristol Parish February the 23d 1757.

Present. The Reverend Mr. Thomas Wilkinson, William Eaton, Theod[k] Bland, C. W., Theophilus Field, James Boisseau, James Murray, Thomas Williams.

[146] Stephen Dewey, Alexander Bolling, Theodorick Bland, William Eaton persons appointed to consider of the Work House made their report, which being approved by the Vestry is Ordered to be registered, and it is Ordered that the same persons above mentioned be appointed as a Committee to Petition the General Assembly in conjunction with the Vestrys of Martins Brandon and Bath Parishes, to obtain such Act as aforesaid.

THEO'K BLAND, WILLIAM EATON, JR., C. W.

Test JOHN WOOBANK, Clk Vestry.

At a meeting of the members appointed by the Respective Parishes of Bristol, Martins brandon and Bath as a Committee to Consider of the best and most proper method for Building a Poors House at the Joint Expence of the said Parishes—

It is the opinion of this Committee that a Convenient House ought to be Rented for Entertaining the poor of the said Parishes, if to be had, But if not, that then Land ought to be bought & Convenient Houses to be built for the joint use of the said Parishes in proportion to the number of Tithables in each of the said Parishes. This Committee having taken under their most serious Consideration the unhappy and indeed miserable Circumstances of the many poor Orphans and other poor Children, Inhabitants of the said Parishes whose parents are utterly unable to give them any Education and being desirous to render the said House as Beneficial as possable & that such poor Children should be brought up in a Religious, Virtuous & Industrious Course of Life so as to become usefull members of the Community, Have Resolved earnestly to recommend it to their Respective Vestries that they should join in a Petition to the General Assembly to procure an Act to enable the said Parishes to erect a FREE SCHOOL for Educating the poor Children of the said Parishes in Reading, Writing and Arithmetic at the joint Expence of the said Parishes, and Uniting the same to the said Poorshouse Under such Rules, Orders and Directions as shall be most just and proper for perfecting so usefull and Charitable a Work, And in Order to facilitate the obtaining such Act to propose that the said Vestries should unite in opening Subscriptions that the Rich & Opulent & all other well disposed people may have an opportunity of Contributing towards so pious a design out of that STORE which the FATHER of Bounties hath bestowed on them.

It is the opinion of this Committee that Four of the Members of each of the said Vestries ought to be appointed as a Committee to Petition the General Assembly in the name and on behalf of the said Vestries in Order to obtain such Act as aforesaid And also to put the said resolutions into Execution.

[147] It is the opinion of this Committee that these Resolutions be Communicated to the respective Vestries as soon as possable for approbation or Descent.

Signed According to the Directions of the Committee By

Jany 19th, 1757. RICHARD BLAND.

At a Vestry held at the Brick Church November 15th 1757.

Present. The Reverend Thomas Wilkinson, William Eaton, Theo^{k} Bland, C. Wardens, Theop^{s} Field, James Murray, William Eppes, George Smith, James Boisseau, Alexander Bolling, Hugh Miller.

BRISTOL PARISH. DR.

To the Revd Thomas Wilkinson,	17,280
To George Williams Clk Jones Hole,	1,000
To John Woobank Clk Vestry,	500
To Abraham Alley Sexton,	400
To Thomas Bonner,	400
To William Yarborough as Clk of the Brick Church,	1,125
To John Brown Keep^{g} Ann Newhouse 8 M^{os},	400
To William Butler Keep^{g} Ditto 4 M^{os},	200
To Widdow Alley for her Mother,	1,000
To John Kemp Keep^{g} Poxon,	1,000
To Henry Spire Keep^{g} the widow Tatam 4 M^{os},	266
To Nathaniel Lee Keeping D^{o} D^{o} 8 M^{os},	534
To Daniel Vaughan Keep^{g} Margaret Williams,	1,000

To George Smith Keep^{g} Fra^{s} Dezarne,	600
To Mary Barrett,	800
To George Currie Keep^{g} Cyrus Stewart,	400
To John Crews Keep^{g} Elizabeth Davis	1,000
To Samuel Vaughan Keep^{g} Henry Warne,	1,000
To Daniel Vaughan Senr,	500
To Major Cotton,	600
To Abraham Alley Keep^{g} Judith Nance,	800
To George Nicholas Clk Dinwiddie his Ticket for 2 Copies of Tiths,	32
To Thomas Shrewsbury for a Parish Levey,	30
To Jacob Dunhart Junr Ditto,	33
To William Eaton Insolvents in Dinwiddie,	150
To Ditto D^{o} P^{t} George,	390
To the Late Sherrif of Ditto his Ticket,	243
To William Eppes for a Levy Overcharg'd Last year Tatam's Estate,	30
To Tob^{o} to be sold for the use of the Parish,	4,863
To 6 p Cent for Collecting,	2,334
	38,910

DITTO. CR.

By 1,297 Tithables @ 30^{l} Tob^{o} p Pole,	38,910

[148] Order'd That the Churchwardens enquire of Mr. Thomas Williams about the sum of Forty shillings payable to Elizabeth Brown yearly which sum is due to Thomas Man as p his Acco^{t} given in to this Vestry.

That Stephen Dewey Settle the Parish Acco^{t} wth the Churchwardens and pay the Ballance due in his hands to them.

That the Churchwardens employ some person to Comence process against Mary Hall for not complying wth her Husbands Will in keep^{g} Judith Nance.

That the Churchwardens treat wth Lewis Parham for the Purchase of his Land joyning the South side of the Glebe and make their report to this Vestry.

John Jones, Haulkey Pride, Sheppyallen Puckett being fin'd for gameing by the Judgement of Pr George Court, Order'd that the Churchwardens revive the said Judgment by Sire Facias; and that they apply to John Burge for his Daughters Fine for having a Bastard Child & if he refuses to pay, that they bring Suit against him for his Assumsit.

That Susannah Woodlief be Sexton of Jones Hole Church in the room of Thomas Bonner.

That the Churchwardens pay to the Clk & Surveyor of Prince George their Fees in the procecution of Parham in the Glebe Land out of the Tob^{o} levied to be sold.

That the Churchwardens pay Mr. Thomas Wilkinson Forty Three Shillings for a Corn House built on the Glebe.

That Theo^{k} Bland and James Murray be Churchwarden for the Ensuing Year.

That George Williams be allowed 200^{l} Tob^{o} more than what was allowed him last year.

That the Churchwardens at the most Convenient place put up the Poor of this Parish to the lowest Bidder.

That the Churchwardens receive from every Tithable person in this Parish Thirty pounds Tob^{o} for their Parish Levy for this present year and in case of refusal or nonpayment to levy the same by distress and pay the Parish Creditors as it is proportion'd.

THEO'K BLAND, WILLIAM EATON. Churchwardens.

Test JOHN WOOBANK Clk Vestry.

At a Vestery held at the Brick Church, Novemb^{r} ye 25th 1758.

Present. Theop^{s} Feild, James Murray, Samuel Gorden, Alex^{r} Bolling, Thomas Williams, James Boiseau, Theo^{k} Bland.

Ordered That William Yarbrough be App^{d} Clerk of this Vestry.

[149] 1758 Novr 25th. BRISTOL PARISH. DR.

To the Revd Mr Thomas Wilkerson,	17,280
To William Yarbrough Clk of ye Brick Church,	1,500
To George Williams Clk Jones Hole Church,	1,200
To Abraham Alley Sexton,	400
To Susanna Woodlief Sexton,	400
To William Butler for Ann New-house,	600
To The Widow Alley,	1,000
To John Kemp for keeping Ollive Poxen two months,	166
To Ditto for Burying the S^{d} Poxen,	54

To James Murray for a Coffin for the S^{d} Poxen,	60
To Nathl Lee for Widow Tatum,	800
To Daniel Vaughan for Margret Williames,	1,000
To Benj^{a} Cook for Dezarn,	600
To James Moore for Mary Barrett,	1,000
To George Currie for Cyrus Stewart,	1,000
To John Crews for Elizth Davis,	1,000
To William Browder for Warne,	1,000
To Elizth Vaughan Due to her late Husband Daniel Vaughan,	418
To Major Cotten,	600
To Abram Tucker for keeping Judith Nance four Months,	500
To Ditto for Burying the S^{d} Nance,	114
To Sarah Tomas for Peter Tomas,	500
To Elizth Brown to be p^{d} to Benj. Cook,	400
To Theo^{k} Bland By his Acc^{t},	86
To James Murray Shirff by Rains's Acc^{t},	23
To Samuel Vaughan for keeping Warne one month,	90
To Abram Alley for keeping Judith Nance Ditto,	90
	31,881
To 6 ꝑ C^{t} for Collecting 35,360^{l} Tobaco,	2,121
To Ball^{s} in Collectors hands,	358
	34,360

CR.

By 1,360 Tyths @ 26^{l} Tobaco ꝑ^{r} pole,	35,360

DR.

To Mr. Theop^{s} Feild for Wine for the Church ꝑ^{r} acc^{t},	£	1.	18.	8
To William Davis for Benches for the Church,		1.	5.	0
To D^{o} for Burying Barnaby Moore,		1.	5.	0
	£	4.	8.	8

[150] Orderd That the Church Wardens apply to Noah Brown for three Parish Levies due from him on acc^{t} of Tyths belonging to Duglas Irby which ought to have been listed by the said

Brown, and if the said Brown refuses to pay them that the said Churchwardens prosecute the said Brown for consealing y[e] s[d] Tyths.

That James Murray and Theop: Feild be Church Wardens for the Ensuing year.

Theo[k] Bland Church Warden ret[d] his acc[t] by which there appears to be the Ball[s] of £112. 17. 3½ due to the Parish.

Orderd That Theo[k] Bland pay to Theop[s] Feild £1. 18. 8. as above acc[t] out of the money in his hands.

Orderd That Theo[k] Bland pay to William Davis £2. 10[s] as above out of the money in his hands.

Orderd That the Remaining Ball[s] due from Theo[k] Bland to the Parish be paid to the Church wardens for the Ensuing year.

THEO'K BLAND, JAMES MURRAY, Churchwardens.

Test WILLIAM YARBROUGH, Clk ves[t].

At a Vestry held at the Brick Church of Bristol Parish the 5th of January, 1760.

Present. The Rev[d] Mr. Thomas Wilkerson, James Murray, Thomas Williams, Theop[s] Feild, James Boisau, William Epes, William Eaton, Samuel Gorden, Gent[l]men.

Orderd That the persons following be appointed to Possision the lands in this parish in their several Precincts as Followith.

[151] Orderd That Daniel Cawl and Daniel Vaughan with the freeholders of their precincts Possesion from the Nottoway Road up as far as Munks Neck Road from the head of Black water to the River. That William Persons and Thomas Willson with the freeholders of their precincts Possesion from the Puddle Dock to Leutenants Run between the River and the great swamp on Munks Neck Road. That William Eaton and John Loyal with the freeholders of their Precincts Possesion from Leutenants Run to the Indian Town Run Including Rohowick. That Roger Adkerson and Robert Harrison with the freeholders of their precincts Possesion from the Indian Town Run to the parish line. That Edward Birchett and Drurey Birchett with the freeholders of their precincts Possesion between Black water swamp and second swamp from James Baughs path down to the parish line between the s[d] swamps. That Charles Gee and James Hall with the freeholders of their precincts Pos-

sesion below Jones hole Road between the County and Parish lines & warwick swamp. That John Rains and Thomas Bonner with the freeholders of their precincts Possesion from Warwick swamp to the parish line between Jones hole Road and Nottoway Road. That Hugh Kirkland and William Pirkins with the freeholders of their precincts Possesion from Munks Neck Bridge to Rowante Bridge. That John Browder and Morris Vaughan with the freeholders of their precincts Possesion from Munks Neck Road up the north side of munks neck and Hatchers Run to the Parish line. That Thomas Deavenport and Daniel Sterdevent with their freehold of their precincts Possision from James Baughs Path between Blackwater & second swamp and Munks Neck Road. That Christopher Golikely and Henry Wilkerson with the freeholders of their precincts Possesion from the Parish line up the great branch of Warwick. That Peter Leath and Richard Geary with the freeholders of their precincts Possesion from the great branch of warwick between warwick and second swamp to Munks Neck Road. [152] Orderd That Robert Batte and John Peterson with the freeholders of their precincts Possesion from Puddle dock Run to the Road that goes by Samuel Jourdans former Plantation and from y[e] Parish line to Nottoway road. That William Batte and William Thweatt with the freeholders of their precincts Possesion from the Parish line to the Nottoway Road and from the said Road leading by the s[d] Jourdans Plantation to Black water. That Rob[t] Eavins and William Malone with the freeholders of their precincts Possesion from the County line between Stoney Creek aud the fox branch up the parish line. That David Abbernatha and Bennet Kirbey with the freeholders of their precincts Possesion between the fox Branch and Munks to the Parish line. That James Stirdevent and John Gilliam with the freeholders of their precincts Possesion from Puddle dock run to Citty Creek and from the main Road to the River. That Burrill Green and John Stirdevent with the freeholders of their precincts Possesion from the Citty Creek to the Parish line between the main Road and the River. That John Whitemore and James Cate with the freeholders of their precincts Possesion from the Road Over Warwick Bridge to the Munks Neck Road between the two swamps. That Thomas Eavins and James Harrison with the freeholders of their precincts Possision the lands on the South Side of Stoney Creek in this parish which was taken out of Bath Parish to the Parish line. That Thomas Jones and Thomas Eagleton with the freeholders of their precincts Possision the Lotts in the Town of Petersburg and Blandford.

Orderd That the Several persons afore Menchiond do appoint and Advertise the time of Possesioning the several lands within their several precincts before the last day of Next March and make Return of their Proceeding as the law directs and that they take care to date their several returns.

Orderd That Col^{o} Robert Bolling and George Smith be appointed Vestry Men for this Parish.

[153] BRISTOL PARISH DR.

To The Revd Thomas Wilkerson,	17,280
To William Yarbrough Clerk of Brick Church and Vestry,	2,000
To George Williams Clk of Jones hole Church,	1,200
To Abraham Alley sexton,	400
To Susanna Woodlief d^{o},	400
To William Butler for keeping Ann Newhouse,	800
To the widow Allin. If so much due,	800
To Nathl Lee for the widow Tatam, If so much will doe,	300
To Daniel Vaughan for keeping Margret Williames,	1,000
To Benj^{a} Cook for keeping Dizarn,	600
To James Moore for Mary Barratt,	250
To George Currie for keeping Cyrus Stewart,	1,000
To Robt Waren ℘^{r} order John Crews for Elizth Davis,	1,000
To William Browder for keeping of warne,	1,000
To Maj^{r} Cotten,	600
To Sarah Brown for keeping Peter Brown,	337
To Elizth Brown to be p^{d} Benj^{a} Cook,	400
To Mr. George Nichols,	32
To Col. Theo^{k} Bland,	32
To Mary Barrow for keeping Ann Butterworth 8 months,	533
To Starkey Moore for keeping her 4 months,	267
To Elizth Vaughan,	250

To Mr. Theop^{s} Feild for Peter Brown, ...	104
To William Cawls acc^{t} for Peter Brown, . . .	59
To John Hansel for 2 levies in ye year 1758, . .	52
To William Davis p^{r} 1 Levie, ...	30
	30,726
To 6 p^{r} C^{t} for Collecting 32,680^{l}, ...	1,954
	32,680

CR.

By 1,491 Tyths @ 22^{l} p^{r} pole, ...	32,802
	122

CASH ACC'T DR.

To John Rains for work at Jones hole Church,	£	8	0	0
To Mr. Theop^{s} Feild for wine &c.		2	10	11
To William Davis for Carting Church Benches,			5	0
To William Yarbrough for a Chest lock &c. .			3	7
	£	10	19	6

[154] Orderd That Mr. James Murray & Mr. Theop^{s} Feild continue Church wardens.

That Mr. Stephen Dewey, Mr. William Eaton, & Col Theo^{k} Bland settle their former acc^{ts} with the present Church Wardens, and Either pay their Ball^{ss} or Give Bond and Surety.

Orderd That the Church wardens of this parish do Receive of Every Tythable person within the same by distress, in case of Refusal or non payment Twenty two Pounds of Tobacco ꝑ Pole as their Parish Levie for this present year 1759. And that the Present Church wardens Give Bond.

THEOP'S FEILD, JAMES MURRAY Churchwardins.

Test WM. YARBROUGH Clk Vestry.

At a vestry held at the Brick Church of Bristol Parish the 5th of August 1760.

Present. The Rev^{d} Mr. Thomas Wilkerson, James Murray, Theop^{s} Feild, James Boiseau, Allex^{r} Bolling, George Smith, William Eaton, Robert Bolling, Samuel Gorden, Thomas Williames, Gen^{ts}.

Order'd That Mr. William Poythress be appointed a vestry man for this Parish in the room of Maj[r] William Epps, Deces'd.

That the Church wardens pay unto William Yarbrough the sum of Three Pounds two shillings and Nine pence out of the Parish money as they have or shall have in their hands, for keeping of John Reeves three weeks and three Days in his sickness, and his Funeral Expences.

That the Churchwardens of this Parish apply to the Church wardens of Dale Parish in the county of Chesterfield for the sum of three pounds two shillings & nine pence on acc[t] of the above s[d] John Reeves's Expences in sickness and Funeral & he being a Resident of that Parish.

THEOP'S FEILD, JAMES MURRAY Church wardens.

Test WILLIAM YARBROUGH Clk Vestry.

[155] At a vestry held at the Brick Church of Bristol Parish Decem[r] the 8th 1760.

Present. The Rev[d] Mr. Thomas Wilkerson, James Murray, Theop[s] Feild, James Boisseau, George Smith, Samuel Gorden, Robert Bolling, Thomas Williams, William Poythress.

BRISTOL PARISH. Tobacco. DR.

	l.
To the Rev[d] Mr. Thomas Wilkerson,	17,280
To William Yarbrough Clk of the Church and Vestry,	2,000
To George Smith Clk of Jones hole Church,	1,200
To Ditt[o] for sexton of Jones hole Church,	400
To Mary Alley for sexton of the Brick Church,	400
To William Butler for Keeping Ann Newhouse,	1,000
To Daniel Vaughan for d[o] Margret Williams,	1,000
To Benj[a] Cook for Dezarn 4 months,	267
To George Currey for Keeping Cyrus Stewart,	1,000
To William Browder for d[o] Warne,	1,000
To Starkey Moore for d[o] Ann Butterworth,	800
To Maj[r] Cotten,	600
To Henry Avery for d[o] Peter Brown 4 months,	333
To Henry Dickson for d[o] Eliz[th] Davis,	1,000
To The widow Barrow for Eliz[th] Brown,	400
To Eliz[th] Vaughan,	250

To George Nicholas, ...	16
To Co[l] The. Bland, ...	40
To Theop[s] Feild sen[r], ...	44
To William Yarbrough for sundry services, . .	100
	29,130
To 6 ℔[r] C[t] for Collecting, ...	1,747
	30,877
Cr.	
By 1,563 Tyths at 20[l] Tob[o] ℔[r] pole, ...	31,260
	338

Orderd That the Churchwardens Receive from Every Tythable person within the same by Distress in Case of Refusal or non payment, Twenty Pounds of Tobaco ℔r Pole as their Parish Levie and pay the same to the several C[drs] to whom it is Proportiond.

Orderd That Mr. Roger Adkerson and Mr. George Nicholas be appointed Vestrymen in the Room of Mr. Hugh Miller who is remov'd & Mr. Stephen Dewey who has resind.

Orderd That the Rev[d] Mr. Thomas Wilkerson on his motion to the Vestry has liberty to reside in Chesterfield County.

Orderd That Theop[s] Feild and George Smith be appointed Church wardens for the proceeding year.

Bristol Parish. To Cash acc[t]. Dr.

To John Rains for services done to Jones hole Church, ...	£	1.	0.	0
To Benj[a] Cook for Burying Dezarn, . . .		1.	7.	0
To Henry Averey for Burying Peter Brown,			12.	6
	£	2.	19.	6

Theop's Feild, James Murray.

Test William Yarbrough Clk Vestry.

[156] March the 12th 1760 Rec[d] of Theop[s] Feild as Church warden of Bristol Parish Eight Pounds it being what was

levied by the said Parish for work done at Jones hole Church by . . . . . . John Rains.

April 15th 1760 Rec^{d} of Theo^{s} Feild as Church warden of Bristol Parish five shill^{s} it being levied by the said Parish for services done by . . . . William Davis.

1759 Decem^{r} 6th Paid William Yarbrough by C^{r} in his acc^{t} wth Theo^{s} Feild levied him for a Chest lock 3^{s} 17.

Paid by order of Vestry To The^{o} Feild, £2. 10. 11.

1760 March the 12th. Rec^{d} from Theo^{s} Feild as Church warden of Bristol Parish fifteen shillings for Procecuting a suit in behalf of our Sovereign Lord the King agst Robert Rievs in this Court of Prince George.

A. CLAIBORNE.

1760 March the 12th. Rec^{d} from Theo^{s} Feild as Church warden for the Parish of Bristol fifteen shillings for Procecuting a suit in behalf of our Sovereign Lord the King against Benj^{a} Moody in the Court of Prince George.

A. CLAIBORNE.

1760 Sepr the 9th. Rec^{d} from Theo^{s} Feild as Church warden of Bristol Parish thirty shill^{s} for Procecuting two suits in behalf of our sovereign Lord the King agst John Chamlis J^{r}.

A. CLAIBORNE.

1760 Sepr the 9th. Rec^{d} from Theo^{s} Feild as Church warden for the Parish of Bristol fifteen shill^{s} as my fee for procecuting a suit in behalf of our sovereign Lord the King agst William Brown.

A. CLAIBORNE.

1760 At Prince George Court the 9th of August, before Thedo^{k} Bland Esqr the above Mr. Augus^{n} Claiborne own'd to have Rec'd this fees due from the Parish for Presentm^{ts} against John Peterson, John Butler and William Persons.

1758 BRISTOL PARISH TO THEO'S FEILD DR.

			s	d
Decem^{r}	23	To 2 y^{ds} ozrb^{s} to make a wallet to fetch ye Church Plate, ...	1	1
	25	To 2 Bottles wine for ye Communion Service Brick Church, . . .	6	8
	31	To 2 d^{o} the outward Church, . .	6	8

			£	s.	d.
		To man & Horse to carry out the wine		2	6
1759.					
Ap^{l}	13	To 2 Bottles wine for the Brick Church C service, ...		6	8
	15	To 2 d^{o} the outward Church, . .		6	8
		To man & Horse to Carry out d^{o}, .		2	6
June	3	To 2 Bottles wine &c. for the Brick Church, ...		6	8
	10	To 2 d^{o} the outw^{d} Church, . .		6	8
		To man & Horse d^{o} d^{o}, . . .		2	6
			£ 2	8	7
		To keeping and looking after Peter a molatto fool left by his mother in my Quarter fryday the 19th of Octr 1759. I kept till ye 26th nov^{r} following.			
Decm^{r}	30th	To 2 Bottles wine for the Brick Church,		6	8
			£ 2	15	3

CR.

			£	s.	d.
1758.					d.
Dec^{r}		By 1 bottle caried back ye oth^{r} brok, .			4
	3	By 2 d^{o} brought from ye outw^{d} Church,			8
1759.					
Ap^{l}	13	By 2 from ye Brick Church, . .			8
	15	By 2 from ye outw^{d} d^{o}, ...			8
June	3	By 2 d^{o} from ye brick d^{o}, ...			8
	10	By 2 from ye outw^{d} d^{o}, ...			8
Decm^{r}	30	By 2 d^{o} from ye brick d^{o}, ...			8
			£ 0	4	4

[157] 1759 BRISTOL PARISH DR.

	£	s.	d.
To the amount of the several sums paid ye Parish Creditors 34,002^{l} Tob^{o}, ...	£ 283	7	0
To Mr. Walter Boyd for Clearing the Church Yard, ...	6	15	
To 10 Insolvents, , ...	2	3	4
To 6 Tyths listed in Capt Eatons name for Benj^{a} Harrison not Paid, ...	1	6	0

To Ball[s] due to the Parish, ...		19	8	8
	£	313	0	0

CONTRA CR.

By 35,360[l] Tob[o] levied on 1,360 Tyths @ | 2 .		294	13	4
by Receiv[d] from Rigsby, ...		2	10	0
by d[o] N. Brown Irbys Tyths, ...		1	15	0
by d[o] Cain, ...		5	0	0
by Tyths Rec[d] not listed Vz: Sallathiel Vaughan 7, John Banister Esq[r] 9, M. Williams 1, J. Hawks 1. 18, . .		3	18	0
By Tyths Rec[d] T. Bonner 23, ...		4	19	8
By Commissions on £3. 9. 4 @ 6 p[r] C[t], . .			4	
	£	313	0	0

Erors Excepted JAMES MURRAY.

BRISTOL PARISH IN ACC'T WITH THEOP'S FEILD CHURCH WARDEN DR.

1760.					
M'ch 12	To P[d] Augustin Claiborne 2 fees for procecuting the suit ags[t] Rob[t] Reeves & Benj[a] Moody, . .	£	1	10	0
	To paid John Rains by Order of Vestry Decm[r] 1759 as p[r] rec[d], .		8		
	To paid Theop[s] Feild by D[o], .		2	10	11
April 6	To 2 Bottles wine for Communion ser[s] Brick Church, . . .			6	8
13	To 2 d[o] for Jones Hole d[o], . .			6	8
	To man and horse to carry d[o] out,			2	6
15	To William Davis by order of Vestry Decm[r] 1759, . . .			5	
	To Wm. Yarbrough by d[o] paid to his acc[t] wth T. F. . . .			3	7
May 25	To 2 bottles wine for Jones hole Church, ...			6	8
	To man and Horse to carry out d[o] & plate, ...			2	6
June 1	To 2 bottles wine for the Brick Church, ...			6	8

Sepr 9 To p^d Augustine Claiborne for proc-ecuting 2 suits against John Chamlis Junr,		1	10	0
To p^d Clerk & sheriff 206^l Tob^o their fees as Judgm^t in the suits on John Chamlis Junr he being chargd for ye same, . . .		1	13	4
To Paid Augustine Claiborne his Fee in the suit of Wm. Brown, as p^r Judgm^t to John Chambles J^{rs} note of hand daited April 26th 1760 payable on demand to the Present Church Wardens or successors wth Interest, ...		18	3	4
To Fran^s Ledbetter Penal Bill of the 9th Sepr 1760 payable on demand to ye present Church wardens or their successors with Interest, ...		2	19	10
To my Commissions for Collecting £64. 3. 10 & Taking proper Vouchers & Recepts for the parish @ 5 ℔ C^t, ...		3	4	2
Ball^s due ye Parish from Theop^s Feild here wth,		21	19	8
To P^d Augs^{tn} Claiborn his fee agst Wm. Brown as p^r Judgm^t, ...			15	
	£	64	6	6

CONTRA CR.

1760 March 11 By Cash of Augustine Claiborne due from Christop^r Golightly, he the s^d Claiborne keeping & retaining his fee,	£	5	0	0
by Cash of Robert Reevs for his fine & att^g fee,		5	15	0
12. by d^o Benj^a Moody his d^o & d^o, . .		5	15	0
April 6 by 2 bottles returnd, . . .				8
By John Chamblis J^r fines with the att^g fees & costs of sutes as p^r his note of hand payable on deman^d with Interest, . . .		18	3	4
by 3 bottles returnd, ...			1	0
June 11 by 500^l Tob^o of Wm. Persons as his fine sold @ 2^d, ...		4	3	4
augst ye 9 by Cash of Wm. Davis for his Daughter Ann Davis's fine for having a Bastard Child, ...		2	10	0

12 by Cash of Thos Epes sheriff for John Petersons fine p^{r} Recep^{t}, ...	5	0	0
21 by 500^{l} Tob^{o} a fine due from John Butler sold @ 2^{d} as his fine, ...	4	3	4
Sepr 9 by Cash of Theod^{k} Bland for a fine formerly due from Jno Jones as p^{r} my Recp^{t}	5	0	0
By Cash of Wm. Brown & att^{g} fee his fine, .	5	15	0
By Fra^{s} Ledbetter for his daughter Anns fine for having a Bastard Child with the cost of suit as p^{r} his penal Bill on demand with Interest, ...	2	19	10
£	64	6	6

[158] At a vestry held at the Brick Church of Bristol Parish Novemb^{r} ye 18th 1761.

Theophilus Feild, Samuel Gorden, Robert Bolling, William Eaton, George Smith, George Nicholas, Roger Adkerson, Gen^{t}men.

BRISTOL PARISH IN TOBO. DR.

	l.
To The Rev^{d} Mr. Thomas Wilkerson, ...	17,280
To William Yarbrough Clk of the Brick Church & vestry, ...	2,000
To George Williams Clk Jones Hole Church, . .	1,200
To Ditto as Sexton of d^{o}, ...	400
To Mary Alley sexton of the Brick Church, . .	400
To Daniel Vaughan for Keeping Margret Williams,	1,000
To William Butler for Ann Newhouse, . . .	1,000
To George Currey for Cyrus Stewart, . . .	1,000
To William Browder for Waren, ...	1,000
To Starkey Moore for Ann Butterworth, . . .	800
To Major Cotten, ...	600
To Henry Dickson for Elizth Davis, ...	1,000
To the Widdow Barrow for Elizth Brown, . .	600
To Elizth Vaughan, ...	250
To Col^{o} The. Bland, ...	180
To George Nicholas, ...	16

To Theop^s Field & George Smith for 74 Tyths by mistake last y^r, ...	1,480
To The Collect^r 6 ℔ C^t, ...	1,901
To Henry Todd Counstable 1 Tyth p^d Last Year, .	20
To Depositum in Collectors hands, ...	1,305
	33,432

BRISTOL PARISH. CR.

By 4 Tyths Rec^d last Year not listed 80^l Tob^o,		
By 1,516 Tyths @ 22^l p^r Poll,	33,432	33,432

Orderd that the Church Wardens Receive from Every Tythable person within the same by distress, in case of Refusal or non payment Twenty two Pounds of Tob^o p^r Poll as their Parish Levies and Pay the same to the several Crd^rs to whoom it is Porpotiond.

BRISTOL PARISH. To Cash, DR.

To James McDewell for keeping Brown, .	£ 3.	6.	0
To Bathiah Ivey for making Browns Cloths, .		7.	6
To William Flewellin for keeping Brown, .	2.	10.	0
To William Davis sen^r for setting up horse blocks, ...		7.	6
To John Rains for Repairing the windows of Jones hole Church, ...	12.	9.	2
To William Persons for a coffin for Wm. Blackwell, ...		10.	0
	£ 19.	10.	2

CR.

By money due in Theo^s Feilds hands, ...	£ 9.	8.	0			
By money in m^r Eatons hands wth Interest, ...	23.	17.	5			
	33.	5.	5	33.	5.	5

[159] Order'd That Theop^s Feild & George Smith Junr are appointed Church wardins for the Ensuing Year.

THEOP'S FEILD, GEORGE SMITH, Junr.

Test, WILLIAM YARBROUGH, Clk vestry.

At a Vestry held at the Brick Church of Bristol Parish the 24th of May 1762.

Present. Theophilus Feild, Samuel Gorden, Robert Bolling, William Poythress, William Eaton, George Smith, George Nicholas, and Roger Atkerson—Gen^{t}men.

Order'd That William Eaton settle the parish Acc^{ts} with Stephen Dewey Esqr for the Year 1756 for 6,588^{l}, of Tob^{o} sold for the Parish use.

Order'd That William Yarbrough Clk of the Vestry Apply to Mr. Jam^{s} Murray for all Bonds and Other papers, Relating to the parish affairs.

THEOP'S FEILD, GEORGE SMITH, JR., Church wardens.

Test WILLIAM YARBROUGH, Clk Vestry.

At a Vestry held at the Brick Church of Bristol parish, November the 11th 1762.

Present. James Boiseau, Theop^{s} Feild, sen^{r}, Allex^{r} Bolling, George Nicholas, George Smith Ju^{r}, Roger Adkerson, William Eaton, James Murray, Samuel Gorden, Gent^{l}men.

Order'd That a small Church be Built in some Convenient part in the outward part of this Parish.

Order'd That the Churchwardens do let out the poor of this parish to the lowest bidder.

Caried Over. November the 30th 1762.

William Butler to Keep Ann Newhouse for and Return her sufficiently Clothed at the years End.	975^{l} Tob^{o}	℔ year
That Phillip Moore Keep Ann Butterworth for and Return her as afore said at the years End.	800	d^{o}
That Starkey Moore Keep Elizth Davis for	885	d^{o}
That he Keep Cyrus Stewart for	850	d^{o}
That he Keep Warn for and return them all three sufficiently Clothed at the years End.	950	d^{o}
That John Temple Keep old Wilson for and Return him as afore s^{d} at the years End.	900	d^{o}

[160] Brought Over. November the 11th 1762.

BRISTOL PARISH IN TOBACCO. DR.

	1
To the Revd Mr. Thomas Wilkerson, ...	17,280
To William Yarbrough Clerk of the Church & Vestry & sexton, Brick Church, ...	2,400
To George Smith Clk of Jones Hole & sexton of do, .	1,600
To Daniel Vaughan for Margret Williames, . .	1,000
To William Butler for Ann Newhouse, . . .	1,000
To George Currey for Cyrus Stewart, . . .	1,000
To Starkey Moore for Ann Butterworth, . . .	800
To Major Cotten, ...	600
To Elizth Vaughan, ...	250
To Henry Dickson for Elizth Davis, ...	1,000
To Mary Barrow for Warne, ...	1,000
To Thomas Cheves for Elizth Brown, . . .	400
To the sheriff of Prince George County, . . .	284
To Col. The. Bland, ...	321
To George Nicholas, ...	16
To Mary Wilkerson for 1 Levie over paid, . .	22
To Benja Firdenando for 1 do, ...	20
To the Use of the Parish, ...	11,277
To the Collector, ...	2,570
	42,840

CR.

By 1,530 Tythes @ 28l Tobo ꝑr Tythe, ...	42,840

Order'd That Thoms Bonner Colr Receive from Every Tythable person within the same by distress in case of Refusal or non payment Twenty Eight Pounds of Tobo ꝑr Pole as their Parish levie and pay the same to the several Credtors To whom it is Porpotiond and Give Bond for the same.

Order'd That Roger Daniel & David McColloch senr be Exempted from paying Parish Levies for the future.

BRISTOL PARISH IN CASH DR.

	£		
To Henry Wilkerson for Wilson.	5	16	0
To John Williams, ...	3	0	0

Order'd That the present Churchwardens be Continued for the ensuing year.

THEOP'S FEILD SEN'R, GEORGE SMITH JR., Churchward[ns].

Test WILLIAM YARBROUGH Clk.

[161] At a vestry held for Bristol Parish at Mr. Walter Boyds in Blandford, Novem[r] 22d 1762.

Present. Theop[hs] Feild, Georg Smith, James Murray, James Boiseau, George Nicholas, Roger Adkerson, William Eaton, Samuel Gorden, Allex[r] Bolling—Gentlmen.

The Rev[d] Mr. Thomas Wilkerson this day appeared in Vestry and Resign'd the Parish.

Orderd that the Rev[d] Mr. William Harrison be Rec[d] minister of this Parish in the Room of Mr. Thomas Wilkerson who has Resign'd the same.

Mr. James Boiseau this Day Resign'd his office of a Vestryman of this parish.

That Sir William Skipwith Bar[t] is Elected a Vestryman of this parish in the Room of Mr. James Boiseau and that the Clk of vestry aquaint him therewith.

Orderd That George Williams be Discontinued Clerk of Jones Hole Church.

That James Murray, Allex[r] Bolling, William Eaton & George Smith j[r] or aney three of them do provide a plan for a Glebe House for this parish and Advertise letting the same as soon as it can Conveniently be done.

That Theop[s] Feild, William Eaton & George Nicholas, or aney two of them Examine the several Acc[ts] in the Vestry Books and Report it to the Vestry.

THEOP'S FEILD, GEORGE SMITH Church Wardens.

Test WILLIAM YARBROUGH Clk Vestry.

At a vestry held at the Brick Church of Bristol on Feb[r] 19th 1763.

Present. The Rev[d] Mr. William Harrison, Theop[s] Feild sen[r], Sir William Skipwith, George Nicholas, George Smith, William Eaton, James Murray, Samuel Gorden, Gen[t]men.

Order'd That Sir William Skipwith, Samuel Gorden, Allex[r] Bolling, William Eaton & George Nicholas, or aney two of them do meet the Gen[t] appointed by the Vestry of Martins Brandon parish in Order to Run the Dividing line between the s[d] Parishes agreeable to the Act of Assembly passed at the last Session provided the said line does not Interfere with the line formerly Established.

Order'd That John Young be appointed Clerk of Jones Hole Church in the Room of George Williams who is discharg'd from the same.

THEOP'S FEILD, GEORGE SMITH Church Wardens.

Test WILLIAM YARBROUGH Clk vestry.

[162] At a vestry held for Bristol Parish at the Brick Church July the 26th 1763.

Present. Theop[s] Feild sen[r], Sir William Skipwith, George Smith, George Nicholas, William Eaton, Robert Bolling, James Murray, Gent[l].

Order'd That the persons following be appointed to procession the lands in this Parish in their several precincts as followith Viz:

That Daniel Cawl & Daniel Vaughan with the freeholders of their precincts procession from the Notoway Road up as far as Munks Neck Road from the head of Blackwater to the River. That Nathaniel Harrison & Thomas Willson with the freeholders of their precincts Procession from the Puddle Dock to Leutenants Run between the River and the Great Swamp on Munks Neck Road. That William Eaton & John Blick with the freeholders of their Precincts procession from Leutennants Run to the Indian Town Run Including Rohowick. That Starling Thornton & Rob[t] Ruffin with the freeholders of their precincts Procession from the Indian Town Run to the parish line. That Edward Birchett & Drurey Birchett with the freeholders of their Precincts Procession from Between Black Water Swamp & Second Swamp from James Baughs Path down the Parish line between the s[d] Swamps. That Thomas Whitmore & James Cate with the freeholders of their precincts procession from the Parish line between Jones Hole & warwick swamp up to Munks Neck Road. That Nathaniel Rains & Thomas Bonner J[r] with the freeholders of their precincts Procession from warwick swamp to the parish line between Jones Hole Road & Notaway Road. That Joseph Kirkland & William Pirkins with the freeholders of their precincts Procession from Munks Neck Bridge to Rowanty Bridge. That Morris Vaughan & William Browder J^{r} with the freeholders of their precincts Procession from Munks Neck Road up the north side of munks neck to Hatchers Run to the parish line. That Joseph Reeves & Thomas Deavenport with the freeholders of their precincts procession from James Baughs path between Black water & second swamp and Munks Neck Road. That Thomas Daniel J^{r} & Henry Wilkerson with the freeholders of their Precincts Procession from the parish line up the Great Branch of warwick. [163] Order'd That Peter Leath & Richd Garey with the freeholders of their precincts, procession from the Great Branch of warwick, between warwick and second swamp to munks neck road. That Peter Peterson & Henry Batte with the Freeholders of their precincts, Procession from Puddle Dock Run to the Road that Goes by Samuel Jourdans former Plantation and from the Parish line to Notaway Road. That Miles Thweatt & William Thweatt with the freeholders of their precincts Procession from the parish line to the Notaway Road and from the s^{d} Road leading by the s^{d} Samuel Jourdans former Plantation to Black-Water. That Robert Eavins & William Melone with the freeholders of their precincts procession from the County line between Stoney Creek and the Fox Branch up to the parish line. That David Abbernatha & Joshua Worsham with the freeholders of their precincts procession Between the fox branch and munks neck to the parish line. That John Gilliam & Robert Gilliam with the freeholders of their precincts procession from the Puddle dock Run to the City Creek & from the main Road to the River. That Burrill Green & John Stirdevent with the freeholders of their precincts procession from the City Creek to the parish line between the main Road and ye River. That Thom^{s} Evins & James Harrison with the freeholders of their precincts procession the lands on the south side of stoney Creek in this Parish which was taken out of Bath parish to the parish line. That Thomas Jones & Thomas Eagleton with the freeholders of their precincts procession the Lotts in the Towns of Petersburg & Blandford.

Orderd That the several persons afore mentiond do appoint & Advertize the time of processioning the s^{d} lands within their several precincts before the last day of next March and mak

Return of their proceedings as the Law directs and that they take Care to date their several Returns.

Orderd That William Eaton, George Smith Junr & Thomas Bonner or aney two of them do view the most Convenient place for to Erect a Church in this parish and make Report to the vestry.

THEOP'S FEILD, GEORGE SMITH, Church Wardins.

Test WILLIAM YARBROUGH, Clk Vestry.

[164] At a vestry held for Bristol Parish at Mr. Walter Boyds Jany 21st 1764.

Present. The Reverand Mr. William Harrison, The^{o} Feild, George Smith, Saml Gordon, Roger Adkerson, Geo. Nicholas, Wm. Eaton, Alex^{r} Bolling—Gentlemen.

BRISTOL PARISH IN TOBACCO. DR.

To the Reverand Mr. Wm. Harrison,	17,280
To Wm. Yarbrough Clk of the Brick Church,	1,600
To ditto for d^{o} Vestry & Sexton of d^{o},	800
To Jno Young Clk & Sexton of Jones hole Church,	1,600
To Danl Vaughan for keeping Margrett Williams,	1,000
To Wm. Butler for Ann Newhouse,	975
To Phillip Moore for Ann Butterworth,	800
To Starkey Moore for Eliz^{a} Davis,	885
To ditto for Sirus Stuart,	850
To ditto for Ann West 8 Months,	800
To Mary Barrow for Warne,	950
To ditto for Eliz^{a} Brown,	600
To ditto for keeping Mary May 6 Weeks,	100
To John Temple for Willson,	900
To Maj^{r} Cotten,	600
To Eliz^{a} Vaughan,	250
To Mr. John Pride for Running the dividing Line betwixt Brandom and Bristol Parishes,	636
To Co^{lo} The^{o} Bland,	23
To Ge^{o} Nicholass,	32
For the Use of the Parish,	10,431
To the Parish Collector,	2,624
	43,736

BRISTOL PARISH CR.

By 1,562 Tyths @ 28^{l} Tob^{o} p^{r} tythe, ...	43,736

BRISTOL PARISH IN CASH DR.

To Starkey Moore for burying Eliz^{a} Davis, .	£ 1	6		
To Mr. Chas Duncan, ...	4	12	6	
To the Reverand Mr. Wm. Harrisson a Ball^{s} .	0	17		
To Messrs Feild & Call, ...	8	5	8	
To Doctor Jam^{s} Feild for keeping Jean Jones,	6	1	3	
To Wm. Yarbrough for Expences & Trouble For Going to Search the Record for this Parish, ...	0	17	7	
	£ 22			

Ordered that a Receipt from The^{o} Bland To alex^{r} Bolling for Forty two Pounds five shill^{g}, Due from the s^{d} Bolling for the use of Richd Bland, To the Parish for the Year 1751 be Recorded.

Decr 29, 1752 Received of Alex^{r} Bolling £41. 15. 7½ on Account of Bristol Parish for the Use of Col^{o} Richd Bland Rec^{d} p^{r} The^{o} Bland. 9 | 4½ p^{d} in Sundry Ferriges £42. 5.

[165] Ordered That John Clements be Exempted from Paying Parish Levy.

That Mr. John Ruffin be appointed Vestryman In the Room of Mr. Thos Williams Deceased.

Sir Wm. Skipworth by Letter Resigns being a Vestryman of this Parish any Longer.

Nat^{l} Rains appointed Vestryman in the Room of Sir Wm. Skipworth.

Ordered that the Church Wardens apply To Richd Bland (who undertook the addition to the Brick Church and the Church Walls) and acquaint him Unless he will finish the Work according to agreement within three months that the Church Wardens do agree with some Person to finish it agreeable To the said agreement.

The former Church Wardens be appointed for the Ensuing Year.

THEOP'S FEILD, GEORGE SMITH, Church War^{dns}.

Test WILLIAM YARBROUGH Clk Vestry.

1762 BRISTOL PARISH IN ACC'T WITH THEOP'S FEILD & GEORGE SMITH DR.

	l Tob°.
To p^d the Rev^d Mr. Thos Wilkerson his sallery of, .	17,280
To p^d William Yarbrough Clk of the Brick Church, Vestry & sexton, ...	2,400
To p^d George Williams Clk of Jones Hole Church & sexton, ...	1,600
To p^d Daniel Vaughan for Margret Williams, . .	1,000
To William Butler for Ann Newhouse p^d," . .	1,000
To p^d George Currie for Cyrus Stewart, . . .	1,000
To p^d Starkey Moor for Ann Butterworth, . .	800
To p^d Mary Cotten, ...	600
To P^d Richd Tidmus for Eliz^th Vaughan, . . .	250
To p^d Henry Dickson for Eliz^th Davis, . . .	1,000
To p^d Mary Barrow for Warne, ...	1,000
To p^d Thomas Cheves for Eliz^th Brown, . . .	400
To p^d the Prince George Sheriff, ...	284
To p^d Col. The. Bland for clks fees, . . .	322
To p^d George Nicholas for ditto, ...	16
To p^d Mary Wilkerson for 1 Tyth twice listed, .	22
To p^d Benj^a Ferdenan for 1 Tyth twice listed, . .	20
For Collecting 42,840^l Tob° at 6 p^r Cent, . . .	2,570
To 5 Insolvents as p^r Thom^s Bonners acc^t returd @ 28^l p^r Pole, ...	140
To Tob° sold chiefly on C^r to sundry Persons for the use of the Parish of which 9,318 was at | 2^d p^r p^d & 1,987 at 18 | 6 Payable ye 12 of dec^r next,	11,305
	43,008

1762 BRISTOL PARISH. CR.

By 1,530 Tyths @ 28^l Tob° Each 42,840, . . .	42,840
by 5 Tyths p^d & not listed @ d° p^r Thos Bonners acc^t,	140
by 1 Tyth found short in Col. Blands list, . . .	28
	43,008

[166] At a Vestry held for Bristol Parish at Mr. Walter Boyds Decr 1st 1764.

Present. The Reverand Mr. William Harrison, The° Feild,

Sam[l] Gordon, Geo. Nicholas, William Eaton, Roger Atkirson, Geo. Smith, William Poythress, Nat[l] Rains.

BRISTOL PARISH. DR.

To the Reverand Mr. William Harrison,	17,280
To William Yarbrough Clk Brick Church,	1,600
To ditto for Clk Vestry,	400
To ditto for Sexton,	400
To Jn[o] Young Clk Jones Hole Church,	1,200
To Geo. Williams as Sexton for ditto,	400
To Dan[l] Vaughan for keeping Margrett Williams,	1,000
To William Butler for ann Newhouse,	975
To Jn[o] Phillips for Ann Butterworth,	1,000
To Geo. Currie for Cyrus Stuart,	630
To Mary Barrow for Warne,	1,000
To Jacob Denhart for Willson,	400
To Eliz[a] Vaughan,	250
To Thom[s] Chives for Eliz[a] Brown,	600
To Geo. Nicholas for 3 Copys List of Tythables,	48
To The[o] Bland for 2 Copys & ditto,	36
To William Thweatt six tythes twice listed,	168
To Wm. Jones for one tithe Listed which ought not to be,	22
For The use of The Parish,	6,000
To the Collector for Collecting 36,478 @ 6 ℔ C[t],	2,188
To depositum In Collectors hands To be sold,	881
	36,478
By 1,586 Tythes @ 23 ℔ Poll,	36,478

MONEY CLAIMS.

To Gordon & Ramsay ℔ ac[t],	1.	16.	5
To Jam[s] Feild ℔ ditto,	26.	14.	10
To Feilds & Call ℔ ditto,	5.	9.	2

Ordered That The[o] Feild & William Poythress be appointed Church Wardins for the Ensuing year.

Ordered That Jn[o] Banister be appointed a Vestryman In the Room of Jam[s] Murray Dec[d].

[167] Ordered That Thomas Hayes be appointed Sexton for the Brick Church & that he attend accordingly.

THEO. FEILD, GEO. SMITH JR.

a Copy Test WILLIAM YARBROUGH Clk Vest.

1763 BRISTOL PARISH TO GORDEN & RAMSEY DR.

Decr 27th	To 32 Pains of Glass 8 & 10 @ 10^d,	£	1	6	8
	To 7^l of Putty 1/3^d, ...			8	9
		£	1	16	5

1763 BRISTOL PARISH TO FIELDS & CALL DR.

Feb^r	20th	To 7 yards 21 | 1 p^r shoes 5 | 6, ...	£	1	6	6
		1 p^r hoes 5 | 1 Ell oznabrigs 1 | 6			6	6
		1 oz Thread 1 | 3 1 oz Ditto | 7½, ...			1	10½
		6 Ells Dowlas, . . .			16	6
		2 Hankerchiefs for Ann West,			2	6
Sep^r	11	100^d 20^d Nails 1 | 8 500 8^d ditto 4 | 6, ...			6	2
	27	1 m 8^d ditto p^r the Revd William Harrison			9	0
		11¼ y^ds Irish Lin @ 8 | 6, .		4	13	7½
		1 oz Thead for the suples, .			1	0
			£	8	5	8

1763 BRISTOL PARISH TO FIELD & CALL DR.

May	27	To m 8^d Nails p^r the Revd William Harrison omm^t in the last acc^t				
1764		for 1763, ...	£	0	9	0
Jan^r	11	To 5½ yds of Plaids 12^s | 1 oz Thread | 8^d ℔^r note C. W. .			12	8
	27	To 1 oz thred | 8^d 7½ yds of Dowlas 13 | 1½, ...			13	9½
feb^r	11	To 1 Ivry Comb 10^d for Ann West				10
April	4	To 6 Ells ozbrigs 9^s | p^r order to John Williams, ...			9	0

Octor	1	To 8½ yds of sheff 20 | 7½ 4½ yds of Plaid 9s |	1	9	7½
		8½ yds Lin. 21 | 3d 1 oz thread 1 | for Ann West, . . .	1	2	3
	12	To 1 Ell of Lin 2 | for ditto, .		2	0
		To 1 pr womens Hoes 4 | 6 1 pr shoes 5 | 6 for do, . . .		10	0
		£	5	9	2

Erors Excepted pr FIELD & CALL.

[168] 1762 BRISTOL PARISH IN ACC'T WITH THEO. FEILD & GEO. SMITH JR. CHURCHWARDENS OF YE S'D PARISH DR.

To Paid the Reverand Mr. Thos Wilkirson his Sallery of	17,280
To Paid William Yarbrough Clk of the Brick Church, Vestry & sexton, ...	2,400
To Paid Geo. Williams Clk & Sexton of Jones hole his Sallery of	1,600
To Paid Danl Vaughan for Margret Williams, . .	1,000
To Paid William Butler for Ann Newhouse, . .	1,000
To Paid Geo. Currie for Cyrus Stewart, . . .	1,000
To Paid Starkey Moore for Ann Butterworth, . .	800
To Paid Mary Cotten, ...	600
To Paid Richd Titmas for Eliza Vaughan, . . .	250
To Paid Henry Dickson for Eliza Davis, . . .	1,000
To Paid Mary Barrow for Warne, ...	1,000
To Paid Thos Cheves for Eliza Brown, . . .	400
To Paid ye Sherriff of Prince George, . . .	284
To Paid Colo Theo Bland for Clerks fees, . . .	321
To Paid Geo. Nicholas for ditto, ...	16
To Paid Mary Wilkerson one tithe twice listed, .	22
To Paid Benja Fernando 1 tythe twice listed, . .	20
To Collecting 42,840l Tobo @ 6 ℔ Ct of . . .	2,570
To five Insolvants as pr Thos Bonner acct Retd at 28 ℔ Pole, ...	140
For Tobacco sold (Chiefly on Credit) to sundaries Persons for the use of the Parish of wch. 9,318l	

	was at 2^{d} p^{r} p^{d} & 1,987 at 18 | 6 p^{r} C^{t} Payable the 12th Dec. next, ...	11,305
		43,008
1762	By 1,530 Tiths at 28^{l} Tob^{o} Each, ...	42,840
	By 5 Tiths p^{d} & not listed at D^{o} as ℔ Thos Bonners acc^{t}, ...	140
	By one tithe found short. Cast in Col^{o} Bland's list, ...	28
		43,008

D^{o} Twice Recorded by mistake.

[169] 1762 BRISTOL PARISH DR.

			£	s	d
Decem.	7th	To Cash Paid Henry Wilkison by Order of Vestry as p^{r} Rec^{t}, ...	5	16	
	22d	To Cash Paid Fields & Call on ye Acc^{t} of Jno Williams by Ord^{r} of Vestry as p Rec^{t}	3		
		To one bottle Clarrot for the Communion at Jones Hole Church, ...		4	6
		For man and horse to go out with & bring back ye Plate &C. from D^{o}, ...		2	6
1763. Februry	8	To Cash Paid A. Claiborne for a Judgment obt^{d} & secur'd agst Wm. Carpenter p^{r} Rec^{t}, ...		15	
	13	To 2 bottles Clarrot for ye Communion at the brick Church, ...		9	
Mach	29	To Cash Paid Mrs. Taylor as p^{r} her Acc^{t} & Receipt, .		17	
April	1st	To 2 bottles Clarrett for ye Communion at the brick Church one of wch accidently broke, ...		9	

			£	s	d
	17	To 2 D° D° for the Communion at Jones Hole Church,		9	
		To man & horse to go out with & bring back the Plate &C. from D°, ...		2	6
June	5	To 1 bottle Clarrett for the Communion at the brick Church, ...		4	6
	18	To Cash Paid Alex^r Gibbs for 33 Days work due at the Glebe as p^r Rec^t, . .	5	15	6
	26	To one bottle Clarrett for the Communion at Jones hole Church, ...		4	6
		To man & horse to go with & bring back ye Plate &C. twice thro bad weath^r, .		5	
	29	To Paid the P. George Sherriff tickitt of 45^l N^t Tob° @ 2^d, ...		7	6
July	12	To Mr. James Murrys note of hand of this Date in fav^r of ye Parish for, . . .	12	12	8
		To Wm. & Jn° Lanthrops Joynt bond Payable 12th Xber next in fav^r of D°, .	18	7	8
Octob^r	23	To 1 bottle Clarrett for the Communion at ye brick Church, ...		4	6
	24	To Paid Doct^r Jameson Acc^t ag^t the Parish for ann West as p^r Rec^t, . . .	6	19	4½
		To Paid Mr. William Eaton for ye 1st payment to the undertaker of the Parsons Glebe house as ℘ Rec^t, .	100		
	30	To Man & horse to go with & bring the Plate &C. from Jones hole C^h, . . .		2	6

Nov^r^	2	To Paid William Yarbrough by order of Vestry as p^r^ Rec^t^, ...	3	2	9
	13	To 2 bottles Clarritt for ye Communion at Jones hole Church, ...		9	
		To man & horse to go wth and bring back the Plate &C. from D^o^.		2	6
Dec.	16	To Paid Peter Warren the the rever^d^ Mr. Wm. Harrissons order for the Delivery of 2 H^ds^ Shells at the Glebe, ...		17	6
	22d	To p^d^ Mrs. Sarah Tayler Acc^t^ of this date ag^t^ the Parish as p^r^ Rec^t^, ...	1	6	
		To Commissions for selling 11,305^l^ Tob^o^ sold for 96. 0. 8 as p^r^ Contra, . . .	4	16	
		To Commissions for securing & Collecting the nine several fines &C. amounting to 24. 12. 8 as appears on ye Contra side, . . .	1	4	7½
		To ball^a^ Due the Parish (Exclusive of four specialtys amounting To 56. 16. 2. wch are Mr. Wm. Eaton 23. 17. 6, Mr. Richd Bland 5. 6. 0, James Day 15. 0. 0, Mr. Jam^s^ Murray 12. 12. 8,	2	16	3½
			172	2	10½

1762.

Nov. 11 By ball^a^ due ye Parish as p^r^ acc^t^ Rendered in my hand Exclusive of four specialtys w'ch were William Wm Eaton Chas Sullivant R^d^ Bland and Jam^s^ Day amount^g^

	in ye whole (Exclusive of Int^{t}) to 49. 1. 10, ...	£ 28	2	1½
Dec. 22	By Cash of Wm. Carpenter & Chas. Sullivant Penal bill Lawyers fee Therein in Cluded, . . .	4	18	4
	By 3 month 22 Days Int^{r} Due on 4. 18. 4 is, ...		1	5
1763.	By a Judgm^{t} of P. Geo. Court ag^{t} Mr. Jam^{s} Murray as Sherriff for fines Rec^{d} by Peter Peterson his under Sherriff Due the Parish including Cost of suit & att. fee wch is not yet Paid A Claiborne,	12	12	8
June 12	By 1,987^{l} Tob^{o} sold W Lantrope at 18 | 6 ℔ C^{t} Payable as p^{r} his and his Brother Johns bond the 12th Dec. next, ...	18	7	8
July	By 9,318^{l} Tob^{o} sold sundry Persons a great p^{t} C^{r} @ 2^{d}, ...	77	13	
Novr. 3	By Eliz^{a} Crooks Child for a fine,	2	10	
	Carr^{d} forw^{d}, ...	144	5	2½
[170]	Debit bro^{t} Forward, .	£ 172	2	10½
	C^{r} Bro^{t} Forward, . .	144	5	2½
	By Richd Harrison & R^{d} Harrison Junr and Peter Aldridge for Profane swearing 5 | Each, . .		15	
7	By Mary Tuckers fine for a bastard Child Paid by Richd Taylor, .	2	10	
16	By Wm. & Jno Lantrops bond p^{d} 26 Days before Due, . . .	18	7	8
Dec. 22	By Cash p^{r} Nathan^{l} Rains for a fine as p^{r} Judgm^{t} Peter Peterson wherein A Claiborns fee is included, ...	5	15	
	By Cash of Nat^{l} Rains for a fine of 5 | agst Thos Lee & 5 | for a fine agst James Sturdivant, . .		10	
		172	2	10½

By a ball[a] due the Parish Exclusive of y[e] 4 specialtys for 56. 16. 2 Errors Excepted y[e] 22[d] of Dec. 1763 T. Feild Churchwarden, .	2	16	3½

Recorded Test WILLIAM YARBROUGH Clk Vestry.

1763. BRISTOL PARISH IN ACC'T WITH THE'O FEILD & GEO. SMITH JR CHURCHWARDENS OF YE S'D PARISH. DR.

To p[d] the Rever[d] Mr. William Harrison his Sallery of,	17,280
To Wm. Yarbrough p[d] his Sallery as Clk and Sexton of the Brick Church, ...	2,400
To p[d] Jn[o] Young his Sallery as Clk and Sexton of Jones hole Church, ...	1,600
To p[d] Dan[l] Vaughan for Margret Williams, . .	1,000
To p[d] Wm. Butler for Ann Newhouse, . . .	975
To p[d] Phillip Moore for Ann Butterworth, . .	800
To p[d] Starkey Moore for Eliz[a] Davis, . . .	885
To p[d] Ditto Ditto for Cyrus Stewart, . . .	850
To p[d] Ditto Ditto for Ann West, ...	800
To p[d] Mary Barrow for warne, ...	950
To p[d] Ditto Ditto for Mary May, ...	100
To p[d] Col. Theo. Bland, ...	23
To p[d] Mr. Geo. Nicholas, ...	32
To p[d] Mr. Jn[o] Pride for Runing y[e] Parish line, .	636
To p[d] Jn[o] Temple for Willson, ...	900
To p[d] Rich[d] Titmash for Eliz[a] Vaughn, . . .	250
To p[d] Mary Barrow for Eliz[a] Brown, . . .	600
To the Collector for Collecting 43,736[l] Tob[o] @ 6 ℔ C[t],	2,624
To Tob[o] sold at Publick auktion y[e] 10th may & 14 ag[t] 1764 for the use of y[e] Parish of which . .	600
Was Carried for Maj. Cotten an Inhabitant of y[e] Lower Parish.	
On C[r] To Mr. Jn[o] Baird 6,076[l] @ 15 | 1 The[o] Feild 1,526[l] @ 14 | 11 Mr. Ja[s] Murray 792[l] @ 16 | 1 The[o] Feild 1,482[l] @ 14 | . Richard Hanson 1,155 @ 14 | . The hole being as p[r] ac[t] annext 81. 11. 11,	11,031
	44,336

JAN'Y 1764 DITTO CR.

By 1,562 Tythes at 28l Tob° pr Tythe, .	43,736	
By Levy'd for Majr Cotten who I found was and is an inhabitant in ye Lowr Parish,	600	44,336

[171] 1763 BRISTOL PARISH IN ACC'T W'T THE'O FEILD CHURCHWARDEN DR.

			£	s	d
Dec.	25th	To one bottle Clarrett for the Communion at Jones Hole Church, ...		4	6
		To man & horse to go and return wth the Plate twice from Ditto, ...		5	
	31st	To Paid Walter Bateman for glazing & Repairing the Church winds pr Rect, . .		6	7
1764. Jany	1	To one bottle Clarrett for the Communion at ye brick Church, ...		4	6
	4	To Paid the reverd Mr. William Harrison his acct as pr Rect,		17	
march	29	To pd Starkey Moores (order) as pr order of Vestry as pr Rect, ...	1	6	
April	22d	To 3 bottles Clarrett for ye Communion at the brick Church two of Which was accidently broke, ...		13	6
may	8	To pd A. Claiborne a fee for a Judmt agt Peter Peterson as pr Rect, ...		15	
June	2	To pd Wm. Burk for plasterg and wt washing the Glebe as pr Rect, ...	1		
	10	To 2 bottles Clarrett for ye Communion at Jones hole Church,		9	
		To man & horse to go wth and			

			£	s.	d.
		bring back ye Plate &C. from D^{o}, ...		2	6
	17	To 2 bottles Clarrett for the Communion at the brick Church, ...		9	
	22	To P^{d} Doct^{r} James Feild p^{r} order of Vestry as p^{r} Rec^{t}, .	6	1	3
July	11	To p^{d} John Banister his fee for a Judgm^{t} ag^{t} James Day as p^{r} Rec^{t}, ...		15	
	12	To p^{d} Feild & Call p^{r} order of Vestry as p^{r} Rec^{t}, . .	8	5	8
		To p^{d} Chas Duncan ℘ Ditto as p^{r} D^{o}, ...	4	12	6
Octob^{r}	14	To 2 bottles Clar^{t} for ye Communion at at Jones hole Church,		9	
		To man & horse to go with and bring back ye Plate from D^{o},		2	6
	21st	To one bottle Clar^{t} for ye Communion at ye Brick Church,		4	6
	31	To p^{d} Wm. Yarbrough p^{r} ord^{r} of Vestry as p^{r} Rec^{t}, . .		17	7
		To Commissions for Selling 11,031^{l} Tob^{o} 81. 11. 11. as p^{r} Contra, ...	4	1	7
		To D^{o} for securing and Collect^{g} 10 fines amount^{g} as p^{r} Contra to 12^{s}, ...		12	
Dec.	1	For ball^{a} Due ye Parish Exclusive of two specialties amount^{g} to £36. 10. 2 which are Mr. Wm. Eaton 23. 17. 6 & Mr. Jam^{s} Murry Dec^{t} 12. 12. 8,	87	4	7½
			£119	18	9½

1763. Dec. 22		Do C^{r} By Ball^{a} Due ye Parish as p^{r} acc^{t} Cur^{t} Exclusive of four Specialties for 56. 16. 2. wch are Mr. William Eatons 23. 17. 6. Mr.			

		£	s.	d.
1764.	Richd Bland Jr £5. 6. Jams Murry 12. 12. 8 Jams Day £15, -	2	16	3½
may 8	By a fine from Jno Temple for Profane Swearing, - - - -		5	
June 12	By mary Jones fine for a bastard Child pd by Natl Rains, - -	2	10	
	By a fine from Tho. Whitmour for Profaning the Sabath Day, -		5	
July 11	By Cash of & for Mr. Richd Bland Jr note hand, ...	5	6	
augt 11	By Cash & for Jas Days specialty as pr Judgmt, ...	15		
	By Do for Ints from ye 30th Novr 1762 to ye 10th augt 1764, .	1	5	5
	By Do for Cost atte fee 15 | . Clks & Sherriffs 145l Tobo 24 | 2, .	1	19	2
may 10	By Mr. Jno Baird for 6,076l Tobo on 6 months Cr @ 15 | 1, . .	45	15	8
	By Theo Feild for 1,526l Do on Jordons and hoods 14 | 11, . .	11	7	7½
	By Mr. Jams Murry 792l Do his Levys 15 | 1, ...	5	19	6
augt 14	By Theo Feild 1,482l Do at Jordons 14 | ., ...	10	7	5½
	By Richd Hanson for 1,155l Do at Cabin Point 14 | , ...	8	1	8
Nov. 21	By Danl Sturdivants fine pr Natl Rains, ...		5	
	By Jas Sturdivants fine pr Do Do, .		5	
	By Geo. Davis 2 fines pr Do Do, .		10	
	By Tho. Lee's Jr fine pr Do Do, .		5	
	By Henry Delony Gaming fine 5£ By Sarah Rowtons bastard fine 2£ | 10s., ...	7	10	
Dec. 1	By pr Tho Bonner,		5	
		119	18	9½
	By Balla Due ye Parish exclusive of 2 specialtys 36. 10. 2, . . .	87	4	7½

E. Excepted ye 1st Dec. 1764.

[172] 1764 ACC'T OF TRANSFER TOBO. SOLD AT PUBLICK AUCTION FOR YE USE OF BRISTOL PARISH.

may 10th	To Mr. Jn° Baird 6,076[1] on 6 months Credit @ 15 | 1, . .	£ 45	15	8
	To The° Feilds 1,526 of Jordons and hoods Inspectors @ 14 | 11,	11	7	7½
	To Mr. James Murrey 792 his Levys @ 15 | 1, . . .	5	19	6
Aug[t] 14	To The° Feild 1,482 of Jordons Inspectors @ 14 | , . . .	10	7	5½
	To Mr. Rich[d] Hanson 1,155 of Cabin p[t] Tob° Ditto @ 14 | , .	8	1	8
		£ 81	11	11

11,031 of which 10,431 was Levyed for sale and
600 for Maj[r] Cotten an inhabitant of y[e] Low[r] Parish.

11,031

At a vestry held for Bristol Parish at the Glebe Octob[r] 14, 1765.

Present. the Reverand Mr. William Harrison, The° Feild Sen., George Nicholas, William Poythress, John Banister, Jn° Ruffin, Roger Atkirson, Samuel Gordon, Gen[t].

BRISTOL PARISH IN TOBO. DR.

To the Reverand Mr. William Harrison, . . .	17,280
To William Yarbrough Clk of the Brick Church & Vestry, ...	2,000
To Thomas Hayes Sexton of D°, ...	400
To D° D° for Extraordinary Services, . .	200
To John Young Clk Jones Hole, ...	1,200
To Geo. Williams Sexton, ...	400
To Dan[l] Vaughan for Margret Williams, . . .	1,000
To William Butler for Ann Newhouse, . . .	975
To Jn° Phillips for Ann Butterworth, . . .	1,000
To Geo. Currey for Cyrus Stewart, ...	630
To Mary Barrow for Warne, ...	1,000
To Jacob Denhart for John Willson, . . .	1,000

To William Aldridge for Eliz[a] Brown, ...	500
To Geo. Nicholas for 3 Copys List Tithes 16 Each, .	48
To William Yarbrough for washing Church Linnen,	400
	28,033
To the Collectors for Collecting 30,400, ...	1,824
To Depositum in Collectors hands, ...	543
	30,400

CR.

By 1,600 Tithes @ 19[l] Tob[o] ℔ Poll, ...	30,400

[173] MONEY CLAIMS.

To Feilds & Call ℔ Acc[t], ...	£	1	9	4½
To William Harrison ℔ Acc[t], ...		2	2	4
To Ann Lambath Davis ℔ Ac[t], ...		3	18	6
To Th[o] Arbuthnot for a Coffin for Cha[s] Mearns, ...			10	
	£	8	0	2½

Ordered That Theodrick Bland Jun. be appointed Vestryman in the Room of William Eaton who is Removed out of the Parish.

Church wardens to Call Several Parish Debtors to Acc[t] for the ballance due to the Parish and to acc[t] for the same at next Laying the Levy.

William Harrison & Jn[o] Ruffin appointed to See the Glebe house is finish't according to agreement and to agree with Some Person to build a Kitchen 20 by 16 with a Brick Chimney and Good brick floor and to agree with Some Person to wainscoat the two Lower Rooms in the Glebe house four feet high.

William Harrison to Purchase 100 Choice apple trees for the benefit of the Glebe.

John Ruffin & Nat[l] Rains appointed Church wardens the Ensuing year.

THEO. FEILD, WM. POYTHRESS.

Test WILLIAM YARBROUGH Clk Vestry.

At a vestry held at Bristol Glebe Friday July 10th 1766.

Present. Revera[d] William Harrison, John Ruffin, John Banister, The[o] Feild, Theod[k] Bland Jun[r], Rob[t] Bolling, George Nicholas, George Smith J[r], Vestrymen.

Ordered That Christopher Ford be allowed twenty Pounds for additions to the Glebe house as ℔ acc[t] & agreement made with him.

Ordered That Peter Legrand be allowed ten Pounds for Sundry additions to the Glebe house as p[r] acc[t] acc[t] & agreement with Mr. Wm. Eaton one of the Commissioners.

Ordered That Mr. The[o] Feilds acc[t] &C. be Recorded.

Ordered That Theo. Feild do Pay to Christopher Ford by order of Peter Legrand the Sum of one hundred & twenty Pounds the ball[a] of his acc[t] for building the Glebe house which is this Day Received & also to Christopher Ford the Sum of twenty Pound & to Peter Legrand the further Sum of ten Pounds agreeable to the above allowances & for which S[d] Sums the S[d] Feild is to be allowed Interest from this Day till Repaid; & which S[d] Sums of £20 & £10 the Said ford agrees to Except in full of all Demands against the s[d] Parish Either by the S[d] Legrand or Ford.

JOHN RUFFIN Church Warden.

Test WILLIAM YARBROUGH Clk. V[s].

[174] BRISTOL PARISH IN ACC'T WITH THEO. FEILD & WILLIAM POYTHRESS CHURCH WARDENS S'D PARISH DR.

To p[d] y[e] Rever[d] Mr. William Harrison his Sallery of,	17,280
To p[d] Wm. Yarbrough his Sallery as Clk & Clk of Vestry & Sexton of Brick Church, . . .	2,400
To p[d] John Young Clk of Jones hole Church by Geo. Smith Jr., ...	1,200
To p[d] Geo. Williams Sexton of D[o] to Jn[o] Hall by do,	400
To p[d] Dan[l] Vaughan for keeping Margret Williams by T. F., ...	1,000
To p[d] William Butler for keeping ann Newhouse by G. Smith J[r], ...	975
To p[d] Jn[o] Phillips for Eliz[a] Butterworth by Theo. Feild,	1,000

To p^{d} Geo. Currie for keeping Cyrus Stuart ꝑ his order to N. Rains by do, ...	630
To p^{d} Mary Barrow for keeping Eliz^{a} Vaughan by Geo. Smith J^{r}, ...	1,000
To p^{d} Jacob Denheart for keeping Willson by The^{o} Feild, ...	400
To p^{d} R^{d} Titmash for keeping Eliz^{a} Vaughan ꝑ order to Feild & Call, ...	250
To p^{d} Thom^{s} Cheves for keeping Eliz^{a} Brown by Geo. Smith Jr., ...	600
To p^{d} George Nicholas Esqr by The^{o} Feild, . .	48
To p^{d} Col^{o} The^{o} Bland by ditto, ...	36
To p^{d} William Thweatt for 6 Tythes twice Listed by The^{o} Feild, ...	168
To p^{d} William Jones for one Tithe twice Listed by George Smith Jr., ...	22
To p^{d} Jno Hall ye Sherff William Potters att^{a} vs Geo. Smith and The^{o} Feild as Church Wardens of this Parish from Lunb^{g} Cot^{r} as p^{r} Rec^{t}, ...	1,640
To 6 ꝑ C^{t} for Collecting 36,478^{l} Tob^{o} as ꝑ the Parish Acc^{t}, ...	2,188
To Sundrys Insolvents as ꝑ Jno Halls List, . .	968
To p^{d} the Prince George Clk Ticket of, ...	154
To p^{d} the Prince George Sheriff a Ticket of, . .	27
For Tob^{o} taken & sold for ye use of the Parish @ 2d,	4,138
	36,524

1764 Decr. Do. Cr.

By 1,586 Tithes @ 23^{l} ꝑ Poll, ...	36,478
By 2 tithes Rec^{d} by The^{o} Field which was Sr Payton Skipwiths & Thom^{s} Hayes found not incerted in the Clks List of Tithables 23 Each, ...	46
	36,524

Insolvents for Bristol Parish for the year 1764.

William Burk	3
Robert Bonner	14
William Carpender	1
William Davis	2

Edward Epes	1	BRISTOL PARISH CR.
Henry Hobbs	1	Tyths, by Theop[s] Feild found, not
Rob[t] Jesper	1	inserted in Clks list. Sir Payton
Anthoney Jesper	1	Skipwith & Tho[s] Hayes by Each 23. 46.
David Lee	1	
Osbon Ledbetter	1	
Honorious Powell	3	
Fra[s] Poythress	2	
Burrill Reeves	3	
William Spears	1	
John Warpole	1	
William Gibbs	5	
Joseph Kirkland	1	
	42	@ 23 p[r] Pol 968
		46
		922

Errors & omitions Excepted p[r] John Hall Collector.

nov[r] y[e] 11th 1765.

[175] BRISTOL PARISH IN ACC'T WITH THEO. FEILD AS CHURCH WARDEN DR.

1764.					
Dec[r]	11th	To p[d] Mr. Peter Legrand on acc[t] of the Glebe p[r] order of Mr. Wm. Eaton as p[r] Rec[t], ...	£ 60		
1765.					
Jan[y]	6	For man & horse to go with & bring back the Plate from Jones hole Church In very frosty Cold Weather, ...		4	
March	27	To p[d] Mr. Ch[r] Ford on acc[t] of Mr. Legrand p[r] order of Wm. Eaton on acc[t] of the Glebe as ℘ Rec[t], . . .	60		
ap[l]	14	For man & horse to go with and bring back the Plate from Jones hole Ch[ch],		3	
May	26	For do do do		3	
June	15	To p[d] D[r] James Feild by order of Vestry of y[e] 1st Dec. 1764 as p[r] Rec[t],	26	14	10

	To p^d Feild & Call by order of D^o of the 1st Dec. 1764 as p^r Rec^t, .	5 9 2
Octob. 10	To p^d Mess Gordon & Ramsay Levied them by the vestry do. as p^r Rec^t	1 15 5
	as with Great Diffaculty it was I Could Procure Good Claritt at Such times as the Church Wanted induced me where such offered to buy up Sufficient (as I thought) for two years. accordingly I so Provided but thro. (an uncommon Winter) and the Long & Continued Severity of it 9 bottles of Clarrett turn^d sow^r & useless, ...	2 0 6
16	To p^d Walter Boyd acc^t for Clarret had for the Sacramental use of the two Churches between 24th Decr 1764 & 23 may 1765 being Nine bottles as p^r Rec^t, . . .	2 14
30	To Col^o Bolling his acc^t as (p^r Rec^t) of	1 10
		£160 13 11

1764 Decr 1st. Do. Cr.

	By ball^a Due the Parish (as p^r Acc^t Ren^d in my hands Exclusive of 2 Specialties for £36. 10. 2. which is Wm. Eatons £23. 17. 6 & Mr.	
1765.	Ja^s Murrays dec^d for £12. 12. 8,	87 4 7½
March 14	By Cash for Mr. William Eatons Specialty of, ...	23 17 6
	By Int^st due thereon for 3 years & near 3 months, . . .	3 17 4
May 16	By a fine of Ja^s Sturdivants (℘ N. Rains) for profane swearing, .	5
	By the nine Empty bottles wch Contain'd the Clar^t y^t sow^d, . .	3
Novr 11th	By 4,138^l Tob^o Taken & Sold for the use of ye Parish @ 2^d, . .	34 9 8
	Ball^a due from the Parish as the	

above Mr. James Murray Dec[d] Specialty of £12. 12. 8 is Return'd to the Present Church Wardens To The[o] Feild Late Church Warden, . . .	10 16 9½
	160 13 11

Errors and omissions Excepted the 11th nov[r] 1765.

THEO. FEILD.

Test WILLIAM YARBROUGH.

[176] At a Vestry held for Bristol Parish In Blandford Tuesday January 27th 1767.

Present. John Ruffin, Nathan[l] Rains, George Smith J[r], William Poythress, Theodrick Bland J[r], John Banister, George Nicholas Vestrymen.

BRISTOL PARISH IS DR.	lb. Tob.
To the Reverend Mr. William Harrison, ...	17,280
To William Yarbrough Clk of the Brick Church & Vestry, ...	2,000
To Thomas Wright Sexton of the brick Church, .	400
To Ditto for Extraordinary Services, ...	200
To John Young Clk of Jones hole Church, . .	1,200
To George Williams Sexton for do, ...	400
To Daniel Vaughan for keeping Margret Williams,	1,000
To William Butler for keeping Ann Newhouse, .	975
To John Phillips for keeping Ann Butterworth, .	1,000
To George Currie for keeping Cyrus Stewart, . .	630
To Jacob Denheart for keeping John Willson, . .	1,000
To William Aldridge for keeping Eliz[a] Brown, .	500
To George Nicholas for three Copys list Tithables, .	48
To William Yarbrough for Washing the Church Lin[g] the Last year, ...	120
To John Hall for Levying Ex[t] on Mr. Feild a Ch. Warden, ...	36
For the use of the Parish, ...	11,851
	38,640

To the Collector for Collecting 41,106, ...	2,466
	41,106

CR.

By 1,581 Tithes @ 26l Tob° ℔ Poll, ...	41,106

Ordered That Nathaniel Rains & John Ruffin be appointed Church Wardens of this Parish the Ensuing year.

MONEY CLAIMS VIZT.

To Theophilus Feild ℔ acc^t, ...	£ 16	5	10½
To Thomas Egleton ℔ Ditto, ...	4	10	0
To The Reverend Mr. William Harrison for building Kitchen at the Glebe when finished & Receiv'd, ...	35		
	£55	15	10½

That Thomas Bonner be appointed Collector for the Lower Part of the Parish of Bristol that lies in Prince George County and John Jones Junr. for the upper part of the s^d Parish in Dinwiddie County on their Giving Bond & Security as the Law Directs and that they Collect from Every Tithable Person twenty Six Pounds of Tob° for the Parish Levy for the year 1766 and In Case of Refusal or non Payment to Levy the Same by distress and Pay the Parish Creditors as it is Proportion'd.

JOHN RUFFIN & NATH'L RAINS, Church Wardens.

Test WILLIAM YARBROUGH Clk.

[177] At a Vestry held at Blandford for Bristol parish Augt 31st 1767.

Present. The Reverend Mr. William Harrison, John Ruffin, Nathan^l Raines, C. Wardens, The° Feild Senr, Samuel Gordon, Geo. Nicholas, George Smith, Robt Bolling, Gent^m.

Persuant to the orders of the Last Courts held for Prince George & Dinwiddie Counties this Vestry has divided the Parish into Convenient Precincts and appointed the times and Persons for Processioning Every Particular Persons Land within the same as Followeth,

Ordered That the Precincts from the Nottoway Road up as far as munks Neck Road from the head of Black water to the River be processioned gone Round and the Landmarks Renew'd On the First Monday in Nov[r] Next and That Anthony Williams & Dan[l] Vaughan be appointed to See the Same performed and to make & Return to the Vestry an Account of every persons Land they shall procession and of the persons present at the same & what Land in their precincts they shall fail to procession and particular Reason of such failure. That the precincts from the puddle dock to Lieutenants Run between the River & the Great or munks Neck Road be processioned gone Round and the Land marks Renewed on the first Wensday in Nov[r] Next and that Nathan[l] Harrison & William Poythress be appointed to see the same perform'd and to make and Return to the Vestry on Acc[t] of Every Persons Land they shall procession and of the persons present at the same and what Land In their precincts they shall fail to procession & Particular Reason of such failure. That the precincts from Lieutenants Run to the Indian Town Run including Rohowick be procession'd gone Round and the Land marks Renewed on the First friday in Nov[r] Next and that William Eaton and John Blick be appointed to see the same perform'd &C. That the precincts from the Indian Town Run to the Parish Line be processioned gone Round and the Land marks Renewed on the Second monday in Nov[r] Next and that Robert Ruffin and Roger Atkinson be appointed to see the same perform'd &C. That the precincts from between Black water Swamp and Second Swamp from Baughs path to the Parish Line be processioned gone Round and the Land marks Renewed on the Second Wensday in Nov[r] Next, and that Edward Birchett & Drury Birchett be appointed to see the same perform'd &C. That the precincts from the parish Line between Jones hole & Warwick Swamp up to munks Neck Road be processioned gone Round and the Land marks Renewed on the Second Friday in Novem[r] Next and that Thomas Whitmore & James Cate be appointed to see the same perform'd &C. That the precincts from Warwick Swamp to the parish Line between Jones hole Road and Nottoway Road be processioned gone Round & the Land marks Renew'd on the third monday in Nov[r] Next and that James Cureton & Thom[s] Bonner be appointed to see the same perform'd &C. That the precincts from munks Neck bridge to Rowantay Bridge be processioned gone Round and the Land marks Renewed on the third Wensday in Nov[r] Next and that Jo[s] Kirkland & William Perkins be appointed to see the same perform[d] &C. That the precincts from munks Neck Road up the North Side of munks Neck to hatchers Run to the parish Line be processioned gone Round & the Land marks Renew'd on the Third Friday in Nov[r] Next & that Morriss Vaughan and William Browder Jur. be appointed to see the same perform'd &C.

[178] Ordered That the precincts from James Baughs path Between Black water and Second Swamp and munks Neck Road be procession'd gone Round and the Land marks Renewed on the fourth monday in Nov[r] Next and that Jo[s] Reves and William Edwards be appointed to see the same perform'd &C. That the precincts from the Parish Line up the great Branch of Warwick be procession'd gone Round and the Land marks Renewed on the fourth Wensday in Nov[r] Next and that Thomas Daniel Jur & Henry Wilkerson be appointed to see the same perform'd. That the precincts from the Great Branch of Warwick between Second Swamp, to munks Neck Road, be processioned gone Round & the Land marks Renewed on the fourth Friday in Novem[r] Next and that John Wicks & Peter Leath be appointed to see the same perform'd &C. That the precincts from Puddle dock Run to the Road that goes by Samuel Jordans former Plantation and from the Parish Line to the great Road, be procession'd gone Round and the Land marks Renew'd on the first Tuesday in Nov[r] Next and that Thomas Lewis & James Murrey be appointed to see the same perform'd &C. That the precincts from the Parish Line to the Nottoway Road and from the Road Leading by Samuel Jordans former plantation to Black Water be processioned gone Round and the Land marks Renewed on the first thursday in Nov[r] Next & that John Thweatt & John Cureton be appointed to see the same perform'd &C. That the precincts from the County Line between Stony Creek & the fox Branch up to the Parish Line be procession'd gone Round and the Land marks Renew'd on the Second Tuesday in Nov[r] Next and that Robert Eavans and William Melone be appointed to see the same perform'd &C. That the precincts from between

the fox Branch and munks Neck to the Parish Line be procession'd gone Round & the Land marks Renew'd on the Second thursday in Novr Next and that David Abernatha and Bennet Kirby be appointed to see the same perform'd &C. That the precincts from the puddle dock Run to the City Creek and from the main Road to the River be procession'd gone Round & the Land marks Renew'd on the third Tuesday in Novr Next & that John Gilliam and Robert Gilliam be appointed to see the same performed &C. That the precincts from the Parish line between the main Road and the River be processioned gone Round and the Land marks Renew'd on the third thursday in Novr Next and that Burwell Green and John Sturdivant be appointed to see the same perform'd &C. That the Lands on the South Side of Stony Creek in this Parish which was taken out of Bath Parish to the Parish Line be procession'd gone Round and the Land marks Renew'd on the fourth Tuesday in Novr Next & that Thomas Eavans & James Harrison be appointed to see the same perform'd &C. [179] Ordered That the Lots in the towns of petersburg & Blandford be procession'd gone Round and the Land marks Renew'd on the fourth thursday in Novr Next and that Thomas Jones and Peter Jones Jun. be appointed to see the same perform'd &C.

That the several persons afore mentioned do appoint and advertise the time of processioning the Said Lands within their several precincts before the last day of Next March and make Return of their proceedings as the Law directs and that they take Care to date their Several Returns.

That Nathaniel Harrison be appointed a Vestryman in the Room of Alex^r^ Bolling Gen^t^ dect. and that he be acquainted with the same by the Clk.

That the Church Wardens of this parish do apply to the Church wardens of Dale parish to know what has become of the money the Glebe Lands sold for by Vertue of an act of assembly made in the year 1757 & to Receive the proportion due to this Parish and to make Report to the Vestry.

JOHN RUFFIN, N. RAINES C. Wardens.

Test WILLIAM YARBROUGH Clk. Vestry.

At a Vestry held for Bristol Parish, Blandford Nov[r] 13th day 1767.

Present. The Reverend Mr. William Harrison, The[o] Feild Sen[r], George Smith, The[o] Bland, George Nicholas, Nathan[l] Harrison, Sam[l] Gordon, Col[o] John Ruffin, Gent'men.

BRISTOL PARISH DR.

To the Reverend Mr. William Harrison,	17,280
To William Yarbrough Clk Church & Vestry,	2,000
To ditto for washing the Church Linnen,	120
To Thomas Wright Sexton for the Brick Church,	400
To John Young Clk Jones hole Church,	1,200
To Geo. Williams Sexton of ditto,	400
To Dan[l] Vaughan for keeping Margret Williams,	1,000
To William Butler for keeping Ann Newhouse,	975
To Wm. Aldrige for keeping Ann Butterworth,	1,000
To Geo Currie for keeping Cyrus Stuart,	630
To Jacob Denheart for keeping John Willson,	1,000
To William Aldridge for keeping Eliz[a] Brown,	500
To ditto for ditto for Extraordinary Trouble,	1,000
To William Scoggin for assistance in maintaining him,	500
To Benj[a] Johnston Constable for Removing Eliner Morgan Alce McDonald and her daughter Margret poor persons, to the Parish & County of Henrico 31 miles p[r] acc[t],	186
To ditto for ferriges & accomodations 7 | 6,	45
To Morgan Council for keeping Mary Tammond 6 months,	500
Debit Carried Over,.	28,736
	℔ Tob[o]
[180] Amount of Debit Bro[t] Over,	28,736
To Col[o] The[o] Bland for Copy List Tithes,	36
To George Nicholas for 3 ditto ditto,	48
	28,820
To 6 ℔[r] C[t] for Collecting 50,010[l] Tob[o],	3,000
To Tob[o] to be Sold for the use of the Parish	18,190
	50,010

By 807 Tithes in Dinwiddie County }
By 860 ditto in Prince George ditto }

1,667 Tithes @ 30[l] is	50,010

MONEY CLAIMS.

	£	s	d
To Starkey Moore, ...	£1	14	
To Alice Brown, ...		15	
To Wm. Stainback, ...		4	
To The° Feild, ...	4	19	8
	£7	12	8

Nathaniel Raines & Rob[t] Bolling appointed Church Wardens for the Ensuing Year.

JOHN RUFFIN, C. Warden.

Test WILLIAM YARBROUGH, Clk. V.

1765 THE PARISH OF BRISTOL IN ACC'T WITH JOHN RUFFIN CH. WARDEN DR.

	£	s	d
1766.			
To paid Thomas Egleton in part of his Acc[t], .	£ 2	10	
To p[d] Geo. Nicholas for 48[l] Tob° @ 2[d], . .		8	
To p[d] Old Jones for Removing a woman from this parish ℘ order, ...		5	
To sending Elements to both Churches at Xmas,		5	
To ditto ditto at Easter, ...		5	
To ditto ditto at whitsuntide, ...		5	
To ditto ditto in Sep[r], ...		5	
To ditto ditto at Xmas, ...		5	
1767 January 27th.			
To p[d] Mr. N. Raines C. W. in full of his Acc[t], .		4	
To p[d] Field & Call in full, ...	2	2	10½
To p[d] Th° Abuthnot for a Coffin, ...		10	
To sending Elements to both Churches at Easter,		5	
To ditto at Whitsuntide, ...		5	
To Thomas Bage for 10 Bottles Clar[t] @ 5 | , .	2	10	
	£10	4	10½
Ball[a] Due to the Parish, ...		17	9½
	£11	2	8

1796 Sepr 12. Cr.

By John Jones Jr. Collector for Last years depositum 543^{l} Tob^{o} 18 | , ...	£ 4	17	8
By Cooks fine for a Bastard, ...	2	10	
By William Meanly for swearing, . . .		5	
1767 By John Donlavies fine for Selling by unlawfull measure, ...	1		
By Hansalls fine for a Bastard, ...	2	10	
	£11	2	8

[181] At a vestry held at Blandford for Bristol Parish Feby 20th day 1768.

Present. The Reverend Mr. William Harrison, Col^{o} John Ruffin, John Banister, Theo^{k} Bland Junr, Nathan^{l} Raines, Col^{o} Robt Bolling, George Nicholas, Theo. Feild Senr, Nathan^{l} Harrison, Samuell Gordon, Gentlemen.

Mr. Nathan^{l} Harrison appeared in Vestry and Resign'd being Vestryman.

Mr. William Call appointed a Vestryman in the Room of Nathaniel Harrison who has resign'd, and that he be acquainted of the same by the Clerk.

Thomas Bonner be appointed Collector for the part of Bristol Parish that lies in Prince George County, and Millington Smith for the upper part of the said Parish in Dinwiddie County, on their giving bond and security as the Law directs.

Col^{o} John Ruffin & William Call be appointed to view the work done at the glebe by Mr. William Harrison.

That John Jones Junr (late Parish Collector having failed to settle his accounts of his last years Collection and to pay the Tobacco according to his bond given) be applyed to by the Church Wardens and on Refusial, his bond to be prosecuted.

To Morgan Council for nursing finding a Coffin and Burying Mary Tammons since the laying of the Levy, £3. 0. 6.

That Edmund Conway be appointed sexton for the Brick Church and that he attend accordingly.

Nathan'l Raines, Robt. Bolling, C. Wardens.

a Copy Test William Yarbrough Clk Vestry.

[182] At a vestry held at Blandford for Bristol Parish Octob^{r} 6th 1768.

Present. The Reverend William Harrison, Robert Bolling C. W., George Smith Junr, Theophilus Feild Senr, Roger Atkinson, John Ruffin Senr, William Call J^{r}, George Nicholas, Vestrymen.

BRISTOL PARISH DR.	ls N^{t} Tob^{o}
To the Reverend William Harrison, ...	17,280
To William Yarbrough Clk Brick Church & Vestry,	2,000
To ditto for washing Church Linnen, ...	120
To Edmund Conway Sexton for the Brick Church, .	400
To ditto for Extraordinary Services, ...	100
To John Young Clk Jones Hole Church, ...	1,600
To George Williams Sexton for ditto, ...	400
To Daniel Vaughan for keeping Marg^{t} Williams, .	1,000
To William Butler for keeping Ann Newhouse, .	975
To Wm. Aldridge for Ann Butterworth, ...	1,000
To George Currie for Cyrus Stewart, ...	630
To Jacob Denheart for John Willson, ...	1,000
To Wm. Aldridge for Elizabth Brown, ...	1,000
To William Seoggin for assistance in maintain^{g} him,	500
To Jno Butler for maintain^{g} his son Lewis Butler, .	600
To George Nicholas Clk Dinwid^{ie} for 2 Cop. List Tithes, ...	32
To sherriff for 13 Insolvents return'd @ 30l each, .	390
To Miles Williams 1 Levy twice Charg'd Last Year,	30
To The Collector for Collecting 40,725l. @ 6 p^{r} C^{t}, .	2,443
For the use of the Parish, ...	9,225
	40,725
By 785 Tithes in Dinw^{ie} } By 844 d^{o} P. George } 1629 @ 25^{l} Tob^{o} p^{r} poll, .	40,725

MONEY CLAIMS TO WITT.

	£	s	d
To Feild & Call, ...	£1	12	6
To John Hall for sum^{g} 3 witn^{ss} ag^{t} Brand^{m} Parish 27l. Tob^{o}, ...		4	6
To Neil Buckannon j^{r} for wine, ...	2	2	0
	£3	19	0

John Ruffin return'd his acc[t] of his Church Wardenship Ball[a] 3 | 3 as appears by Acc[t] Paid To Rob[t] Bolling present Church Warden.

George Nicholas & William Call appointed Church Wardens for the Ensuing year.

George Smith j[r] appointed Collector in that part of Bristol Parish that liės in Dinwiddie and Tho. Bonner in that part that Lies in Prince George and to give bond and security for their due Collect[n].

ROBT. BOLLING C. Warden.

Test WM. YARBROUGH Clk Vestry.

[183] THE PARISH OF BRISTOL IN ACC'T WITH JOHN RUFFIN DR.

1766.				
Sep[r] 12th	To paid Geo. Nicholas for 481 Tob[o] @ 2[d], ...	£ 0	8	0
	To p[d] Thomas Egleton in p[t] of his Acc[t], ...	2	10	0
	To p[d] Old Jones for removing a woman out of this parish p[r] order, ...	0	5	0
	To Sending Elements to both Churches at Christmass, . .	0	5	0
	To ditto at Easter, . . .	0	5	0
	To ditto at whitsuntide, . .	0	5	0
	To ditto in Septem[r] or Octob, .	0	5	0
1767.	To ditto at Christmass, . .	0	5	0
Jan[y] 27	To p[d] Wm. Raines in full of his Acc[t], ...	0	4	0
	To p[d] Mess[rs] Feild & Call in full, .	2	2	10¾
	To p[d] Tho. Arbuthnot for a Coffin,	0	10	0
	To Send[g] Elem[ts] to both Churches at Easter, ...	0	5	0
	To ditto at whitsuntide, . .	0	5	0
	To Tho. Bage for 10 Bottles Clarrett	2	10	0
		10	4	10¾
	To Ball[a] as ℘ acc[t] ren[d] to vestry, .		17	9¼
		11	2	8

CR.

By last years deposition 343l Tob° @ 18 | .	£ 4	17	8
By Jn° Donlavy for selling Corn by unlawfull measure, ...	1	0	0
By Cooks fine for a Bastard, ...	2	10	0
By Mary Hansells fine for d°, . . .	2	10	0
By Wm. Meanly for swearing, . . .	0	5	0
	11	2	8
1768. To paid Bolling Clarke p^r acc^t, .		14	6
Octob. 6 To Cash p^d Col° Bolling C. Warden in full, ...		3	3
	£ 0	17	9
By Ball^a as p^r Contra, ...	£ 0	17	9¼

Octob^r 6th 1768. E. E. ℘. JOHN RUFFIN.
a Copy Test

[184] At a Vestry held at Blandford for Bristol Parish June 10th day 1769.

Present. The Reverend William Harrison, Col° John Ruffin, Doctor The° Bland, George Nicholass, Samuel Gordon, William Call, George Smith, Roger Atkirson, Nathan^l Raines, Vestrymen.

Ordered That there be a new Church built in the upper part of this Parish that Lies in dinwiddie County to be Sixty Feet Long and 28 feet wide and that, The Reverend William Harrison, Capt George Smith, Capt Nathaniel Raines, Capt Joseph Tucker & Capt Bennett Kirby or any three of them be appointed to view, & report to the next Vestry the most Convenient place for building the said Church, and that they prepare a Plan of the Same and give Publick notice for undertakers to appear at the next Vestry in order to undertake the building the Same.

That Mr. Theophilus Feild Junr be appointed a Vestryman in the room of Capt William Poythress dec^d and that he be serv'd with a Copy of the Same by the Clerk.

That Capt George Smith (Collector) do pay Mary Cook 800^l Tobacco out of the parish Tobacco that he has in his hands.

That the Church wardens do agree with Some Person to Rail in the oak Tree at the brick Church and to fix Convenient benches for the same, also to rail in a place at Jones Hole Church & Fix the Same.

John Roberts agrees to board ann Hanks at Ten Shillings ℔ month to be paid at laying the next parish Levy.

[185] Ordered That the Church wardens (at the Selling the Parish Tobacco) do give Credit till october next on taking bond & Security.

GEO. NICHOLAS, WILLIAM CALL, Church Wardens.

Test WILLIAM YARBROUGH, Clk Vestry.

At a Vestry held at Blandford for Bristol Parish October 14th Day 1769.

Present. The Reverend William Harrison, Mr. Geo. Nicholass, Mr. William Call, Chu. W., Col° John Ruffin, Col° Robert Bolling, Capt Geo. Smith, Doct^r The° Bland, Capt The° Field, Vestrymen.

BRISTOL PARISH DR.	lb. Tob°	
To The Reverend William Harrison, .	17,280	
To William Yarbrough Clk Church & Vestry, ...	2,000	
To do do for washing Church Linn., ...	120	
To John Young Clk Jones Hole Church,	1,600	
To Edmund Conway Sexton Brick Church,	400	
To d° for extraordinary services, . .	200	
To Geo. Williams Sexton of Jones Hole Ch.	400	
To Danl Vaughan for keeping Marg^t Williams, ...	1,000	
To William Butler for Ann Newhouse, .	975	
To William Aldridge for Ann Butterworth,	1,000	
		24,975
To Geo. Curry for Cyrus Stewart, . .	630	
To William Aldridge for Eliz^a Brown, .	350	
To William Scoggin for assistance in maintaining him, ...	500	
To John Butler for his Son Lewis, . .	600	

To Geo. Nicholass for 2 Copys List Tythes,	32	
To John Browder for Ann Hauks, . .	400	
To John Roberts for d°, ...	100	
To Nathan[l] Parriot for d°, ...	322	
To do. for burying besides her Clothes & beding, ...	40	
		2,974
Amo[t] Carried over, ...		27,949
[186] Amo[t] Bro[t] over, ...		27,949
To Thomas Bonner for y[e] use of ann Phillips 1770, ...	300	
To Cap[t] Wm. Call for use of mary Lantrops Children d°, ...	400	
To martins Brandom Parish for Judg[t] Cer[t] &c. .	920	
To John Hall assignee of Jo[s] Reves for atten. as a witness against Brandomn Parish, .	225	
To Thom[s] Bonner for atten. as a witness ag[t] d°,	250	
		2,095
To Jacob Denheart for John Willson, . . .		1,000
		31,044
To Cap[t] Geo. Smith for keeping & burying Mary Coocke, ...		1,000
		32,044
To the Collector for Collecting 34,629 l Tob°,	2,077	
To Ballance due The Parish, ...	508	
		2,585
		34,629
By 805 Tythes in Dinwiddie. By 844 d° in Prince Geo.		
1,649 @ 21 l ℔ Poll, ...		34,629

Ordered That Millington Smith be appointed Collector in Dinwiddie County and Tho[s] Bonner be appointed Collector in Prince George and that they give bond & security according to Law.

That William Call & Geo Nicholass appointed Church wardens for the ensuing year.

MONEY CLAIMS.

To The° Fied Ex[r] in full of his acc[t],	4	13	7½
To Field & Call,	5	8	5½
To Geo. Williams,	0	5	0

Ordered That Geo. Smith late Parish Collector do Pay the Ball[e] due from him & Thomas Bonner the same To Wm. Call Church Warden.

Richard Taylor appointed a vestryman in the room of The° Feild gent. dec'd, and that the Clerk furnish him with a Copy of this order.

[187] Ordered That The Church Wardens do settle with Col° Richard Bland for Building the addition to the Brick Church and pay the Ball[e] to Col° The° Bland ℔ his order.

The gentlemen appointed to view the Place for building a new Church, having failed to make report agreeable to the former order of Vestry Ordered that no further proceedings be had therein.

GEO. NICHOLASS, WILL'M CALL C. Wardens.

Test WILL. YARBROUGH Clk Vestry.

At a Vestry held at Blandford for Bristol Parish April 23d day 1770.

Present. The Reverend William Harrison, Nathaniel Raines & William Call, Church Wardens, John Banister, George Nicholas, Robert Bolling, George Smith, Theophilus Feild & Richard Taylor Vestrymen.

It appearing to the Vestry that an acre of Land purchased by the Parish of John Lowe, in the year of our Lord one Thousand Seven Hundread and Thirty Five is not entirely inclued within the Church Wall and it being necessary that the Boundaries thereof should be ascertained, it is therefore ordered that the Church wardens do lay of the Surplus of the Said acre from the west side of the wall sqare with the same, giving Lewis Parham the present proprietor of the adjoining land notice of the time when the Said Line is to be run, in addition to the above order the quantity of Land included in Col° Poythresses Burying Place is to be laid off over and above the Said acre according to the agreement of the Vestry with the Said Poythress in the year of our Lord One Thousand Seven Hundread and Fifty Four.

[188] Ordered That Col^{o} Theodorick Bland have Credit for the Sum of One Hundread and Twenty Pounds one Shilling and five Pence farthing it being the ballance due to Col^{o} Richd Bland for building the addition to the Brick Church and for building a wall Round the Church Yard he having undertaken to Repair and fix the gates properly before the first day of october next.

The gent. appointed to view the Chimney built to the Kitchen at the glebe of this Parish this day Reported that the Same is insufficient, ordered that the Said Chimney be Rebuilt and that the undertaker be paid for the Same when Sufficiently done and Received.

That a Petition be preferr'd to the next assembly to dispose of the Glebe Land belonging to this Parish & that the Money arising from the Sale of the Said Lands be Laid out on the purchase of a new Glebe.

Col^{o} Robert Bolling appeared in Vestry and resign'd being a Vestryman. It is ordered that Capt Peter Jones be appointed a Vestryman in his Room and be furnish'd with a Copy of the Same by the Clerk.

GEO. NICHOLAS, WM. CALL, Ch. Wardens.

Test WILLIAM YARBROUGH Clk Vestry.

[189] At a Vestry held at Blandford for Bristol Parish September 11th Day 1770.

Present. The Reverend William Harrison, Geo. Nicholas William Call Church Wardens, George Smith, Richard Taylor, Roger Atkerson, Nathan^{l} Raines, The^{o} Bland Jun. Theodrick Field, Vestrymen.

Orderd That the Glebe land belonging to this Parish (agreeable to the act of assembly) be sold on Thursday the 15th day of November next to the highest bidder and that 12 months Credit be given for one half the purchase money and 12 months after for the other half and on failure of the payments on the days appointed to Carry Interest from from the date of the Bonds and that it be advertised in the Virginia Gazette till the day of Sale.

That the sum of Thirty Pounds ꝑ^{r} Annum be Paid to the

Rev[d] Will[m] Harrison to Commence from the first Day of dec[r] next as an Equivolent for a Glebe untill a Sufficient one be got for the Use of the Parish.

That an Addition be built to the Jones Hole Church to be 30 by 24 to be of the Same Pitch of the Old Church & that the Church Wardens prepare a plann of the same & that George Smith Jun[r] Natha[l] Raines & Will[m] Call or any two of them do Advertize the letting the Building the Same one one third to be paid at the Raising & the other two Thirds to Paid on the Receiving the Same to be Compleated in twelve Months.

Oct[r] 22 1770 At a Vestry held at Blandford for Bristoll Parish.

Present. The Rev'd Will[m] Harrison, Will[m] Call, Churchwarden, Col[o] Jn[o] Ruffen, Col[o] John Banister, The[o] Feild, Georg Smith, Mr. Rich[d] Taylor, Nathaniel Raines, Vestremen.

BRISTOLL PARISH DR.	lb. of Tob[o]
To the Rev[d] Will[m] Harrison,	17,280
To Will[m] Yarbrough Clk Church & Vestry,	2,000
To d[o] for Washing Church Linnen,	120
Carried Over,	19,400

	lb. of Tob[o]
[190] Amount brought over,	19,400
To John Young Clk of Jones Church,	1,600
To Edmund Conway Sexton of Brick Church,	400
To d[o] for Extraordinary Services,	200
To Georg Williams Sexton Jones hole Ch.,	400
To Daniel Vaughan keeping Mar[t] Williams,	1,000
To Will[m] Butler for Ann Newhouse,	975
To Georg Currie for Cyrus Stewart,	630
To Will[m] Aldridge for Ann Butterworth,	1,000
To Rich[d] Beggins for John Willson,	1,000
To Will[m] Scogin to Assist him in Man[t],	500
To John Butler to Maintaine son Lewis,	600
To Geo. Nicholass Clk D[n] Court for Copp. list Tithes,	48
To Will[m] Call for the use Ann Fhipps,	600
To d[o] for use Mary Lantropes Children,	200

To Mr. Nathaniel Raines late Church Warden for Will[m] Edwards Acc[t] as a Witness for Bristoll Parish, ...	250
To Col[o] The[k] Bland Clk Court for Tickets, . .	230
To Cap[t] Nathaniel Raines ℔[r] Acc[t], ...	115
To Jo[s] Kirkland for 1 tith twice listed, . . .	21
	29,169
To The Church wardens to be Sold for Cash payable in Octo. 1771 for the use of the Parish, . .	7,931
To Collection 6 ℔ C[t] off 39,468, ...	2,368
	39,468
By 922 Tithes in Prince George Cot[y]	
By 872 do in Dinwiddie	
1,794 @ 22 l Tob[o] ℔ Poll, ...	39,468

The former Church wardens to be Continued the Ensuing Year.

Order'd That Millington Smith be appointed Collector for Dinwiddie County & Thomas Bonner for Prince George County, on Giving Bond & Security according to Law.

Col[o] The[o] Bland a former Church warden Returned his Acc[t] including Col[o] Rich[d] Blands Acc[t] for repairing the Church &c. by which there appears to be a Ballance (due to the Parish) of Twenty one Pounds Ten Shillings.

[191] That Wm. Call (Church Warden) do furnish ornaments for Jones Hole Church.

WM. CALL Ch. Warden.

Test WM. YARBROUGH. Clk Vestry.

At a Vestry held at Blandford for Bristol Parish March [th] 21, 1771.

Present. The Reverend William Harrison, William Call & John Banister Church Warden's, Theophilus Field, George Smith, Theodrick Bland J[r], Richard Taylor, Nath[l] Raines, Peter Jones, Gentlemen.

Ordered That Robert Armistead be appointed Clerk of the Vestry in the Room of William Yarbrough Dec[d].

Ordered That John Banister be Appointed Church Warden for the Rest of the Year, in the Place of George Nicholas Dec[d].

Ordered That Robert Bolling be Appointed a Vestryman, in the Place of John Ruffin Remov'd, & Thomas Jones in the Place of George Nicholas Dec[d], & that the Above Gentlemen be Furnished with A Copy of the Same by the Clerk.

Agreable to the Sale made on the 15 of Nov[m] 1770, of the Glebe Lands the Vestry have this Day Executed a Deed to William Brown the Purchacer Thereof, for the Same, and Have Recieved Bonds for the Consideration, which Sum's when they Become Due, the Church Warden's for The time being are by an order of the Vestry Impower'd to Recieve in behalf of the Parish,

WILLIAM CALL, JOHN BANISTER, Church Warden's.

Test ROBERT ARISMTEAD Clerk Vestry.

[192] At A Vestry held at Blandford for Bristol Parish Nov[r] 21 1771.

Present. The Reverend William Harrison, William Call, John Banister Church Wardens, George Smith, Robert Bolling, Theop[us] Field, Roger Atkerson, Richard Taylor, Peter Jones, Nath[l] Raines, Thomas Jones, Gentlemen.

BRISTOL PARISH DR.	Lb[s] of Neat Tob[o].
To the Reverend William Harrison, . . .	17,280
To Robert Armistead Clerk Brick Church & Vestry,	2,000
To John Young CLK of Jones Hole Church, . .	1,600
To Edmond Conway Sexton Brick Church, . .	400
To D[o] for Extrodinary Service, ...	200
To George William's Sexton of Jones Hole, . .	400
To Ann Vaughan for Keeping Margaret William's, .	1,000
To William Aldridge for Ann Butterworth, . .	1,000
To Theo[k] Munford for Cyrus Stewart, . . .	630
To Rich[d] Beggin's for John Wilson Dead, . .	800
To William Scoggin to Assist him in his Maintanance,	500
To D[o] for to enable him to Build A house, . .	500
To William Call for the Use of Ann Phillips, . .	800
To Thomas Ruffin CLK, Court of Dinwiddie for Copy List Tithes, ...	32

To Theo^{k} Bland for D^{o}, ...		36
To Henry Spears of One Levy Twice Listed, . .		22
To Robt Armistead for Extra. Service's, . . .		400
To Daniel Camble for Board of Robt Elder 14 Weeks @ 5 | p^{r} Week £3. 10 Paid in Vestry.		
To Millinton Smith as p^{r} Acct, ...		17
To Thomas Bonner as p^{r} D^{o}		135
To William Butler for Burying Ann Newhouse, ...	1 2 6	
To John Butler for Burying Son Lewis, .	12 6	
To Robt Tucker for a Coffin for Lewis Butler, ...	15	
To the Church Wardens to be Sold for Cash for the Use of the Parish, . .		7,000
		34,752
To the Revd William Harrison for Building A house at the Harricane Church, .	10 10	
	£13	

Wm. Call Late Church Warden, Returned his Acct. which Was Recieved & Ordered to be Recorded. Ballance Due to the Parish £18. 12. 8. as ℘^{r} Acc^{t}.

[193] Ordered, That George William's be Appointed CLK of Jones Hole Church in the Room of John Young Dec^{d} And that he Attend Accordingly.

	Lb^{s} Tob^{o}.
Brought Over, ...	34,752
By 806 Tithes in Dinwiddie.	
By 946 D^{o} Prince George.	
1,752 Tithes @ 21 Lb^{s} is 36,792.	
To 6 ℘^{r} C^{t} for Collecting, ...	2,095
	Lb^{s} 36,847

Ordered. That John Banister & Theo^{us} Field Gent^{n} be Appointed Church Warden's the Ensueing Year.

Ordered, That the Church Wardens Recieve from Every Titheable Person 21 Lb^{s} of Neat Tobacco Per pol, & in Case of Non Payment or Refusal to Levy the Same by Distress.

Ordered, That John Thweat be Appointed a Vestryman in the Place of Samuel Gorden Gen^t Dec^d & That the Above Gentlemen be Furnished with a Copy of the Same by the Clerk.

Ordered, That the Church Warden's furnish a Regester Book For the Use of the Church & That they find a book for the Use of the Desk.

Ordered, That R. Armistead fix the Gates in a Proper Manner at the Church, & bring in his Acc^t to the Church Warden's.

BRISTOL PARISH IN ACC'T WITH MR. WILLIAM CALL, CHURCH WARDEN FOR 1769, 1770 & 1771.

1769.	DR.	£.	s.	d.
Feby 12	To Cash Paid Theop^s Field, ...	29	10	4
July 24	To D^o To Field's & Call, ...	1	12	6
	To Paid Patt Bird for attending Edmond Browder & his Wife, Poor people of this Parish, on Sufferance & ordered by Robert Bolling Esqr late Church Warden, & Doctor James Field who attended the S^d Browder was Called upon by Robt Bolling Esqr & my Self, who said, They Desirved 40 | , . .	2		
Augt 4	To Henry Wilkerson for Corn & Meat, To Mary Lanthroph, ...	1	11	6
Sepr 27	To Mary Lanthroph Half Barrel of Corn,		5	
Octr 14	To D^o D^o		5	
Decr 6	To Theop^s Field ℔^{r} Order of Vestry, .	4	13	7
	To Field & Call ℔^{r} D^o, ...	4	18	5½
23	To Robert Row for a Coffin for Obediah Hamblet Ordered by G. Nicholas, C. W,		10	
1770.				
April 9	To Thomas Bage his Acc^t for Glazing Church Windows, Paid Col^o Bolling,		8	6
June 2	To Cash to Richd Lamb, for 4 Bottles of Wine for ye Church, ...		12	
	To Paid Niel Buchanan his Acc^t Again the Revd W. Harrison For Wine for the Use of the Church ℔^{r} Direction of the Vestry, ...	2	8	

		£	S.	D.
	To Henry Lockead, for 4 Bottles Wine November 1769,		12	
	To D^{o} 4 D^{o} Decr 1769,		12	
	To D^{o} 4 D^{o} Apr^{l} 1770,		12	
Octr 22	To John Christian for Burying Lucy Clark by Order of Vestry,	1	13	7½
	To George William's so much allow'd him for Extra Services,		5	
Novr 1	To Edmond Conway by Order of Vestry,	1		
	Carried Over,	£53	9	6

[194]

		£.	S.	D.
	Brought Over,	53	9	6
1771.				
July 30	To Cash Paid Peter Willis, in Part for the Addition to the Church,	5		
	To Errow in Cred^{t} William Browder's 50 | which he Said was Paid George Nicholas, but Never has been Paid into my hands, I have his Note,	2	10	
	To Mary Barrow for takeing Care of Mary Hatfield,	6		
Nov^{r}	To 4 Bottles of Wine for the Church,		12	
	To The Rev^{d} Mr. Harrison so much Allow'd him in Lieu of A Glebe,	30		
	To a Grave Diger for Edmond Browder 2 | 6,		2	6
	Sundrys to his Widows Viz^{t} 2 Quarts of Rum 2 | 6 ¼^{lb} Tea 1 | 6 1½ ℔^{r} rum,		5	
		£97	19	

[195]

CONTRA CRD'T.

			£	S	D
1769.					
Jan^{y}	11	By John Jones Collecter for John Ruffin Senr,	20		
Feb^{y}	6	By Fields & Call for John Ruffin,	9	4	11
Omitted y^{e}	4	By Thomas Bonner,	1	3	

			£	s	d
July & Oct^r		By D^o Rec^d of himself Thomas Harris & Walter Peter for Tob^o Sold Them, ...	17	11	9
1770		By Cash Rec^d of Nathl Raines a fine for Some Disorderly Person's Swearing, ...		5	
May	3	By Cash of Robt Ruffin for his Dues when Col^o Ruffin was C. W., .	11	10	1½
July	13	By D^o Rec^d of Richd Booker A fine of Some Person Sold Oats by false measure at ye Bridge, ...	1		
Oct^r	22	By John Wicks, for Part of Amey Hills fine for a Bastard Child, .	1	10	
Nov^r		By Capt George Noble for Tob^o Sold him Payable in Octr 1769, . .	6	16	5
		By Intrest Received, ...		7	4
		By Edmond Ruffin for D^o Sold Payable in Octr 1769, ...	11	5	
		By Intrest Rec^d on D^o, ...		11	3
1771		By Willm Browder a fine for Eliz^h Williams Had a Bastard Child, .	2	10	
Aug^t	22	By Cash Rec^d of Thomas Bonner for Ballance Due of his Acc^t for 1769,		4	1
		By D^o of D^o for 1,039^{lb} of Tob^o unacounted for, for 1771 @ 17 | 2, .	8	18	11
		By John Wicks for the Remainder Part of Amey Hills fine, . . .	1		
		By 1,581^{lbs} Tob^o Sold Edward Brisbane for the use of the Parish @ 16 | 9, ...	13	4	6¾
		By 995^{lbs} D^o To Field & Call @ 17 | 2,	8	10	9¾
		By my Order on Capt George Smith to William Parson's For Railing in the Oak at the Church, . . .	17		
		By my D^o in favour of Peter Willis, Part of his first Payment For the Addition to the Outward Church,	15		
		By Cash of Capt George Smith,		1	3

By D° of Richard Taylor for Millington Smith, ...		5		
		152	13	4½
D[r] Carried up, ...	£ 97 19			
To Wm. Parsons for Railing in the Oak & benches a Round the Church, ...	17			
To Peter Willis Part of his first Payment for Building y[e] Addition to the Church, ...	15			
To Daniel Camble for keeping of R° Elder, ...	3 10	133	9	0
Balance Due the Parish from Mr. William Call,		£19	4	4½

[196–197] BRISTOL PARISH IN ACC'T WITH THOMAS BONNER COLLECTOR FOR 1769.

To Paid The Reverend Mr. William Harison, . .	5,000
To Wm. Yarbrough, ...	2,120
To George William's, ...	400
To Daniel Vaughan, ...	1,000
To William Butler, ...	975
To William Aldridge, ...	2,000
To George Currie, ...	630
To Jacob Denheart, ...	1,000
To William Scogging, ...	500
To John Butler, ...	600
To the Sheriff for 13 Insolvents, ...	390
To 17 Tithes, Listed, that are Inhabitant's of Brandom Parish, Viz, Sarah Hunnicut 9 Robert Hunnicut 3 Edward Walker 4 William Lee 1, . .	425
To 3 D° no Inhabitant Viz Samuel Heath—Christopher Hood, & John Speires, ...	75
To 9 D° Twice Listed, Viz John Raines, 6 & Henry Wilkerson, 3, ...	225
To Tob° Sold @ 20 |	3,614
To D° D° @ 18 |	1,206
To my Com[s] for Collecting @ 6 ℘[r] C[t] On 20,675 Lb[s] Tob°, ...	1,240
	21,400

CONTRA CR.

By 844 Tithes @ 25 Lb^{s} Tob^{o} ℔^{r} Pol, ...	21,100
By Eliz^{h} Yates 8 Tithes not Listed, ...	200
By James Patterson 2 D^{o} D^{o}, ...	50
By John Hall 1 D^{o} D^{o}, ...	25
By Lisenby William's 1 D^{o} D^{o}, ...	25
	21,400

	L	S	D
To Mr. William Call which he has Recieved L15. 11. 9½, ...	15	11	9½
To D^{o} George Noble's note of hand when Rec^{d} for,	6	16	5
To D^{o} Edmond Ruffin's D^{o} for, . . .	11	5	
To D^{o} for William Brown Cash, ...	1		
To D^{o} John Hall D^{o}, ...		4	6
To D^{o} in Cash, ...	2		
	£36	17	8½
To D^{o} Paid Willm Call's Order in favour of Peter Willis Date'd 22 of May 1771 & Willi's Recie't of 13 of June for ye same, ...	12		
To Cash Paid Wm. Call for Ball^{o} the 22 of Augt 1771,		4	1
	£49	1	9½

	L	S	D
By 3,614 lb^{s} Tob^{o} Sold @ 20 |	36	2	9½
By 1,206 Lb^{s} D^{o} D^{o}, @ 18 |	10	17	
	£46	19	9½
By 210 lb^{s} Levy^{d} for Insolvents Last Year & was Paid in Cash, ...	2	2	0
	£49	1	9½

[198–199] THE PARISH OF BRISTOL IN ACC'T WITH THOMAS BONNER COLLEC'R FOR YEAR 1770.

To Paid The Reverend William Harrison, . . .	6,356
To William Yarbrough, ...	2,120
To Field & Call for Wm. Aldridge Ann Phillips & Nathl Parrot, ...	2,012

To George Williams,	400
To Daniel Vaughan,	1,000
To William Butler,	975
To George Curry,	630
To Jacob Denhart,	1,000
To William Scoggin,	500
To Thomas Bonner,	250
To Martin's Brandon's Parish for Judgmet & Costs &c.	920
To John Hall Assignee to Josepth Rieves,	225
To the Collecter,	1,066
To Mary Lanthrope,	400
Solomon Thrift no Inhabitant,	21
Thomas Smith Molatto D°,	21
James Long twice Listed two Tithes,	42
	17,938

1770 CONTRA CR.

By 844 Tithes @ 21 Lb^s Tob° ℘^r Poll,	17,724
Capt Charles Gregory Paid 4 Tithes not Listed,	84
	17,808
By Ballance Due Thomas Bonner,	135
	17,943

THE PARISH OF BRISTOL IN ACC'T WITH THOMAS BONNER, COL'R FOR THE YEAR 1771.

To the Revd William Harrison,	7,200
To Wm Yarbrough, ,	2,120
To George Williams,	400
To Daniel Vaughan,	1,000
To Wm Butler,	975
To George Currie,	630
To Wm Aldridge,	1,000
To Ric^d Biggins,	1,000
To William Scoggin,	500
To Wm Call for Ann Philips,	600
To Mary Lanthrop,	200
To Nathl Raines for Wm Edwards,	250

To Col° Theo^k Bland,			330
To Nathl Raines,			115
To Joseph Kirkland,			21
To the Collecter,			1,217
			17,558
To Sundry Insolvents, Viz Charles Hood Run to Carrolina,	Lb. 1. 22		
John Pace Removed to Brumswick,	4. 88		
James More Removed, but do not know where,	4. 88		
Matthias Crow run to Carrolina,	1. 22		190
			17,748
To Ballance Remaining in my hands to be sold for ye use of the Parish,			2,726
			20,474
To Paid into ye hands of Wm Call Church Warden & was sold Augt Court,	Lbs. 1,212 @ 17 | 2		
To Paid in hands of D° @ D° 280 @ 16 | 9,	280 @ 16 | 9		
To Paid in the hands of Field & Call,	195		
To Cash Paid D° if the Vestry approves of is £8. 18. 11. for 1,039 Lb^s Tob° Unaccounted for at 17 | 2,	1,039		
	2,726 Lb^s		

1771 CONTRA CR.

By 922 Tythes at 22 Lb^s Tob° ℔^r Poll,			20,284	
By Sundrys not Listed, Viz,				
John Raines,	6	132		
Joseph Butler,	2	44		
John Phillips,	1	22		
John Thrift,	1	22	220	
	10		20,504	20,474
By Ballance Remaining in my hands to be sold for the use of the Parish,				2,726

Test R. ARMISTEAD, Clk Vestry.

[200] At a Vestry Held at Blandford For Bristol Parish Jany 15, 1772.

Present. the Revd William Harrison, Theop^{s} Field, C. W., Robert Bolling, John Thweat, Dr. Theo^{k} Bland, Richard Taylor, William Call, Nathl Raines, Peter Jones, Gentlemen.

Ordered, That the Claim of Lewis Parham to the Acre of Ground, on which the Brick Church Stands, on Well's Hill, And his offer of the Said Land, on Paying him five Hundred Pounds for the Same be Rejected, he having no Right Thereto, in the Opinion of the Vestry.

Ordered, That the Church Wardens, Pay unto William Craise The Sum of Twenty two Shillings & Six Pence for finding A Coffin & Funeral Expenses for Burying Robt Whiting.

THEOP'S FIELD, Church Warden.

Test R. ARMISTEAD, CLK Vestry.

At A Vestry held at Blandford for Bristol Parish May 21, 1772.

Present. the Revd William Harrison, Theop^{s} Field, John Banister, Church Wardens, Robert Bolling, Thomas Jones, William Call, Nathl Raines, John Thweatt, Richd Taylor, Doc^{r} Theo^{k} Bland, Gentlemen.

Ordered, That the Several List of Processions, be Recorded That has been this Day Deliv^{d} & Rec^{d} Wm Perkins & Joseph Kirkland's, James Cureton & Thos Bonner's, Robt Evans & Robt Tucker's, John & George Blicks, Thomas Evans & James Harrison's, Isham Baughs & Ath^{y} Williams's, Willm Gary & Fred^{k} Archer's, Drury Alley & Lesb^{y} Williams's, John Thweatt & John Cureton's, James Overby's & Robt Newsum's, Edward & Drury Burchetts, Henry Wilkerson & Thomas Daniel's, Thomas Jones & Partrick Ramsey's.

Ordered That the Church Warden's Pay unto Wm Craise the Sum of One Pound Seven Shillings & Six Pence for a Coffin for Jane Long and a Stranger.

Ordered, That the Church Warden's Pay unto Wm Brice the Sum of Four Pounds for board & Maintanance of Jane Long as Ꝑ^{r} Acct.

Ordered, That the Church Warden's apply to the Church

Warden's Elisabeth Parish, for the Expences of Jane Long's board & funeral Expences.

Ordered that the Church Warden's Pay unto Rob[t] Rose for Burying of Henry Grigg, The Sum of Twelve & Six Pence. Carried up.

[201] The Rev[d] William Harrison haveing asked Leave of the Vestry to be absent for eleven Months is Granted him.

Ordered that the Church Warden's Put up Advertisements at both Churches to this Purpose, Whereas the Parish is in Want of a Tract of Land Suitable for a Glebe, This is to Give Notice, that we the Church Wardens are Ready to Treat with any Person who Hath Land's Convenient for this Purpose, for which Ready Money will be Givein.

Ordered that the Church Warden's, Pay unto the Rev[d] William Harrison, from this Day, the Sum of Twenty Six Pound's ℔[r] Year, instead of a Glebe, he haveing Agreed to it in Vestry.

At A Vestry held at Blandford for Bristol Parish Oct[r] 9. 1772.

Present. John Banister, Theop[s] Field Church Warden's, Robert Bolling, George Smith, William Call, Richard Taylor, Peter Jones, John Thweat, Gentlemen.

The Church Warden's haveing Returned There Tob[o] Acc[t] And the Same after Examination being Approved of is Ordered to be Recor[ed].

The Vestry haveing this Day entered into an agreement with Mrs. Elizabeth Yates for the Purchace of A Tract of Land Containing four Hundred And Ninety Acres Agreeable to the Annexed Plot, Have Ordered That the Sum of Three Hundred and Fifty Pounds Laufull Money of Virginia, The Consideration agree'd upon for the Said Tract of Land be Paid Her in the following Manner, That is to Say—One Hundred & Seventy five Pounds Part Thereof in the Month of November next ensueing, and the Remaining one Hundred and Seventy Five Pounds in Month of December Next, Out of the Fund Ariseing upon the Sale of the Late Glebe of this Parish, Provided that Previous to the Said Payments the Said Elizabeth Shall make to the Vestry and Church Warden's of the Parish of Bristol And to there

Successers a good and indefeasable Estate in fee Simple of in and to the Said Tract of Land & Premisses.

JOHN BANISTER, THEOP'S FIELD Church Warden's.
Test R. ARMISTEAD Clerk of the Vestry.

[202–203] 1772 Octr. BRISTOL PARISH TO THE CHURCH WARDEN'S AS COLLECTER'S IN LB'S TOB'O DR.

To Paid The Revd William Harrison,	17,280
To Robert Armistead,	2,000
To D^o for Extra Service's,	400
To Paid John Young,	1,600
To Edmond Conway,	600
To George William's,	400
To Ann Vaughan,	1,000
To William Aldridge,	1,000
To Theo^k Munford,	630
To Richard Biggins,	800
To William Scoggin,	1,000
To William Call for Ann Phillips,	800
To Thomas Ruffin,	32
To Theo^k Bland,	36
To Henry Spears,	22
To Millington Smith,	17
To Thomas Bonner,	135
	27,752
To 43 Insolvents @ 21 Lb^s Tob^o ℔^r Poll,	903
To 6 ℔^r C^t for Collecting,	2,095
To 7,000 Sold for Cash,[*]	7,000
	37,747
Ballance Due the Parish Sold,[‡]	704
	38,451

Octr 1772. CONTRA CR.

By 1,752 Tithes Collected @ 21 ℔^r Poll,	36,792
By 79 Tithes Collected that was not Listed,	1,659
	38,451

[*] 2,523 @ 15 | & 2,477 @ 14 | 6 Carried to Cash Acc[t], ...	£44 7 6
[‡] 704 @ 15 | Carried to Cash Acc[t] not yet Returned, ...	5 5 6
	£49 12

Errors Ex[d]. JOHN BANISTER, THEOP'S FIELD, Church Wardens.

[204] 1772 Oct[r] 23. At A Vestry held at Blandford for Bristol Parish.

Present. John Banister, Theop[s] Field C. Warden's, Robert Bolling, Doct[r] Theo[k] Bland, Rich[d] Taylor, William Call, Nath[l] Raines, John Thweat, Gentlemen.

BRISTOL PARISH DR.	£ S D	Lb[s] Neat Tob[o]
To the Rev[d] Wm. Harrison, ...		17,280
To Robert Armistead CLK. of Brick Church and Vestry, ...		2,200
To John Young Clerk of Jones Hole Church, . .		1,600
To D[o] Sexton of D[o] . .		400
To Edmond Conway Sexton Brick Church, . .		400
To D[o] for Extra Service, . . .		300
To Ann Vaughn for Keeping Margaret William's, .		1,000
To Wm. Aldridge for Keeping Ann Butterworth, .		1,000
To Theo[k] Munford's Ex[rs] for Keeping Cyrus Stewart,		630
To Wm. Call for the Use of Ann Phillips, . . .		1,000
To Wm. Gary for Rob[t] Elder, ...		1,000
To Theop[s] Field for Collecting 704 Lb[s] of Tob[o] of Persons Not Listed Last Year, 6 ℔[r] C[t] Omitt[d] in his Acc[t], ...		42
To Henry Wilkerson for one Tithe Overp[d] Last Year,		21
To John Conway Constable for one D[o], ...		21
To Theo[k] Bland Ballance of his Acc[t] Last Year, .		36
To D[o] for List of Tithes this Year, . . .	7. 6.	
To Thomas Ruffin Ballance of his Acc[t] Last Year, ...		16

	£	s.	d.	Lbs.
To Dº for List of Tithes this Year 60 Lbs @ 12 | 6, ...		7.	6.	
To Wm. Scoggin to assist him in Maintaneance, ...				500
To the Church Wardens to be Sold for Cash for Parish use, ...				10,000
				37,456
To the Collecter for Collecting @ 6 ꝑr Ct,				2,247
				39,703
By 937 Tithes in Prince George.				
By 735 Dº in Dinwiddie.				
1,672 @ 24 Lbs Tobº ꝑr Poll, . .				40,128
To Mary Archer as ꝑr Acct, . . .	3	2	6	
To John Murry as Exr of James Murry's Este, ...		12	6	
Ordered, That the C. Warden's Pay unto Wm. Harden Out of the Depositum,	5			

Ordered, That Theops Field & Peter Jones Gentm be appointed Church Warden's for the Ensueing Year.

Ordered, That the Church Warden's, Recieve from Every Titheable Person 24 Lbs of Neat Tobº Per Poll, and in case of Non Payment, or Refusall, to Levy the Same by Distress.

JOHN BANISTER, THEOP'S FIELD, Church Warden's.

Test ROBT. ARMISTEAD Clerk of the Vestry.

[205] 1773 July 22. At a Vestry held for Bristol Parish on the Glebe Lands Purchased of Eliza Yates.

Present. Revd Mr. Harrison, Theops Field, Peter Jones, Robert Bolling, William Call, Nathl Raines, Richd Taylor, & John Thweat, Gent.

Ordered, that the Present Dwelling House be Repaired and A Chimney Built to the N. End for a Kitchen, the Roof Repaired, and the Windows Repaired, and the House Tar'ed; the Chimney Eight feet in the Clear four feet Deep Two and a Half Brick Jam's, The S. Chimney Well repaired with a New back, The Lime to be Good and Properly Mixt; the flours to be takeing up and filled in with Dirt;

Ordered, That a Shed Twelve feet be built to the End of the barn for a Stable Substantially fitted with Stalls Racks and Mangers, Shingled and Weatherboarded, Sealed four feet inside, The Shed Ten feet from the House out; The Barn properly Repaired and floured with Inch and Half Plank trunneled Down & Proper Sleepers and well Tar'd;

Ordered, That a Dwelling house be built forty Six feet Long & Eighteen feet Wide, Two story high, the first Story Eleven feet, and the Second Nine feet both in the Clear, with a box Cornice Neatly sett The feather edge Plank well Planed and Quarter Rounded with Corner Boards neatly Put up, Good flouring Plank, well Tong'd & Groved, the Ends well Wainscoated, and one room wainscoated chair board high, the other Room and Passage, to have wash & Chair boards & Sir Base; A neat Stair case to Run in the Passage, three out Closets Beside the Chimney's and an end Door with a Cap over the Top, Two Portches Ten, by Seven feet out, Weatherboareded hand rail high, with Good featheredge Plank and Good flours, Neatly finished with out Side Cornice's, and Sealed in Side, with Good wide benches &c. The Chimney's and Cellar of Good Well burnt bricks, which Cellar is to be twenty eight feet and Six feet Deep, Three feet above Ground and Three feet under Ground, The other Part of the underpining to a good foundation, and Three feet above as the Other Cellar Part, the Whole to be compleatly finished Agreeable to the Plan which will be produced at the time of Letting; a Smoak house Ten feet Square, A Dairy Sixteen by Ten to be built and one end to fitted up Close for a Lumber Room Turn Over [206] The present dairy to be fitted up for a house of Office And the present smoak house for a hen house, to be moved and Placed as the Directer's thinks Proper;

A Garden to be built a Hundred and fifty feet Square the posts of Good young Post Oak, with Saw'ed Rails and Pails of Hart of Pine or of Poplar, the Posts Seven or Eight Inches Square and well Hewe'd;

Ordered that the work be advertised in the Gazette; And that the Church Warden's for the time being Reve[d] Mr. Wm. Harrison, William Call and Nath[l] Raines Gen[t] or any two of them are Appointed to Let and Superintend the Same, who are to take bond and Sufficient Security of the Undertaker for his faithfull Performance of the Said works by the Last of October Seventeen Hundred and Seventy Four;

Ordered That there be an Oven built in a proper Manner and that the Well be bricked with Good well burnt bricks and to have a Proper Kirb Over it with Windlas and Buckett;

Ordered, That Joseph Jones be Appointed A. Vestryman in the Place of Thomas Jones Gen[t] Dec[d] and that he be Served with a Copy of the Same by the Clerk;

THEOP'S FIELD, PETER JONES CH. WD[s].

Test ROBERT ARMISTEAD CLK of the Vestry.

[207] Oct[r] 15. 1773. At a Vestry Held at Blandford for Bristol Parish.

Present. The Rev[d] Mr. William Harrison, Roger Atkerson, Geo. Smith, Peter Jones, Joseph Jones, Theop[s] Field, William Call and John Thweat; Gentlemen.

BRISTOL PARISH DR.		L.	S.	D.
To the Rev[d] Wm. Harrison, ...		133	6	8
To R. Armistead CLK of the Brick Church & Vestry, ...		18	6	8
To Geo. William's CLK & Sexton of Jones Hole Church, ...		16	3	4
To Edmond Conway Sexton of the Brick Church,		5		
To D[o] for Extra Service's, ...		4		
To Ann Hare for Keeping of Margaret William's,		12		
To William Aldridge for Ann Butterworth, . .		8	6	8
To Granny Stewart for Cyruss Stewart, . .		5	5	
To William Call for the use of Ann Phillips, .		8	6	8
To Alex[r] Coothrell, for Keeping of Rob[t] Elder, .		1	10	
	Lb[s] Tob[o].			
To Col[o] Theo[k] Bland for Copying List of Tithes, ...	60			
To Recording the Deed of the Glebe Land,	100			
To Entering Order for Witness attendance 10[lb] Copy 10 D[o], ...	20	1	3	9
	180			
To Wiliam Butler for Keeping Eliz[h] Sears, . .		12		

To William Scoggin to assist him in His Maintanance, ...	4	3	4
To the Church Wardens, for the Support of Will. Harden, ...	5		
To Doc^r James McCartie, for Attending of Elisha Lester as p^r Acc^t, ...	10	14	3
To Ro^t Roe, for a Coffin for Alex^r Burnett, . .		15	
To Norman Ash for Keeping Jeremiah Bishop, .	1	10	
To Cash to Pay for Building a Glebe House, .	200		
To the Revd William Harrison in Lieu of a Glebe,	26		
To the C. Wardens for a Deposite for Parrish use,	42		
	516	11	4
To Commissions for Collecting the above, . .	31		
	547	11	4

Ordered That the C. Wardens Recieve from Every Titheable Person 52 Lb^s of Tob^o or 6 | 6. Cash; in Case of Refusall or non Payment, Levy the Same by Distress.

Ordered That Walter Thomson, be allowed at the Laying of the Next Levy, Twelve Pound's for His board, and Three Pounds for Cloaths the Ensueing Year;

Ordered That Col^o Theo^k Bland have leave to Build Side Windows in the Brick Church, adjoining His Family Pew. At his own expence, without Injuring the Church.

Ordered That the C. Wardens do Endeavour to agree with Some Capt to Carry Jeremiah Bishop to the Port of London and to Pay His Passage.

Ordered That, Norman Ash, at the Rate of eight Pounds Six & Eight Pence, for board of the s^d Bishop, untill a Passage Can be Procured.

Ordered that the C. Warden's be Continued. Theop^s Field C. Warden Returned his Tob^o Acc^t for Last Year and Ordered to be Recorded.

Ordered That the C. Wardens pay unto Some Proper Person at the Rate of Twenty five Shillings ℔^{r} Month for the Support of Thomas Egleton.

THEOP'S FIELD, PETER JONES, C. W.

Test ROB'T. ARMISTEAD, Clk of the Vestry.

[208–209] 1773. BRISTOL PARISH (THERE TOBO. ACCT) IN ACC'T WITH THEOP'S FIELD CH WDN. DR.

To Paid the Revd William Harrison,	17,280
To Paid Robert Armistead CLK. Church,	2,200
To Paid Geo. Williams CLK. and Sexton,	2,000
To Paid Edmond Conway Sexton Brick Church,	700
To Paid Ann Vaughn for Margaret Williams,	1,000
To Paid William Aldrige for Ann Butterworth,	1,000
To Pd Theok. Munfords Exrs for Cyrus Stewart,	630
To Paid William Call for the use of Ann Phillips,	1,000
To Paid William Gary for Robert Elder,	1,000
To Theops Field for Collecting 704 Lbs Tobo Last Year Not Listed at 6 ℘r Cent,	42
To Paid Henry Wiikerson for a Tithe twice Listed Last Year,	21
To Paid John Conway Do Do Do,	21
To Paid Theok Bland Ballance of his acct Last Year,	63
To Paid Thos Ruffin Ballc List of Tithes for 1771,	16
To Paid William Scoggin to Assist Him,	500
To the C. Wardens Sold for Parish Use, [*]	10,000
	37,456
To the Collr for Collecting @ 6 ℘ Ct,	2,247
	39,703
To Difference for use of the Parish, [†]	425
	40,128

1773 CR.

By 937 Tithes in Prince George.	
By 735 Do in Dinwiddie.	
1672 @ 24 Lbs ℘r Poll is,	40,128

[*] Carry'd To Cash Acct 1,175 @ 13 | 6 & 8,825 @ 13 | 5,	£67 2 6
[†] at 13 | 5 Carryd to Cash Acct at 13 | 5 is,	£ 2 16 10
	£69 19 4

At a Vestry Held for Bristol Parish at Pet[s] April 20, 1774.

Present. Theop[s] Field, Peter Jones, John Banister, Nath[l] Raines, John Thweat, Rob[t] Bolling, Rich[d] Taylor, William Call, Gentlemen.

Peter Willis, this Day came in Vestry, in Order for the Gent[n] to Recieve His work on Jones Hole Church, Persuant to an Order of Sep[r] 10, 1770. In Repairing and adding to the S[d] Church, is done agreeable to the Said Willis's Contract is Rec[d].

Order'd That the Present C. Warden's settle the Same with the Said Willis, and Pay him the Ballance;

THEOP'S FIELD, PETER JONES, CH WD[s].

Test. ROB'T. ARMISTEAD, CLK. of the Vestry.

[210] At a Vestry Held at Petersburg for Bristol Parish Oct[r] 18, 1774.

Present. The Reve[d] William Harrison, Peter Jones, Theop[s] Field, Theo[k] Bland, Nath[l] Raines, Rob[t] Bolling, John Thweat, Roger Atkerson, Rich[d] Taylor and Joseph Jones, Gentlemen.

BRISTOL PARISH DR.	L	S	D
To The Rev[d] Mr. William Harrison, ...	144		
To Rob[t] Armistead Clerk of Brick Church & Vestry, ...	18	6	8
To Geo. William's Clerk & Sexton of Jones Hole Church, ...	16	13	4
To Edmond Conway Sexton of Brick Church & Extra Service's, ...	9		
To Ann Hare for Keeping of Margaret William's,	12		
To William Aldridge for Keeping Ann Butterworth, ...	8	6	8
To Granny Stewart for Cyrus Stewart, . . .	5	5	
To William Call for the Use of Ann Phillips. .	8	6	8
To Wm. Butler for Eliz[h] Sear's, ...	8	6	8
To William Scoggin to Assist him in Maintanance,	4	3	4
To The Church Warden's for Support of Wm. Harden, ...	5		
To John Archer for Keeping Rob[t] Elder, . .	8	6	8

	£	s.	d.
To Doc^r^ Theo^k^ Bland for Copying List of Tithes (40 Lb^s^ Tob^o^).			
To Doc^r^ James M^c^Cartie for attending Elisha Lester, ...	2	9	7½
Ordered, That £15 be Leveyed for Walter Thompson & Deposited in the Hands of the C. Wardens, & Paid as Soon as Collected, .	15		
To Jeremiah Bishop in the Hands of the C. Warden's, ...	8	6	8
To Thomas Egleton, to be Paid at 25 | ℘^r^ Month By the Church Warden's, ...	15		
Ordered, That Eight Pound Six & Eight Pence be levyed For Robert Elder & Paid him in hand, to Carry him A Broad, on his Givein Bond & Security to the Church Wardens, not to be Chargeable to this Parrish for Twelve Months, ...	8	6	8
To William Creaise for Two Coffins one for Walter Dick & One for Daniel Cambel @ 10 | each,	1		
To Peter Aldridge to assist Him in his Maintanance, ...	4		
To D^o^ for His Wife, ...	4		
To William Temple for Nancy Davies, . .	4		
To Peter Rosser, for One Tithe Twice Listed, .		6	6
To James Burge for One D^o^, ...		6	6
To John Walker for Nursing of Margaret Gibbon's, ...	3	8	4
To William Brown for Nine Tithes Twice Listed,	2	18	6
To Thomas William's for One D^o^ D^o^ .		6	6
	317	4	0½

A Memorandum, That Eliz^h^ Deacon, Eliz^h^ Deacon Ju^r^, Mary Shorey, Jane Deacon, Sarah Deacon & Rebecca Browney Were Removed by a Warrant to Brandom Parish And has since Returned to this Parish, The Church Wardens of the S^d^ Parish of Brandom Undertaking That they shall not be Chargeable to this Parish, Which was done in Presence of Col^o^ Theo^k^ Bland, John Lewis Ju^r^, Thomas Thweat and Charles Gilliam.

[211] The Amount brought up, . .	£317	4	0½
To Thomas Bonner for Removeing the s[d] Person's, ...	1	4	6
	£318	8	6½
Ordered, That the C. Wardens, apply to the C. Warden's of Brandom Parish for the above sum.			
To the C. Warden's for a Deposit for Parish use, ...	45		
	363	8	6½

By 903 Tithes in Prince George.
By 872 We Suppose for Dinwiddie.

1,775 Tithes.

Theop[s] Field Late Church Warden Haveing Returned his Accounts from the year 1771 to 1773, and is Ordered to be Recorded, Ballance Due the Parish £329. 3. 4½.

Thomas Bonner Collecter for Bristol Parish, haveing Returned His Account and ordered to be Recorded.

Ordered That Theop[s] Field & Peter Jones, the Present Church Warden's be Continued.

Ordered That the Church Warden's Recieve from Every Titheable Person 4 | 2 Cash or 25 Lb[s] of Neat Tob[o] in Case of Refusal or Non Payment Levy the Same by Distress.

Ordered That the Rev[d] Mr. Harrison the C. Warden's Rob[t] Bolling Doc[r] Theo[k] Bland, or any Three of them, be appointed For the Parish of Bristol, to agree with the Vestry of Brandom Parish, in Order to Purchace a Place To Errect a Poor House for the use of Bristol and Brandom Parish's.

THEOP'S FIELD, PETER JONES, Church Warden's.

Test. ROBERT ARMISTEAD, Clerk of the Vestry.

[212] DR BRISTOL PARISH IN ACC'T WITH THEOPHILUS FIELD CHURCH WARDEN.

Nov[r] 1771	To Cash Paid makeing a Coffin Obediah Ham[i]lton, . . .	£	10	
	To Cash Paid Diging Edmond Browder's Grave, ...		2	6

			£	s	d
		To 2 Quarts of Rum 2 | 6 ¼ Lb. Tea 1 | 6 Edmond Browders Widow, ...		4	
		To 1½ Pints Run for Ditto, . .		1	
		To Sundrys for Mrs. Hatfield Viz. 3 lbs of Candles 3 | Cash 2 | 6 ½ Lb. of Tea 2 | 6 Cash 7½d 2½lb Sugar Refined 3 | 1½ 9 Lbs of Bacon 4 | 6, ...		16	3
		To 1 Prayer Book Pd Rob. Armistead, ...		10	
Decr	24	To ½ Gallon of Wine for ye Communion, ...		5	
1772.					
April	21	To 1 Ledger for Regester Book, .	2	4	
May	2	To 2 quarts of Rum To Bury Jane Long, ...		2	6
		To 2 quarts of Wine for yo Communion, ...		5	
	27	To Cash pd Wm. Brice ℘r Order of Vestry, ...	4		
June	9	To 2 qts of Wine } for ye Communion			
	20	To 2 qts Ditto } for ye Communion		10	
	27	To Field & Call pd Francies Cook by Order pr Capt Geo. Smith, .	1	8	1½
Augt	12	To Cash pd Docr Bland for attending Robt Elder ℘r Order of Colo Banister as ℘r Recept, . . .	8	1	9
		To Cash pd Peter Willis in Part for Building the Addition to Jones Hole Church, ...	7		
Oct.	2	To 1 Stock Lock for the Church, .		2	3
	23	To 1 Gallon & 1 qt of Wine for ye Communion, ...		12	6
Novr	25	To Cash pd John Murray for Mrs. Yates First Payment of the Glebe Land, ...	175		
Decr	1	To Cash pd Revd Wm. Harrison in			
1773.		Lieu of a Glebe Due to this time,	27	17	10
Jany	29	To Cash Paid John Murray for Mrs.			

			£	s	d
		Yates Last Payment, in full for Glebe Land, ...	175		
Feb^y	1	To 14½ yards Linnen, } To make two surplusces, one for each Church, } 7 | 6,	5	13	9
		17 yards Ditto, } 7 | ,	5	19	6
		To 1 Oz. of Fine Thread, . .		3	6
	3	To 5 pints of Wine for Communion,		6	3
	20	To Sundrys as Reliefe for John Lantrop 6 Ells of ozna. 7 | 6 4 Ells of Roles 3 | 4 1 q^t of Rum 1 | 3 1 Handk^r 1 | 1 p^r yarn hoes 1 | 5,		14	6
	23	To 1 q^t of Wine for ye Communion,		2	6
March	18	To Paid James Baugh & Burwell Lea, Lev^yd By Vestry for William Harden, ...	5		
April	21	To 54^lb of Bacon 27 | , 6 Lb^s of Cheese, 4 | 6 John Lanthrop, .	1	11	6
	23	To Cash p^d Mrs. Park, Mak^g two Surplusses ℘^r Recp^t, . . .	2	12	
	27	To Cash p^d Jeremiah Bishop which he s^d was to Pay His Passage away, ...		18	
		Carried up, ...	£400	18	10
[213]		Brought from the Other Side,	400	18	10
May	22	To 3 qts of Wine for ye Communion,		7	6
June	3	To 5½ yards of Sheeting for Elisha Lester, ...		11	
	16	To Sundry's for Bishop To 3½ Yards of Chex. 5 | 3. 2½ Ells Ozna^bgs 2 | 8½ Oz of Thread 10^d. Cash 5 | , ...		13	9½
Aug^t	10	To Cash p^d Peter Willis, in p^t of work to J Hole Church, . .	57	3	11
	31	To 1 Regester Book p^r Ro. Armistead, ...		9	
Sep^r	18	To 12 Lb^s of Bacon for John Lantrop, ...		6	
Oct^r	13	To p^d Qristopher Manlove for Board			

		& Cure of Anthony Johnston of a Sore Leg, ...	3	10	
Decr	1	To Cash pd Revd Wm. Harrison in Lieu of A Glebe due to this time,	26		
	1	To Cash pd Wm. Creaise pr Order of Vestry Jany & May 1772, .	2	10	
		To Cash Paid Revd Wm. Harrison for Building A House at Jones Hole Church, ...	10	10	
		To pd Wm. Butler pr Order of Vestry in the year 1771, . . .	1	2	6
		To pd John Butler pr Ditto 1771, .		12	6
		To pd Robt Tucker pr Do 1771, .		15	
		To pd Theok Bland pr Do 1772, .		7	6
		To pd Thomas Ruffin pr Do 1772, .		7	6
		To pd Mary Archer pr Do 1772, .	3	2	6
		To pd James Murrays Exrs pr Do 1772,		12	6
		To Sundrys for Robert Elder, .	3		
		To Do for John Lantrop, . .	2	12	7½
		To Do for Jeremiah Bishop, . .	1	13	10½
		To Sundrys for Margaret Gibson, .	1	3	5
Decr	23.	To 3 Bottles of Wine from Andrew			
1774.		Johnston, ...		9	
Jany	1.	To 3 Bottles Do from Do, .		9	
March	5.	To Joshua Wise 8 Bottles Wine at Times ℘r Acct, ...	1	8	
Apl	2.	To Andrew Johnson for 3 Bottles of Wine, ...		7	6
	20.	To pd Peter Willis in full, . .	22	16	1
May	20.	To Wm. Beattie 4 Bottles Wine Omited 1771, ...		12	
	27.	To Edward Brisbane 6 Bottles of wine, ...		15	
		To Andrew Johnston 2 bttls of Wine Omitted in April, . . .		5	
		To Sundry's for Thomas Egleton pr O. Vestry, ...	15	3	11¼
July		To Cash Pd Edmond Conway pr O. Vestry	9		

			£	s.	d.
		To pd William Harden's Order ℘ Do	5		
		To pd Granny Stewarts Order ℘r Do	5	5	
		To pd Wm. Scoggin Do ℘r Do	4	3	4
		To pd Wm. Aldridge Do ℘r Do	8	6	8
		To pd William Butler Do ℘r Do	12		
		To pd Alexr Coothrell ℘r Do	1	10	
		To pd Wm. Call for Ann Phillips ℘r Do, ...	8	6	8
		Carried Over, . . .	£641	2	0½
		[214–215] Brought Over from the other Side, ...	£641	2	0½
		To pd Robert Roe for a Coffin for Alexr Burnett, ...		15	
		To pd Colo Theok Bland his Tickett 180 Lbs Tobo ℘r Order V. . .	1	3	9
		To pd The Revd Wm. Harrison ℘r Order of Vestry, ...	133	6	8
		To pd Geo. William's ℘r Do Do, .	16	13	4
		To pd Robert Armistead ℘r Do, .	18	6	8
		To pd Ann Hare ℘r Order of Do, .	12		
		To pd Docr James McCartie ℘r Do,	10	14	3
		To pd Norman Ash ℘r Do, . . .	1	10	
1774.		To pd The Revd Wm. Harrison in Lieu of a Glebe, ...	26		
Sepr	16.	To Wm. Beattie for 3 qts of Wine,		7	6
	24.	To 2 Bottles of Wine from Do, .		5	
			£862	4	2½
		Ballance Due the Parish carried to A new Acct which will be Due to John Woodward, ...	329	3	4¼
			£1,191	7	6¾

CONTRA CR.

			£	s.	d.
1771.					
Novr		By Cash Recd of Wm. Call late Church Warden For Ballance of his Acct Rendered, ...	£ 19	4	5½
		By Cash of Wm. Brown pd by			

		£	s	d
1772.	Charles Duncan His first Payment for Glebe Land, . . .	260		
Aug^t	By Cash for 7,000 Lb^s Tob° Levy^d in 1771, for Parish Use sold at 14 | 6 & 15 | for 3,477, . . .	51	12	6
	By 704 Lb^s Tob° Collected of People not Listed After Deducting Insolvents 15 |	5	5	6
Dec^r	By Cash of Wm. Brown p^d by Charles Duncan Due ye Parish for the Glebe Land. Sold him as in			
1773.	full, ...	260		
Aug^t	By Cash for 10,000^lb Tob° Lev^d in 1772 for Parish use sold @ 13 | 5 and 13 | 6 1,175, . . .	67	2	6
	By a Difference, in the Tob° Levy^d & the Tob° due And to be paid in			
1774.	1772 426^lb 13 | 5, . . .	2	16	10
March 24	By Cash in part of Theo^k Bland's Acc^t, ...	10		
	By Cash of Richd Bland J^r full of His Acc^t, ...	11	8	9
	By Cash of Thomas Daniel for a fine of ye Grand Jury, . . .		5	
	By Cash for a fine James Bonner. Rec^d of John Weeks, . . .	5		
	By Cash Rec^d of Thomas Bonner, for the Ballance of his Acc^t as parish Collecter for the Year 1773, .	498	12	
		£1,191	7	6½

Errow's Ex^d. ℔^r THEOPS. FIELD.

Test ROBERT ARMISTEAD Clerk of the Vestry.

BRISTOL PARISH IN ACC'T WITH THOMAS BONNER COLLEC'R. DR.

		£	s
1774. Oct^r	To 30 Tithes of Col° John Banister, Listed in this Parish which Belonged to Bath Parish, ...	£9	15

	To Commission's for Collecting £540. 15. 11¾ at 6 ℔r Ct,	32	8	11¾
	To Paid the Church Warden's,	498	12	
		£540	15	11¾

1774. CONTRA CR.

Octr	By 853 Tithes Collected in Tobo at 52 Lbs ℔r pole, Sold to Sundry's for,	£269	1	11¾
	By 836 Tithes paid in Cash @ 6 | 6,	£271	14	
	1,689	£540	15	11¾

Errows Excepd ℔r Thos Bonner Collecr for Theops Field & Peter Jones C. Warden's.

Test. ROBERT ARMISTEAD CLK. Vestry.

[216] At a Vestry Held at Petersbg for Bristol Parish Jany 26. 1775.

Present. The Revd Wm. Harrison, Peter Jones C. Warden, Robert Bolling, William Call, Nathl Raines, John Thweat, Joseph Jones & John Banister Gentn.

William Call Gent was Appointed a Church Warden, to Succeed Theops Field Gentl Decd, And Qualified Accordingly.

Ordered, That four Pounds be Levy'd for Thomas Clements Jur at the Laying the Next Parish Levy.

PETER JONES, WM. CALL C. Warden's.

Test ROBT. ARMISTEAD Clerk of the Vestry.

At a Vestry Held at Bristol Glebe in the County of Prince Geo. Sepr 26. 1775.

Present. the Revd Mr. Harrison Rector, William Call, Peter Jones C. Wardens, Geo. Smith, John Banister, Nathl Raines, Richd Taylor, And John Thweat Gentlemen.

It is the opinion of the Vestry that the Garden is finished According to Agreement.

It is the opinion of the Vestry that the Dairy shall be Recieved After a Lattice Window is made Opposite to the one already made And after the Meal Room is Plaistered.

An Unanimous Reception of the Smoak House.

The shed to the stable & Reperation of the Barn pass.

The old Dwelling House after it is Shelved & Glazed and a Shutter Renewed, ought to be Recieved.

The Well we think proper to Recieve.

The Dwelling House is Rec[d] But the Shed over the Çellar door is to be Shingled, in part where it is Defective, And the Chimney pieces above stairs to be Whitewashed again, &. all Other Stains in the House Occasioned by the Gust, to be also whitewashed.

The Undertaker to pay Seven Months Rent to the Vestry for his Failure to Comply with his Contract, within the Time Stipelated By Agreement, This Allowance to be Deducted out of the Money Due to the Undertaker from the Parish.

The Glebe with its Appertenances, Recieved this Day By the Rev[d] Mr. Harrison, The Incumbent.

WILLIAM CALL, PETER JONES Church Warden.

Test ROB'T ARMISTEAD Clerk of the Vestry.

[217] At a Vestry held at the Brick Church Oct[r] 19. 1775.

Present. The Rev[d] Wm. Harrison, William Call, Peter Jones, Church WarDen's, Geo Smith, John Banister, Nath[l] Raines, Rich[d] Taylor & John Thweat, Gen[t].

BRISTOL PARISH DR.		S	D
To the Rev[d] Mr. Harrison, ...	£144		
To Robert Armistead Clk of Brick Church and Vestry, ...	18	6	8
To Geo. William's Clk. & Sexton of Jones Hole,	16	13	4
To Edmond Conway Sexton of the Brick Church & Ext[a] Ser[s], ...	9		
To Ann Hare for Keeping Margaret William's,	12		
To William Aldridge for Ann Butterworth, .	8	6	8
To Grany Stewart, for Cyrus Stewart, . . .	5	5	
To Goditha Sear's for Elizabeth Sear's, . .	15		
To William Scoggin to Assist him in his Maintance, ...	4	3	4
To the Church Wardens, for Jeremiah Bishop's Support, ...	8	6	8
To the C. Warden's for the Support of William Harden, ...	5		

To William Temple for Nancy Davis, . . .	4		
To R. Armistead for Clerk of the Possessions,	3	6	8.
To Walter Thomson £12 As £3 was Overpaid last year, ...	12		
To Edith Daniel, for Keeping her Daughter Jane, ...	3.	2	6.
	£268	10	10.

By 1,840 Tithes. at 3 | or Seventeen Lb[s] Tob[o].

Ordered, That Every Titheable person pay three shillings. Or Seventeen Lb[s] of Tob[o].

Ordered, That Nath[l] Raines, and Joseph Jones, Gentlemen. Be appointed C. Warden's, for the Ensewing Year.

Mr. William Call, Late C. Warden Returned his Acc[t] And ordered to be Recorded. & pay the Ballance in his Hands to the present C. Warden's. The Ballance, £3. 9. 8¾.

Ordered, That Rob[t] Skipworth, be Appointed a Vestryman in the Room of Robert Bolling Es[qr] Dec[d].

Ordered, That William Brown, be Appointed, a Vestryman in the Room of Theop[s] Field Gen[t] Dec[d] And the Above Gentlemen Be served with a Copy of the Same by the Clerk,

Whereas, The Callamitious State of the Country renders it Doubtfull whether a Sufficient Sum Can be Collected from the people, for payment of the Parochial Debt, in Money. And by the Restrained Laid on Exports, By publick Consent, The Parishoners are Precluded of the Election which the Law Had Giveing them, in paying there Due's in Tob[o] or Money. It is Determined by Vestry That the Ministers Salary Shall be Estimated, at One Hundred And Forty four Pound's, to be Collected as Nearly as possible in Money Unless the prohibition on Exports Should be Removed, And in that Case the People to be at Liberty to pay in Tob[o] at Eighteen Shilling's ℔ Hundred, In Lieu of Money, According to there Own Choice. And it's further to be Understood that the Rev[d] Mr. Harrison shall wait for the Ballance, After the Collection is made, three Years without Intrest, unless it Shonld Please HEAVEN to Put an End before that time, To the Troubles of our Country, And then it is understood, that the Encumben[t's] Salary shall be Demandable in the usal and accustomed Way.

WILLIAM CALL, PETER JONES Church Warden's.

Test R. ARMISTEAD CLK Vestry.

[218] 1775 BRISTOL PARISH. IN ACCOUNT WITH WILLIAM CALL. CHURCH WARDEN. DR.

	£	s.	d.
To Cash Paid the Rev[d] Mr. Harrison,	£144		
Robert Armistead,	18	6	8
Geo. Williams,	16	13	4
Edmond Conway,	9		
Ann Hare,	12		
William Aldridge,	8	6	8
Granny Stewart,	5	5	
William Call for Ann Phillips,	8	6	8
William Scoggin,	4	3	4
For the Support of William Harden,	5		
John Archer,	8	6	8
Theo[k] Bland Ju[r] for Copying List of Tithes,		6	8
James McCartie,	2	9	7½
Walter Thomson,	15		
Henry Wilkerson for Keeping Jeremiah Bishop,	8	6	8
Thomas Egleton,	15		
Boswell Goodwyne for Keeping Rob[t] Elder,	8	6	8
William Creaise,	1		
Peter Aldridge & His Wife,	8		
William Temple,	4		
Peter Rosser,		6	6
James Burge,		6	6
John Walker,	3	8	4
William Brown &C[o],	2	18	6
Thomas Williams,		6	6
Thomas Bonner,	1	4	6
William Butler,	8	6	8
Sundry's furnished John Lanthrop, a poor person,	2	6	2½

To Wine for the use of the Churche's, . .	3	4	11½
To 21 Insolvents @ 4 | 2, ...	4	7	6
To 6 p C^t for Collecting £370. 16. 8, . .	22	5	
	£351	5	3½
To John Woodward a Ballance Due him for Building the Glebe House, ...	107		
11 Ells of Orazinbrigs for Thomas Egleton @ 1 | 3, ...		13	9
	£458	19	0½

[219] 1775 CONTRA CR.

By 1,775 Tithes @ 4 | 2, ...	£369	15	10
By 26 Tithes not Listed @ 4 | 2, ...	5	8	4
By ballance to Recieve in the hands of Theop^s Field Late Church Warden, ...	101	3	4½
	£476	7	6¼

To Amount Brought Over, ...	£458	19	0½
To Richd William's as ℘ Acc^t, ...	1	2	6
To Alex^r Taylor do	1		
To R. Armistead do		10	
To John Ruffin do		16	3
To Thomas Ruffin for Copying 6 Lists of Tithes for 1774, 120 Lb^s Tob^o, ...	1	13	4
To Doc^r Theo^k Bland for Copying 2 Lists of Tithes for 1775, 40 Lb^s @ 2^d, ...		6	8
To Eliz^h Smith, for her Trouble, & Expence in Burying of Thomas Egleton, ...	1		
To Richard Lunsford for Keeping two Children of Robert McCullock a poor man of this Parish, three Months @ 10 | Each, . . .	3		
To Mary Jennings for keeping one of the S^d McCullock's Children 3 months D^o, . . .	1	10	
To Walter Thomson Overpaid, to be Short Levyed for next Year, ...	3		
	£472	17	9½

By Ballance Due the parish in the Hands of the Collecter, for 1775, ...	3	9	8¾
	£476	7	6¼

Errow's Excepted ꝑ^{r} WILLIAM CALL. Church Warden.
October 19, 1775.

Test. ROBERT ARMISTEAD Clerk of the Vestry.

[220] At a Vestry held for Bristol Parish. Feby 1. 1777.

Present. The Rev^{d} Wm. Harrison, Nathl Raines, Joseph Jones, C. W., Geo Smith, John Banister, Wm. Call, Richd Taylor, Roger Atkerson & John Thweat Gen^{t}.

BRISTOL PARISH DR.	Lb^{s} of Neat Tob^{o}.		
To the Rev^{d} Mr. Harrison, ...	Lb^{s} 20,880		
To Robt Armistead C Brick Church, . . .	£21	13	
To Geo Williams C. Jones. Hole. & Sexton, .	16	13	4
To Edmond Conway Sexton, ...	5		
To James Day Deputy Sexton, ...	4		
To Ann Hare for Margaret William's, . .	14		
To Granny Stewart for Cyrus Stewart, . .	6		
To William Aldridge for Ann Butterworth, . .	10		
To Goditha Sears for Elizabeth Sears, . . .	14		
To William Scoggin to Assist Him in Maintanance,	5		
To the C. Warden's for Support of Wm. Harden,	5	15	
To William Temple for Nancy Davis, . . .	8		
To Walter Thomson, ...	15		
To Margaret Dick for Elizabeth Carpenter, . .	6		
To Amey Dowley for Keeping Elisha Lester, .	27		
To the C. Warden's for Support of John Lanthrop,	10		
To Mary Clements, ...	4		
To David Vaughn for Mary Jennings, . . .	5		
To Richard Lunsford for Keeping Robt MColler Children, ...	7		
To Doc^{r} McCartie &C^{o} as ꝑ^{r} Acc^{t}, ...		10	9
To Mary Adams for Keeping Robt McColler Children, ...	3	17	6
To John Ruffin, Fee V^{s} John Jones Ju^{r}, . .		16	8
	£189	7	11

CR.

By 1,840 Tithes @ 5 | 3 or Forty Lb[s] of Tob[o].

Ordered, That Every Titheable person pay 5 | 3 or Forty Lb[s] of Tob[o].

To 6 p[r] C[t] for Collecting.

Ordered, That Nath[l] Raines & Joseph Jones Gen[t] be appointed C. W. The Ensueing Year.

Ordered, That, John Burwell be Appointed a Vestryman in the Room of Peter Jones, Removed. &. Dr. James Field in the Room of Wm. Brown Dec[d], & that the above Gen[t] be Served with a Copy by the Clerk.

Rob[t] Gilliam in the Room of John Thweat, Resigned & that He be Served with a Copy of the Same by the Clerk.

Ordered That Thomas Bonner & Peter Williams be Appointed Collecters for this Parish, And that they Give Bond & Sufficient Security for the Same.

NATH'L RAINES, JOSEPH JONES, C. Wardens.

Test ROBT. ARMISTEAD Clerk of the Vestry.

[221] At a Vestry held for Bristol Parish April 23, 1778.

Present. the Rev[d] Wm. Harrison, Nath[l] Raines, Joseph Jones, C. Wardens, William Call, Robert Skipwith, John Burwell, James Field & Rich[d] Taylor, Gen[t].

BRISTOL PARISH DR.	L.	S.	D.
To Susannah Tucker for Jane Daniel, . .	11		
To William Temple for Nancy Davis, . .	8		
To Ann Hare for Margaret Williams, . .	14		
To Granny Stewart for Cyrus Stewart, . .	6		
To William Aldridge for Ann Butterworth, .	10		
To Goditha Sears for Elizabeth Sear's, . .	14		
To Wm Scoggin to Assist him, ...	5		
To the C Warden's for Support of Wm. Harden,	5	15	
To Walter Thompson for Maintanance, . .	15		
To Margaret Dick for Eliz[h] Carpenter, . .	11		
To Amey Dowley for Elisha Lester, . . .	13	10	
To Robert Armistead CLK of the Vestry, .	35		
To John Roberts for Keeping Wm. Evans from July 1777 till Oct[r] 1777, ...	3	6	8

To Joseph Jones, Cash Advanced for Elizabeth Carpenter, ...	5		
To Doc[r] James Greenway for John Pettipool, .	33	11	9
	£190	3	5
Ordered, That the Church Warden's for the Ensueing Year Pay unto the former C. W. The Sum of £66. 1. 4 With Intrest, . . .	66	1	4
Ordered, That the C. Wardens Pay unto Tho[s] Bonner £21. 19. 0¼ with Intrest from August 1775 Untill paid, ...	21	19	0¼
	£278	3	9¼

Ordered that the C. W. Let to the Lowest Bidder the Building of A Chimney at the Glebe which has Lately fallen Down.

Ordered That James Field & Rob[t] Skipwith Gentlemen, Be Appointed Church Warden's the Ensueing Year.

Ordered That the C. W. Recieve from Every Tithable person four & Six Pence Cash. In case of Refusal Levy by Distress. Credit. By 1750 Titheable persons @ 4 | 6 ℘[r] Tithe £393. 15.

Geo. Smith Gen[t] a Vestryman of this Parish begs Leave By the Information of John Burwell Gen[t] to Resign his Office as A Vestryman, & has Leave so to do.

Ordered That Wm. Diggs Gen[t] be appointed a Vestryman in his Place, & that he be Served with a Copy of the Same by the Clerk, & that he Qualify Accordingly.

Nath[l] Raines & Joseph Jones Gentlemen, C Warden's haveing Haveing returned there Accounts for 1775, & 1776, And Ordered to be Recorded,

NATH'L RAINES, JOSEPH JONES, C. W.

Test RO. ARMISTEAD CLK of the Vestry.

[222 & 223] 1775. BRISTOL PARISH IN ACCOUNT WITH THOMAS BONNER COLLECTER DR.

		S	D
To paid Sundry person's as ℘[r] Proportion, .	£268	10	10
To paid for John Lanthrop, ...	2	2	9

	£	s	d
To Insolvents as ꝑr List, ...	7	13	0
To 6 ꝑ Ct Collecting £260. 17. 10, . . .	15	13	0
	£293	19	7
To Ballance ꝑr Contra, ...	21	19	0¼

Cr.

	£	s	d
By 1,840 Tithes @ 3 | , ...	£268	10	10
By Cash Recd of the Former C Wardens, .	3	9	8¾
	£272	0	6¾
Ballance Due the Collecter, ...	21	19	0¼
	£293	19	7

E E ꝑ Thomas Bonner Clr.

1776. Bristol Parish In Account With Thos. Bonner & Peter Williams Collecter's. Dr.

	£	s	d
To paid Sundry persons as ꝑr Proportion, .	£189	7	11
To paid Sundry persons for Tobacco for the Reverend William Harrison ꝑr Accts, .	309	10	1
To 70 Insolvents @ 5 | 3, ...	18	7	6
To 6 ꝑr Ct for Collecting £460. 9. 2, . . .	27	12	6½
	£544	18	0½
To Ballance ꝑr Contra, ...	£ 66	1	4

Cr.

	£	s	d
By 1,840 Tythes @ 5 | 3, ...	£478	16	8
By Ballance Due the Due the Collecters, .	66	1	4
	£544	18	0
	£544	18	0

E. E. ꝑ Tho's Bonner & Peter Williams Colrs.

[224] At a Vestry held at Petersburg for Bristol Parish Feby 1, 1779.

Present. The Revd Mr. William Harrison, James Field, Robert Skipwith C Warden's, Will. Digges, Will. Call, Roger Atkerson, Richd Taylor, Nathl Raines & Joseph Jones Gent.

Bristol Parish Dr.	£.	S.	D.
To Susannah Tucker for Jane Daniel, . .	11	5	
To William Temple for Nancy Davis, . .	15		
To Ann Hare for Margaret William's, . .	26	5	
To Granny Stewart for Cyruss Stewart, . .	11	5	
To William Aldridge for Ann Butterworth, .	30		
To Goditha Sears, for Eliz^h Sear's, . . .	26	5	
To Will. Scoggin, to Assist him as a Poor person, ...	9	7	6
To The C. Wardens for Support of Will. Hardin, ...	10	15	7½
To Walter Thompson to Assist him as a poor person, ...	28	2	
To Margarett Dick for Eliz^h Carpenter, . .	17	10	
To Amey Lester for Elisha Lester, . . .	16	17	6
To Robert Armistead CLK of the Vestry, .	50		
To John Roberts for Will. Evans, . . .	10		
To Will. Temple for Burying of Nancy Davis,	10	9	
To Duke Bonner for horse block's at the Out Church, ...	6		
To Margarett Dick, for Keeping Eliz^h Carpenter from Octr 1778 Untill Feby 1, 1779, .	12	16	6
To the C Wardens to Assist Thos Pillion, .	40		
To Mary Allen for Elisha Lester, . . .	8	8	9
To Edmond Conway to Assist him as a Poor person, ...	40	0	0
Ordered That James Day be Allowed, The Sum of Twenty Five Pounds, as an Object of Charity, ...	25		
	£405	6	10½

Ordered, That the Church Warden's endeavour to Borrow Money Towards the Support of the poor, as it Appears to the Vestry, that it will be Verry Benificial to this Parish.

Cr.

By 863 Tithes in Dinwiddie. } at 10 | each.
By 727 D^o in P. Geo. }

1,590

Ordered That the Church Warden's Recieve from Every Tithable Person The sum of Ten Shilling's & in Case of Refusal or Non Payment, Levy the Same by Distress.

To Six p^r C^t for Collecting.

John Burwell Gen^t Appeared this Day in Vestry Likewise Theo^k Bland Ju^r Gen^t and Resigned there Office's of Vestrymen.

Ordered That John Kirby be Appointed, in Place of John Burwell And William Roberson in Place of Theo^k Bland, And that the Above Gentlemen be Served with a Copy by the CLK.

Ordered That James Field & Joseph Jones, Gen^t be appointed Church Wardens the Ensueing Year. And that they Qualify Accordingly.

JAMES FIELD, JOSEPH JONES C W.

Test R ARMISTEAD CLK of the Vestry.

[225] At A Vestry Held at the Brick Church May 1. 1779.

Present. The Rev^d. Mr. Harrison, Joseph Jones, Wm. Call, Roger Atkerson, Richard Taylor, Robt Gilliam, Wm. Robertson & John Kirby Gentl^n.

Whereas, at A Vestry held Feby 1. 1779. for the Parish of Bristol the Said Vestry Lev^yd A Sum for the Clerks & Sextons. and Whereas they find the Same Contrary to an act of Assembly, Ordered therefore that the Sum Levy^d for the Same Clerks & Sextons be Rescin'ed.

JOSEPH JONES. C W.

Test R ARMISTEAD C V.

At a Vestry held for Bristol Parish Feby 4. 1780.

Present. James Field, Joseph Jones C W., Wm. Call, John Banister, Roger^r Atkerson, Richd Taylor, Robt Gilliam & John Kirby Gen^t.

BRISTOL PARISH DR.	£ S. D.
To the C Wardens for Jane Daniels Support, . .	210 00 0
To Mary Allen for Elisha Lester, ...	210 00 0
To Will. Aldridge for Ann Butterworth, . . .	210 00 0
To Ann Hare for Margarett Williams, ...	210 00 0
To Thos Armistead for Eliz^h Stewart & Son Cyrus, .	210 00 0
To Will. Scoggin to Assist him, ...	90 00 0
To the C W. for Support of Will Harding, . .	20 00 0
To Walter Thompson for Maintanance, . . .	210 00 0

To John Roberts for William Evans, . . .	90 00 0
To James Day to Assist him, ...	60 00 0
To Edmond Conway D°, ...	120 00 0
To Peter Aldridge D°, ...	100 00 0
To the C W for Support of Hannah Kenner, . .	225 00 0
To Boswell Goodwyn for Rob[t] Elder, . . .	100 00 0
To R. Armistead C V. and Possession's, . .	360 00 0
To Peter Aldridge for Eliz[h] Carpenter, . . .	150 00 0
To the C W. for Thom[s] Pillion's Support, . .	210 00 0
To Rich[d] Williams as ℘[r] Acc[t], ...	153 7 0
	£2,938 7 0

C[r] By 863 Tithes in Dinwiddie.
D° By 737 D° P. George.

1,600 Titheable @ 42 | each £3,360.

Ordered That the C W. for the year 1778 Settle There Acc[ts] with The Present C W. and Pay them the Ballance.

This day the Late Recter, the Rev[d] Mr. Harrison, wrote in his Resignation of his Cure of this Parish, Which is accepted.

The Late C W. Returned there Acc[ts] for the year 1779.

The Ballance Due the Parish £335. 16. 10½.

Ordered, That William Digges & Rob[t] Gilliam Gen[t] be Appointed C W. The ensueing year, And that they Recieve from every Titheable person 42 | each. And in Case of Refusall or Non Payment Levy the Same by Distress.

James Field, Joseph Jones C W.

Test R. Armistead C V.

At a Vestry held for Bristol Parish Jan[y] 19. 1782.

Present. Rob[t] Gilliam C W., The Honourable John Banister, James Field, Nath[l] Raines, Joseph Jones, Roger Atkerson & Wm. Roberson Gen[t].

Rob[t] Gilliam Late C W. Returned his Account, for P. Geo. & Ordered to be Recorded.

Ordered. That Rob[t] Bolling Ju[r] Es[qr] be Appointed a Vestryman. In Place of Rob[t] Skipwith Gen[tn] Dec[d] and that he be Served with A Copy of the Same by the Clerk.

Rob't. Gilliam C W.

Test R Armistead C V.

[226] At a Vestry held for Bristol Parish March 16. 1782.

Present. William Robertson, John Kirby C W., Nath[l] Raines, James Field, Richard Taylor, Robert Gilliam & Rob[t] Bolling Gentlemen.

Bristol Parish Dr.	£	S	D.
To Susannah Tucker for Jane Daniel,	10	00	0
To Fedrick Archer for Ann Butterworth,	10	00	0
To Amey Hacker for Elisha Lester,	15	00	0
To Ann Hare for Margarett Williams,	13	00	0
To the C Wardens for Will. Harding's Support,	6	00	0
To Walter Thompson D°,	15	00	0
To John Roberts for Will Evan's,	5	00	0
To James Day to Assist him,	5	00	0
To Peter Aldridge Sen[r],	3	00	0
To Judith Goodwyn for Eliz[h] Carpenter,	7	10	0
To the C W. for Thomas Pillion,	12	00	0
To Robert Armistead Clerk of the Vestry,	10	00	0
To Hartwell Raines for 24 Tithes Insolvents of Alex[r] Shaw for the year 1775 @ 4 | 2 each,	5	00	0
To the C W. for Cyrus Stewart Support,	10	00	0
To the C W. for Rob[t] Elder D°,	10	00	0
N. B. this Levyed for the Year of our Lord 1780.			
To the C Wardens for Jane Daniel's Support,	£15	00	0
To Amey Hacker for Elisha Lester,	15	00	0
To Ann Hare for Margarett Williams,	13	00	0
To the C W. for Support of Will. Harding,	6	00	0
To Walter Thompson D°	15	00	0
To John Roberts for Wm. Evans (to be bound Apprentice),	5	00	0
To Ann Phillips for Ann Butterworth,	13	00	0
To James Day to Assist him,	5	00	0
To Peter Aldridge Sen[r] D°,	3	00	0
To the C W. for Rob[t] Elder's Support,	10	00	0
To Judith Goodwyn for Eliz[h] Carpenter,	7	10	0
To the C W. for Tho[s] Pillion's Support,	12	00	0
To Robert Armistead Clerk of the Vestry,	10	00	0
To the C W. for Cyrus Stewart,	10	00	0
N. B. this Levyed for 1781.			
	£298	00	0

C^{r} By 763 Tithes in Dinwiddie.
D^{o} By 637 D^{o} in Prince Geo.

1,400 Tithes @ 4 | 6 each £315 00 0.
To 6 p^{r} C^{t} for Collecting £ 18 4

Ordered, That William Robertson & John Kirby Gentlemen be Appointed C Wardens the Ensueing Year. And That they Recieve from Every Titheable Person 22½ Lb^{s} of Neat Tob^{o} or 4 | 6 Speicie, in Case of Refusal or Non Payment, Levy the Same by Distress.

Ordered That the Church Wardens, Let the Repaireing of the Glebe (Such as are Nessary) to the Lowest Bidder.

ROBERT GILLIAM.

Attest R. ARMISTEAD C V.

[227 Blank] [228–229]

1780 BRISTOL PARISH IN ACCOUNT RO'T GILLIAM C W. DR.

To the Church Warden for Jane Daniel, . .	£ 210	00
To D^{o} for Ann Butterworth (Wm. Aldridge), .	210	00
To Ann Hare for Margarett Williams, . . .	210	00
To Thos Armistead for Stewart & Son, . .	210	00
To William Scoggin to Assist him as a poor person,	90	00
To William Hardings Support, ...	20	00
To William Thompson D^{o} D^{o}, .	210	00
To James Day as a poor person D^{o}, .	60	00
To Robt Armistead Clerk Vestry & Possessions, .	360	00
To Richd Williams as p^{r} Acc^{t} Rendered, . .	153	7
To John Salmon a poor Person, ...	71	
To Wm Harding D^{o}	19	
To John Roberts Acc^{t} of William Evans, . .	30	
To Margarett Dick for Eliz^{h} Carpenter, . .	36	10
To John Salmon a poor person D^{o}, . . .	87	15
To Clothes found Jane Daniel, ...	242	
To Salmons Acc^{t} of Betty Skinner, . . .	42	15
To Commissions in Collecting, ...	92	17
To Cash for Jane Daniels Support, . . .	96	13
	£2,451	17

CONTRA CR.

By Cash Recieved of Doc^r James Field, . .	£335	18
By D^o for a fine, ...		5
By D^o D^o, ...		5
By D^o of Robert Skipwith, ...	87	15
By 737 Tythes in Prince George @ 42 | each, .	1,547	14
By Support of Jane Daniel, ...	210	
By James Day, ...	60	
By William Aldridge paid by Col^o Digges, . .	210	
	£2,451	17

1780 THOMAS PENISTONE DR. BRISTOL PARISH.

To One Years Rent of the Glebe, . . 1,500^lbs Tob^o.

[230] At a Vestry held for Bristol Parish November 27th. 1782.

Present. William Robertson & John Kirby Church Wardens, Nathl Raines, James Field, Richard Taylor, Robert Gilliam & Joseph Jones, Gentlemen.

BRISTOL PARISH DR.	£	S	D.
To the C Wardens for Jane Daniels Support, .			
To Obedience Hacker for Elisha Lester. . .	15	00	
To Ann Hare for Margarett William's, . .	15	00	
To the C Wardens for Will Harding, . . .	6	00	
To the Widow Day for her Support, . . .	5	00	
To Judith Goodwyn for Eliz^h Carpenter, . .			
To the Church Wardens for Thos Pillions Support,	12	00	
To the Church Wardens for Cyrus Stewart, . .	10	00	
To R Armistead Clerk of the Vestry, . . .	10	00	
To the Church Wardens for Robert Elder, . .	10	00	
To Sarah Sadler for Edward Griffins Child Mary,	10	00	
To Peter Aldridge Senr for Keeping Eliz^h Carpenter 3 Months, ...	1	17	10

C^r By 763 Tithes in Dinwiddie.
D^o By 761 D^o in Prince George.

1,524 Tithes @ 1 | 3, . £95 5 0

William Digges a former Church Warden for Dinwiddie, haveing Returned his Acc[t] p[r] Mr. Kirby, which is Ordered to be Recorded.

William Digges. Gen[t] Wrote his Resignation of Vestryman of this Parish, which is Recieved.

Ordered That Bennett Kirby be Appointed A Vestryman in The Room of William Digges Resigned, And that the Said Gentleman be Served with a Copy of the Same by the Clerk.

John Kirby Gentl[n] C Warden for Dinwiddie for the year 1781 and 1782 Returned his Acc[t] And was Ordered to be Recorded.

Ordered That John Kirby & William Robertson Gentl[n] Be Continued Church Wardens the Ensueing Year, And that they Recieve from Every Titheable Person 1 | 3. Cash. In Case of Refusal or Non payment to Levy the Same by Distress.

WILLIAM ROBERTSON C W.
JOHN KIRBY D[o]

Attest R ARMISTEAD CLK V.

[231 Blank] [232–233]

1780 BRISTOL PARISH, IN ACC'T WITH WILLIAM DIGGES CHURCH WARDEN DR.

To Cash Paid Peter Aldridge, ...	£ 250	00	0
To Mary Alley, ...	210	00	0
To William Aldridge, ...	210	00	0
To John Roberts, ...	90	00	0
To James Day, ...	60	00	0
To What the Collecter p[d] Boswell Goodwyn,	100	00	0
To D[o] paid Sarah Conway, ...	69	10	0
To Commissions for Collecting, ...	102	11	0
Oct[r] 24. 1782.			
To Cash p[d] John Kirby present C W. £9. 17. 3¾ Special Which Equal as p[r] Scale Oct[r] 1780 to	720	5	0
	£1,812	6	0

CONTRA CR.

By 863 Tithes @ 42 | each, ...	£1,812	6	

1782 November 9. BRISTOL PARISH IN ACC'T WITH JOHN KIRBY, CHURCH WARDEN DR.

	£	s	d
To Cash paid John Roberts, . . .	10	00	0
To Peter Aldridge, ...	6	00	0
To Judith Goodwyn, ...	15	00	0
To Thomas Pillion, ...	24	00	0
To R Armistead, ...	20	00	0
To Emmanuel Lewis, for Cyrus Stewart, .	20	00	0
To Robert Elder, ...	20	00	0
To Obedience Hacker for Elisha Lester, .	30	00	0
To Commissions for Collecting, . . .	10	6	0
To Sarah Conway, for Edmond Conway, for year 1779, ...		13	10
To Thomas Pillion for year 1779, . . .	2	17	6
To Cash p^d Isaac Gilmore, for Cloathing Wm. Brandom, ...	1	18	3
	£160	15	7

CONTRA CR.

	£	s	d
By 763 Tithes @ 4 | 6 each, ...	£171	13	6
By what William Digges paid me, . .	9	17	3¾
	£181	10	9¾

[234] At a Vestry Held for Bristol Parish Oct. 16. 1783.

Present. William Robertson & John Kirby C Wardens, John Banister, James Field, Robert Gilliam, Bennett Kirby & Richd Taylor; Gentlemen.

BRISTOL PARISH DR.	£	S	D
To Ann Perkins, for Jane Daniel, Due Decr 1. 1784,	10		
To Obedience Hacker for Elisha Lester, . .	13		
To Ann Hare for Margaret Williams, . . .	12		
To The Widow Day, for her Support, . .	6		
To The C Wardens, for Thomas Pillion, . .	12		
To The C Wardens for Cyrus Stewart, . .	10		
To Sarah Sadler for Ed^d Griffins, Child Mary, Due May 8th 1784, ...		7	10
To The C Wardens for, Eliz^h Carpenter, . .		7	10
To The C Wardens, for Eliz^h McCulluck, . .	10		

To The C Wardens for Rob[t] Elder's Support, .	10
To Robert Armistead Clerk Vestry & Possessions,	15
	£113

C[r] By 763 Tithes in Dinwiddie.
D[o] By 761 D[o] in Prince George.

1,524 Tithes @ 1 | 6 p[r] poll, . . . £114 6

The Church Wardens through these Indisposition's, haveing it not In there power's to Collect the Money's Due for the Last Year.—Ordered, That there Acc[t] Lay Over, to the Next Vestry.

Thomas Pennistone, the present Tennant of the Glebe, Haveing this Day, Returned his Acc[t] in full and Ordered to be Recorded. The whole, with his former Acc[t] Amounting to £11. 13. 00.

Mr. Thomas Pennistone D[r] Bristol Parish. 1780 Jan[y] 1. To Jan[y] 1st 1784 @ 1,500 Lb[s] of Tob[o] p[r] year.

The Gentlemen Of the Vestry, this day Agree'd with Mr. Pennistone The present Tennant and have Rented the Said Glebe to him the Next year, for 1,500 Lb[s] of Neat Tob[o]. Likewise it is to be Payed with Tob[o] Inspected on Appomattox River.

Ordered That Rob[t] Bolling Ju[r] & Bennett Kirby Gentlemen Be appointed C Warden's the Ensueing Year, And that they Recieve from Every Titheable Person, 1 | 6 Cash p[r] poll. In case of Refusal or Non payment Levy the Same By Distress.

Ordered. That the Church Wardens Advertise in the publick Gazette, That the Parish of Bristol, is Vacant for want of a Minister.

WILLIAM ROBERTSON }
JOHN KIRBY C. Wardens } C Ws.

Attest. R. ARMISTEAD. C. V.

[235] At a Vestry held for Bristol Parish. March 17. 1784.

Present. Robert Bolling, Bennett Kirby, Church Wardens, Nath[l] Raines, Rich[d] Taylor, James Field, Joseph Jones, Wm. Robertson & John Banister, Gentlemen.

Ordered That Henry Bonner & Joseph Kirkland with the freeholders of there Precinct, Possession from the S[o] Side of Jones Hole Swamp to the Sussex Line, And Rowanty Road.

Ordered, That the Several Returns of Possession's, be made

as Soon as Possible, to the Clerk of the Vestry & that he Record them as Soon as Rec[d].

Agreeable to an Order of Vestry, Bearing Date October 16th 1783.

That the Church Wardens Advertise for a Minister, Which Advertisement was Duly Complyed with; Agreeable to the Said Order, The Rev[d] Mr. John Cammeron and the Rev[d] Mr. Thomas Kenedy, Appeared, and were both Nominated.—The Rev[d] Mr. John Cammeron was Elected for One Year,—And that the Glebe, is Now Rented, he is to have the profits of, from this Date for Twelve Months.

ROB'T. BOLLING, BENNETT KIRBY C W'S.

Attest R ARMISTEAD C V.

At a Vestry Held for Bristol Parish, in Petersburg November 1. 1784.

Present. Rob[t] Bolling C W., Rich[d] Taylor, Wm. Robertson, Rob[t] Gilliam, John Kirby, Nath[l] Raines, & John Banister, Gentlemen.

BRISTOL PARISH DR.	£	S	D
To William Harding for his Support, . .			
To Thomas Pillion for D[o] . . .	12	00	0
To Cyrus Stewart for D[o] . . .	10	00	0
To Sarah Sadler for Edw[d] Griffins Child Mary,	7	10	0
To Ann Perkins for Jane Daniel, . . .	10	00	0
To Rob[t] Bolling Gen[t] C W. for Sundrys as p[r] Acc[t], ...	10	1	10½
To Rob[t] Elder for his Support, . . .	10	00	
To Ann Vaughn, for James McCullock, . .	5	00	0
To Nath[l] Raines Gen[t] for Rachel Redings Support, ...	5	00	0
To William Jones for Rich[d] Lunsford's Child, .	5	00	0
To R Armistead Clerk of the Vestry, . .	10	00	0
To Alex[r] Taylor for a Coffin for Hannah Kenner,	1	00	0
	£85	11	10½

C[r] By 763 Tithes in Dinwiddie.
By 761 D[o] Prince Geo.

1,524 Tithes @ 2 | £152. 8.

Ordered, That the C W. Recieve from Mr. Penistone the present Tennant The Last year's Rent, and pay unto the Rev^{d} Mr. Cammeron, the Same.

This Day John Kirby Late C W. Returned his Acc^{t} & Ordered to be Recorded.

The Rev^{d} Mr. John Cammeron, came this day in Vestry When the Vestry Unanimustly, Elected him Rector of this Parish.

Ordered, That the Church Wardens Recieve from Every Titheable Person Two Shillings Cash or 16 Lb^{s} of Tob^{o} In case of Refusal or Non Payment, Levy the Same by Distress.

Ordered, That Robt Turnbull, Gentleman be appointed A Vestryman in the Room of Roger Atkerson Gentleman who has Resigned. And that he be be Served with a Coppy of the Same by the Clerk.

ROBERT BOLLING C W.

Attest R ARMISTEAD C V.

[236–237] Octr 19 1784. BRISTOL PARISH IN ACC'T WITH JOHN KIRBY FORMER CHURCH WARDEN DR.

To paid Thomas Pillion as p^{r} Reciept, . .	£12		
To p^{d} Emanuel Lewis, for Cyrus Stewarts Support, ...	10		
To p^{d} Ann Perkins for Jane Daniel's D^{o}, . .	9		6½
To p^{d} Richd Lunsford, for Eliz^{h} McCullock, .	1	4	
To p^{d} Ann Vaughn for Support of Eliz^{h} McCullock 3 Months, ...	1	16	
To p^{d} Judith Goodwyn, for Eliz^{h} Carpenter, .	4	3	4
To Obedience Hacker, for Elisha Lester, . .	15		
To p^{d} John Thompson, for Robt Elder, . .	10		
To Commission for Collecting, ...	2	17	2
	£66	1	0½
To cash p^{d} Robt Bolling Church Warden Novr 1. 1784, ...	2	8	
	£68	9	0½

CONTRA CR.

By 763 Tithes @ 1 | 3 each, ...	£47	13	9
By the Depositt for Last Year, ...	20	15	2¾
	£68	8	11¾

1784 BRISTOL PARISH IN ACC'T WITH ROBERT BOLLING, CHURCH WARDEN DR.

		£	s	d
March	To Advertiseing for a Minister three Weeks, ...	£ 0	7	0
	To a Bushell of Corn Meal for Mrs. Chriswell, ...		4	
	To a Bushell of Wheat for D^{o} 5 | 22 Lb^{s} Bacon 9^{d}, ...	1	1	6
July	To 8 Barrells of Corn for Wm. Harding @ 20 |	8		
	To 12 Yards Oznabrigs for Ditto @ 9^{d},		9	4½
		£10	1	10½

[238] We do hereby engage ourselves to be conformable to the Doctrine Discipline & Worship of the Protestant Episcopal Church. September 3d 1788.

John Banister,	Thomas G. Peachy,
Robert Bolling,	Alexander G. Strachan,
James Feild,	Isaac Hall,
William Robertson,	James Geddy,
Robert Turnbull,	Richard Gregory,
John Shore,	
April 10th 1789.	Jesse Bonner.

[239 Blank] [240] 1785 March 28th.

Persuant to an Act of Assembly, passed Last Session Entiled an Act, for Incorporating the protestant Episcopal Church, An Election was held, When the following Gentlemen were duly Elected, For the Parish of Bristol Viz—

John Banister, Robt Bolling, James Field, Robt Turnbull, Richd Taylor, Joseph Jones, William Robertson, Nathl Raines, Christopher McConnico, Isaac Hall, Alex^{r} Glass. Strachan, & John Baird Senr.

April 11th.

A Meeting of the Minister and Vestry, of the Protestant Episcopal Church in the Parish of Bristol, Being Called The Following Gentlemen Mett, and previous to there entering on the Office of Vestrymen, Have Subscribed in Vestry, to be Conformable to the Doctrine, Discipline And Worship of the Protestant Episcopal Church,

Robert Bolling,	Joseph Jones,	Isaac Hall,
Rob[t] Turnbull,	William Robertson,	Alex[r] Glass Strachan,
Rich[d] Taylor,	Chris[r] M[c]Connico,	John Baird.

Ordered. That John Banister & Rob[t] Bolling Gentlemen be appointed Church Wardens.

Ordered. That R Armistead, be Appointed Clerk, Collecter & Treasurer And that he Recieve Seven & a Half per Cen[t] for his Trouble.

Ordered. That the Rev[d] Mr. Cammeron Employ a Sexton for the Brick Church And that no Other person Open the ground, nor digg a Grave in the Said Church Yard, but the Sexton, And that the Said Sexton be Allowed Six Shillings, for Digging a Grave & his Attendance.

Ordered. That the Church Wardens, Lett the Makeing of Proper Gates to the Church Walls, to Some undertaker, And have them Properly Fitted, Likewise the Repairs of the Church, And pay for the Same out of The late Rents of the Glebe Lands of this Parish.

Ordered. That the Church Wardens Furnish The Elements for the use of the Churches, and that they draw on the Treas[y] to Pay the Same.

Ordered. That the Church Wardens (after the Church is in Order, have all the pews Numbred, Reserving two for the use of the Studien's, and four for the use of the Poor. And lett The same, to the highest Bidders.

[241] Robert Bolling Esq[r] is Duly Elected to Meet the Convention in the City of Richmond, on the 18th of May Next. And that he be Served with a Copy of the Same by the Clerk Agreeable to his Appointment.

Ordered, That Robert Bolling, Christopher M[c]Connico, Wm. Robertson and Nath[l] Raines, Gen[t] are Appointed to Prepare Subscriptions for the Support of the Protestant Episcopal Church. And that they are to be Returned, by the 30th of Oct[r] Next Ensueing.

Resolved That it is the Opinion of the Vestry that a Petition be presented to the Next Assembly for Permission to Dispose of the Glebe Lands of this Parish;

ROBERT BOLLING Church Warden.

Attest R ARMISTEAD C. V. B. Parish.

At a Meeting of the Minister & Vestry of the Protestant Episcopal Church in the Parish of Bristol, held at Petersburg, on the Fifth Day of February 1787.

Present. The Reverend John Cameron Rector, John Banister, Robert Bolling, Robert Turnbull, John Baird, William Robertson, Isaac Hall, Alexr G. Strachan, John Shore, & Christopher McConnico, Vestrymen.

John Shore Esqr is appointed a Deputy to attend the annual Meeting of the Convention of the Protestant Episcopal Church in Virginia, on the Third Wednesday in May next.

David Organ is appointed Sexton of St. Pauls Church, commonly called the Brick Church in Petersburg.

ROBERT BOLLING JR C. W.

[242] In Conformity to an Act of General Assembly passed last Session, directing the Appointment of Trustees & other purposes, the Members of the Protestant Episcopal Church in the Parish of Bristol, assembled in the Town of Petersburg on the Seventh day of November 1787, & elected the following Gentlemen as Trustees & Vestrymen for the said Parish to serve in that Office untill the Monday in Easter week in the Year one Thousand seven hundred & Ninety. Viz John Banister, Robert Bolling, James Feild, William Robertson, Robert Turnbull, John Shore, Thomas G. Peachy, Alexander G. Strachan, Isaac Hall, James Geddy, Joseph Jones, & Richard Gregory.

ROBERT BOLLING JR C. W.

Attest ROBERT ARMISTEAD Clk V.

At a meeting of the Trustees & Vestrymen of the Parish of Bristol, held at Petersburg on the Third day Sepr 1788.

Present. The Reverend John Cameron Rector, Robert Bolling jr, Thomas G. Peachy, John Shore, James Feild, William Robertson, James Geddy, Robert Turnbull, Isaac Hall, Alexr G. Strachan, & Richard Grigory, subscribed to be conformable to the Doctrine, Discipline, & Worship of the Protestant Episcopal Church, & took their seats as Trustees & Vestrymen for this Parish.

Robert Bolling j^r^ & Thomas G. Peachy Gentlemen are appointed Church Wardens.

Ordered That David Organ Sexton receive Six Shillings for his own services in digging a Grave, and Three shillings for the Liberty of burying in the Church Yard, before he breaks Ground, & that he make Return of such Money to one of the Church Wardens, once in every month.

ROBERT BOLLING, JR C. W.

[243] At a meeting of the Trustees & Vestrymen of the Parish of Bristol held at Petersburg, on the Thirty first day of December 1788.

Present. The Reverend John Cameron Rector, Bobert Bolling j^r^, Thomas G. Peachy, Church Wardens, John Shore, Alexander G. Strachan, Robert Turnbull, Isaac Hall, James Geddy, William Robertson Trustees & Vestrymen.

Peter Williams & Jesse Bonner Gentlemen are appointed Trustees & Vestrymen in the room of John Banister & James Feild deceased.

Ordered That Donald Cameron collect the Subscriptions for the Year 1788. & make Return to the Vestry on or before the first day of February next. & that he be allowed Five ℘^r^ Cent for his Trouble.

Ordered That the Sexton make up his Accounts & pay up all the Money now due for privilige of burying in Church Yard, immediately into the hands of the Church-Wardens;—& that for the future he make up his Accounts monthly, & Settle with the same.

ROBERT BOLLING JR C W.

[244] At a Meeting of the Trustees & Vestrymen of the Parish of Bristol held at Petersburg on the Eighteenth Day of April A. D. 1789.

Present. The Reverend John Cameron Rector, Robert Bolling j^r^, Thomas G. Peachy Church Wardens, William Robertson, John Shore, Richard Gregory, & Isaac Hall Trustees & Vestrymen.

Jesse Bonner Gen[t] came into Vestry & having subscribed to be conformable to the Doctrine Worship & Discipline of the Protestant Episcopal Church took his seat as a Vestryman & Trustee for this Parish.

William Robertson Esq[r] is appointed a Deputy to attend the annual Meeting of the Convention of the Protestant Episcopal Church in Virginia, on the first Wednesday in May next.

Ordered, that Peter Williams & Jesse Bonner do provide a sufficient Lock & Key for Jones Hole Church & give publick Notice that if any Person or Persons shall here after open the Doors or Windows of said Church, or officiate therein without Leave first obtaind of the Minister & Church Wardens of this Parish, He or They so offending shall be dealt with according to Law.

Ordered that David Organ, Sexton for the Church in Petersburg, employ a Bricklayer upon the best Terms He can to repair the South-west corner of the Church Yard-Wall & secure the same by a strong Post of Oak or some other durable Wood, & apply to the Church Wardens for Payment.

ROBERT BOLLING JR, THOS. G. PEACHY C W.

REGISTER.

A

Ephraim son of Wm. & Amy Andrews born 4th feb^{r} last bap^{t} sep^{tr} 1st 1721.

George son of Wm. & Anne Archer born 31st July last bap^{t} sep^{tr} 3d 1721.

Mary dau of Robt & Mary Abernathy born 16th Aprill last bap^{t} 9th Octob^{r} 1721.

Tho: son of Tho: & Ann Addison born 1st Aprill last bap^{t} 27th May 1722.

Isham son of Rich & Mary Andrews born 19th Aprill last bap^{t} July 7th 172–.

Tally son of Hen: & Mary Alley born 24th Augs^{t} 1721 bap^{t} March 27th 1722.

Ann dau of Abra & Mary Alley born 25th Instant bap^{t} 31st May 1722.

Fran: dau of Geo: & Mary Archer born 8th May last bap^{t} 19th August 1722.

Wm. son of Tho: & Mary Adaman born 2d July last bap^{t} 17th feb: 1722–3.

Geo: son of Wm. & Avis Andrews born 14th Jan^{r} last bap^{t} July 10th 1723.

Mary D. of Tho & Jane Andrews born 14th Aprill last bap^{t} July 10th 1723.

Judith D. of Geo & Mary Archer born 23d Aprill last bap^{t} 5th sep^{tr} 1724.

Winifred D of Wm. & Avis Andrews born 1st June last bap^{t} 16th sept^{r} 1724.

Drury son of Abra & Mary Allen born 1st X^{br} 1724.

Fran: son of Rich & Mary Andrews born 10th August last bap^{t} March 28th 1725.

Tho: Son of Tho: & Mary Adaman born 6th octob^{r} 1724 bap^{t} 12th Sep 1725.

John son of Rob[t] & Mary Abertnartha born 21th bap[t] 1723.
Mary Da[t] of Ann Andrews being Illigitimate born 18th octber last 1725.
Martha A negro of George Archer born Jan[r] 1725.
David Son of Rob[t] and Mary Abertnarthy born May 29th bap[t] June 6th 1726.
Wm Son of Elkana and Sarah Allen born 3d sep[r] 1726.
Sarah D of John and Catherine Adams born 30th Ap[r] 1726.
Winefritt D of Abraham and Mary Alle born 22d Aprill 1727.
Eliz D of Th[o] and Jane andrews born 11th Novem[r] 1726 bap[t] 15 1727.
Wm S of Rich[d] and Mary andrews born 13th May 1726 bap[t] 15 novem[r] 1727.
avice D of Wm and avice andrews Born 7th Dec[m] 1727 Bap.
Martha D of Wm. and ann Archer born 19th Bap[t] 19th Janr[y] 1727.
Mary D of George and Sarah Archer Born 25th June 1728.
Eliz[a] D of henry and Eliz[a] anderson Born 14th aprill 1729.
Ellinor female slave of Ditto Born 14th aprill 1729.
Sarah D of Elcanah and Sarah allin Born 28th Dec[r] Bap[t] 4th March 1728.
Henry Son of Richard & mary andrews Born 3d feb[r] 1729 Bap[t] 28th aprill 1730.
John Son of Wm and avis andrews Born 7th July 1729 Bap[t] 10th May 1730.
Mary D of abraham and Mary Alle Born 13th July 1730.
Thomas Son of Christophar and Mary Addison Born 12th Sept[r] 1730.
Eliz[a] D: of Robert and Mary Abernarthy Born 20th May 1730 Bap[t] 20th Sep[tr].
Frances D of William and Ann Archer Born 14th august 1730 Bap[t] oct[r] 12th.
Sarah D of George & Mary Archer Born 31th Dce[r] Bap[t] 21th feb[r] 1730.
anne of Thomas & ann addison Born 1th feb[r] 1730.
Martha Dat[r] of Tho[s] & Jean Andrews born 16th March 1731 bap[t] June 1st 1732.
Luciana dat[r] of W[m] & Avis Andrews born 9 Sep[r] 1731 bap[t] July 30th 1732.

Phebœ dater of Rich^{d} & Mary Andrews born 26th March 1732 bap^{t} July 30th 1732.

Jean Dat^{r} of Geo & Mary Archer born 12th July 1732 bap^{t} Sepr 3d 1732.

Clyborn of Henry & Elisabeth Born anderson 21th Decr 1732 Bap^{t} Jan^{r} 14th 1732.

amy D of Robert & mary abernarthy Born 30th Jan^{r} 1732 Bap^{t} 26th March 1733.

Eleonore D of abraham & mary allen Born 11th ap^{r} 1733 Bap^{t} 27th may 1733.

Winifred D^{r} of Christopher & mary addison Born 8th octb^{r} 1732 Bap^{t} 17th June 1733.

Phebe D: of Wm & ann archer Born 3d Sepr 1733 Bap^{t} octb^{r} 18th 1733.

Robert Son of John & martha alexander Born 2d Jan^{r} 1733 Bap^{t} 30 feb^{r}.

John Son of James & Elisabeth Anderson Born 4th May 1734 Bap^{t} 4th august.

Field Son of field & Elisabeth archer Born 1th July 1734 Bap^{t} 2d July.

George Son of Richard & Tabitha Archer Born 30 April 1734.

Ruth D. of Jane Anderson born July 12th 1733.

Amey D. of John & Elizabeth Anderson Born 18th June 1734.

Henry S of Henry & Elizabeth Anderson Born 4 Jan^{ry} 1734.

Thomas S of Thomas & alice Archer Born Octob^{r} 3d 1734 Baptiz'd the 25th.

Lucey D. of Abraham & Mary Allen Born Sep^{t} 12th 1735.

Fredrick S of Thomas & Alce Archer Born November ye 13th 1740.

Mary D of Peter & Elisabeth Aldridg Born febuary ye 22nd 1739.

Miles S of Abraham & mary Allen Born may ye 18th 1741.

Lucy D. of David and Ann Abernothy B Feb^{ry} 14th 1740.

John S of William & Agnis Abbet Feb^{ry} 26th 1740.

William S. of Richard & Tabitha Archers born Sep^{tr} 20th 1738 & Bap^{t} Octob^{r} 30th 1741.

Roger S. of Richard & Tabitha Archers Born May 10th 1741 & Bap^{t} Octob^{r} 30th 1741.

Mary D. of John & Elizabeth Atkinsons Born Sep^{tr} 5th 1741 & Bap^{t} Apr 11th 1742.

Robert S. of Robert & Sara Abernethys Born March 27th 1742 & Bapt June 13th 1742.

William S. of Charles & Ellis Abernethys Born Apr 4th 1742 & Bapt June 13th 1742.

Joanna D. of William & Ellis Aldrige Born Jany 10th 1741–2 & Bapt May 11th 1742.

Elizabeth D. of Richard & Mary Aycock born Decr 4th 1742 & Bapt Feb 20th 1742.

Martha D. of Elizabeth Allen born Octobr 28th 1742 and baptd Aprile 10th 1743.

John S. of Peter & Elizabeth Aldrige born June 14th 1743 & baptd May 9th 1743.

Sara D. of William & Mary Archers born Janr 28th 1742–3 & baptd June 12th 1743.

Mason D. of Abram & Mary Allens born Novr 20th 1743 & baptd Janry 1st 1743–4.

Mille D. of Peter & Elizabeth Aldridge born Janry 25th 1744–5 & baptd Aprile 28th 1745.

Mary D. of William & Mary Archers born Septr 16th 1745 baptd Octob —— 1745.

Frederick S. of John & Lucy Aberneathys was born Sept 2d baptd Novr 10th 1745.

Shade Son of Winifreid Alley born —— —— Baptized May 12th 1751.

David Son of William & Jean Andersons born Novemr 29th 1750.

James Son of Ditto born January 21st 1753.

Sukey D of Drury and Abigail Alley born August 28th 1752.

Binns Son of Howell Adkins (of Sussex) & Susannah his Wife, born March 13th & bap. May 13th 1792.

Branchey a Negro Boy slave belonging to Roger Atkerson was Born April 23d 1761.

Samuel, Son, of Thomas Adams, & Mary his Wife, born August 11th & baptized September 22nd 1793.

William Archer (of Dinwiddie) was buried 23d June 1795.

B

Robt son of Majr Robt & Anne Bolling born 30th octobr Last bapt 13th Nov: 1720.

Wm. son of Wm. & Mary Belsher born 4th June last bap[t] 24th octob[r] 1720.

Ruth dau: of Rich: & Agnis Barber born 14th octob[r] last bap[t] Jan[r] 1st 1720–1.

John son of Moses & Mary Beck born 4th Nov last bap[t] March 21th 1720–1.

Eliz: dau: of Andrew & Eliz: Beck born 26th octob[r] last bap[t] March 21th 1720–1.

Tho son of Tho: & Mary Burge born 31th may last bap[t] 17th sep[tr] 1721.

Rich: son of John & Eliz: Brown born 3d July instant bap[t] July 19th 1721.

Tho: son of Wm. & Mary Batt born 3d July last bap[t] Sept[r] 27th 1721.

Agnis dau of Edw: & Margret Birchet born 6th Jan[r] last bap[t] 27th August 1721.

Vide D: for Banks.[*]

Wm. son of Jo & Rebecca Bryerly born 9th sep[t] last bap[t] octob[r] 22th 1721.

James son of Rob[t] & Ann Bevell born 2d nov: Last bap[t] 25 decemb[r] 1721.

Jane dau of peter & Eliz Baugh born 15th Nov: last bap[t] March 5th 1721–2.

John son of Wm. & Anne Brown born 30th Augs: last bap[t] March 11th 1721–2.

Tho: son of Tho & Eliz Bott born 14th decem 1721 bap[t] Aprill 1722.

Cha: son of James & Mary Banks born sep[t] 18th Anno 1716.

Mary d: of ditto born Nov: 21th 1718.

Sarah d. of ditto born 10th Nov: 1721.

Tho son of Wm. & Mary Belcher born 28th June last bap[t] July 7th 1722.

Wm. son of Hugh & Mary Bragg born 20th March last bap[t] July 15th 1722.

John son of Rich: & Jane Burch born 7th March last bap[t] June 11th 1722.

---

*Three leaves, containing the first (and much the larger) part of the register of names in D, E and F, are missing.—C. G. C.

Annakin A Slave belonging unto Capt Drury Bolling born in April 1720.

Sue A slave belonging unto ditto born in Nov: 1720.

Mingo A negro boy belonging unto ditto born in July 1722.

Benja son of Benja & Eliz Blick born 26th March 1721 bapt March 29th 172–.

John son of Rich & Agnis Barber born 21th Aprill last bapt 31th May 172–.

Cha son of Nico: & Ann Butterworth born 6th Jan: last bapt feb 14th 172–.

Agnis dau of Edw & Margaret Birchett 6th Jan: last bapt 27th August 1721.

Wm. son of Jno & Anne Bradshaw born June 9th 1719.

John son of ditto 1st febr 1721–2.

Wm. son of Edw & Mary Burchet born 30 xbr last bapt July 7th 1723.

Wm. son of Ja. & Eliz Baugh born 5th Aprill last bapt July 21th 1723.

Wm. son of John & Eliz Browder born 7th July last bapt 18th August 1723.

Tho. son of Geo. & Ann Brooks born 20th feb. last bapt Augt 21th 1723.

prissilla dau of Jam. & Mary Banks born 31th Janr last bapt Augt 22th 1723.

Robt son of Robt & Ann Bevell born 10th octr 1723.

Gabe A negro boy belonging to Capt Drury Bolling born 10th of 9br 1723.

Bety A negro girl belonging to Mad. Anne Bolling born 28th Aprill 1723.

John son of Tho & Letitia Broadway born 10th May 1720 bapt Janr 30th 1723–4.

Abigail D. of Rich: & Agnis Barber born 27th octob last bapt feb. 6th 1723–4.

Anne D. of Tho. & Eliz Bott born xbr ult bapt feb 1st 1723–4.

prud. dau. of Jno & Rebeca Broyely born 16th xbr last bapt feb. 15th 1723–4.

Wm. son of Edm. & Mary Broadway born 4th June last bapt Aug 30th 1724.

Mason d of Maj^{r} Robt & Anne Bolling born 14th August last bap^{t} sep^{t} 22th 1724.

Andrew s of Andrew & Eliz Beck born 4th March last bap^{t} 18th Aprill 1725. '

Randolph s. of Patrick & Rose Bardin born 12 March last bap^{t} May 2d 1725.

Tho. s. of Tho & Ester Backly Born 24th June last bap^{t} 7th March 1724-5.

Ann daughter of ditto born 28th May 1722.

Jam s. of Edw. & Margaret Burchet born 19th Nov. last bap^{t} June 13th 1725.

——— of John & Anne Bradshaw ———

Mary D. of Moses & Mary Beck born 27th May last bap^{t} 25th July 1725.

Luis s of Jno & Eliz. Baugh born 25th June last bap^{t} may 7th 1725.

John son of John burton and Catherine born 7th Sep^{tr} bap^{t} 12th oc^{tr} 1725.

Catherine burton Decs^{t} 10th Sep^{tr} 1725.

John Son of benj^{n} & Elis^{a} blick born 27th octb^{r} 1725.

Gower Son of Jno & Ann Bradshaw oct^{m} 24th 1724.

martha da^{t} of George and Ann brooks born 31th March 1725.

George son of henry and ann baly born 2d Day o June 1725.

Eliz^{a} Dat of Hugh and mary brag born 8th July 1725.

Mary Dat of George and Eliz^{a} Browder born 20th Augt 1725.

Eliz Dat of abraham and mary Burton born ap^{r} 1726.

Anne Da^{t} of simon and Martha Bursby born Jan^{r} 28th bap^{t} march 20th 1725.

Samuel burton son of Judith nunsry born august 8th 1725.

Wm son of James and Mary bankes born Ap^{r} ye 17th 1725.

Mol Slave of Capt Drury bolling Deceast. born 24th Sep^{t} 1726.

Mary D of Joseph and Margarit brewer born oct^{m} 7th 1725 bap^{t} 2d oct^{m} 1726.

Wm son of Robert and Ann Bevill born 2d oct^{m} bap^{t} 30th 1726.

Sarah D of Mary bly born 29th Aprill bap^{t} Dec^{m} 18th 1726.

Eliz^{a} D of Francis and Eliz bracy born 23d Dce^{r} 1724.

Handstess D of Edmond and martha browder born 30th Novr 1721.

James son of Ditto born 24th Aug^{s} 1725.

Edward son of Edward and Mary Brawdiway born 7th Decem[r] 1726.

Abram son of Lazarus and Winefred berten 17th Dce[m] 1726.

Mol female slave of Abr[a] burton born 4th Jan[r] 1722.

lego slave of Ditto born 14th february 1724.

peter slave of Ditto born 15th aprill 1726.

Robert son of Wm and Mary batte born 16th octem 1727.

Dorithy D of John and Rebekah Bryally born 30th feb[r] 1726.

Eliz D of John and ann Bradsho Born 20th July 1727 bap[t] 1. oct[m].

Eliz[a] Dater of Ishmail Bullock and Bersheba Chiswell Born 17th March 1721.

Frances D of Ditto born 2d March 1722 Bapt oct[m] 1th 1727.

Abraham son of Abr[a] and Mary Burton Born 28th Jan[r] 1727.

Rich[d] son of John and frances Byrge Born 29th March 1728.

Amie D. of Th[o] and Dorcorrs Booth Born 5th June 1728 Bap[t] 3d June.

John son of Henry and Avis Balie Born 23d oct[m] 1727 Bap[t] July 28th 1728.

Lucy D of John and Mary Beavil Born 19th Nov[m] 1727 Bap[t] July 4th.

Dol female slave of abraham Burton Born 18th July 1728.

Th[o] son of Wm and Mary Bryan Born 29th May 1728.

Mary D of John and Sarah Burton Born 15th June 1728.

Robert son of Wm. and Eliz[a] Bowman Born 14th March 1728.

Ann D of Rich[d] and agnis Barber Born 22d august 1728.

Edward son of Wm and Mary Belcher Born 10th March 1728.

Joel son of Hugh and Mary Bragg Born aprill 10th 1729.

William son of Edmond and martha Browder. Born 31th oct[m] Bap[t] 12th Jan[r] 1728.

Sarah D of Wm and Dorithy Browder Born 22d Dec[m] Bap[t] aprill 20th 1728.

amy D of andrew and Eliz[a] Beck Born 22d oct[m] Bap[t] feb[r] 16th 1728.

Peter male slav of John Burton Born 4th May 1729.

David son of Lasurous and Winfrit Benton Born 16th sep[r] 1729.

Sarah D of Mary Blaton 24th Jan[r] Decs[d] 1th feb[r] 1729.

Wm son of Jn[o] and Mary Blackston Born 9th May Bap[t] 27th June 1729.

John son of Th^{os} and ann Brooks Born 21th Dce^{m} Bap^{t} 15th Jan^{r} 1729.

John son of Wm and Mary Batte Decs^{d} oct^{r} 8th 1729.

ann D of Ditto Dces^{d} oct^{r} 6th 1729.

Ceasor male slave of Ditto Dces^{d} oct^{r} 6th 1729.

Ditto Margery Sue. Jone Dinah Tom 11th 1729.

Eliz^{a} D of John and frances Byrg Born 11th Decm^{r} Bap^{t} 12th March 1729.

Jeane D of George and Eliz^{a} Browder Born 29th Decr 1729 Bap^{t} 10th May 1730.

Martha Da^{t} of George and Ann Brooks born 31th March 1725.

George son of henry and amy baley born 2d June 1725.

Eliz^{a} Da^{t} of hugh and mary brag born 8th July 1725.

Mary Da^{t} of George and Eliz^{a} browder born 20th aug^{t} 1725.

Martha Da^{t} of Richard and Jane burch born 27th feb^{r} bap^{t} 29th May 1726 1725.

Tho. son of John and Eliz^{a} Blanchet Born 22d feb^{r} 1729 Bap^{t} 10th May 1730.

John son of John and ann Butler Born 15th aprill 1730 Bap^{t} 10th May.

Wm. son of William and amy Bowen Born 2d Dcem^{r} 1729 Bap^{t} 10th May 1730.

Phebe D of John and ann Bradsho Born 21th Decr 1729 Bap^{t} 10th March 1730.

Eliz^{a} D of Simon and Martha Bursby 7th Jan^{r} 1729 Bap^{t} 2d March.

——— Dater of John and Mary Bentley Born 19th May 1730.

Phebe Dater of Abraham and Mary Burton Born 11th Sepr 1730 Bap^{t} 7th Dce^{r}.

Henry son of John and Johannah Burrough Born 26th octb^{r} 1730 Bap^{t} 15th Nov^{m}.

Amy D of Richard and agnis Barber Born 30th august 1730.

Lucie D of Robert and avis Bowen Born 23th august 1730.

Abraham son of Edward and Margret Burchet Born 15th June 1730.

David son of David and Mary Barret Born 23d octob^{r} 1730 Bap^{t} 12th Jan^{r}.

Joseph son of Robt & ann Beavil Born 11th Dce^{r} 1730 Bap^{t} 14th feb^{r}.

John son of Eliz^{a} Butler Born 10th feb^{r} 1725 Bap^{t} 19th Sepr 1731.

Sarah D of William and Eliz^{a} Butler Born 8th Dec^{m} 1714 Bap^{t} 11th Sepr 1731.

Eliz^{a} D of Sam & Catharine Bartlet Born 25th Janr^{y} 1730 Bap^{t} 12th Sepr 1731.

Mary D of francis & Eliz^{a} Bressie Born 3d 1731 Bap^{t} 15th august 1731.

Sarah D of Mary Bly Born 29th ap^{r} 1726.

Thomas son of Thomas & anne Brooks Born 10th June Bap^{t} 11th octb^{r} 1731.

Miles son Liewes & Eliz^{a} Bobbitt 22d Janu^{r} 1731 Bap^{t} ap^{r} 23^{d} 1732.

Jo. male slave of abr^{a} Burton Born Novr 1730.

Jane female slave of Ditto Born Jan^{r} 1730.

Benj^{a} Son of Jno & Ann Bradshaw born April 6th 1732.

Sam a Negro of James Boisseau born May 14th 1732.

Wm. son of William & Eliz^{a} Bowman born Ap^{l} 3d 1731 bap^{t} May 21. 1732.

Sarah dat^{r} of Jno & Mary Bently bap^{t} June 1. 1732.

Martha dat^{r} of Jno & Ann Butler born 23d Ap^{l} 1732 bap^{t} June 11. 1732.

George Son of Wm. & Mary Belcher born 18th July 1731. bap^{t} 9th July 1732.

John son of Wm. & Mary Bugg born 1st Feby 1731 bap^{t} 16th July 1732.

Jno son of Andrew & Eliz^{a} Beck born 30th Ap^{l} 1732 bap^{t} 23d July 1732.

David of Wm. & Amy Bowen born 13th Novr 1731 bap^{t} 30th July 1732.

Ephraim Son of Robt & Avis Bowen born 12th Feby 1731 bap^{t} 30th July 1732.

Fra^{s} dat^{r} of Robt & Ann Burton born Octr 11h 1732 bap^{t} Sepr 20th 1732.

Martha dat^{r} of Jno & Sarah Burton born 25th May bap^{t} Sepr 23d 1732.

Rice son of Jno & Mary Blaxton born Sepr 16th 1732 bap^{t} Novr 5 1732.

Drury & Miles Sons of Simon & Martha Busby born 11th Decr bap^{t} ye 23 Decr 1732.

Frances dat^{r} of Robt & Ann Bevell born ye 12th of Decr bap^{t} Decr 24th 1732.

William Slave of Robt Bolling born	18th Decr 1730.		bap^{t}
Bouzer Slave of D^{o}	24th Novr 1728.	}	Decr 26
Anthony Slave of D^{o}	12 Octr 1732.		1732.

Robert Son of Abra & Mary Burton born 24th Augt 1732 bap^{t} 26 Decr 1732.

John son of John & Frances Burg Born 10th nov^{r} 1732 Bap^{t} dce^{r} 29th.

George son of John & Eliz^{a} Browder Born 5 dce^{r} 1731 Bap^{t} 30 Jan^{r}.

Richard son of Richard & agnis Barber Born 17th feb^{r} 1732 Bap^{t} ap^{r} 9th 1733.

Peter Son of William & Elisabeth Butler Born 20th octb^{r} 1732 Bap^{t} 26th. 1733.

Martha D. of John & Wilmet Banister Born 21th Decem^{r} 1732 Bap^{t} feb^{r} 4th.

Thomas Son of Francis & Eliz^{a} Bracy Born 25th March 1733 Bap^{t} 22d ap^{r} 1733.

Susanna D^{r} of John & mary Beavil Born 4th Jan^{r} 1732 Bap^{t} 27th may 1733.

amy D^{r} of Thomas & anne Brooks Born 17th feb^{r} 1732 Bap^{t} 7th ap^{r} 1733.

William son of Henry & avice Baly Born 10th may 1733 Bap^{t} 17th June.

David son of David & Frances Burn Born 25th March 1733 Bap 2d June.

Will male slave of John Burton Born 5th March 1732.

amy D of william & Dorothy Browder Born 11th July 1733 Bap^{t} 9th sep^{r}.

Robin male slave of abraham & ann Burton Born 3d august 1733.

Judy of Ditto Born 15 sep^{r} 1733.

William Son of Samuel & Cattorn Barttlet Born 6th July 1733 Bap^{t} 28th Sep^{r}.

Mary D. of James & Catherine Burow Born 1th Novr 1733 Bap^{t} Novr 4th.

Robert Son of George & Eliz^{a} Belcher Born 4th Novr 1733 Bap^{t} Dce^{r} 10th 1733.

Robert Son of William & lettis Barten Born Dce^{r} 1th 1733 Bap^{t} feb^{r} 3d.

Phebe D. of William & Elisabeth Baldin Born 16th dec^r 1733 Bap^t Jan^r 30th.
Sarah D. of Thos & ——— Brawdiway Born 28th Sepr 1733 Bap^t 10th feb^r.
John Son of Daniel & amy Wall Born 10th dce^r 1733 Bap^t 27th Jan^r.
James Son of peter & Letisia Brewer Born 1th Novr 1733 Bap^t Jan^r 27th.
Jemmy slave of abr^a & Sarah Burton Born 13th Dce^r 1733.
Maryellis D. of John & Mary Bently Born 12th Dce^r 1733 Bap^t 10th March.
William Son of John & Eliz^a Blanchet Born 25th feb^r 1733 Bap^t 10th March.
anne D. of John & Eliz^a Browder Born 13th feb^r 1733 Bap^t 24th March 1734.
Lucy D. of John & Suffiah Blackman Born 29th Decr 1733 Bap^t 28th ap^r 1734.
Francis Son of John & Elisabeth Baugh Born 3d ap^r 1734 Bap^t 30th July.
William Son of George & Elisabeth Belcher Born 12th March 1733 Bap^t 28th July 1734.
Miles Son of Thomas & Elisabeth Bott 21th feb^r 1733 Bap^t 28th July 1734.
Presilia D. of George and Eliz. Brouder Born ye 2d of June 1735. Bap^t 6th July.
James S of John and Ann Butler Born 14 March 1734 Bap^t 17 Ap^l 1735.
Martha D. of John and Mary Bevel Born 4 March 1734 Bap^t 17 Ap^l 1735.
George S. of Thomas and Ann Brooks Born 28 May 1734 Bap Ap^l 19. 1735.
Nonney Male Slave belong^g to Theodirick Bland born Ap^l 22d 1735.
Rachell D. of John and Sarah Burton born 13th Feb^ry 1734.
Anthony Male Slave belonging to Richard Booker Born 11th January 1734.
Henry Son of Charles & Lovedy Burton Born 17th January 1734 Baptiz^d 26 March 1735.
Peter S. of William & Elizabeth Bowman Born ye 30th Xb^r 1734.

Elizabeth D of William & Elizabeth Burrow Born 5th Feb^{ry} 1734-5.

John Son of John & Willmuth Banister Born 26th December 1734.

Robert Male Slave belong^{g} to Ditto Born 2d Octob^{r} 1734.

Mary F. Slave belong^{g} to Ditto Born 25 July 1733.

Lady F. Slave belong^{g} to Ditto Born 28th Xb^{r} 1734.

Francis F. Slave belong^{g} to Ditto Born 28th Xb^{r} 1734.

Mary D. of John & Mary Blackstone Born 8th Novr 1734.

Martha D. of Henry & Avis Baley Born March 30th 1735 Baptizd 4th May.

Jesse S. of Wm. & Amy Bowyon Born March 11th 1734.

Martha D of Benjamin & Elizabeth Blick Born 5th May 1734 Bap. Octo. 25.

William S. of James and Margrett Baugh Born Octob^{r} 7th 1735.

Martha D. of William and Margrett Butler Born 24th Sep^{t} 1735.

James S of James & Martha Baugh Born December ye 2nd 1740.

Nehemiah S of Henry & Ann Beckwith Born November ye 6 1740.

Abraham S of John & Sephirah Blackmun Born may ye 14 1741.

John Son of Thomas & Martha Butler B. June 25th 1740.

Woody Son of George & Lucy Belchair B Feb^{ry} 22d 1740-1.

Debora D. of Richard & Joyce Burnet B Feb^{ry} 17th 1740-1.

Sarah D of Wm. & Margaret Butler B June 30th 1740.

Eliz Daughter of James & Mary Boisseau B Septr 20th 1733.

James Son of the above Jam^{s} & Mary B May 22d 1736.

Sarah Daughter of the above James & Mary B March 3d 1738.

Nan Slave of the above Ja^{s} & Mary B July 3d 1740.

Fanny Slave of Ditto B Augs^{t} 16th 1740.

Patt Slave of John Bullington B July 14th 1740.

Sam^{el} S of Francis & Elisabeth Brasey B Feb^{ry} 12th 1740.

Susanna D. of Capt James & Mary Boisseaus Born Octr 17th 1741 & Bap^{t} Octob^{r} 30th 1741.

Philip S. of Philip & Martha Burrows Born July 20th 1741 & Bap^{t} Novr 1st 1741.

Frederick S. of Thomas & Mary Burges was Born Novr 5th 1741 & Bap^{t} Jan^{ry} 3d 1741-2.

Anne D. of Richard & Elizabeth Biggins Born June 24th 1741 & Bap^{t} Jan^{ry} 3d 1741-2.

Francis D. of John & Francis Burges Born July 7th 1741 & Bap^{t} Jan^{ry} 3d 1741–2.

Burwell S. of William & Elizabeth Browns Born Decr 13th 1741 & Bap^{t} Jan^{ry} 17th 1741–2.

Joseph S. of Senr John & Elizabeth Browders Born Feb^{ry} 2d 1741–2 & Bap^{t} Feby 28th 1741–1.

Winnie D. of George & Elizabeth Browders Born Jan^{ry} 7th 1741–2 & Bap^{t} Feb^{ry} 28th 1741–2.

Jane D. of George & Jane Bollings Born Decr 31st 1740 & Bap^{t} March 21st 1741–2.

Theoderick S. of Capt Theodorick & Francis Blands Born March 21st 1740 & Bap^{t} Ap^{r} 26 1742.[*]

Anne D. of James & Catharine Burrows Born March 28th 1742 & Bap^{t} May 2d 1742.

James S. of William & Mary Baxters Born Feb^{ry} 17th 1741–2 & Bap^{t} May 11th 1742.

Mary D. of George & Lucy Belchers Born May 9th 1742 & Bap^{t} June 13th 1742.

Isham S. of Thomas & Susanna Bonners Born Feby 7th 1741–2 & Bap^{t} June 13th 1742.

Edward S. of Robert & Jane Birchets Born March 17th 1741–2 & Bap^{t} May 30th 1742.

Patt A Negro Girll belonging to Robt Birchet Born March 15th 1741–2 & Bap^{t} May 30th 1742.

Phœbe D. of Joseph & Mary Becks Born Ap^{r} 16th 1742 & Bap^{t} June 27th 1742.

Thomas S. of Thomas & Francis Browns Born Aug. 12th 1741 & Bap^{t} July 25th 1742.

Mason D. of John & Mary Browders Born June 30th 1742 & Bap^{t} July 4th 1742.

Jesse S. of William & Margret Butlers Born Aug 2d 1742 & bap^{t} Octob 17th 1742.

Elizabeth D. of William & Margret Butlers born Septr 4th 1737.

Anne D. of Joseph & Mary Burreys born Aprile 1st 1742 & bapt^{d} Novr 14th 1742.

Thomas S. of Henry & Anne Bickwiths born Aug 17th 1742 & bapt^{d} Octob 31st 1742.

---

* Erased in original.—C. G. C.

Margret D. of William & Margret Browders born Novr 16th 1742 & bapt^d Decr 19th 1742.

John S. of Mary Brandom was born Octob 22d 1740 & bap^t June 12th 1743.

Charles S. of Mary Brandom born March 1st 1742 & bapt^d June 12th 1743.

Joseph S. of William & Elizabeth Butlers born Jan^ry 5th 1719–20 & bapt^d Septr 8th 1743.

Anne D. of John & Anne Butlers born Sep^tr 25th 1743 & bapt^d Octob 9th 1743.

Mary D. of John & Anne Baughs born Novr 22d 1743 & bapt^d Jan^ry 6th 1743–4.

Lucretia D. of Richard & Elizabeth Biggins born Novr 7th 1743 & bapt^d Decr 25th 1743.

Mary D. of Richard & Constance Bundy born Decr 25th 1743 & bapt^d Feb. 19th 1743–4.

Adam S. of James & Martha Baughs born Feb 1st 1743–4 & bapt^d March 18th 1743–4.

Betty D. of Henry & Anne Berrys born Aug. 16th 1743 and bapt^d March 18th 1743–4.

Charles S. of Joseph & Mary Becks born Jan^ry 29th 1743–4 & bapt^d Aprile 8th 1744.

Mary D. of Wm. & Agnes Batts born Ap^r 16th 1744.

Charles S. of Charles & Elizabeth Butterworths born Apr. 18th & bapt^d May 13th 1744.

Dinah a female slave belonging to Edward Burchet born Feb. 27th 1743–4.

Frederick S of Thomas & Mary Burge born Nov 21st 1741.[*]

Woodie S. of Thomas & Mary Burges born March 22d 1743–4 & bapt^d March 25th 1744.

Mary D. of Thomas & Martha Baughs born March 20th 1743–4.

William S. of William & Frances Birchets born Decr 20th 1744 & bapt^d Jan^ry 27th 1744–5.

Charles S. of Henry & Anne Beckwith born Octob^r 28th 1744 baptized Feb^r 3d 1744–5.

Robert S. of Robert & Jane Birchets born Apr 8th 1744.

---

* Erased in original.—C. G. C.

Noah S. of Noah & Elizabeth Browns born Jan^ry 26th 1744–5 baptized Aprile 7th 1745.

Wood S. of John & Sophia Blackmans was born March 22d 1744–5 & bapt^d May 19th 1745.

Frederick S. of John & Mary Browders was born Feb 22d 1744–5 & bapt^d June 23d 1745.

Susanna D. of William & Marg^t Browders was born June 18th 1745 & bapt^d July 3d 1745.

Nannie A Negro Child belonging to Mr. William Brodnax was born Octob^r 1st 1745.

Agnes D. of Henry & Mary Wilkisons born Septr 8th & bapt^d Octob^r 1745.[*]

William S of Mr. William Brodnax & Ann his wife born Novr 26th & bapt^d Decr 27th 1745.

Patty D. of Nathanael & Mary Burrows born Sep^t 22d & bapt^d Novr 3d 1745.

John S of Peter & Susanna Boilsys was born Octob^r 5th & baptd Novr 12th 1745.

Arthur S. of Richard & Elizabeth Biggins was born Octob^r 26th baptd Decr 8th 1745.

Hannah D of James & Margaret Bruce was born March 22d 1745–6.

Mary D. of Charles & Elizabeth Butterworths was born Jan^ry 16th 1745–6 bapt^d March 16th.

Phebe D. of Thomas & Martha Baughs was born Octob 13th 1745 bapt^d Feb 16th 1745–6.

Henry S. of William & Agnes Batts was born Feb 17th 1745–6 bapt^d Ap. 6th 1746.

Agnes } Negroes belonging to Mr James Boisseau
Billie }

born { Aug 15th 1745 / March 31st 1746 } baptd May 1746.

William son of Richard & Constant Burge born March 23d 1746.

Alexander S. of Thomas & Mary Burge was born June 6th 176.

Betty D of Sarah Brown Mulatto born March 28th 1745.

Ruth Female Slave of Noah & Eliz^a Browns born Feb^ry 14th 1747–8.

---

*Erased in original.—C. G. C.

James Son of Wm & Ann Baughs, Born July the 3d, Bap^{t} October 5th 1749.

Elizabeth D of Theod^{k} & Frances Bland born 4th Jan^{ry} 1739.

Mary D of Ditto born 22d of August 1745.

Ann D of Ditto born 5th Septem^{r} 1747.

Jane D of Ditto born 30th Septem^{r} 1749.

Drury Son of John and Frances Birchet born 2d July bap^{t} Novem^{r} 2d 1749.

Lucy Female Slave belonging to Edward Birchet Senr born Ap^{r} 13th 1749.

Anthony Male Slave belonging to Ditto born 27th Septem^{r} 1749.

John Son of Robt & Jane Birchetts Born 17th October 1749.

Robert Son of Alexander & Susannah Bollings born —— March bapt^{d} 28th Ap^{r} 1751.

David Son of Edward Birchett Junr & Sarah his wife born April 15th 1749.

Peter Son of Ditto born May the 6th 1750.

John Son of James & Mary Boisseau born Feb^{ry} 12th 1747–8.

Dinah Female Slave belonging to ditto born June 1st 1746.

Tom Male Slave of ditto born 18th August 1747.

Millee Female Slave of Ditto born October 24th 1749.

Kate Female Slave of ditto born August 6th 1751.

Clitty Female Slave of Ditto born February 14th 1752.

Theoderick Son of Theod^{k} & Frances Blands born 21st March 1741–2.

Rebeckah Daughter of Noah & Elizabeth Brown born 19th Novem^{r} 1738.

Betty Daughter of Ditto born 27th Septem^{r} 1740.

William Son of Ditto born 16th October 1742.

Noah Son of ditto born 26th January 1744.

Jesse Son of Ditto born 6th May 1747.

Burwell Son of Ditto born 11th Septem^{r} 1749.

Boswell Son of Ditto born 1st May 1752.

Amy a Negro belonging to Ditto born 7th October 1738.

Roger male Slave belonging to D^{o} born 29 March 1741.

Nanny Female Slave to ditto born 18th April 1743.

Titus Male do to d^{o} born 5th Novem^{r} 1745.

Ruth Female do to d^{o} born 14th Febru^{ry} 1747.

Bobb Male d^{o} to d^{o} born 27th Septem^{r} 1750.

Martha D of Robt and Jane Birchetts born October 14th 1752.

1752 Jane Daughter of Benjamin & ——— Blicks born ——— Bap^{t} 12 Xber 1752.

Benj^{a} Son of James & Mary Boisseau born 28 February 1753.

York Male Slave of Ditto 11th July 1752.

Joan Female Slave of d^{o} 18 April 1753.

Quako Male Slave of d^{o} 2d October 1753.

Frances Daughter of Theo^{d} Bland born 24th Sep^{t} 1752.

James Son of Robert and Jane Burchetts born 6th August 1755.

Molley holt Boisseau Daughter of James & Mary Boisseau Born Sepr 25 1756.

Charles a Negro Slave belonging Ditto son of Patt Born March 28 1755.

Nancy Ditto Daughter of Bess Born June 12th 1755.

Peter Ditto son of Chloe Born July 31 1756.

Silva a Negro Slave belonging to James Boisseau Born feb^{r} 12 1757.

Hannaball Ditto son of Bess Born Jan^{r} 29 1758.

Anthony Ditto son of Patt Born October 26 1758.

William son of Drury and Elizth Birchett Born may the 12th 1756.

Elizth Daughter of Drury & Elizth Birchett Born January the 4th 1760.

Elizth Daughter of John and Sarah Butler was born Jan^{r} 23 1753.

Mary Daughter of John & Sarah Butler was Born Novr 28 1755.

William son of John and Sarah Butler was Born Novr 11 1758.

John son of Sarah and John Butler was Born July 6 1762.

Daniel Son of James & Anner Boiseau was born march ye 4th 1760.

James son of James & Anner Boiseau was born Novr ye 13 1761.

A negro Girl slave belonging to Ditt^{o} Namd Hannah born June 28 1760.

One Ditt^{o} named Phillis belonging to Ditt^{o} was born Jan^{r} ye 1 1762.

Agness Birchett Daughter of Edward & Sara Birchett was Born April ye 6 1753.

d^{o} Edward their son was Born June ye 6 1755.

d^{o} Ephraim their son was born March the 5th 1758.

d^{o} Henry their son was Born August the 5th 1761.

Drurey son of Drurey & Elizth Birchett was Born July 23 1762.

William Son of William & Sarah Batte was Born November 19th 1763 About one in the Morning Baptiz^{d} Jan^{r} 12th 1764.

Daniel Birchett son of Edward & Sarah Birchett was Born ———— may the 12th 1764.

Ann daughter of Joseph & Fanny Butler born dc^{r} 8 1766.

Elizth Brandon Daughter of Mary Brandon was born April: 11th 1758.

John son of Mary Brandon was born Octob^{r} the 4th 1760.

Aaron son of Mary Brandon was Born august the 1st 1762.

Judith Daughter of Mary Brandon was born July the 16th 1764.

Peter son of Mary Brandon was born Jan^{r} ye 16th 1766.

Gabril son of Mary Brandon was born Octo^{r} ye 2d 1767.

Robt Bird son of Martha Bird was born July the 24th 1756.

Theoderick son of Edward & Sarah Birchet was born Jan^{r} 23d 1769.

Nancy Brice Daughter of Wm & Margarett Brice was born Dec. 2d. 1766.

Molley their other Daughter was born Dec. 22. 1768.

Richard Bird Son of Elizabeth Bird was born July 7th 1767.

Susanna Burchet Daughter of Drury Burchet Baptised July 7. 1771.

Charlotte, Dau of Letty, a Negro Woman belonging to Sarah Brown, born December 29th 1791, & baptized Feby 27th 1792.

James, Son of John Baxter & Patsey his Wife, born Novr 4th 1791, & baptized March 11th 1792.

William, Son of Jeany, a Slave belonging to David Buchanan, born in December 1791 & baptized March 25th 1792.

John Bate, Son of John Baird & Polly his Wife, born February 8th & baptized March 31st 1792.

Mary D^{r} of Richard Booker & Margaret his Wife, born March 19th & baptized June 3d 1792.

Aggy, D^{r} of Aggy, a Negro Slave, belonging to the same, born Sepr 12th 1790, & bap. June 3d 1792.

Rebeccah D^{r} of James Barnes & Elizabeth his Wife, born March 17th & bap: June 17th 1792.

Silias Dunlop Buchanan, the Child of David Buchanan, died the 15th & was buried the 16th of August 1792.

John. S. of William Bingham & Mary his Wife born March 27th, and baptized Septr 19th 1792.

Mary Anne Jones, Daur of Thomas Batte & Frances his Wife, born March 10th, and baptized October 2nd 1792. Chesterfield.

Robert Birchett, of Prince George County, was buried October 7th 1792.

Thomas, S. of Suck, a Negro Slave belonging to the Estate of Robert Birchett was born July 10th 1789. & baptized October 7th 1792.

Lid, Daur of Sukey, belonging to the same, was born August 31st 1789, & baptized as above.

Milly, Daur of Bet, belonging to the same, was born Novr 20th 1789, & bap: as above.

Anna Buck. Dr of John Bland & Mary his Wife, born March 12th & bap: June 25th 1792.

Robert Stith, Son of Robert Bolling was buried October 18th 1792.

Rebecah, Daur of Thos T. Bolling & Seigniora his Wife, was born March 18th & baptized October 20th 1792.

Mary Chambless Daur of Nathaniel Barker, & Sally his Wife, born January 9th & baptized Novr 15th 1792.

Patrick, S, of John Blick junr, & Sarah his Wife, born October 10th, & baptized Novr 25th 92.

Sterling, S, of Sion Butler, & Dionicia his Wife, born Septr 11th & baptized Decr 23rd 1792.

Rebecca, Daur of Robert Bolling & Catharine, his Wife, was born February 23rd & baptized May 12th 1793.

Anne, Daur of John Blackwell & Martha his Wife, was born February 15th & baptized May 19th 1793.

Mary-Anne, Daur of Joseph Benwood and Amy his Wife, born February 3rd & baptized June 9th 1793.

Mary Brooks Daur of Richard Booker of Chesterfield County died July 24th & was buried August 7th 1793.

Richard Booker of Chesterfield County died August 27th & was buried Septr 17th. 1793.

Betsey, Daur of Thomas Brockwell & Jemimah his Wife, born Septr 10. 1793.

Mary Johnson, Dau^r of Robert Baugh. & Martha his Wife, born Septr 30 & baptized Decr 8th 1793.

Lucy Ann dau^r of Robt Bolling & Catharine his wife born 3d May and baptized 12th June 1795.

——— Broadie of the Town of Petersburg died Decr 22d & D^o 23d 1794.

Betsey Butler (of Petersburg) died Septr 16th & buried 18th D^o 1794.

John Bland (of P. George) died —— Dec^r & buried 11th D^o 1794.

Mrs Bonar Spouse of Jesse Bonar died ——— and buried May 1st 1795.

Robert Baugh was buried 26th April 1795.

Yelverton de Mallet Bolling Son of Thomas Bolling & Seigniora his wife born 10th Decr 1795 & bapt^d 29th Octr 1796.

C.

Luis [ ] son of Barsheba Cristwell born 18th August 1718 bap^t 26th feb: [ ].

Margaret dau of ditto born 16th Aug: 1720 bap^t 26th Feb 1[ ].

peter son of Wm & Faith Coleman born 25th June last bap: feb: 9th 17[ ].

John son of Fran: & Mary Coleman born 11th June last bap: May 14th 17[ ].

Rich: son of Rich: & Mary Carlile born 2d May 1719.

Anne dau of Robt & Mary Chappell born 8th feb^r bap^t may 21th 172[ ].

peter-hannor son of Rich: & Eliz: Cook born feb^r 28th last bap^t July 16th 17[ ].

Nutty a negro girl belonging unto Jno Cureton born 25th of August 17[ ].

Bartho: son of Barth^o & Eliz: Crowder born 3d June last bap^t July 9th 17[ ].

Anne dau of Edw: & Tabitha Colvill born 10th August last bap^t 17th sept^r 1721.

Geo: son of Cha: & Margery Cousens born 9th sept^r last bap^t nov 2d 1721.

Nath: son of Rich & Mary Carlile born 2d Jan^r Last bap^t feb^r 1st 1721–2.

Nutty a negro Girl belonging to Jno Cureton departed this life March 172[ ].

Cooke A negro slave belonging to John & Eliz: Edwards born Jan: 22th 1721–2.

Eliz dau of Jno & Mary Caudle born 17th Jan^{r} last bap^{t} May 20th 1722.

John son of Cha: & Fran: Chapman born 26th Aug: last bap^{t} June 16th 1722.

Hannah Wife of Titus Crecher bap^{t} 30 octob^{r} last 172[ ].

Mourning dau of Titus & hannah Crecher born 5th xb^{r} 1716 bap^{t} 30th octob^{r} 17[ ].

Millesin dau: of ditto born 25th Jan^{r} 1719 bap^{t} 30th octob^{r} 172[ ].

Agnis dau: of ditto born 24 of Aug: last bap^{t} 3th octob^{r} 172[ ].

peter son of Wm & Faith Coleman born & bap^{t} in August 17[ ].

Kasiah dau of Rich & Mary Carlile born August 24th 1715.

Eliz dau of ditto born Sep^{t} 4th 1717.

Amy dau of Tho: & ——— Clay born 9th March last bap^{t} May 5th 172[ ].

Ruth dau of Rich: & Eliz: Cook born 1st Aprill last bap^{t} Aug: 22th 17[ ].

Amy Dau of Fran: & Mary Coleman born 23d of May last bap^{t} sep^{tr} 29th 17[ ].

Wm son of Barth & Eliz: Crowder born 23th Augst last bap^{t} Nov 7th 172[ ].

Tho: son of John & Mary Caudle born 5th Jan^{r} Inst bap^{t} Jan^{r} 30th 172[ ].

Susanna d of Jno & Fra: Cureton born 19th Jan. last bap^{t} March 7th 17[ ].

Moses s: of Robt & Katharine Cannell born 8 feb^{r} last bap^{t} 10th Aprill 17[ ].

Robin a negro belonging to John & Fran Cureton born 19th July 1724.

Rich son of Hen: & Mary Crowder born 26th March last bap^{t} Aug 30th 172[ ].

Sarah d of Cha & Fran: Chapman born 18 feb last bap 6th Novr 172[ ].

Frances D of Abra: & Fran: Crowder born 14th xb^{r} last bap^{t} feb: 7th 172[ ].

Benj^{a} s: of Dan: & Eliz: Coleman born 14th decem: last bap May 10th 172[ ].

Nutty A negro beling to Jno Cureton Died.

Wm son of patrick & Jane Doram.

Mary Dat^{r} of Jno & Mary Cawdle born [ ] 8th last bap^{t} Jul 22^{d} 172[ ].

Sarah Dat of Rich^{d} & Eliz^{a} Cook born 18th Dec^{m} 172[ ].

Jno Son of Robt and winiford Cook born 29th sep^{tr} 1724.

David Son of Samuel and hannah Crew born 28th Janr^{y} 1725.

Betty Slave of John and frances Cureton born march 16th 1725.

Amy D of batholomiew and Eliz^{a} Crowder born 20th Sep^{tr} 1725.

Jack m Slave of Jno and Mary Coalman born 6th febr 1726.

Martha D of Daniel and Eliz^{a} Coalman born 20th nov^{m} 1726.

John Son of John and Elliner Curtis born 22d feb^{r} 1726.

Febe D of Abraham and frances Crowder born 3d Jan^{r} 1726.

Lucretia D of John and Mary Cordle born 7 May 1727.

Eliz^{a} D of John and frances Curiton born 20th Jan^{r} 1726.

Jo male Slave of henry Cox born 10th oc^{tm} 1727.

William Son of Cornelias Cargell and Eliz^{a} Daniell born 15th June 1727.

Matthew Son of Th^{o} and Eliz^{a} Couch born 24th July 1725.

Peter M. S of Walter Childs born 14th January 1727.

[ ] of Wm and Mary C [ ] on Born 12 August 1727.

[ ] D of Wm and Sarah Coalman born 18th August.Bap^{t} Sep^{t} 20th 17[ ]8.

[ ] D of Samuell and Ann Crews Born 19th Dec^{m} 1727 Bap^{t} 2d June.

[ ] female Slave of Henry Cox Born 2d sept^{m} 1729.

[Ge]orge & Richard sons of Bath^{o} and Eliz^{a} Crowder Born 13th oct^{r} 1727.

[Hen]ry son of Henry and amy Crowder Born 15th June Bap^{t} 24th Jan^{r} 1729.

[Ric]hard son of Jno and Dinah Cook Born 27th July Bap^{t} 24th Jan^{r} 1729.

[A]braham son of Robt and Eliz^{a} Chappell Born 6th May Bap^{t} 15 June 1729.

George son of Daniel and sandilla Carnill Born 31th March Bap^{t} 27th June 1729.

[J]one female slave of henry Cox Born 22d Nov^{m} 1729.

David son of Jno and Mary Cawdle Born 27th feb^{r} Bap^{t} 19th March 1729.

Alexander son of alexander and Mary Chisnall Born 25th Dcem: 1729.

Jamme male slave of Jno and francis Curiton Born 18th July 1730.

agnis female slave of Ditto Born 17th July 1728.

Thomas Son of John and Mary Crowder Born 19th July 1730 Bapt: 6th Sep^{tr}.

Abraham Son of abraham and frances Crowder Born 30th august 1730.

Abraham Son of abraham and Mary Cock Born 30th Sepr 1730 Bap^{t} 14th Dec^{r}.

Martha D of William and Sarah Coalman Born 10th Sepr 1730 Bap^{t} 8th octb^{r}.

Maryligon Coalman of John and Mary Coalman Born 18th July 1731 Bap^{t} august 10th.

anne D. of Charles & margry Cousins Born 8th Jan^{r} 1730 Bap^{t} ap^{r} 19th 1731.

Martha D of George & Eliz^{a} Crook Born 9th ap^{r} 1715.
Mary D. of Ditto Born 28th March 1717.
Tabitha D. of Ditto Born 8th feb^{r} 1719.
Joseph Son of Ditto Born 28th august 1722.
James Son of Ditto Born 27th Jan^{r} 1725.
Bap^{t} 11th Sepr 1731.

Nickols Son of Robt and Winnifred Cook Born 28th July 1731 Bap^{t} 12th Sep^{r}.

anne D. of Wm & Margaret Coalman Born 11th ap^{r} 1731 Bap^{t} 19th Sep^{r}.

Daniel Son of Daniel & Eliz^{a} Coalman Born 24th May 1731 Bap^{t} 14th Sep^{r}.

John Son of John and francis Curiton Born 27th Sepr 1731 Bap^{t} octb^{r} 20th.

Oather son of Robt Cobb born Jany 1st 1731.

Robt son of Robt & Eliz^{a} Chaple born 2d April 1732 bap^{t} May 7th 1732.

Drury Son of Edwd & Mary Burchett born Jany 1st 1731 bap^{t} May 29. 1732.

Wm Son of Wm & Sarah Coleman born 23d June 1732 bap^{t} Augst 13th 1732.

Jno Son of Thos & Mary Cheaves born 3d Augt 1732 Bap^{t} 14th Sepr 1732.

John son of Jno & Mary Crouder born 11th Sepr 1731 Bap^{t} May 22d 1732.

Frances d of Henry & Frances Chamlis born 7th Novr 1732 Bap^{t} 29th dce^{r}.

Mary d of ditto, born 26th May 1729 Bap^{t} Decr 29th 1732.

Isham son of John & Sarah Clayton Born 1th Novr 1727 Bap^{t} feb^{r} 27th.

Sarah D: of John & Mary Cordle Born 19th octob^{r} 1732 Bap^{t} Jan^{r} 14th.

Frances of Henry & amy Tucker Born 25th ap^{r} 1733 Bap^{t} 3d June 1733.

Isaac son of William & Eliz^{a} Chandler Born 15th ap^{r} 1732 Bap^{t} 7th ap^{r} 1733.

Susana D^{r} of Robert & agnis Childers Born 28th august 1732 Bap^{t} 7th ap^{r} 1733.

Filis female Slave of William Crawley Born 15th July 1731.

Jenne female Slave of Ditto Born 29th March 1733.

Warner son of william & Eliz: Coalman Born 20th March 1732 Bap^{t} 26th august 1733.

Jenne female slave of Walter Childs Born Decr 1732.

Margery lucas D: of William & Margaret Coalman Born 24th Sepr 1733 Bap^{t} 21th octb^{r}.

Rebeckah D: of Thomas & Martha Clemmonds Born 10th Novr 1733 Bap^{t} 5th Dce^{r}.

John son of Charles & Mary Clay Born 2d Jan^{r} 1733 Bap^{t} feb^{r} 10th.

Sare female Slave of John Curiton Born 27th March 1734.

anne D: of Cornelias & Sarah Clensy Born 10th feb^{r} 1733 Bap^{t} 10th March.

Sarah D: of William & Sarah Coalman Born 20th March 1734 Bap^{t} 28th ap^{r}.

Robin male Slave of Ditto Born 11th Decr 1733.

Catharine D: of Thomas & Mary Covington Born 16th feb^{r} 1733 Bap^{t} 15th May 1734.

Tom male Slave of Saml Cobbs Born 1th Sep^{t} 1729.

Mol fe: slave of Ditto Born 7th Dce^{r} 1732.

William Son of Francis & Mary Coalman Born 2d May 1733. Bap^{t} July 2d.

David Son of abr^{a} & frances Crowder Born 26th may 1733 Bap^{t} July 2d.

Susanah daughter of Thos & Mary Cheives Born Augt 1st 1734.

William S of Joseph and Eliz Coleman Born 8th March 1734.

John S. of Robert and Agnis Childres Born 20 Ap^{l} 1734 Bapt: Ap^{l} 19th 1735.

Ben male Slave belong^{g} to the Colledge of Wm & Mary Born March 1734.

Abraham Son of William & Elizabeth Chandler Born 26th Feb^{ry} 1734.

Susanna Male Slave Belonging to Saml Cobbs Born 11th June 1732 Bap^{t} Octo^{r} 6th 1734.

Fredirick S. of Robert & Winifrid Cook Born 15th Xb^{r} 1734.

Dunnim S. of John and Elizabeth Coziear Born 28th July 1734 Baptiz'd 18th Octo.

William S of John and Mary Crowder Born ye 1st Octob^{r} 1734.

Freeman S. of Thomas & Martha Clemmonds Born 26th June 1735.

Ann Ford D. of Martha Holy Cross being Illigitimate Born 24th Sep^{t} 1735.

Sarah D of John and Lucretia Cox Born Novr 2d 1735.

Martha D of Evin & affa Colbreth Born Febuary ye 8 1740.

William S of William & Mary Cheves Born December ye 22 1740.

Elisabeth D of John & Elisabeth Clark Born March ye 16 1740.

Daniel S of John & Margret Clark Born March ye 17 1740.

Joshua S of Henry & Francise Chambles Born May ye 15 1741.

Martha D of Solomon & Martha Crook B Feb^{ry} 1st 1740–1.

George S. of George & Mary Cavanist B Jan^{ry} 30th 1740.

Joseph S. of Abraham & Frances Crowder B Ap^{l} 22d 1741.

Mary D. of William & Judith Caries Born Decr 11th 1741 & Bap^{t} Decr 26 1741.

George S of John & Lucretia Cox Born Jan^{ry} 12th 1741 & Bap^{t} March 1st 1741–2.

Mary D. of James & Mary Christians Born May 31st 1741 & Bap^{t} March 21st 1741–2.

William S. of Joseph & Elizabeth Clarkes Born Janry 6th 1741-2 & Bapt March 21st 1741-2.

Mary D. of Benjamin & Francis Coxs Born Apr 28th 1742 & Bapt June 6th 1742.

John S. of John & Anne Chevers Born Janry 18th 1741-2 & Bapt July 25th 1742.

Thomas S. of Thomas & Martha Clemans born Decr 12th 1742 & baptd Feb. 6th 1742-3.

Silvia D. of Henry & Francis Chalmers born Decr 5th 1743 & baptd Janry 22d 1743-4.

Elizabeth D. of Richard & Elizabeth Carliles born Aug 22d & baptized Septr 30th 1744.

James S. of John & Elizabeth Chamles born Octob 6th & baptized Novr 11th 1744.

Robert S of Thomas & Martha Clemmonds born Septr. 13th & baptd Novr 11th 1744.

Martha D. of Mr. Burnell & Hannah Clairbornes born Feb 19th and baptd March 20th 1744-5.

Sarah D. of Thomas & Mary Cheeves born Janry 2d & baptd March 24th 1724-5.

Elizabeth D. of Benjamin & Frances Cooke was born March 15th 1745-6.

John Son of Richard & Elizabeth Carliles was born March 9th 1745-6 baptd Ap. 27th 1746.

William S. of Bolling & Phebe Clarke was born Janry 26th 1745-6.

Lockie D. of Thomas & Martha Clemmonds was born Febry 20th 1748.

Frances D. of John & Sarah Chambles was born Janry 24th 1748-9.

Prissilla Daughter of John & Mary Clemonds born June 30th 1750.

Tabitha Daughter of Thos & Mary Cheeves born Septr 27th 1750 bapt 3d March 1750-1.

Thomas Son of Thomas & Mary Cheves born 13th November 1738.

Elizabeth Daughter of Thomas & Mary Cheves born September 15th 1748.

Jemina D. of ditto born April 1st 1753.

Joshua Son of Thos and Martha Clemonds born November 24th 1752.

Mary Daughter of John & Mary Clemonds born 16th May 1754.

John Cureton son of John & Winneford Cureton was born Novr 13 1757.

Margret Daughter of John and Mary Clemons was born December th 3d 1757.

Louisey Cureton Daughter of John & Winneford Cureton born Jan^{r} 28 1760.

Elizabeth Cox Daughter of Saml & Ellinor Cox was born Augus^{t} 29th 1759 Baptiz^{d} Octo^{r} 21 1759.

Elizth Daughter of John & Mary Clemons was born Decem^{r} 25 1762.

Fran^{s} Cureton daughter of John Cureton & Winifred his wife was born decem^{r} 13th day 1762.

Charles Cureton Son of John & Winefred Cureton was born Sepr 20th 1765.

Henry, Son of Richard Cook, & Jean his Wife, born August 22d 1790, & baptized April 6th 1792. Sussex County.

Lucy Grice, Dau^{r} of Richard Christian, (of Sussex County) & Anne his Wife, born March 10th 1791, & baptized April 6th 1792.

William son of William Cole & Anne his Wife, born Janu^{y} 22d, & bap. June 19th 1792.

Jeany Dau^{r} of Hannah a Negroe Slave belonging to William Call, born April 24th & baptized July 22nd 1792.

Walker, S of George Cheatham & Nelly his Wife, born April 2nd and baptized October 2nd 1792.

Maitland Mary Currie Maitland dau^{r} of Mr. David Maitland of Blandford died 26th Jany and was buried 27th D^{o} 1795. [*]

Elizabeth Corbin Daughter of William & Rosey Corbin was born April the 20th 1760.

William Son of John & Mary Clements was Born may the 28th 1760.

Rosey Daughter of William & Rosey Corbin was born feb^{r} ye 27 1764.

---

* Erased in original.—C. G. C.

Joseph, S, of Ann Crews, was born Sept[r] 27th 1792 & bap: January 8th 1793.

Augustus Cæsar, S. of Susy a Negro Slave belonging to John Causy, was born November 25th 1792, & baptized March 31st 1793.

Thomas Son of the Revd John Cameron and Anne Owen his Wife, was born Jan[y] 16th and baptized April 1st 1793.

Richard Keith, Son of William Call jun[r] & Hellen his Wife, was born Octr 24th 1792 & baptized June 2nd 1793.

Clements, Son of James Clements, was buried 10th May 1795.

D.

Mary Davis Daughter of William & Maxey Davis, Born April 22d 1747.

Thomas Jones, son of William & Maxey Davis, was Born the 1st Nov[r] 1752.

Samuel Davis the son of Ditto was born March y[e] 23d 1757.

Shepherd Davis their son was born June the 28 1759.

Mary Magdalene a Negro Girl slave belonging to Stephen Dewey Born March 1st 1761.

Maxey Daughter of Rob[t] & Sarah Smelt was born Decem[r] 30th 1763.

Eliz[th] Davis Daughter of Wm & Maxey Davis was born March 22 1744.

Lewis Burwell, Son of Thomas Dun & Lucy his Wife, born Oct 22d 1792, and baptized May 13th 1792.

Mary, Dau[r] of William Dun (of Sussex) & Jean his Wife, born July 4th & bap: May 13th 1792.

John Creagh, Son of John Denton & Margaret his Wife, born Dec[r] 12th 1789.

Rebeccah Hathorn D[r] of the same, born Sep[r] 9th 1791, & bap: June 24th 1792.

Polly Baugh Dau[r] of Shepherd Davis & Martha his Wife, born Dec[r] 17th 1792 and baptized July 7th 1792.

Samuel, S. of Samuel Davis & Sarah his Wife, born January 26th & bap: July 7th 1792.

Aggy Franklin, Dau[r] of William Dodson, and Mary his Wife, was born Jan[y] 11th and baptized March 21st 1793.

Mary Durand, was born June 1st 1776 & baptized July 1 1793.

Lucy Ann Kimbow Dau[r] of James Day & Levina his Wife, born April 20th & was baptized Oct[r] 13th 1793.

E

Lucretia, D[r] of John Eppes & Susanna his Wife, was born Feb[y] 7th 1791. & baptized March 11th 1792.

Richard Son of Buckner Ezell (of Sussex) & Elizabeth his Wife born Aug[t] 15th 1791. & bap. May 13th 1792.

Elizabeth Hall D[r] of Tinah, a Negro Slave belonging to Frank Eppes, was born January 27th & baptized May 27th 1792.

Richard Eppes (of City point) in Prince George County died the 8th and was buried the 23rd of July 1792.

Mary Danforth Dau[r] of Lewis Edwards & Mary his Wife, was born Jan[y] 4th & baptized April 1st 1793.

Mary Edwards, wife of Lewis Edwards, died Oct[r] 30th & was buried Nov[r] 1st 1792.

F

Thom[s] Francis, Son of Fran[s] & Sarah Finn was Born April 25 1753.

William Son of Ditto: was born January the 12th 1756.

John Son of Ditt[o] was Born the 18th May 1761.

Sarah Fernendo third Daughter of Benj[a] & Mary Feranondo was Born may the 16th 1764 about 4 oClock in the morning on a Wednsday.

Joel Son of Fra[s] & Sarah Fin was Born aug[st] 8th 1758.

Rosey Daughter of Ditt[o] was Born Octo[r] 13 1763.

David son of Fra[s] Lisenburg Finn and Sarah his wife was Born augs[t] 7th 1765.

Ann Fernando, y[e] 4th daughter of Benj[a] & Mary Fernando was born the 21st Day of September 1766. On a Sunday about 5 OClock in the Evening.

Ann Laughton, Dau[r] of Simon Fraser & Elizabeth his Wife, born January 18th, & baptizd April 7th 1792.

Arthur Son of Liza, a Negro Slave belonging to Simon Fraser, born March 8th, & baptized May 27th 1792.

Daniel, Son of John K. Fisher & Elizabeth his Wife, born the 2d & baptized the 7th June 1792.

Daniel Baugh, Son of Joel Fenn & Mary his Wife, born April 12th 1791, & baptized June 10th 1792.

Richard, S, of D^{o} & D^{o} born June 28th 1789.

Simon Fraser, of the Town of Petersburg, died October 28th, & was buried Novr 2nd 1792.

Clarissa Birchett, Dau^{r} of Betsey, a Mulatto Slave, belonging to the Estate of James Feild, born February 25th, & baptized Decr 9th 1792.

Lucy Dau^{r} of Edward Featherstone, & Sarah his Wife, born June 20th 1791 & baptized December 28th 1792.

Martha Edwards, Dau^{r} of D^{o}, born Septr 3rd & baptized as above.

Maria Deas, Dau^{r} of Thomas Fraser & Ann Loughton his Wife, was born July 3rd 92 & baptized January 16th 1793.

G

Peter son of Luis & Fran: Green born 16th Innstan. bap^{t} 20th octob^{r} 1720.

Nance son of Tho: & Eliz: Grigory born 10th Nov: last bap^{t} Jan 22th 1720–1.

Mary dau: of Hugh & Jane Golightly born 24th July last bap^{t} 7^{br} 18th 1720.

Margaret A Mollatto belonging unto Godfry & Eliz: Radgsdale born 7th Nov: last baptiz: May 28th 1721.

Tabitha dau of Tho: & Martha Goodwin born 25th Jan^{r} last bap^{t} July 18th 1721.

Nash son of Robt & Eliz Glidwell born 19th June last bap^{t} July 21st 1721.

Rebecca dau: of Harris & Frances Gillam born 18th July last bap^{t} Sep^{t} 30th 1721.

Anne dau: of John & Susanna Garret born 22th Sep^{tr} last bap^{t} Octob^{r} 2d 1721.

Anne dau of Wm & Mary Gent born 4th Aprill last bap^{t} 9th octob^{r} 1721.

Mary dau: of John & Mary Gibbs born 18th Sep^{tr} 1716.

Eliz dau: of ditto born 6th octob^{r} 1718.

John son of ditto born 30th Aprill 1719.

Wm son of Stephen & Martha Gill born 6th Inst bap^{t} Jan^{r} 20th 1721–2.

John son af Robt & Rachel Glascock born 3d feb last bap 21th Aprill 1722.

Ann dau of John & Mary Gibbs born 23th decem last bap^t 15th Aprill 1723.

Susan dau of Wm & Eliz: Grigg born 11th June 1720 bap^t Aug 25th 1722.

Mary dau of John & Abigaell Green born 9th Aug: last bap^t 4th Sep^t 1722.

Abra son of Tho: & Mary Gent born 7th July last bap^t 13th August 1722.

John son of Tho & Eliz: Grigory born 1st instant bap^t Jan 30th 1722.

David son of Tho & Martha Goodwin born 27th Aug last bap Jan^r 30th 1722.

John son of Tho: & Eliz Grigory born 1st Jan^r bap^t 31th instant 1723.

Ann dau of Joss: & Eliz: Gill born 30th May last bap^t June 15th 1723.

Jno son of Jno & Ann Gillam born 2d May 1713.

Eliz: dau of Ditto born 16th Jan^r 1716.

John son of Tho: & Martha Gunter born 19th octob^r last bap^t August 21th 1723.

Moses son of Wm & Mary Gent born 15th May last bap^t August 22th 1723.

Susanna D: of John & Susanna Garret born 1st Sep^tr & bap^t 25th instant Sep^t 1723.

Susanna D: of Luis & Susanna Green born 14th July last bap^t octob^r 21th 1723.

John S: of Hen: & Eliz: Green born 10th Jan^r last bap^t Septr 22th 1724.

Mary D of Tho Gregory born 9th Sep^t last bap^t 1st Nov 1724.

Ralph S of Rich: & Mary Griffon born 16th feb^r last bap^t May 16th 1725.

Wm S of Harris & Fran: Gillom born 29th Jan^r 1723 bap^t 12th Aprill 1724.

Tho S of Hugh & Jane Golightly born 27th May lest bap^t 3d June 1725.

Betty A Negro Girl belonging to ditto born 7th May 1725.

hugh lee golikely son of Jno Golikely born 27th sep^tr 1725.

Mary Dat of Thomas and Martha Gunter born 17th Dec^{m} 1724.
Wm Son of Wm and Ann Gower born 30th Aprill 1725.
Agnis D of Jno & Mary Gibs born Oct^{m} 6th 172[ ].
Jno son of Jno and Susannah Garrot born 10th July last 1726.
John Son of harris and francis Gilliam born 18th Ap^{r} 1726.
John Son of benj^{a} and Anne Grainger born 24th Dec^{m} 1726.
John Son of Joshua and Sarah Glass born 10th oct^{m} 1726.
Ann D of John and Abigall Green born 12th January 1725.
Dorcus D of henry and Eliz^{a} green born 27th Sepr 1726.
Wm Son of Wm and Mary Gamliin born 24th July 1727.
Mary D: of George and Rosamond Green born 24th ffeb^{r} 1721.
Eliz^{a} D of Wm and Ann Gower born 18th March 1726.
Eliz^{a} D of James and frances Grigg born 24th aprill 1726.
Phebe female Slave of John and ann gilliam born 29th June 1727.
Joseph Son of benj^{a} and Ann Grainger born 10th feb^{r} 1727.
Eliz^{a} Dater of Joshua and Sarah Glass born 15th aprill 1728.
John son of John and Ann Gilliam born 2d May 1712.
Eliz^{a} Dater of Ditt^{o} born 16th Jan^{r} 1714.
Edward Son of Wm and Susannah Gates Born 6th Novm^{r} 1727.
John Son of Richard and Mary Griffin Born 22d June 1727 Bap^{t} oct^{m} 1.
John Son of John and Eliz^{a} Gilliam Born 13th Dce^{m} 1725.
Lucy D of Ditto Born 17th Dce^{m} 1727.
Amie D of harris and frances Gilliam Born —— aprill 1728 Bapt 28th Sep^{t}.
Susan D of Robt & Eliz^{a} Glidewell Born 13th Novm^{r} 172[ ].
Margret D of John and Abigal Green Born 15th feb^{m} 1727 Bap^{t} 2d June.
Martha D of peter and Mary Green Born 27th May 1728 Bapt 2d June.
Susannah D of John and Mary Gibs Born 1th Dce^{r} 1728 Bap^{t} 20th aprill 1729.
Isack Son of John and Susan Garrot Born 9th Dce^{r} 1729.
James son of James and francis grigg Born 7th Jan^{r} Bap^{t} 24th 1729.
amy of stephen and Martha Gill Born 25th May Bap^{t} 30th august 1729.
Robt Son of Robt and Eliz^{a} Glidewell Born oct^{r} 23d 1722 Bap^{t} March 19th 1729.

Josiah son of Charles and frances Gilliam Born 30th March Bap^{t} 30th 1730.

Sarah D of Joshua and Sarah Glas Born 24 Jan^{r} Bap^{t} 22d feb^{r} 1729.

ann D of George & Rosomond Green Born 1th feb^{r} 1729.

Harris Son of Harris and frances Gilliam Born 8th Sepr 1730.

Phebe D: of John and Mary Gibbs Born 1th Sepr 1730 Bap^{t} 4th octb^{r}.

Thomas son of John & susannah Garrat Born 6th Dce^{r} Bap^{t} 4th Jan^{r}.

Benjamine son of Benjamine & ann Grainger Born 21th feb^{r} 1730.

William Son of William & amy Hill Born 14th feb^{r} 1731 Bap^{t} ap^{l} 23d 1732.

Winnifrid D of Henry & Eliz^{a} Green Born 17th March 1731 Bap^{t} 23 ap^{r} 1732.

Abraham Son of John & Susan Garratt Born 3d July 1729.

Thomas son of Ditto Born 6th Dce^{r} 1730.

Fanny female slave of Wm Green Born 4th Jan^{r} 1731.

Tom a Male Slave of Jno & Mary Gibbs Born 10th Feby 1731.

Richd Son of Corn^{s} & Susanna Gibbs 22d June 1724 bapt May 29th 1732.

Susanna dat^{r} of Ditto born 31 Jany 1726 bap^{t} Ditto.

Lucie dat^{r} D^{o} 15 Ap^{l} 1728 Ditto.

Thos Son D^{o} 14 March 1730 Ditto.

Joshua Son of Joshua & Sarah Glass born 26th Ap^{l} 1731.

Eliz^{a} dat^{r} of Charles and Francis Gilliam May 7th 1732.

Frances dat^{r} of Benj^{a} & Ann Granger born 2d Sepr 1731 bap^{t} May 22d 1732.

Peter Son of James & Fra^{s} Grigg born 6 March 1731 bap^{t} Nov 5th 1732.

Mathew Son of Jno & Mary Gibbs born 25th Sepr 1732 bap^{t} Novr 19th 1732.

Patty female slave of abraham Green Born 18th Dce^{r} 1731.

Jemima d of John & abigal Green born 28th July 1731 Bap^{t} 2d Jan^{r}.

Drury son of Thomas & Jane ————

Mary D^{r} of Joshua & Sarah Glass Born 17th feb^{r} 1732 Bp^{t} 8th ap^{r} 1733.

James son of Harris & Frances Gilliam Born 13th May 1733 Bap[t] 24th June.

Johannah female Slave of abraham Green Born 25th May 1731.

Jonathan Son of John & Esther Green Born 29th Dce[r] 1732 Bap[t] 25th august 1733.

Mary D: of William & Susanna Gates Born 26th feb[r] 1732 Bap[t] 6th Sep[r] 1733.

Stephen Son of John & Susan Garret Born 9th ap[r] 1733 Bap[t] octb[r] 20th.

Mol fe slave of Wm Green Born 18th March 1733.

Tarance lamb son of Eliz[a] Glidewell Born 14th Jan[r] 1733 Bap[t] 24th March 1734.

ann son of Richard & Eliz[a] Green Born 25th feb[r] 1733 Bap[t] 26th May 1734.

Dol fe slave of Stephen Gill Born 5th feb[r] 1728.

Peg of Ditto Born 10th ap[r] 1733.

Joshua son of Charles & francis Gilliam Born 20th March 1733 Bap[t] 2d June.

Nan Slave of John & ann Gilliam Born 20th May 1734.

Martha D: of William & Amey Green Born 8th May 1734 Bap[t] 4th July.

Lucey daug[r] of Tho[s] and Jane Gregory Born 9 July 1734.

Lucey daughter of John & Mary Gibbs born 14 Novem[r] 1734 Bap[t] 9 Feb[ry] 1734-5.

Dick Male Slave belong[g] to Abraham Green Born February. 26. 1734.

Inde female Slave belong[g] to Ditto Born March y[e] 6th 1734.

Ann D. of Alex[r] and Mary Gray Born 20th May 1734 Baptiz'd Sep[t] 22d.

Edith D. of Benjamin & Ann Granger Born the 15th June 1734.

John S of John & Anne Fitz-Gareld Born July y[e] 25 1741.

John of Matthew and Ann Goodwyn B Ap[l] 20th 1740.

Susannah D. of Ditto B. December 17th 1736.

Toney Negro of The Same B: August 2d 1737.

Jimmey Slave of the Same B March 20th 1740-1.

Patty Slave of the Same B November 23d 1740.

Wm S of Richard & Mary Griffin B Nov[r] 21st 1740.

Burrell S. of Jessey & Amey Grigg B Aprill 28th 1741.

Wm of Abner And Mary Grig B March 6th 1740.

Lewis Burwell S of Burwell & Mary Greens Born Aug. 25th 1741 & Bap[t] Nov[r] 9th 1741.

Thomas S. of Thomas & Mary Ghents Born Dce[r] 8th 1741 & Bap[t] March 22d 1741–2.

Elizabeth D. of Richard & Hannah Garys Born Dce[r] 2d 1741 & Bap[t] Apr 4th 1742.

Peter S. of Nash & Martha Gloydwells Born Octob[r] 9th 1741 & Bap[t] June 13th 1742.

Katharine D. of Angus & Isabel Galbreaths born Octob 23d 1742 & bapt[d] Jan[ry] 15th 1742–3.

William Randolph S. of Burwell & Mary Greens born March 26th 1743 & bapt[d] May 24th 1743.

Daniel S. of Duncan & Barbara Galbreaths born May 31st 1743 & bapt[d] June 5th 1743.

Mary D. of William & Margret Galbreaths born Aug. 15th 1743 & bapt[d] Sept[r] 11th 1743.

John S of Richard & Hannah Gary born Dec[r] 4th 1743 & bapt[d] Janry 22d 1743–4.

Sarah D. of Charles & Mary Gees born Aug 22d 1743.

Peter S of Joseph & Elizabeth Grammers born Octob 11th & bapt[d] Nov[r] 11th 1744.

William S. of John & Elizabeth Gilliams born Nov[r] 29th 1744 & bapt[d] Jan[ry] 27th 1744–5.

John S of William & Martha Gibbs born Dec[r] 17th 1744.

John S of Charles & Mary Gees born Jan[ry] 18th & bapt[d] March 3d 1744–5.

Anne D. of Mr. John & Anne Geralds born June 17th & bapt[d] July 9th 1745.

James Williams son of Jane Gent born Aug. 21st 1745.

Richard S. of Richard & Hannah Gary was born Sep[tr] 9th 1745.

Joseph S. of Joseph & Elizabeth Grammars was born March 14th 1745–6.

Pattie Daughter of Wm & Martha Gibbs born Nov[r] 12th 1750.

Sarah Rogers, Daughter of Archibald & Hester Gracie, was born December 14th 1791. & baptized February 12th 1792.

Mary Wright, Daughter of John & Priscilla Grammer, was born January 30th, & baptized February 26th 1792.

Wilson, Son of Richard Grigory & Elizabeth his Wife, born Sept[r] 28th 1791. & baptized March 18th 1792.

John, Son of John Gibbs & Martha his Wife, (of Chesterfield) born March 7th & baptized May 12th 1792.

Martha, Dau^{r} of the same D^{o} D^{o}.

Bristol, Son of Betty a Negro Slave belonging to John Gilliam, was born March 14th & baptized May 20th 1792.

Elizabeth Cain, D^{r} of John Goodcy & Susannah his Wife, born Octr 15th 1791, & baptized May 28th 1792.

Sarah D^{r} of the same, was born July 18th 1790.

Betsy Philipps, Dau^{r} of Peninah, a Negroe Slave belonging to William Gilliam, was born March 4th and baptized September 9th 1792.

Lucy Jones, Dau^{r} of Erasmus Gill & Sarah his Wife, was born September 7th and bap: the 23rd 1792.

Lucy Jones, Dau^{r} of D^{o} buried September 23rd 1792.

Fanny, Dau^{r} of little Aggy, belonging to Erasmus Gill, born the 2nd and baptized the 23rd of September 1792.

Erasmus, S. of Elsey, belonging to Erasmus Gill, born April 22nd & baptized Septr 23rd 1792.

Hannah Scot, Dau^{r} of Amy, a Negro Slave, belonging to John Grammar, born Sep^{t} 27, & baptized Nov 4th 1792.

Elizabeth, Dau^{r}, of Josiah Gary & Sarah his Wife, was born Decr 16th 1791 and baptized January 11th 1793.

Nancy Harrison Dau^{r} of Richard Gary & Mary his Wife, was born May 10th 1792 & baptized January 11th 1793.

Delilah Peterson, Dau^{r} of James Grantham, & Jean his Wife, born Decr 17th 1792 & baptized January 27th 1793.

Harriott Dau^{r} of Richard Gregory and Elizabeth his Wife, was born October 27th 1792 and baptized April 4th 1793.

Elizabeth, Daughter of William Gilliam & Christian his Wife was born Octr 26th 1792, & baptized May 16th 1793.

Charles, Son, of Charles Gee & Susannah his Wife, was born April 9th 1792 & baptized June 2nd 1793.

Elizabeth Kid Dau^{r} of James Geddy jun^{r} & Euphan his Wife was born Feby 14 & baptized July 7th 1793.

Thomas, Son of Charles Gee and Susanna his Wife, born 21st Novr 1793 and baptized 20th Decr 1794.

John Gilliam, Son of William Gilliam & Christian his wife born 15th April 1795 & bapt^{d} 5th Feby 1796.

William, Son of D^{o} born ———— & bapt^{d} 9th March 1798.

H

James son of Instant & Mary Hall born Jan^r 3d 1701–2.
Judith daughter of ditto born 17th June 1705.
Instant son of ditto born 28th october 1707.
John son of ditto born 18th Jan^r 1709–10.
Frances dau: of ditto born 20th July 1716.
George son of ditto born 20th Jan^r 1718–9.
James son of Tho: & Jane Hardaway born 10th July 1719.
Betty a negro girl belonging unto Allin Howard born 19th sep^t 1720.
Arthur son of Gab: & Grace Harrison born 15th Jan: bap^t 30th Jan 1720–1.
Mary dau: of Tho: & Mary Hobby born 29th Jan: last bap^t feb: 9th 1720–1.
Tim: son of Tim: & Anne Harris born 1st Aug: last bap^t 24th octob^r 1720.
Joseph son of John & Mary Hye born 28th March last bap^t July 18th 1721.
John & Rich: two sons born at one birth of Edw & Eliz Hall 1st of Octob^r last bap^t 18th July 1721.
Obedience dau of Rich: & Martha Hudson born 7th July 1720 bap^t 30th July 1721.
Anne dau: of Tho: & Jane Hood born July 26th last bap^t 19th August 1721.
Wm son of Inst: & Mary Hall born 22th Aprill 1721.
Robin a negro boy belongin unto ditto born 16th Aprill 1714.
Jeney a negro girl belonging to ditto born 18th Aprill 1717.
Micaell son of Micall & Eliz: Hill born 20th feb^r last bap^t Nov 2d 1721.
Jane Dau: of tho: & Jane Hardaway born 26th March last bap^t June 1st 1721.
A negro Man belonging to Bullard & Mary Herbert died April 7th 1722.
Wm son of James & phebe Hudson born 11th Jan: last bap^t June 17th 1722.
John son of Jeffry & Sarah Hauks born 10th feb: 1721 bap^t March 27th 1722.
John son of Christ & Marg^a Hinton born 29th July last bap^t 30th Aug: 1722.

Isaac son of Hall & Eliz: Hudson born 7th July last bap[t] May 5th 1723.

Wm son of James & ——— House born 25th decem last bap[t] June 16th 1723.

Grace dau of Wm & Joan Johnson born 31th octob[r] 1721 bap August 21th 1723.[*]

Wm son of Tho: & Jane Hardaway born 12th June last bap[t] 13th Octob[r] 1723.

Geo: son of Timoth & Anne Harris born 27th feb[r] last bap[t] July 10th 1723.

Johanna D of Tho: & Jane Hood born 7th nov: last bap[t] 30th Jan 1723–4.

Eliz: D: of Tho: & Johanna Hobby born 26th decem last bap[t] 30th Jan[r] 1723–4.

Tho: son of Chris: & Marg[a] Hinton born 31th Jan[r] last bap[t] feb 6th 1723–4.

Wm s: of Tho: and Jane Hood born 14th of May 1711.

Sam son of James & Mary Huccaby born 19th May 1721.

Ann d of ditto born 9th of octob[r] 1723.

John son of Bullard & Mary Herbert born 4th Aprill last bap[t] 24th ditto 1724.

Eliz: d of John & Eliz: Hemans Born ———

Mary D: of ditto born 1st feb[r] last bap[t] Aprill 8th 1724.

Mary D: of Hall & Eliz: Hudson born 27th xb[r] last bap[t] sep[tr] 12th 1724.

Heuen son of Tho & Eliz: Hudson born 4th Augs[t] last bap[t] 4th Nov[r] 1724.

Mary d of Rich & Martha Hudson born Octob[r] 9th bap[t] 4th Nov 1724.

James son of James & Mary Hudson born 1[ ]th Augs[t] last bap[t] 6th Nov[r] 1724.

John son of Christopher Hinton died Ult. October 1724.

Wm s: of Tho & Sarah Hackney born 28th Sep[t] last bap[t] 18th Aprill 1725.

Frances D: of Tho: & Jane Hardaway born 4th Aprill last bap[t] 1725.

James S. of James & phebe Hudson born 10th July last bap[t] June 13th 1725.

---

* Erased in original.—C. G. C.

Fran: D. of James & Ruth Hall. born 8th feb: last bap[t] March 10th 1725.
Johannah D of thom and Johannah hobby born 14th march 1725.
Mary D of Samuel and Anne homes born 29th november bap[t] 6th March 1725.
Lucainna Dat of Jn[o] and Susan harwell born 18th oct[m] 1725.
David son of Jn[o] and mary high born 2d march 1725.
Patrick son of Edwd and Eliz[a] hall. born 4th may 1724.
James son of John and Eliz[a] hill born 17 July 1726.
Edward Son of timothy and Ann harris born 27th March 1726.
——— son of James and Ruth hall born 27th nov[r] 1726.
John Son of Mical and Agnis hankings born 7th Jan[r] 1721.
Jane Daughter of Ditto born 7th August 1723.
Joshua Son of Hall and Eliz[a] Hudson born 9th June 1727.
John Son of Christopher ann Rowland born 20th May 1727.
Ann D: of buller and Mary herbert born 21th March 1726–7.
Blennum male slave of Ditto born 16th June 1727.
Moll female slave of Ditto born 10th Dce[m] 1727.
David Son of Michael and agness hawkins born 3d June 1727.
James Son of Jo[n] and Rebeckah Harwell born 9th June 1727.
Th[o] Son of Th[o] and Eliz[a] hudson born 1th ffeb[r] 1724.
Joshua Son of Micael and agnis haukins born 25th July 1725.
Susanah D of John and Mary high born 12th aprill 1727.
Sarah D of John and Eliz[a] harwell born 22d aprill 1725.
Th[o] Son of Ditto born 29th March 1727.
Theodrick Son of James and Ruth hall born 27th Nov[m] 1726.
Tabitha D of Th[o] and Eliz Hudson Born 29th march 1728 Bap[t] July 28th.
John Son of Th[o] and Jane Hood Born 1th octob[r] 1728.
Mary D of Edward and frances Hill Born 15th Sep[t] 1728 Bap[t] No[r] 12th.
Benj[a] Son of Hall and Eliz[a] Hudson Born 15th Jan[r] Bap[t] 3d March 1728.
Charles Son of Richard and Martha Hudson Born aprill 14th 1729.
Joseph Son of Th[o] and Jane Hardiway Born 9th March 1728 Bap[t] 7th aprill 1729.
frances D of Wm and amy Hill Born 2d Jan[r] Bap[t] 2d feb[r] 1728.
Isack Son of sam[l] and ann homes Born 16th Novm[r] 1727.

Betty female slave of Mary herbert Born 12th oct^m 1729.

Liewes son of Jno and frances Hill Born 12 July Bap^t 12th august 1729.

Richard son of James and Phebe Hudson Born 18th July Bap^t 10th august 1729.

John son of James and Ruth Hall Born 2d march Bap^t 1728.

Wm Son of Jno & Rebeckah Harwell Born 20th august Bap^t Sep^t 6th 1729.

Eliz^a D of Jno and Mary High Born 17th June Bap^t 23d august 1729.

James Son of Christophar and Margret Hinton Born 25th Jan^r Bap^t 1729.

Frances D of Th^o and Sarah Hackney Born 20th Jan^{ry} 1729 Bap^t 30th May 1730.

William Son of William and Judith Jones Born 8th aprill 1730 Bap^t 10th may 1730.

Ann D of Wm Harris Born 7th March 1729 Bap^t 8th aprill 1730.

James markam son of Jno Frances Hardiway Born 21th Jan^r 1729 Bap^t 8th aprill 1730.

Frances D of Richard and Phebe Herbert Born 6th octb^r 1729 Bap^t 8th aprill 1730.

Catherine D of Robert and Jane Humphris was Born 20th July 1730.

Betty Slave of Saml Harwell Born 1th octb^r 1719.

John male Slave of Ditto Born 25th Novm^r 1724.

John Son of David and Eliz^a Hamleton Born 22d August 1728 Bap^t 13th Dec^r.

Ann D: of Ditto Born 5th may 1730.

Ruth D: of John & Eliz^a Hammond Born 8th feb: 1730 Bap^t 22d ap^r 1731.

Eliz^a D of Mical & agnis Hawkins Born 7th June 1731 Bap^t 12th august.

Samuel Son of Samuel & ann Homes Born 27th May 1731 Bap^t 7th Octb^r.

Thomas Son of John & mary High Born 22d Sepr Bap^t Novmb^r 7th 1731.

Jeane D: of John & Francis Hardiway Born 21th March Bap^t 14th November 1731.

William Son of william & amy Hill Born 14th feb^{r} 1731 Bap^{t} 23d ap^{r} 1732.

Ludwell Son of Wm & Mary Jones Born 6th march 1731 Bap^{t} 24th ap^{r} 1732.

Frances D: of James & phebe Hudson Born 28th Jan^{r} 1732 Bap^{t} 24th ap^{r} 1732.

Hanah Slave of Buller & Mary Herbert Born Novemb^{r} 2d 1730.

Robert Slave of D^{o} was Born Decem^{r} 26th 1730 Baptized ——.

Martha dat^{r} of Wm & Margery Hood born 8th May 1732 bap^{t} June 1st 1732.

Thos Boon Son of Edward & Eleanor Hawkins born May 3d 1720 bap^{t} July 16th 1732.

Eliz^{a} dat^{r} of Thos & Eliz^{a} Hudson born March 9th 1731 bap^{t} July 16th 1732.

Mary dat^{r} of Wm & Fra^{s} Harris born 11th July 1732 bap^{t} 27th Augt 1732.

Peter of Thos & Phebœ Hamlin born 6th Augt 1732 bap^{t} Sepr 23d 1732.

John son of Jno & Fra^{s} Hardaway born 14th Sepr 1732 bap^{t} Novr 5th 1732.

Christopher Son of Christopher & Margrit Hinton Born 2d Decr 1731 Bap^{t} feb^{r} 23d.

——— son of Wm & mary Hulem Born 29th Jan^{r} 1732 Bap^{t} March 10th.

Eliz^{a} D: of william hudson and Charity smithis Born 18th octob^{r} 1732 Bap^{t} 14th Jan^{r}.

Drury Son of Thomas & Jane Hardiway Born 2d ap^{r} 1733 Bap^{t} ap^{r} 7th 1733.

Mary D^{r} of Isaac & anne Hudson Born 2d feb^{r} 1732 Bap^{t} 7th June 1733.

anne D^{r} of John & Rebeckah Harwell Born 18th march 1732 Bap^{t} 20th may 1733.

George Son of Joseph & Susanah Harper Born 24th Dce^{r} 1732 Bap^{t} 17th June 1733.

ann d: of John & ann Hill Born 19th Sepr 1732 Bap^{t} 22d ap^{r} 1733.

Drury Son of William & Martha Hawkins Born 25th may 1733. Bap^{t} 29th July 1733.

John Son of William & margret Hatcher Born 13th July 1733 Bap^{t} 25 august.

Anne D: of Thomas & Phebe Hamlin born 21th august 1733 Bap^{t} 20th octb^{r}.

Sarah D: of Thomas & Jane Hood Born 21th feb^{r} 1733 Bap^{t} March 22th.

Joakim Son of Hall & Elisabeth Hudson Born 11th feb^{r} 1733 Bap^{t} 10th March.

William Son of William & Mary Hulone Born 13th ap^{r} 1734 Bap^{t} 5th May.

Hannah D: of Solomon & lucy Hawkins Born 15th Dce^{r} 1733 Bap^{t} 27th June 1734.

Robert Son of Christopher & Margrit Hinton Born 14th ap^{r} 1734 Bap^{t} 4th July.

anne D: of Thomas & Eliz^{a} Hodges Born 19th June 1734 Bap^{t} 28th July.

John Son of John & Eliz^{a} Hammons Born 17th may 1733 Bap^{t} July 15th.

Negro's belonging to Wm Hockins.

Amey female 12. August 1727.

Lewis male 1 May 1719.

Willo d^{o} 26 Sep^{t} 1719.

Scipio d^{o} 4 March 1731.

Wm son of Willm & Martha Hawkins, Born 9 March 1734 Baptiz'd 4 May 1735.

Edward S: of Edward and Fránis Hill Born 22d January 1734.

Thomas S: of John and Franis Hardaway Born the 20th Sep^{t} 1734.

John S. of Thomas and Sarah Hackney Born March 9th 1734.

Phillis female Slave belong^{g} to Thomas Hickman Born 4th day of June 1735.

Sawney Male Slave Belong^{g} to Ditto. Born 22d day of June 1735.

Edmund S. of David and Mary Hattaway Born 31st January 1734.

Abraham S. of William and Magery Hood Born 11th December 1734.

Isham S of Edward & Jane Hawkins Born January ye 15 1740.

Harbud S of John & Ruth Hawkins Born December ye 22 1740.

Sibbinor female Slave belonging to Instance Hall Born may y[e] 15 1741.
Susannah D of Thomas & Agnis Hardiway B Sep[r] 27th 1740.
Richard S of John & Rachell Hardey B. Aug[t] 20th 1741.
James S of John & Katharine Hansell B Feb[ry] 29th 1740-1.
Richard S of Richard & Elizabeth Harris B Feb[ry] 18th 1740-1.
Hannah D. of Richard & Winnifred Heylins Born Ap[l] 17th 1741 & Bap[t] Nov[r] 15th 1741.
John S. of Ussery & Mary Hitchcocks Born Dec[r] 9th 1741 & Bap[t] March 21st 1741-2.
Thomas S. of William & Elizabeth Harwells Born March 27th 1742 & Bap[t] June 6th 1742.
Obedience D. of Robert & Sina Hudsons Born June 9th 1742 & Bap[t] July 24th 1742.
Keren-happuch D. of John & Francis Hardaways Born Jan[ry] 27th 1741 & Bap[t] May 30th 1741.
Ainsworth S. of John & Francis Hardaways Born June 30th 1742 & Bap[t] July 3d 1742.
William a Slave of William Hudson Born Sep[tr] 11th 1741 & Bap[t] July 25th 1742.
Winnifred a fem. Slave of William Hudson born Nov[r] 25th 1739 & Bap[t] July 25th 1742.
Lucy D. of Richard & Mary Hawkins Born May 14th 1742 & Bap[t] Sep[tr] 13th 1742.
John S. of Abram & Lucy Hawks born Dec[r] 7th 1742 & bapt[d] Jan[ry] 9th 1742-3.
Edwards S. of William & Mary Hobbes born Dec[r] 29th 1742 & bapt[d] Feb[r] 20th 1742-3.
John S. of John & Martha Halls was born Feb[r] 3d 1742-3 & bapt[d] March 27th 1743.
David S. of William & Elizabeth Harwoods born Jan[ry] 28th 1742-3 & bapt[d] May 29th 1743.
Elizabeth D. of Michael & Susanna Hills born July 18th 1743 & bapt[d] Sept[r] 4th 1743.
Lucy D. of Francis & Frances Haddons born July 15th 1743 & bapt[d] Octob 16th 1743.
Mary D of Peter & Barbara Harwoods born Aug 5th 1743 bapt[d] Apr 29th 1744.

Sarah D of Willm & Mary Hobbes born Apl 22d & baptd June 10th 1744.

William S. of Willm & Elizabeth Harvey born Apr 9th & baptd June 10th 1744.

Anne D. of Robert & Margret Hudsons born July 31st & baptd Septr 17th 1744.

Edward S. of Francis & Frances Haddons was born Aprile 8th & baptd June 9th 1745.

Will a Negro Child belonging to Instance Hall born Septr 23d 1745.

Anne D. of John & Martha Halls was born June 22d & baptd Aug —— 1745.

Randolph S. of Peter & Barbara Harwells was born May 22d & baptd Septr 1st 1745.

Benjamin S. of Richard & Elizabeth Harrisons was born Janry 25th 1745-6 baptd Ap. 27th 1746.

Anne D. of Thomas & Anne Harmers was born March 2d 1745-6 baptd Ap. 27th 1746.

John S. of William & Elizabeth Harwells was born March 4th 1745-6 baptd Ap. 27th 1746.

Jesse Son of William & Mary Hobbs was born June 6th 1746.

Amie D. of Michal & Susanna Hills was born April 27th & baptd June 22d 1746.

Mary D. of Frances & Francis Haddons was born May 13th 1748.

Frederick son of John & Christian Hawks born 22d January 1750-1 bapt 3d March.

Nann Female Slave of Instance and Mary Hall born September 30th 1749.

John Male Slave of Ditto born June 5th 1750.

George Male Slave of Ditto born February 7th 1752.

Frank Female Slave of Ditto born April 30th 1752.

Lucey Daughter of Joseph & Ann Hardaway was Born May the 25th 1755.

Drurey Hardway son of Ditto was Born August 13th 1756.

Mason Hardiway Daughter of Ditto Born February 6 1758.

Ann Hardaway Daughter of Ditto Born Septemr ye 24 1759.

Rossey Hunt, Daughter of Samuel Hunt & Ann Lamboth Davis was Born August the 7th 1760.

Daniel Hair son of Thomas and Ann Hair was born y[e] 18th Decemb[r] 1760 and Baptiz'd at Blandford Church, Bristol Parish March y[e] 1st 1761.

Mary Herringham Daughter of William & Prudence Herringham was Born august y[e] 3d 1739.

William Herringham their son was Born May the 15th 1742.

Betty Their Daughter was Born October the 11th 1744.

James son of Thomas and Ann Hair was Born April y[e] 7th 1762 and Baptiz'd at Blandford Church by Mr. McRoberts may y[e] 16th 1762.

Mary their Daughter was Born november y[e] 14th 1763.

Joel Stirdevent Hall son of Mary Hall was Born July the 30th 1760.

Sarah, D[r] of Benjamin Hobbs & Molly his Wife, born March 11th 1789, & baptized March 11th 1792.

Edward, Son of Michael Heathcote & Mary his Wife, born Dec[r] 29th 1791, & bapatized March 19th 1792.

Dolly Agness, Dau[r] of William Heth & Elizabeth his Wife, born March 19th 1789, died Oct[r] 31st 1791, & was buried April 5th 1792.

Dolly Anne, Dau[r] of the same, born November 28th 1791, & baptized April 5th 1792.

Williamson Bonner, Son of Jesse Heth & Agnes his Wife, born February 16th & bap: May 13th 1792.

John Holmes, Son of Holmes Jones (of Sussex) & Susannah his Wife, born March 20th 1791, & bap: May 13th 1792.

Peyton, Son of Henry Harrison (of Sussex) & Elizabeth his Wife, born March 3d & bap: May 13th 1792.

Salley, Dau. of William Hall, & Elizabeth his Wife, born February 14th & bap: May 13th 1792.

Benjamin Stith, S, of Drury Hardaway & Anne his Wife, born Dec[r] 30th 1791. and baptized July 8th 1792.

Peggy Dau[r] of Nancy a Negroe Slave belonging to Edmund Harrison born February 15th & baptized July 22d 1792.

Edward Heathcote, Son of Michael Heathcote, deceased, of the Town of Petersburg was buried October 30th 1792.

Thomas Hope, of Petersburg, died Nov[r] 3d & was buried Nov[r] 5th 1792.

Peterson, S, of Francis Haddon & Becky his Wife, born March 8th & baptized Novr 25th 1792.

Mary Herbert Stith, Dau^r, of Instance Hall & Eliza his Wife, born May 20th & baptized Decr 13th 1792.

Drury Heath, of Prince George County, died Decr 16th 1792 & was buried January 27th 1793.

William Rives, S, of Thomas Heath & Selah his Wife, born September 6th 1791 & baptized January 27th 1793.

Armistead, S, of Drury Heath, & Elle his Wife, born Decr 25th 1792 & baptized January 27th 1793.

Robert, Son, of William Hiland & Lucy his Wife, was born April 15th & baptized June 30th 1793.

Delilah Ann Southall Dau^r of Thomas Hatton & Ann his Wife, born March 29th & baptized August 4th 1793.

Marry Murray Dau^r of Edmund Harrison & Mary his Wife, was born ———— & baptized May 2d 1793.

Andrew Hamilton of the Town of Petersburg died 8th and was buried 11th March 1794.

Martha Ann, and Mary Murray, Daughters of Edmund Harrison & Mary his Wife, died ———— and were buried 17th April 1794.

I–J

Peter son of Rich: & sarah Jones born 17th Nov: last bap^t Jan^r 8th 1720–1.

Frederick son of peter & Mary Jones born 4th decem last bap^t Jan^r 8th 1720–1.

James a Moll: belonging unto Mr peter Jones born 23d June 1720.

Susanna a Moll belonging unto Capt peter Jones born 24th July 1720.

Samuell son of Tho: & Mary Jones born 12th August last bap^t Aprill 30th 1721.

Eliz dau: of Ledbetter & Martha Jones born 7th Jan^r last bap^t feb^r 25th 1721–2.

peter A Moll: belonging to Abraham & Sarah Jones born 10th of May last 1721 & bap^t x^{br} 21th 1721.

Abra son of Abra: & Sarah Jones born feb: 16th 1720 bap^t Aprill 30th 1721.

James A Moll: belonging to Capt peter Jones born 10th of x^br 1722.

Hen: A Moll belonging to ditto born in March 1722-3.

Mary A Moll: belonging to ditto died 12th of Aprill 1723.

Edw: Son of Rich & Sarah Jones born 18th Aprill last bap^t July 28th 1722.

——— Son of John & Eliz: Johnstone born 21th Jan^r 1722-3.

Lucy dau of Wm & Mary Jones born 9th octob^r last bap^t 14th feb 1722-3.

Isaac son of John & Eliz: Johnstone born 22th Jan^r last bap^t may 5th 1723.

Prissilla dau: of Tho: & ——— Jones Born ——— bap^t June 2d hard word 1723.

Grace dau of Wm & Joan Johnson born 31th Octob: 1721 bap^t August 21th 1723.

Dan: son of Rich & Sarah Jones born 30th Octob^r last bap^t feb^r [ ]th 1723-4.

Ann D: of Abra: & Sarah Jones born 11th May 1724.

Wm son of John & Eliz: Johnson born 25 Octob^r last bap feb^r 28th 1724-5.

Eliz: D: of Rich: & Eliz: James born the 8th Inst. bap^t feb 14th 1724-5.

Pru: D: of Rich & Sarah Jones born 19th feb: last bap: 19th Aug 1725.

Sara A negro Girl belonging to Sam Jurden born 17th June 1725.

Francis and Amy Daughters of Ledbetter and martha Jones born 19th July last 1725.

Jane Dat of Wm and Mary Jent born 26th July 1725.

Wm son of Peter and Mary Jones born 25th March 1725.

Tom Slave of Abr^a and Sarah Jones born 10th feb^r 1725.

Benj^a son of Wm and mary Jones born 8th feb^r 1725.

Lucrece D of philip and Amy Jones born 11th March 1726.

Eliz^a D of John and Susan Jones born 27th Jan^r 1726.

Rebeckah Daughter of Wm and frances Jones born 16th Jan^r 1726.

John Son of John and Eliz^a Johnston born 4th March 1726.

Benjamine Son of Wm and Mary Jones born 19th ffeb^r 1726.

Betty female Slave of Samuel and Mary Jordain born 18th oct^m Decs^d 2d Jan^r 1727.

henry Son of Abr^{a} and Sarah Jones born 9th Jan^{r} bap^{t} 18th feb^{r} 1727.

Martin Son of Wm and Johannah Johnson Born 13th Novr 1713.

Wm Son of Ditto Born 16th Decr 1717.

Ann Dater of Ditto Born 8th June 1710.

Grace Dater of Ditto Born Octo^{r} 1720.

Ridly D of peter and Dorithy Jones born 5th august 1728 Bap^{t} 25th august.

Cadwaller Son of peter and Mary Jones Born 19th June 1728 Bapt 25th august.

Wm Son of Phillip and amie Jones Born 23d Sep^{t} 1728.

Dick Male Slave of Saml Jordain Born 30th Novm^{r} 1728.

Phebe female Slave of Abr^{a} and Sarah Jones Born 8th Dce^{m} 1728 Bap^{t} 23d august.

Mary D of Richard & Mary James Born ye 2d Jan^{r} Bap^{t} 2d feb^{r} 1728–9.

ann D. of ledbetter and martha Jones Born 15 Jan^{r} 1727.

Eleonar Dat^{r} of John and Susaner Jones Born 20th august 1729.

Pelletiah of Wm and Mary Jones Born 27th July 1729.

Mary of Wm and frances Jones Born 25th May Bap^{t} 30th June 1729.

William Son of William and Judith Jones Born 8th aprill Bap^{t} 10th May 1730.

Joshua Son of Joshua Irby and Mary Blyth Born 1th aprill 1730.

William Irby Son of Wm Irby and Mary Green Born 30th Decmb^{r} 1730.

Batte Son of Richard and Margrat Jones Born 30th Dce^{mr} 1729 Bap^{t} 2d may 1730.

Ridlie Dater of Dorithy and Peter Jones Born 9th August 1730 Bap^{t} 19th Sep^{r}.

William Son of abr^{a} and Sarah Jones Born feb^{r} 19th 1730 Bap^{t} 23^{d} May 1731.

Peter male Slave of Samuel and Mary Jordain Born 30th June 1731.

ann D of Thomas & Eliz^{a} Ivy Born 28th Jan^{r} 1730 Bap^{t} 21th feb^{r}.

Neptune Son of Thomas & Judith Jackson Born 30th Novm^{r} 1730 at sea Bap: 25th ap^{r} 1731.

Mary D: of James & Mary Jones Born 5th July 1731 Bap[t] august 29th 1731.

peter Son of Peter & Mary Jones Born 28th March 1731 bap[t] 14th Sep[r].

Sarah mulatto Slave of peter and mary Jones Born 11th March 1730 Bap[t] 14th Sep[r].

Nathaniel Son of Tho[m] & amy Jones Born 17th ap[r] 1731 Bap[t] 14th Sep[r].

Elisabeth D of Daniel & ——— Jackson Born 2d June 1731 Bap[t] 1th august.

Peter Son of William & francis Jones Born 11th feb[r] 1731 Bap[t] 23d ap[r] 1732.

Ludwell Son of Wm & Mary Jones Born 6th March 1731 Bap[t] 24th ap[r] 1732.

Eliz[a] dat[r] of Peter & Dorothy Jones Born 19th March 1731 Bap[t] 30th May 1732.

Emanuel Slave of Ditto 30th Sep[r] 1731 Do.

Gideon Slave to Martha Jones Born 14th Aug[t] 1731 Do.

Wilmoth dat[r] of Joshua & ——— Irby born ——— Bap[t] 4th 1732.

Richarda dat[r] of Wm & Mary Jones born 18th Nov[r] 1731 Bap[t] Dec[r] 26th 1732.

Rebecca of Rich[d] & Margett Jones born & bap[t] 28th Dec[r] 1731.

Will a Melatto of Abra & Sarah Jones born 3d July 1730 bap[t] 14th Sep[r] 1731.

Ja[s] son of Wm & Judith Jones born 3d June 1732 bap[t] July 16th 1732.

Dianah dat[r] of Jno & Eliz[a] Johnson born 16th May 1732 bap[t] Sep[r] 29th 1732.

Thomas son of Thomas & Tabitha Jacob Born 14th Nov: 1731 Bap[t] 30th dce[r].

Richard Son of William & Mary Jones Born 12th Nov[r] 1732 Bap[t] 28th Dce[r].

Jenne female Slave of Samuel Jordain Born 25th ap[r] 1733.

Rachel D[r] of Thomas & amy Jones Born 12th feb[r] 1732 Bap[t] 7th ap[r] 1733.

Charles male Slave of Sam[l] Jordain Born 26th May 1733.

Ursula D: of James & Mary Jones Born 28th July 1733 Bap[t] 14th august.

Margrett D: of peter & Dorithy Jones Born 14th august 1733 Bapt 28th Sepr.

Phillip Son of Daniel & mary Jones Born 6th July 1733 Bapt 28th Sepr.

Isabell fem Slave of Thos & amy Jones Born 14th Sepr 1731.

Elisabeth D: of Thomas & Elisabeth Ivy Born 25th novr 1732 Bapt 21th octbr 1733.

Peter Son of abra & Sarah Jones Born 2d novr 1733 Bapt 1th Decr.

George a mulatto Slave of Ditto Born 2d august 1732 Bapt Dcer 1th 1733.

Ned a mulatto of ditto Born 21th Dcer 1732 Bapt Dcer 1th 1733.

William Son of William & Mary Jones Born 21th Janr 1733 Bapt March 15th.

William Son of William & Mary Jones Born 21th Janr 1733 Bapt 14th apr 1734.

Joseph Son of Daniel & Eliza Jackson Born 5th febr 1733 Bapt 10th March.

John Son of Thomas & Tabitha Jacobs Born 26th apr 1734 Bapt 27th June.

Berriman Son of William & Mary Jones Born 18th March 1733 Bapt 4th august 1734.

Moses Son of Joshua & Eliza Jane Born 1th July 1734 Bapt 1th Sepr.

David Son of Phillip and Amy Jones Born 4 March 1734 Bapt ye 4 May 1735.

Amey D of Thomas and Easter Jones. Born 30 Novemb. 1734 Bapt 4 May 1735.

Judith female Slave of Saml Jordan Born 27 March 1735.

Jenny female Slave belongg to Do Born 11 Apl 1735.

Aggey female Slave belongg to Do Born 18 October 1735.

Jane Female Slave belongg to Daniel Jones Born 1st Novr 1734.

Elisabeth Slave Belonging to Abraham Jones Born May ye 8th 1741.

Toby male Slave of Samuel Jurdens Sr Born April ye 14 1741.

Thomas Son of Thomas & Tabitha Jones B July 21st 1740.

Mordica Son of Daniel & Mary Jones B July 22d 1741.

Anne D. of Mr. John & Elizabeth Jones Born May 29th 1742 & Bapt aug 1st 1742.

John A Slave of Capt Richard Jones born Novr 15th 1741 & Bap^t July 4th 1742.

Francis & Sara Negro Children belonging to Mrs Tabitha Jones Born July 4th 1741 & Bap^t May 2d 1742.

Judith D. of William & Judith Jones born July 22d 1742 & bapt^d Octob^r 17th 1742.

John S of Abram & Sarah Jones born Decr 14th 1742 & bapt^d Jan^ry 25th 1742–3.

Edward S. of Samuel & Milson Jordans born Feb 2d 1742–3 & bapt^d March 27th 1743.

Anthony A Male Slave belonging to Mr. Abram Jones born Jan^r 22^d 1743–4.

Betty D. of Mr. John & Elizabeth Jones born Novr 18th & bapt^d Decr 24th 1744.

Dorothy D. of Major Peter & Dorothy Jones born Jan^ry 29th 1744–5 & bapt^d May 5th 1745.

Mary D. of Samuel & Milson Jordans was born Aprile 30th & bapt^d June 2d 1745.

Ann Daughter of Thos & Lucy Jones born —— bap^t 3d March 1750–1.

Frederick Son of William Jones Junr born —— baptized 9th April 1751.

John Hall Jinkins son of William & Mary Jinkins was Born May the 13th 1768.

Sarah Johnson Daughter of Hubbard Johnson was Born Novr 18th 1766.

Elizabeth D. of Tabitha Johnson, a free Mulatto, born May 4th 1791, & baptized March 4th 1792.

Anne Jeffries died Oct —— 1792 & was buried July 4th 1793.

K

Olive dau: of Charles & Anne King born 30th decem: last bap^t July 18th 1721.

Mary dau of Hen: & Mary King born 12th July 1720 bap^t July 18th 1721.

Eliz: dau: of Rich & Agnis Kennon Born 12 day decem 1720.

Harry a negro boy belonging to ditto born Jan^r 1720.

Tho Kent born about 50 years past baptized March 14th 1721–2.

John son of Rob[t] & Cath: Kennell born in xb[r] 1722 bap[t] 3d feb 1722–3.
Ann dau of Cap[t] Rich: & Agnis Kennon born 30th Nov: last bap[t] 30th xbr 1722.
Rich son of Wm & Anne Kennon born 15th Aprill 1712.
Wm son of ditto born 9th feb 1713.
Fran: son of ditto born 3d sep[tr] 1715.
Hen: Isham son of ditto born 22th Aprill 1718.
John son of ditto born 20th decem: 1721.

Negroes Belonging to Maj[r] Wm Kennon.

Nutty born 3d octob[r] 1711.
Pegg born March 18th 1716.
Lewis born 20th Aprill 1719.
Annake born 14th feb[r] 1720.
Hannibal born 17th decem 1722.
Kate born 3d June 1723.

Sarah dau: of Hen: & Mary King born 31th Jan[r] last bap[t] Aug 21th 1723.
John son of Cha & Anne King born 4th Jan: last bap[t] 10th Aprill 1724.
John son of Cornelias and Eliz[a] Keeth born 24th Dec[m] 1724.
Rebeckah Dat of henry and mary King born 1th July 1725.
John Son of Jn[o] and Hannah King born 22d au[g] 1724.
Sa[m] Son of Cornelias and Eliz[a] Keeth born 13th Dec[m] 1725.
Sarah Da[t] of Jo[s] and Sarah Kimbal born 20th feb[r] 1725.
Mary D of Wm and Mary Kally born 22d Sept[r] 1725.
Ann D of Charles and Ann King born 3d oct[m] 1726.
Robert Son of Richard and Agnis Kennon born 14th Aprill 1727.
John Son of John and Ann Kemp born 9th aprill 1710.
Jane Dater of Ditt[o] born 11th May 1713.
Mary D: Wm and Sarah Kelly born 22d Sep[t] 1725.
Nimrod Son of Rob[t] and Jane Kileress born 28th July 1728.
Bille male Slave of Rich[d] and agnis Kennon Born May 1723.
Mol female Slave Ditt[o] Born august 1725.
Janne female slave of Ditto Born feb[r] 1725.
Sue female Slave of Ditto Born Dcem[r] 1727.
Dick male Slave of Ditto Born March 1727.
Mary D of Rich[d] and agnis Kennon Born 29th Jan[r] 1728.

Martha D of Charles and ann King Born 5th Dce^{m} 1728 Bap^{t} aprill 6th 1729.

Negros Belongine to Maj^{r} Wm Kennon.

Hannah female Born 2d June 1723.
Harry male slave Born 1th March 1725.
Phillis female slave Born 1th March 1725.
Scippio male Slave Born 3d March 1727.
Lucy female Slave Born 10th July 1729.
Juno female Slave Born 5th July 1729.
Sampson Male Slave Born 1 decemb^{r} 1729.
Phebe female Slave Born 2d Jan^{r} 1730.
Sam Male Slave Born 4th January 1730.

Martha D: of Richard & agnis Kennon Born 30th august Bap^{t} 17th octb^{r} 1731.

Thomas Son of John & Mary Lenard Born 18th March 1733 Bap^{t} ap^{r} 7th 1734.

Thomas Son of Wm & Eliz^{a} Loftus Born 27th august 1733 Bap^{t} 7th ap^{r} 1734.

Negro slaves belonging to William Kennon Gentleman.

Daniel male slave Born august 1732.
Cyrus male slave Born July 1733.
Molbrow male Slave Born June 1731.
Cato male Slave Born July 1733.
Prince male Slave Born Dce^{r} 1733.
Adam male Slave Born Dce^{r} 1733.
Jemmy male Slave Born March 1733.

Ann D. of William & Judith King Born 11th Novr 1734.

Mary Slave of Mr James Keith B Decr 20th 1740.

Molly D of John & Hannah Kinton B Jan^{ry} 21st 1740.

James S. of Wm & Jane King B Decr 18th 1740.

John S of John & Elizabeth Kirby. B April 18th 1741.

William S. of John & Hannah Kennons Born June 5th 1742 & Bap^{t} July 4th 1742.

Williaw S. of Julian & Elizabeth Kings born Octob^{r} 18th 1742 & bapt^{d} Decr 12th 1742.

Milly, Dau^{r} of Eleanor Keown, born February 12th 1785 and baptized October 2nd 1792.

John Reading, Son of D° born June 25th 1790, and baptized October 2nd 1792.

Elizabeth Reading, Dau[r] of D° born April 4 and baptized October 2nd 1792.

Betsy Collins, Dau[r] of Stephen Knight, and Leah his Wife. Born December 9th 1791 and baptized October 2nd 1792.

Polly Cheatham, Dau[r] of Josiah Knight & Milly his Wife, born Feby. 15: & bap: Nov[r] 7. 1793.

Billy Stephens, Son of Stephen Knight & Leah his Wife born July 2 & baptized Nov. 7. 1793.

L

Mary dau: of Wm & Rebeca Ledbetter born 28th decem: last bap[t] feb 26th 1720–1.

Fran: dau: of Sam: & Fran: Lee born 23th octob[r] Last bap[t] feb: 26th 1720–1.

Wm son of John & Fran: Ledbetter born 19th feb[r] last bap[t] July 23th 1721.

Tho son of Hugh & Mary Lee born 11th Nov: last bap[t] March 4th 1721–2.

Mary dau of Jn° & Cath: Lee born 21th Jan[r] Last bap[t] Aprill 22th 1722.

Peter son of Tho: & Ann Leeth born 22th sep[tr] last bap[t] March 31th 1723.

Eliz: dau of peter & Abigaell Leeth born 19th octob[r] last bap[t] 16th xb[r] 1722.

Jane dau: of Fran: & Jane Lajohn born 28th August bap[t] 18th Nov: 1722.

John son of Wm & Elizth Laws born 29th March last bap[t] Aug: 25th 1722.

Mary dau of ditto born 1th feb: 1719 bap[t] Aug: 25th 1722.

Hannah dau of Tho & Eliz Lockett born 28th decem last bap[t] March 10th 1722–3.

Peter son of Tho & Ann Leeth born 22th sep[t] last bap[t] 31th March 1723.

Wm son of Sam & Fran: Lee departed this life 29th Sep[tr] 1723.

Eliz: dau of John & Mary Lewis born 21th Nov 1705.

Mary d: of ditto born 12th June 1707.

Ann: d of ditto born 16th Aprill 1710.

John son of ditto born 26th Sept[r] 1711.
Wm son of ditto born 22th Aprill 1713.
Fran: dau of ditto born 11th feb[r] 1715–16.
Susan: dau: of ditto born 11th Aprill 1718.
Tho: son of ditto born 29th Aprill 1720.
Frances dau: of Peter & Abigael Leeth bor 2d Nov[r] last bap[t] Jan[r] 19th 1723–4.
Sarah D of Matthew Lee & his Wife born 26th august 1721.
Amy D of ditto born 25 decem: 1722.
Eliz: dau: of Tho: & Mary Luis born July 27th 1722.
Susanna d: of Hugh & Mary Lee Jun[r] born 10th feb last bap[t] May 24th 1724.
Martha d of John & Anne Lile born 28th June last bap Nov. 2d 1724.
John Son of Joss & Mary Lantroop born 27th 8[br] last bap[t] 11th xb[r] 1724.
James S: of Wm & Elishaba Laws born —— March ——— bap[t] May 16th 1725.
Tho: S of Matt: & Eliz: Ligon born 7th feb: 1724–5.
Joss S of Wm & Elishaba Laws born 27th Jan[r] 1716.
Wm Son of ditto born 20th of feb[r] 1718.
John Son of ditto born 29th March last bap[t] August 25th 1722.
Mary D: of ditto born 1st feb[r] 1719 bap[t] August 25th 1722.
Mary D: of Matt: & Anne Lee born 30th May last bap[t] 4th Aug: 1725.
samuel son of Samuel and frances lee born 30th Aprill bap[t] 5th sep[tr] 1725.
Sarah Slave of bej[a] locket born 24th march 1725.
Charles Son of Th[o] & ann Leith born 23d Aug[t] 1725.
Robin Slave of Jn[o] Ledbetter Decst 30th march 1726:
tab Slave of Jn[o] & Mary Ledbetter born June 18th 1726.
Sarah D of Peter and Abigill Leath born 8th March 1727.
lucy female Slave of benj[a] and Winefrit locket born 12th May 1727.
Thomas Son of Thomas and Sarah lee born 12th Jan[r] 1726.
Joseph Son of Joseph and Mary lantrope born 16th Dce[m] 1726.
Eliz[a] D: of Wm and Elishabah Laws born 17th March 1725.
John Son of John and ann liles born 23d March 1726.

Eliz[a] D of Matthew and Eliz[a] Ligon born 9th Dece[m] bap[t] 9th feb[r] 1727.

Thomas Son of John and anne Lanthrop born 30th Dce[m] 1727 bap[t] 14th aprill 1728.

Sam female Slave of matthew Elisabit Ligon born y[e] 12th may 1728.

ann D of Wm and Eliz Loftis Born 2d august 1728.

Edwd of Edward and Martha Liewes Born 3d octb[r] 1728.

Mary D of Joseph and Mary lanthrope Born 24th Nov[m] Bap[t] 13th March 1728.

Winnifrit Wife of Benj[a] locket Dces[d] 25th Nov[m] 1729.

Mary D of Peter and Abigal Leeth Born 5th aprill Bap[t] 26th oct[r] 1729.

Eliz[a] D of John and Sarah Lovett Born 4th May 1730 Bap[t] 10th May.

Margrat D of John and ann lantroup Born 21th May 1730 Bap[t] 27 sb[r].

John Son of Thomas Liewes Born 3d august 1730.

William son of Joseph & mary Lantrop Born 13th Jan[r] 1730 Bap[t] ap[r] 18th 1731.

Sarah D of Sam'l & Frances lee Born 20th March 1731 Bap[t] august 30.

William Son of William & Eliz[a] loftis Born 11th May 1731 Bap[t] Sep[r] 6th.

Mary D of John & mary Leonard Born 20th august 1731 Bap[t] Sep[t] 6th.

Thomas son of Matthew & ann Lee Born 6th Dec[m] 1731 Bap[t] octbr 17th.

William son William & Jane Lovesy Born 14th March 1730 Bap[t] 10th octbe[r].

John Son of Jn[o] & Mary Lenoard Born 30th Jan[r] 1731.

Martha D of peter & Tabitha Lee Born 16th octb[r] 1731.

William son of Jn[o] & Eliz[a] Lile born July 3d 1732 bap[t] 13th Aug[t] 1732.

Joanah dat[r] of Wm & Eliz[a] Lewis born 7th July 1732 bap[t] Oct[r] 8th 1732.

Mary Wife of Joseph lantroup Decs[d] 10th De[r] 1732.

Elisabeth D: of Thomas & Elisabeth Lewis Born 16th Jan[r] 1732 Bap[t] 25th March 1733.

John Son of John & Sarah Loveit Born 14th Jan^r 1732 Bap^t feb^r 25th.

Thomas Son of Samuell & Frances Lee Born 22d ap^r 1733 Bap^t 1th august 1733.

Henritta Dater of Williams & Frances Margret Lockley Born 9th ap^r 1733 Bap^t 1th august 1733.

Burrill Son of Thomas & Sarah Lee Born 30th august 1733 Bap^t 11th Nov^r.

Littleberry Son of William & Elishaba Laws Born 23d June 1733 Bap^t 14th July 1734.

Joshua Son of Catharine Lee Born 11th May 1734 Bapt 4th august.

William Son of Thomas & ann Lister Born July 7th 1734 Bap^t 7th august.

Jesse Son of Thomas & anne Lewelin Born 11th March 1733 Bap^t 28th July 1734.

Patrick Son of John & Mary Lenard Born 31st July 1734 Bap^t ye Ap^l 16. 1735.

Mary D. of John and Sarah Lovett Born 20. March 1734 Bap^t 4 May 1735.

Mary Lee departed this Life the 8th day of January 1734-5 wife of Hugh Lee j^r.

Sarah D of John and Sarah Leveret. Born ye 2d November 1734.

Drury S of Richard & Johannah Ledbetter Born ye 24 Novr 1734.

Elizabeth D. of Christopher & Mary Lane Born August 2d 1735.

Osbun s of Frances & ann Ledbetter Born Febuary ye 14 1740.

Elisabeth D of John & Rebacah Leeth Born January the 22 1749.

Frederick s of John & Mary Lenard Born March 22 1740.

Roland s of Daniel & Elisabeth Lee Born may ye 6th 1741.

Ann D of Richard and Mary Newman B March 30th 1741[*].

William S of Richard & Ha[ ] Ledbiter B March 22 1740.

Thomas S. of Thomas & Mourning Lenoye born Aug. 11th 1741 & Bap^t Octob^r 18th 1741.

Obedience D. of Joseph & Mary Lewis's Born Novr 15th 1741 & Bap^t Jan^ry 17th 1741-2.

James S. of Thomas & Elizabeth Lewis's Born May 28th 1741 & Bap^t Jan^ry 17th 1741-2.

---

* Erased in original.—C. G. C.

Anne D. of William & Anne Lee Born Apr 22d 1742 & Bapt Septr 19th 1742.

Mary D. of John & Elizabeth Lantrops born Octobr 25th 1742 & baptd Feby 20th 1742.

Mary D. of Frances & Anne Leadbetters born Decr 5th 1742 & baptd Febry 20th 1742.

Mary D. of Nathanael & Rebecca Lees born March 11th 1742–3 & baptd May 29th 1743.

Mary D. of George & Katharine Lewis born June 3d 1743 & baptd July 3d 1743.

Ephraim S of John & ——— Leadbetter born Decr 30th 1742.

Winifred D of John & Mary Lenard born May 31st 1743.

Anne Lee ——— Died Feb. 4th 1743–4.

Joseph S. of Willm & Mary Liffsay born March 20th 1743–4 & baptd May 27th 1744.

Drury S. of Daniel & Elizabeth Lees born Aug. 31st & baptd Octob. 28th 1744.

Frederick S. of Thomas & Mary Lees born Feb. 1st 1744–5 & baptd May 5th 1745.

Peter S. of John & Elizabeth Lantropes was born Aprile 2d & baptd May 19th 1745.

Woodie S. of Francis & Anne Leadbetters was born Aprile 5th & baptd June 9th 1745.

Mille D. of John & Keziah Loffsetts was born Novr 15th 1745 & baptd Janry 5th 1745–6.

Frederick S. of William & Mary Loffsay was born Decr 19th 1745 & baptd March 16th 1745–6.

Shadrach Son of Thos and Hannah Lantrop Born 14th Decemr 1749 bapt 1st April 1750.

Winifred Daughtr of Amoss & Mary Love born 8ber 7th 1750.

Benjamin Son of Benjamin and ——— Lawsons born ——— bap. 3d March 1750–1.

Burwell Son of Thomas and Mary Lee born december 3d 1750 bapt 17 March.

Elien Lang Daughter of James Lang & Elizth his wife was Born December the 20th 1766.

Elien Lang Departed this life the 4th of august 1767.

Elizth Lang Daughter of James & Elizth Lang was born July the 9th 1768.

Betsy, Dau^{r} of Euclid Landford (of Sussex County) & Elizabeth his Wife, born October 19th 1789, & baptized April 6th 1792.

Henry, Son of the same, born December 16th 1791, & baptized April 6th 1792.

Patsey, dau: of Robert Land (of Sussex County) & Martha his Wife, born October the 6th 1791, & baptized April 6th 1792.

Rebeccah Parham, D^{r} of John Lewis & Frances his Wife, born April 8th & bap: June 25th 1792.

Thomas S. of Samuel Leigh & Susannah his Wife, born Octr 21st 1791 & bap: July 6th 1792.

Francis Littlepage, S, of Winny Laurence, a free Mulatto, was born June 20th 1791, and was baptized August 26th 1792.

Mary Dau^{r} of John Taylor Leigh & Sarah his Wife born July 18th, and baptized September 30th 1792.

Becky, Dau^{r} of John Cotton, & Celah his Wife, born April 2nd and baptized September 30th 1792.

Rebecca Dressony, Dau^{r} of John Lanier & Catharine his Wife, was born June 5th 1791 & baptized Novr 2nd 1792.

Peter Singleton. S, of Francis Lard & Nancy his Wife, born Novr 2nd & bap: Decr 27th 1791.

Mrs Laniere (wife of ——— Laniere of the town of Petersburg) was buried 3d Novr 1794.

Samuel Son of Jesse Lee & Polly Marcum his wife born 1st May 1793 & baptized Jany 1st 1795.

Isham Randolph. Son of John Lanier & Anne his Wife born May 5th & baptized August 8th 1793.

M

Mary dau: of Sam & Mary Moor born 26th x^{br} 1719 bap^{t} Aprill 10th 1720.

Mary dau: of Dan: & Mary Mellone born 20th March 1719–20 bap^{t} ———.

John son of John & Cath: Moor born 8th decem 1720 bap^{t} 19th March 1720–1.

John Bass son of Margaret Micabin born 26 July last bap^{t} March 21th 1720–1.

Rosamund dau: of Fran: & Margaret Morrimont born 26th July 1719 bap^{t} 22th June 1721.

Joshua son of Peter & Eliz: Mitchell born 26th feb: 1718 bap[t] July 18th 1721.

Tho: son of Tho: & Prissilla Man born 24th May last bap[t] July 6th 1721.

Marth: d of John & Julian Mays born 8th June Last bap[t] 18th ditto 1722.

Lucy dau: of Fran & Eliz: Man born 20th Aprill last bap[t] July 7th 1722.

Priscilla dau of James & Mary Moor born 1st June last bap[t] July 7th 1722.

Tho: son of Wm & Mary ——————.

Dan: son of Peter & Eliz: Mitchell born 26th sep[t] last bap[t] June 11th 1722.

Ann dau of Rich: & —— Massy born about Jan[r] or feb[r] last bap[t] June 14th 1722.

Eliz: dau of Sam & Mary Moor born 13th octob[r] last bap[t] 5th Aug: 1722.

Morgan son of Morgan & Sibilla Mackinney born 7th June last bap[t] 7th octob[r] 1722.

Fran: dau of James & —— Matthews born 28th Aprill last bap[t] Sep[t] 30th 1722.

Joab son of Tho & Hannah Mitchell born 11th feb last bap[t] sep[t] 16th 1722.

John son of Ann Mackdaniell bass born 21th August 1721 bap[t] feb 3d 1722-3.

Eliz: dau: of John & Mary Maise born 30th sep[t] last bap[t] Jan 10th 1722.

John son of John & Cath: Moor born —— bap[t] March 19th 1720-1.

Sara dau of Ditto born 20th March last bap[t] 29th Aprill 1723.

John son of Tho & Ann Mitchell born 26th May 1704.

Tho: son of ditto born 19th Aprill 1705.

Fran: son of ditto born 18th June 1708.

Mary dau: of Tho: & Barbary Mitchell born 18th August 1713.

Barbary dau of ditto born 8th March 1715.

Nath: son of ditto born 4th decem: 1717.

Peter son of ditto born 3d Jan: 1719.

Sam son of ditto born 16th June 1722.

John son of Rob[t] & Anne Moody born 18th May 1723.

Mark son of Mark & Eliz: Moore borne 26th July last bap Nov 7th 1723.

John son of Morgan & Sibbilla Makinny born 12th feb^{r} last bap^{t} 10th Aprill 1724.

Sarah d of Rich & Ann Massy born 27th Nov last bap^{t} 10th Aprill 1724.

Rich son of Sam: & Mary Moor born 9th feb^{r} last bap^{t} August 2d 1724.

Rich son of Hen: & Eliz: Mays born 1st of Aprill last bap^{t} 6th Novr 1724.

Anne d of Fran & Marg^{a} Merimon born 26th June last bap Nov 6th 1724.

Mary d of John & Mary Mays born 2d last June bap^{t} Octob^{r} 11th 1724.

Seth Moor son of great John Moor born 9th Aprill 1692.

Rhuben son of phillip & Mary Morgan born 11th novb^{r} bap^{t} 20th feb^{r} 1725.

Anne Dat of Jno and Julia Mayes born 13th feb^{r} bap^{t} 20th 1725.

John son of John & Julia Mayes born 29th feb^{r} 1719.

Martha Dat of John and Julia Mayes 8th June born 1722.

Thomas son of Thom and Jane Man born 4th June last bap^{t} 30 July 1725.

Amey Da^{t} of Joseph and Eleonore Mathes born 9th Dec^{m} 1724.

frances Da^{t} of peter and Eliz^{a} Mitchel born 28th oc^{tm} 1725.

martha Da^{t} of henry and Martha Morris born 2 June 1725.

Priscilla Da^{t} of Th^{o} and Jane Man born 13th Dec^{m} 1725.

Winiford Da^{t} of Wm and Eliz^{a} Mayes born 22d Aug^{s} 1725.

Jno and Rich^{d} sons of Ric^{d} and Ann Massey born 14th feb^{r} 1725.

Jno Son of David and Eliz Murcollow born 14 Dec^{m} 1725.

Wm Son of Samuel and Mary More born 6th July bap^{t} Octob^{r} 9th 1726.

Wm Son of Jno and Mary Mayes born 11th June bap^{t} oct^{m} 4th 1726.

Mark Son Mark and Eliz^{a} More born 10th June 1726.

James Son of Jno and Catherine More born 18th augst bap^{t} 16th oct^{m} 1726.

Mary D: of Jno and dorithy Morland born 23d Sep^{t} bap^{t} 30th octm 1726.

Mary gardiner D of Gardiner and Eliz^{a} Mayes born 13th Oct^{m} 1726.

Edward Son of Robert and Martha Munford born 1th No^{br} 1726.

James Son of Morgan and Sybellah Makinny born 7th feb^{r} 1725.

James Son of John and Mary May born 6th feb^{r} 1726.

Eliz^{a} D of henry and Susanah Morris born 6th Oct^{m} 1726.

Lucrecee D of Wm and Ann Mallone born 11th Jan^{r} 1726.

Robert Son of Jerimiah and Grace Mize born 10th May 1721.

Joshua son of Ditto born 10th March 1726.

Mary D of David and Eliz^{a} Murcollo born 7th June 1727.

Michaell son of Wm and Eliz^{a} Mixon born 15th aprill 1727.

Eliz^{a} D of henry and Susanah Morris born 6th oct^{m} 1726.

David son of David and Jane Miles born 17th aprill 1727.

Drury Son of Matthew and Eliz^{a} Mayes born 15th Jan^{r} bap^{t} feb^{r} 20th 1727.

Lucy Dat^{r} of Georg hunt and frances More born 22d Dce^{m} 1727.

James Son of John and Julia mayes born Monday ye 18th March 1727.

Agnis D of John and Mary Man Born 31t May 1728.

George Son of John and Mary Mayes Born 19th July 1728 Bap^{t} 6 ocb^{r}.

Jean D of John and Dorithy Moreland Born 21th Sep^{t} 1728 Bap^{t} 7th No^{r}.

Phebe Dat^{r} of John and Catherine More Born 22d oct^{m} 1728 Bapt 25th Dce^{m}.

henry Son of Henry and Susan Morris Born 22d octm^{r} Bap^{t} March 3d 1728.

Margret D of Th^{os} and Elionar More Born 13th aprill Bap^{t} 16th aprill 1729.

Dorithy D of John and Mary May Born 9th Dce^{mr} Bap^{t} 21 Dec^{m} 1728.

Martha D of James and Eliz^{a} munford Born 29th Sepr Bap^{t} 6th Jan^{r} 1728.

David Son of David and Eliz^{a} Murcollo Born 28th May Bap^{t} 3d august 1729.

Susannah D of Roger and Eliz^{a} More Born 27th aprill Bap^{t} 27 June 1729.

Lucia D of Jno and Mary More Born 24th May Bap^{t} 27th June 1729.

Frances D of David and Jane Miles Born 21 June Bap[t] 10th august 1729.

Zacariah son of John and Rachail Martin Born 22d Jan[r] 1729.

ann D of John and Mary Man Born 29th august Bap[t] 2d oct[r] 1729.

Lucy D of Th[os] & Jeane May Born 8th Jan[r] 1729 Bap[t] 28th aprill 1730.

Henry Male Slave of Wm and Mary Mayes Born 24th March 1725 Bap[t] 3d March 1729.

James Male Slave of Ditto Born 26th Jan[r] 1727 Bap[t] 3d March 1729.

Nancy female Slave of Ditto Born 27th Jan[r] Bap[t] 3d March 1729.

Phillip Son of Phillip and Mary Morgan Born 15th Dcem[r] Bap[t] 10th May 1730.

Joseph Son of Josep and Hellen Matthy Born 17th Janr: 1729 Bap[t] 10th May 1730.

Tabitha D of Richard and ann Massie Born 8th Jan[r] 1729 Bap[t] 30th May 1730.

Michal Son of Henry and Mary Matthews Born 27th Dce[m] 1729 Bap[t] 10th May 1730.

Eliz[a] D of George and frances More Born 1th Jan[r] Bap[t] 22d febr: 1729.

Robert Son of Wm and ann Marshall Born 23d Dcem[r] 1729 Bap[t] 3th March 1730.

Zachariah Son of Jn[o] and Rachald Martin Born 22d Jan[r] 1729 Bap[r] 1th March 1729.

Moses male Slave of Jn[o] and Julia Mayes Born 19th June 1730.

Sarah Dater of John and Julia Mayes Born 13th Decm[r] 1730.

Elisabeth Dater of John and Mary May Born 2d octber 1730.

Thomas Son of Roger and Eliz[a] more Born 20th Sep[r] 1730 Bap[t] 15th Nov[r].

Matthew Son of Marke & Mary fowler Born 4th Jan[r] 1730 Bap[t] augst 29th 1731.

Lucy D of John & mary mayes Born 26th Jan[r] 1730 Bap[t] 21th feb[r].

Sarah D: of michael & Eliz[a] Mackey Born 16th Dcm[r] 1730.

Betty rutherford Dater of John and Catharine more Born 25th June Bap[t] 2d octb[r] 1731.

mary D of Samuel & Mary More Born 29th ap^{r} Bap^{t} 7th Novmb^{r} 1731.

Elisabeth D: of Wm and ann marshal Born 13th July Bap^{t} 24th Sep^{tr} 1731.

Ja[ ] Son of David & Elisabeth Maccollo Born 29th Sepr 1731 Bap^{t} Decr 25th.

Laurana D: of Robert & ann Moody Born 29th Jany^{r} 1731 Bap^{t} ap^{r} 23: 1732.

Martha D: of Joseph & Eleanore Matthews Born 8th Jan^{r} 1731 Bap^{t} 23d ap^{r} 1732.

Frank male Slave of Jno & Julia mayes Born 28th Novr 1731.

John Son of Phillip & mary morgan Born 30th Novr 1731 Bap^{t} 23d ap^{r} 1732.

William Son of Rich^{d} & Eleanor McDearmon born May 18th 1732.

Jonathan son of Jonath^{a} & Sarah Mote born ——— bap^{t} Sepr 23d 1732.

Willm Son of Alex^{r} & Ruth Moor born 14th Sepr 1731 bap^{t} May 22d 1732.

Eliz^{a} Dat^{r} of Saml & Mary Morgan born Ap^{l} 20 1732 bap^{t} Decr 17th 1732.

James Son of James & Eliz^{a} Munford born Sepr 16th bap^{t} Decr 26th 1732.

Thomas Son of David & Jane Mils Born 29th dce^{r} 1731 Bap^{t} Jan^{r} 30th.

Johanna D: of Wm & Elisabeth Mayes Born 14 sep^{r} 1732 Bap^{t} Jan^{r} 19th.

William son of John & Mary May Born 28th Dce^{r} 1732 Bap^{t} 24th feb^{r}.

Dick male slave of Robt & martha munford Born 21th Decem^{r} 1732 Bap^{t} feb^{r} 4th.

Daniel son of James & leah more Born 11th feb^{r} 1732 Bap^{t} 2d ap^{r} 1733.

Roger son of Roge & Eliz^{a} more Born 8th Decr 1732 Bap^{t} 25th feb^{r}.

Robert Son of Francis & Eliz^{a} Man Born 7th feb^{r} 1732 Bap^{t} 8th ap^{r} 1733.

George Son of John & Mary More Born 23d Novr 1732 Bap^{t} 8th ap^{r} 1733.

Daniel Son of Nath^a & Mary Molone Born 15th Sepr 1732 Bap^t 17th June 1733.

avis D^r of Thomas & Eleonore More Born 27th March 1733 Bap^t 17th June.

Harry Male Slave of Jno & Julia Mayes Born 23d feb^r 1732.

Delilah D: of Matthew Mayes & Eliz: Born 20th July 1733 Bap^t 26th august.

frances D: of Robert & ann Moody Dcest novmber 1732.

David Son of Jonathan & Sarah Mote Born 13th ap^r 1733 Bap^t 20th octb^r.

Peter Son of John & Martha Manson Born 24th Dce^r 1733 Bap^t 30th Dce^r.

John Son of Samuel & Elizabeth Man Born 23d Dce^r 1733 Bap^t March 22d.

Matthew Son of John & Sarah Meuse Born 27th feb^r 1733 Bap^t 7th ap^r 1734.

Mary D: of John & Mary Man Born 28th feb^r 1733 Bap^r 10th March.

anne D: of william & anne Mershall Born 28th Jan^r 1733 Bap^t 10th March.

Joseph Son of George & ann marchbank Born 4th octb^r 1733 Bap^t 10th March 1733.

Susannah D: of James & Elisabeth Munford Born 29th March 1734 Bap^t 28th ap^r.

Richard son of william & Elisabeth Martin Born 27th august 1733 dces^d 22d November.

Micail son of Micail & Catharine Mikedermond Born 25th feb^r 1733 Bap^t 15th May 1734.

John Son of David & Jane Miles Born 27th ap^r 1734 Bap^t 26th May.

Benica female Slave of John & Julia Mayes Born 8th July 1734.

John Son of Saml & mary morgan Born 26th ap^r 1734 Bap^t 23d June.

Elizabeth, Daughter of Robt & Ann Munford born Sep^t 22d 1734 Bap^t 21st Octob^r.

John Son of John and Mary Moore Born ye 9th May 1735 Bap^t 6th July.

Vadrey S. of Wm and Susana Macbie Born 23 decem^r 1734 Bap^t Ap^l 19 1735.

Robert Son of Jam^{s} and Mary Moore Born ye 23d January 1734.
Daniel s. of Robert and Ann Moody. Born ye 2d Xb^{r} 1734.
John S. of John & Elizabeth Morris Born ye 24th Novr 1734.
William S of William Martin & Elizabeth his wife Born Novr 28th 1734.
Anne D. of David & Elizabeth M^{c}choller. Born 29th July 1735.
Jane D. of John and Ann Mooney Born Decr 13th 1735.
Henry Son of Henry & Sarah Mitchell Born 7th Augt 1735.
Betty D: of John & Agnes May was Born the 16th No^{vm} 1740.
William s of Daniel & Susanah Maccloud Born march ye 10 1740.
Martha D of John & Dorithea Moorland B Sepr 12th 1740.
Joel S. of Wm And Sarah Martin B March 18th 1740–1.
Wood S. of John & Mary Moor B March 27th 1741.
Elizabeth D. of David & Elizabeth Maccullochs Born July 23d 1741 & Bap^{t} Octob^{r} 30th 1741.
Anne D. of William & Isabel Martins Born Aug. 30th 1741 & Bap^{t} Octob^{r} 4th 1741.
Reuben S. of William & Anne Melones Born Sep^{tr} 26th 1741 & Bap^{t} Novr 15th 1741.
Lucy D. of Matthew & Elizabeth Martins Born Sep^{tr} 25th 1741 & Bap^{t} Decr 24th 1741.
Isham S. of Daniel & Jane Meadows Born Feb^{ry} 16th 1740–1 & Bap^{t} Jan^{ry} 3d 1741–2.
Hannah D. of Richard & Mary Meanlands Born Novr 13th 1741 & Bap^{t} Jan^{ry} 17th 1741–2.
Theodorick. S. of Capt Robert & Anne Munfords Born Feby 21st 1741–2 & Bap^{t} Feby 26th 1741–2.
Frederick. S. of John & Sara Mayes Born Feby 2d 1741–2 & Bap^{t} Apr 11th 1742.
Catharine D. of Malcom & Catharine MacNeils Born Feb 12th 1741–2 & Bap^{t} Apr. 26th 1742.
Jane. D of Humphry & Elizabeth Moodies Born March 30th 1742 & Bap^{t} June 13th 1742.
Susanna D. of John & Jane Meadlands Born Decr 13th 1741 & Bap^{t} July 25th 1742.
Mary D of Roger & Elizabeth Moors Born May 11th 1742 & Bap^{t} Aug. 15th 1742.
Richard S of John & Agnes May was Born December 20th 1742.

Benjamin S. of James & Elizabeth MacDowals Born Septr 27th 1742 & bapt^{d} Octob^{r} 3d 1742.

Addie D. of Henry & Sarah Mitchels born June 20th 1743 & bapt^{d} Jan^{ry} 6th 1743–4.

Anne D. of Mr Hugh & Jane Millers born March 13th 1742–3 & bapt^{d} Aprile 10th 1743.

Margret D. of Daniel & Susanna MacLauds born Jan^{ry} 8th 1742–3 & bapt^{d} May 22d 1743.

Elizabeth D. of John & Elizabeth Manns born Jan^{r} 28th 1743–4 bapt^{d} May 13th 1744.

Jane D. of John & Jane Meadlands born March 23d 1743–4 bapt^{d} Septr 22d 1744.

John S. of John & Agnes May born Decr 20th 1744 baptized Feb 24th 1744–5.

William S. of John & Elizabeth Man born Decr 11th 1744 bapt^{d} March 3d 1744–5.

Patrick Smith S of Margaret Malone born Feb. 27th 1744–5 baptized April 14th 1745.

Phyllis A female Slave belonging to Mr. Hugh Miller was born March 12th 1744–5.

Anne D of Mr. Hugh & Jane Milles was born March 13th 1742–3 & baptized Apr. 10th 1743.

Robert S. of Ditto was born March 28th 1746 & baptized ——.

Jane D. of Ditto was born Feb^{ry} 21st 1747–8 & baptized ——.

Betty born June 1740	Negroes belonging to Mr. Hugh Miller.
Beck born —— 1742	
Tony born Aprile 1746	
Cutchnia born Sep^{t} 1746	
Rose born Septr 1747	
Isaac born March 1748	

David Son of John May j^{r} and Agnes his wife Born —— 1749 Bap^{t} 5 Octo^{r}.

James Son of James and Anne Murray born July 10th 1743.

John Son of Ditto born September 13th 1744.

Anne Daughter of Ditto born October 30th 1746.

Margaret Daughter of ditto born February 8th 1748–9.

William Son of ditto born May 6th 1752.

Mary Daughter of Do born Feby 22 1754.

Thomas Son of Ditto Born Jany 13th Baptized ye 16th following 1757.

Negroes Belonging to James Murray Viz^t.

Moll a Mallatto Born Octo^r 1735. Patt a Negro B. Octo^r 1736.
Lucy a Negro. B. May 1739. Frank a Negro. B. Decr 1740.
Sarah a Mallato B. March 1742. Charles a Negro. Octo^r 1742.
Doll a Negro. B. April 1744. Billy a Negro. June 18. 1744.
Hannah a Negro. B. Octo^r 1744. Peg a Negro. July 1746.
Sue a Negro. Octo^r 1746. Tom a Mallato. Decr 1746.
Aggy. a Mallato. July 1748. Tom a Mallato Sep^t 1748.
Joe a Mallato. Augt 1749. Cate a Negro Octo^r 1748.
Will a Negro. Feby 1749–50. Kitt Novr 1751.
Nan, April 1753. Cate July 1753. Harry Octo^r 1753.
Jenny, January 1754. Cain March 1754. Poll. Jany 1755.
Latty, July 1755. Moll. Sep^t 1755. Jenny Novr 1755.
Betty, Decr 1757. Cyruss, March 1756. Patt. Decr 1756.
Easter, March 1757. Antony Sep^t 1757. Tabb. Octo^r 1757.
Matthew. Decemb^r 1757. Frank. March 1758.
Bobb, May 1758. Dick Sep^t 1758.

Joseph Moore son of John Moore & Mary his wife was Born Janury the 20th 1767 and Baptiz^d at the Brick Church of Bristol Parish March the 22d 1767.

Henry Son of George Wale Machen & Mary his Wife, Born March 7th 1780 Baptised May 11th 1780.

Elizabeth Daughter of William Edgar & Jane his Wife, Born Feby 6. 1780. Baptised May 11th 1780.

Jamy Cate, Son of Jeremiah Meacham & Milly his Wife, born October 26th 1791, & baptized March 21st 1792.

Louisa, Daughter of Aggy, a Slave belonging to John McLeod, born in March 1790, & baptized March 25th 1792.

Lucy Massenburg, Dau^r of John Mason (of Sussex County) & Lucy his Wife, born October 26th 1791, & baptized April 6th 1792.

John, Son of John McKenny (of Sussex County) & Rebeccah his Wife, born March 4th 1791, & baptized April 6th 1792.

David, Son of William McCarter & Susannah his Wife, born October 6th 1791, and baptized May 9th 1792.

Joshua Son of Fanny, a Slave belonging to David Maitland, born February 1st 1791, & baptized April 29th 1792.

Thomy Branch, son of Reaps Mitchell & Susanna his Wife, born Octr 20th 1791 & bap. May 13th 1792.

John Malcolm died June 23d & was buried in St Pauls' Church-Yard, June 24th. 1792.

Elizabeth McMurdo, Wife of Charles J. McMurdo, died the 13th and was buried the 14th day of Sep:ember 1792.

Martha, Anne, Elizabeth, Dau^r of Charles J. McMurdo, and Elizabeth his Wife, was born *(the 1st) of *(September) & baptized October 11th 1792.

Elizabeth McFarlane of Chesterfield County, was buried October 16th 1792.

Mary Wales, Dau^r of Thomas Machen & Sally his wife, was born June 8th 1791 & baptized November 2d 1792.

Richard, S, of George May & Anna his Wife, born September 3rd & baptized December 29th 1792.

Lettice Hickman, Dau^r of William Meredith & Anne his Wife, born Septr 23rd & baptized Decr 30th 1792.

Pleasant Meredith, a Child of John Meredith, died the 18th & was buried the 20th of January 1793.

John, S. of John McLeod, & Isabella his Wife was born Jany 18 & baptized March 10th 1793.

James. Son of William McDowell & Susanna his Wife, was born January 20th & baptized May 5th 1793.

Elizabeth Agnes, Daughter of David Maitland & Susanna his Wife was born April 23rd & baptized June 20th 1793.

Lewis Lanier—Son of John Marks & Martha his Wife, born May 6th & baptized July 10th 1793.

Jemimah Wyat, Dau^r of Jeremiah Meachen & Milly his Wife, born March 16th & baptized August 10th 1793.

Polly, Dau^r of Edward Marks & Sally his Wife, born July 24th & bap: Sepr 11th 1793.

Johanna, Dau^r William Marks & Eliza his Wife, born August 3rd & bap: Sepr 22 179[ ].

Ephraim May was buried 16th Octr 1794.

---

*These blanks filled up by her son C. J. Gibson Dec'r 12th 1848. The above note is in Dr. Gibson's handwriting.—C. G. C.

Mary Currie Maitland dau^{r} of David Maitland died 26th & buried 27th Jany 1795.

Tazewell Son of Thos Mitchell and Rebecca his wife (of the County of Sussex) born 16th Augt 1794 and baptized 15th March 1795.

Alexander Campbell Maitland Son of William Maitland & Elizabeth his wife was born Augt 2d & baptized 9th D^{o} 1795. Died Octr 25th & buried Octr 26th 1796.

David Currie Maitland Son of Robert Maitland & Susan his wife, born 2d Nov^{r} & bapt^{d} 26th Decr 1796: died Octr 1797.

N

Mary dau: of Tho: & Margret Neel born 7th Nov: last bap^{t} March 31th 1721.

Phebe dau: of Dan & Eliz: Nance born in octob^{r} 1712.

Eliz: dau: of Ditto born 6th July 1719.

Elinor dau of John & Jane Nance born 25th May last bap^{t} July 19th 1721.

Fran: dau: of Raise & Ann Newhouse born 28th March 1720 bap^{t} July 1st 1721.

Tho: Son of ditto: born 1st sep^{t} 1712.

——— Son of Rich & Dina ————

James Son of Wm & Ann Norton born 2d of octob^{r} 1721 bap^{t} 30th octob^{r} 1722.

Elinor dau of Dan & Eliz: Nance born 9th sep^{t} last bap^{t} 28th Octob^{r} 1722.

——— D: of Tho & Margaret Neel born last summer bap^{t} Augs^{t} 6th 1723.

Tho: son of Jno & Jane Nance born 22th sep^{t} last bap^{t} Jan^{r} 19th 1723–4.

Peter son of Tho & Eliz: Nunnely born 3d Jan^{r} bap^{t} 2d feb^{r} 1723–4.

Tho son of Tho: & Marg^{a} Neel born 1 sep^{t} 1712.

John s: of Rich & Mary Nance bor 15 decem last bap^{t} 14th June 1724.

Mary d of Wm & Anne Norton born 9th Jan^{r} last bap^{t} Nov 1st 1724.

Frances Da^{t} of Thom and mary neel born: 7th may bap^{t} 25th July 1725.

Richard son of Jn° and Jane Nance born 24th Jan[r] bap[t] 15th May 1726.

Eliz[a] Da[t] of Rich[d] and mary nance born 7th Nov[m] bap[t] 15th May 1726.

Tho[m] son of Thomas and Eliz[a] nunnally born 27 sber: 1726.

Martha D: of John and Ann Nipper born 19th No[m] 1726.

Mark Son of Rob[t] and Eliz[a] Nobles born 18th May 1727.

Sarhah female Slave of Th° and Eliz[a] Nunally born 11th May 1728.

Sarah D of Th° and Margrat Neal Born 5th Jan[r] 1727.

Eliz[a] Dater of Daniel and Mary Nance Born 19th June 1728.

Wm Son of John and Jane Nance Born 12th July 1728 Bap[t] July 29th.

Nan female Slave of Daniel nance Born Jan[r] y[e] 5th 1727.

Sarah female Slave of Ditto Born aprill y[e] 10th 1728.

Obedience Dat[r] of Rich[d] and ——— Nunally Born 26th Novmber 1728.

John Son of Th° and Eliz[a] Nunally Born 4th Dce[mr] Bap[t] 12th Jan[r] 1728.

Thomas Son of Thomas & Marget Neel Born 4th July 1730 Bap[t] 9th august.

Leanord Son of Richard and Mary Nance Born 15th Decm[r] 1730 Bap[t] 4th Jan[r].

Lucy D of Daniel & Eliz[a] nance Born 24th Dcember: 1730 Bap[t] Jan[r] 10th.

Daniel Son of Thomas & Eliz[a] Nunally Born 28th march 1731 Bap[t] august 15th.

Nathaniel son of Rich[d] & Mary Nance born 9th Dec[r] 1731 bap[t] May 12th 1732.

Winny Slave of Dan[l] Nance born Oct[r] 1. 1732.

Mary D[r] of Thomas & Eliz[a] nunally Born 1th feb[r] 1732 Bap[t] 20th may 1733.

James son of John & margret nevil Born 1th July 1733 Bap[t] 19th May 1734.

Zachariah Son of Thomas and Eliz. Nunnally Born 19th May 1735. Bap[t] 6th July.

Jamey Male Slave Belonging to Dan[l] Nance S[r] Born Sep[t] 1st 1735.

Giles S. of John and Martha Nance Born 4th May. 1735.

Thomas Son of William & Ann Nance Born 29th February 1735 Bap[t] 18th April 1736.

Ann D. of Richard & Mary Newman B March 30th 1741.

Anne D. of Richard & Mary Nances Born Jan[ry] 15th 1741-2 & Bap[t] June 13th 1742.

Sarah D. of William & Ann Nances born Jan[ry] 30th 1742-3 & bapt[d] Feb[ry] 27th 1742-3.

Will a male Slave belonging to Daniel Nance born Feb 6th 1744-5.

Ned a male Slave belonging to Ditto born Dec[r] 1743.

Sarah D. of Thomas & Priscilla Nantzs born Octob 19th 1745 & bapt[d] Jan[ry] 6th 1745-6.

Johney Nash son of John & Mary nash was Born Nov[r] 4th 1758.

Thomas, son of Thomas and Agness Norton was Born January the 23d 1755.

Sarah Norton their Daughter was Born October the 21st 1756.

Patty Norton their second Daughter was Born the 19th October 1758.

Frances Norton their third Daughter was Born June the 1st 1760.

William Norton their son was Born April 22d 1762.

Cressy, Dau[r] of Beck a negro slave, belonging to Mrs Lucy Newsum, was born March 15th and baptized September 23rd 1792.

O

James son of Nico: & Jane Overby born 5th sep[t] last bap[t] 4th octob[r] 1720.

Fran: dau: of Wm & Marg[a] Overby born 20th feb: last bap[t] 20th July 1721.

Rob[t] son of Rich: & Dina Overby born 18th Aprill last bap[t] 18th June 1722.

Adams son of Nico: & Jane Overby born 28th July last bap[t] Nov: 7th 1722.

Nico: son of peter & Ann Overby born 1st sep[t] last bap[t] Nov: 7th 1722.

Eliz: Dau of Drury & Anne Oliver born 8th June 1718.

John son of Ditto born 11th July 1720.

Wm Son of ditto born 26th July 1722.

Martha d of Rich: & Dinah Overbury born 8th decem last bap[t] feb: 6th 1723-4.

Martha D. of Drury & Amy Oliver born Nov: 25th last bap^{t} Jan^{r} 31th 1724–5.

Abraham son of James and Ann Overberry born 26th august last bap^{t} 17th sep^{r} 1725.

Mary D of nicholas and Jane Overberry born 9th August bap^{t} 17th Sep^{t} 1725.

Martha D of Drury and Amy Oliveer Deceast Sp^{r} ye 27th 1726.

Eliz^{a} D of howard and Margarat Owen born 24th July bap^{t} 2d oct^{m} 1726.

Drury Oliver Son of Wm and Eliz^{a} Olivier born 12th Aprill 1685.

Martha D of Drury and Amy olivier born 27th May 1727.

Jaminah D^{t} of Rich^{d} and Dinah overberry born 26th Jan^{r} 1727.

Peter Son of Peter and ann overberry Born 30th July 1727.

John Son of Th^{o} and anne oliver born 18th aprill 1728.

John Son of Howard and Margret owen Born 1th august 1728.

Mary D of Drury and amy oliveer Born 8th march Bap^{t} 20th aprill 1728.

Thomas Son of Howard and margret owen Born 2d July 1730 Bap^{t} 25th octb^{r}.

Rubin Son of Richard & Dinah overberry Born 12th august 1731.

Lucy D: of James & Eliz: overbury Born 29th July 1733 Bap^{t} 26th august.

Thomas Son of Richard & Dinah Overbury Born July 1st 1734.

William Son of Lanceford and Elizabeth Owen Born 23d Decemb^{r} 1734.

Thamar D. of Richard & Dinah Overby Born 1st July 1734.

Ann D. of Drury & Elizabeth Oliver Born Sep^{t} 4th 1734 Baptiz'd Octob^{r} 27th.

Elizbth D of Edward & Joyce Owan Feb^{ry} ye 26th 1740.

Catharine D. of Nicolas & Elizabeth Ogilbys Born March 22d 1741–2 & Bap^{t} May 9th 1742.

Mildred D. of Isaac & Elizabeth Olivers born Octob 15th & bapt^{d} Octob^{r} 17th 1742.

Thomas S. of Isaac & Elizabeth Olivers born Octob 19th & bapt^{d} Decr 25th 1743.

Mary D. of James & Anne Olivers was born Septr 6th & bapt^{d} Decr 8th 1745.

William S. of Isaac & Elizabeth Olivers was born July 7th & bapt[d] Aug 17th 1746.

Jean, Daughter of David Organ & Elizabeth his Wife, was born April 2nd & baptized June 30th 1793.

John Oliphant died the first day of Nov[r] & was buried the 3d of Nov. 1793.

John Harrison Son of John Osborne & Jane his wife, born 19th July 1794 and baptized 4th Dec[r] 1794.

P

Wm son of John & Judith Puckett born 15th sep[t] last bap[t] 17th decem: 1720

Smith son of John & Jane Pattison born 28th Aug: last bap[t] Nov: 27th 1720.

Edith dau: of Wm & Mary Parsons born 7th Aug: 1719 bap: Nov: 27th 1720.

Nathaniell son of John & Fran: peterson born 12th Nov: last bap[t] Jan[r] 19th 1720–1.

Phebe dau: of John & Judith puckett born 11th Jan[r] bap[t] March 5th 1720–1.

Rich son of Rich: & Martha puckett born 7th March 1718–19.

Ephraim son of Womack & Mable Pucket born 24th Jan[r] last bap[t] Aprill 10th 1721.

Martha dau: of Wm & Rebecca Pearcy born 9th Jan[r] last bap[t] 4th June 1721.

Fran: son of John & Eliz: Perkinson born 5th August last bap[t] Octob[r] 8th 1721.

Wm son of John & Susanna Pride born xb[r] 19th 1721 bap[t] Jan[r] 31th 1721–2.

Jeremiah son of Sara Patrum born 1st Jan[r] bap[t] March 21th 1722.

Eliz: dau: of Seth & Martha Pettypool born 8th May 1721 bap[t] Octob[r] 7th 1722.

Jamime dau: of Wm & Mary Parsons born 20th octob[r] last bap[t] 16 sep[t] 1722.

Eliz: dau of John & Mary price born 7th June last bap[t] 16th sep[t] 1722.

Lewis son of Wm & Mary Puckett born 9th Jan[r] 1722–3 bap[t] May 5th 1723.

John son of Joss: & Mary Pritchett born 1st May 1716 bap^{t} Aug: 25th 1722.

Wm son of ditto born 14th octo^{br} 1719 bap^{t} Aug 25th 1722.

Fran dau of John & Jane Paterson bor 28th May last bap^{t} Aug: 13th 1722.

stephen son of Wm & ffrances pettypool jun^{r} born 30th octob^{r} 1721 bap^{t} 14th feb 1722–3.

Wm son of John & Fran: peterson born 25 Octob^{r} last bap^{t} xb^{r} 7th 1723.

Sarah D: of Seth & Martha Pool born 7th Nov: last bap^{t} Jan^{r} 30th 1723–4.

Joel son of John & Judith Pucket born 11th Nov: last bap^{t} 7th March 1723–4.

Joseph son of Wm & Mary Persons born ——— bap^{t} Aprill 12th 1724.

Isham son of Womack & Mable Puckett born 14th octob^{r} last bap^{t} Aprill 23th 1724.

——— A negro belonging to Mr Wm Poythers born 1st of August 1724.

Luis S: of Luis & Sarah Patrick born 17th Aug: last bap^{t} Aprill 18th 1725.

Wm pool jun^{r} had a Child born feb: 15th 1724–5.

Tho: s of Nath & Penellope Parratt born 30th xb^{r} last bap^{t} March 28th 1725.

Lucy D: of Seth & Mary perkinson born 6th instant bap^{t} March 27th 1725.

Anne D: of Olive poxon died 30th July 1725.

Eady Dat of Jno and Jane paterson born 28th July 1724.

phebe Dat of phebe parham born 9th oc^{tm} 1725.

James Son of James and Mary pittillo born 23d Dec^{m} 1725.

Ann Dat of James and mary plat born 13th Oc^{tm} 1725.

Sheppyallin Son of Jno and Judith pucket born 8th Nov^{m} 1725.

Nathaniel Son of Nathaniel and penilopy parot born feb^{r} 12th bap^{t} 29 may 1726: 1725.

Anne Isham Dat of Wm and Sarah Poythris born 9th Ap^{r} bap^{t} 5th June 1726.

Jno Son of Thomas and Isabell phillips born may 8th bap^{t} June 7th 1726.

tabitha Dat of wm and Frances pool born oct^{m} 13th bap^{t} June 6th 1726.

Eliz^{a} D of Wm and Mary pucket born 19th feb 1725.

Wm Son of Wm and Mary parsons born 24th may 1726.

John Son of John and & Mary powel born 16th march 1725 Bap^{t} Augt 22d 1726.

John Son of Seth and Martha pettypool born 6th Jan^{r} 1725.

Sarah D of peter and frances plantine born 27th June 1726.

Joseph Son of John and Ann phillips born 6th Nom^{r} 1726.

Th^{o} Son of Edward and Eliz^{a} Powell born 14th July 1727.

Ann D of Hezekiah and Batiah Powel born 16th June 1726.

Wm Son of Wm and Sarah poythres born 14th March 1727 bap^{t} 26th may 1728.

Anna Dater of John and Mary Powell born 3d May 1728.

peter Son of Seth and Marth Pittypool Born 17th May 1727.

ann D of James and Mary pittillo Born 15th July 1728 Bap^{t} 29th July.

Littleberry Son of liewes and Sarah Partrick Born 18th May 1728.

Batty Son of Wm and mary parsons Born 22d August 1728.

Stephen Son of John and Judith Pucket Born 17th octb^{r} 1728 Bap^{t} No^{v} 10.

Mary D of Nath^{a} and Penilopy Parrot Born 21th Novmber 1728.

Mason of Th^{o} and Isabell phillips Born 23d July Bap^{t} 16th Sepr 1728.

Phebe D of John and Judith Pucket Born 2d Jan^{r} 1728.

Liewes son of John and Mary Patterson Born 28th august Bap^{t} 2d feb^{r} 1728.

Ephraim son of Wm and frances Pucket Born 2d March Bap^{t} 30th June 1729.

William Son of Thos & Mary Parram Born 22d Sepr 1729.

Alice D of Seth & Mary Perkinson Born 15th June 1729 Bap^{t} 27th June.

Martha D of Joshua & Martha pritchett d^{o} 15th April 1729.

William Son of William ——— ———.

William Son of Zedekiah and Bathua Powel Born 26th aprill 1729 Bap^{t} may 31th 1730.

William Son of peter and frances plentine Born 5th Sepr 1729 Bap^{t} 31th mam 1730.

Pucket Son of John and Susana Pride Born 2d Sepr Bap^{t} 1th march 1729.

Eliz^{a} D of francis and hannah Poythris Born 1th feb^{r} 1729 Bap^{t} 8th aprill 1730.

John Son of peter and Rebeckah pott Born 6th Sepr 1729.

Richard price servant of Drury oliver Des^{t} 29th June 1730.

sarah Dater of Edward & Mary Parham Born 16th Dce^{r} 1730 Bap^{t} 24th Jan^{r}.

Mary D of Thomas & Isabel phillips Born 9th march 1730 Bap^{t} 19th ap^{r} 1731.

Isham of Seth pirkinson Born 8th may 1731 Bap^{t} June 22d 1731.

James Son of Nathaniel & penellope Parrott Born 12th febr: 1730.

Phillip Son of Wm & Frances pool Born 13th march 1730 Bap^{t} 12th Sepr 1731.

Sarah D: of William and Sarah poythris Born 7th august 1731 Bap^{t} 7th octb^{r}.

John Son of John & mary Parham Born 26th Sepr Bap^{t} 6th Novmb^{r} 1731.

Mary D: John & anne phillips Born 11th ap^{r} Bap^{t} Nom^{r} 14th 1731.

Nathaniel Son of John & martha Peterson Born 25th ap^{r} 1732.

Rebeccah dat^{r} of Hezekiah & Bathia Powell born 26th ffeb^{y} 1730 Bap^{t} June 18th 1732.

Frances dat^{r} of Saml & Amy Pitchford born 5th Jany 1731 bap^{t} July 9th 1732.

Jane Dat^{r} of Peter & Rebecca Pott born 10th ffeb^{y} 1731 bap^{t} Augt 13th 1732.

Joshua of Josh^{a} & Catherine Pritchett born 9th May 1732 bap^{t} Augt 13 1732.

Robt Son of Wm & Mary Perkinson born 13th Sep^{r} & bap^{t} ye 28th 1732.

Obedience Dat^{r} of Jno & Pricilla Pickins born 26th Octr 1732 bap^{t} Decr 26th 1732.

Elisabeth D of Gower & archer parham Born 20th octb^{r} 1732 Bap^{t} 24th feb^{r}.

Penellope D^{r} of nathaniel & Penellope Parrott Born 8th may 1733 Bap^{t} 20th may 1733.

anne Dr of Edward & mary Parham Born 14th march 1732 Bapt 8th apr 1733.

Eliza Dr of George & Jane penticost Born 3d febr 1732 Bapt 20th may 1733.

Eddith D: of Seth & Elisabeth pirkenson Born 20th July 1733 Bapt 28th august.

Mary D: of Edward & Elizabeth powell Born 12th august 1733 Bapt novr 4th.

Charles Son of Charles & Sarah Pistole Born 15th Sepr 1733 Bapt 11th Novr.

Frances D: of william & Frances Pettipool Born 18th aprl 1733 Bapt Dcer 10th.

anne D: of Seth & martha Pettipool Born 25th Sepr 1733 Bapt dcer 10th.

Henry Son of James & mary Pittillo Born 31th octbr 1730 Bapt febr 9th.

Lucy D: of Ditto Born 11th Novr 1733 Bapt Janr 20th 1733.

anne D: of Seth & martha pettipool Born 25th Sepr 1733 Bapt dcer 6th.

Robert Son of John & Mary powell 17th Novmr 1733 Bapt febr 10th.

Isham Son of Thomas & Mary Parham Born 17th Sepr 1732 Bapt febr 12th.

John Son of Thos & Mary Pott Born 12th octbr 1732 Bapt 12th febr 1733.

Drury Son of John & Judith Pucket Born 25th Janr 1733 Bapt 12th febr.

Rebeckah d of Hezekiah & Bathia Powell decest 26th march 1734.

martha D: of Charles & mary Parrish Born 10th May 1734 Bapt 4th august.

Rachel D: of Philip & Rachel Prescot Born 3d March 1733.

Thomas Son of Charles & Sarah Pistol Born 2d May 1735 Bapt 6th July.

Thomas S of Thomas and Mary Parham Born Septemr 22. 1734 Bap. 4 May 1735.

Jane female Slave belonging to Wm Parsons Born May 1st 1729.

Betty female Slave belonging to Do Born June 15th 1733.

Dick male Slave belonging to Do Born June 19th 1731.

Dick male Slave belonging to D° Died Augt 22 1731.
Batty Son of William and Mary Parsons departed this life Octo^{r} 11th 1734.
James Markham Son of William and Mary Parsons Born the 31 March 1731.
James Markham Son of William and Mary Parsons departed this life Octo^{r} 26th 1734.
William S. of Gower & Archer Parham Born the 2d July 1735.
William S. of George and Jane Penticost Born 2d August 1734.
Sarah D. of William & Juliana Peirce Born 17th Aug^{ts} 1734.
James S. of Thomas & Izabella Phillips Born Sep^{t} 12th 1734.
Lucy D. of George & Jane Pentycost Born January ye 25 1740.
John S. of John & Elisabeth Porter Born ye 20 of febuary 1740.
John s of John & Anne Phillips Born August ye 20 1740.
John Son of Wm. And Juliana Peircy Sepr 30th 1740.
Susannah of Kaleb & Frances Pritchet B Aug 24th 1740.
Patty D of Thomas & Mary Presise B Decr 10th 1740.
Magdaline D of Israell & Elizabeth Peterson Born Novr 21st 1740.
Wm. S. of Charles & Sarah Pistol B Decr 19th 1740.
Ann D of Morgan & Ann Purreah B August 1st 1741.
John S of Aron & Ann Pricheat B Feb^{ry} 26 ye 1740.
Thomas S of Thomas & Mary Presise Born Decr 27 1735.
Mary Daughter of D° Born March ye 29th 1738.
Elizabeth. D. of Major Willm & Sara Poythress's Born Sep^{tr} 21st 1741 & Bap^{t} Novr 22d 1741.
Henry. S. of William Petty & Francis Pools Born Jan^{ry} 27th 1740–1 & Bap^{t} Novr 29th 1741.
Sara. D. of Daniel & Francis Pegrams Born Decr 29th 1741 & Bap^{t} Feb^{ry} 28th 1741–2.
Mary. D. of Gower & Archer Parhams Born Decr 23d 1741 & Bap^{t} March 14th 1741–2.
William. S. of Thomas & Mary Perrys Born Ap^{r} 19th 1742 & Bap^{t} May 9th 1742.
William. S. of Edward & Mary Pegrams Born June 18th 1742 & Bap^{t} July 4th 1742.
Mary D. of Edward & Amy Paynes Born Oct. 16th 1741 & Bap^{t} July 24th 1742.

Anne D. of Joshua & Lucy Porters born Octob 7th 1742 & bapt^{d} Decr 12th 1742.

George S. of John & Anne Phillips born Feb^{ry} 15th 1742-3 & bapt^{d} May 29th 1743.

Anne D. of George & Jane Pentecost born Sep^{tr} 8th 1743 & bapt^{d} Octob^{r} 9th 1743.

Reuben S. of Abram & Esaia Peebles was born Aprile 11th & bapt^{d} June 9th 1745.

Frances D of Mr John & Martha Petersons was born Septr 3d & bapt^{d} Octob. 27th 1745.

Elizabeth D. of John & Anne Phillips was born Feb. 5th 1745-6.

Luke S. of Edward & Elizabeth Powels was born May 8th & bapt^{d} Aug. 3d 1746.

William Son of Joseph & Frances Parsons born May 9th bapt^{d} 29th May 1750.

Edith Daughter of Wm. & Mary Parsons jun^{r} Born 22nd May bap^{t} Sep^{t} 16th 1750.

Two Twins, Mary & Elizabeth Brown Daughters of William Brown & Servant Probey was Born July 20th 1761.

William Son of Lewis & Sarah Parham was Born april the 22d 1761.

William Paterson son of James Paterson & mary was born Sepr 12th 1768.

David Parrish Son of James Parrish Baptised July 4. 1771.

Henry, Son of Lewis Parham (of Sussex County) & Rebeccah his Wife, born January 28 & baptized April 6th 1792.

Lotty Williams, S. of Page a Negroe Slave belonging to Thos G. Peachy, born July 1st and baptized August 19th 1792.

William Parsons, and his Wife (of Prince George) were buried September 3rd 1792.

Jean Peachy Dau^{r} of Samuel Peachy, was buried October 11th 1792.

David, S, of William Perkins & Margaret his Wife, born October 11th & baptized December 23rd 1792.

Ann, Dau^{r} of Wm Parry & Phœbe his Wife, born September 7th 1789 & bap: Decr 28th —9[ ].

Peggie, Dau^{r} of James Peebles & Betsy his Wife, born Sept 19th & bap: January 27th 1793.

William Poythress died 15th and was buried 18th Octr 1794.

Hannah Dau of Baldwin Pearce & Rebeccah his Wife, was born February 23rd and baptized April 2nd 1793.

Sarah H. Pope. Dau^{r} of Ralph Pope, died June 19th & was buried June 20th 1793.

James Son of William Prentis & Mary his Wife, born August 3. & baptized Septr 23rd 1793.

Mary, Dau^{r} of William Poythress & Mary his Wife, born Septr 24 & bap: Nov. 7. 1793.

R

Mary dau: of Christ^{o} & Sarah Robinson born 3d June last bap^{t} 17th decem: 1720.

Wm A Moll belonging unto Hen: & Eliz: Royall born 7th Aug: 1720 bap^{t} Jan^{r} 30th 1720–1.

Martha dau of Hen: & Martha Rottenbery born 1st sep^{t} last bap^{t} 12th octob^{r} 1720.

Matthew son of Israel & Sarah Robinson born 22th Nov: last bap^{t} Aprill 30th 1721.

Margaret A Mollatto belonging to Godfry & Eliz: Ragsdale born 7th Novr last bap May 28th 1721.

Daniel son of Wm & Fran: Rowlet born 10th June last bap^{t} July 30th 1721.

John of John & Mary Rackly born 14th day of June 1720 bap^{t} 18th July 1721.

Fran: Son of Hen: & Eliz: Royall born 10th Jan^{r} last bap^{t} July 4th 1721.

Mary dau of Wm & Mary Russell born 2d decem 1719 bap^{t} octob^{r} 9th 1721.

Martha dau of Wm & Eliz Russell born 14th decem^{br} Last bap^{t} Aprill 8th 1722.

Tab: dau of Godfry & Eliz Radgsdale born 13th March last bap^{t} May 20th 1722.

Jack a negro boy belonging to Dan: Radgsdale born Octob^{r} 8th 1722.

Ann dau of Hen: & Eliz: Robinson born Jan: 6th 1719 bap^{t} August 25th 1722.

Faith dau of peter & Alice Radgsdale born 24th octob^{r} last bap^{t} 27th decem 1722.

peter son of Hen: & Eliz: Robinson born 27th ——— last bap^{t} Jan: 10th 1722.
Nath son of Christ & Sara Robinson born 21th octob^{r} last bap^{t} Jan 10th 1722–3.
Rich son of Jno & Rebecca Raburn Born 28th May last bap^{t} Aug: 21th 1723.
John son of Israel & Sarah Robinson born 8th May last bap^{t} Aug 21th 1723.
Nath: son of John & Mary Robinson born 21th June last bap^{t} Aug^{s} 21th 1723.
Edward son of Godfrey & Eliz: Radgsdale born 8th decemb^{r} last bap^{t} Jan 12th 1723–4.
Rich: son of Hen: & Marg^{a} Rottenberry born 30th June last bap^{t} 29th July 1724.
Dan: son of Benj^{a} & Martha Radgsdale born 7th May last bap^{t} sep^{t} 6th 1724.
Mary d of Ja & Eliz Rigsby born 10th octob^{r} last bap^{t} 11th x^{br} 1724.
Patt a negro girl belonging to Mr. Peter & Mary Rowlett born 15th feb: 1724–5.
Joseph son Peter & Alice Radgsdale born 17th Jan^{r} last may 23th 1725.
Israil Son of Israil and Sarah Robertson born 14th nov^{m} 1725.
Abr^{a}ham Son of Jno and Mary Robertson born 20th July 1725.
Daniel A negro slave of Ge^{o} and mary Rob^{t}son born Decr 1723.
Matthew A negro of D^{o} born sep^{r} 1724.
Harry A negro of ditt^{o} born May 1726.
Cesar a negro of ditto born aprill 1726.
Daniel Son of Josep and Sarah Reeves born 31th august bap^{t} 11 sep^{t} 1726.
John Son of tho^{m} and Eliz^{a} Rhaynes born 5th July bap^{t} 2d oct^{m} 1726.
Mary D of thomas and Hannah Roberts born 17th August 1726.
Sarah slave of George and Mary Rob^{t}son born 17th July 1726.
Lot Slave of Ditto born 17th 1726.
Rachail D of benj^{a} and martha Ragsdail born 28th June 1726.
Martha D of Christopher and Sarah Robinson born 27th ffebu-ary 1724.
Liewes Son of henry and Eliz^{a} Robinson born 17th March 1723.

Thomas Son of John and Rebeckah Rayborn born 16th Sep[tr] 1726.
ann Daughter of James and Eliz[a] Rigsby born 19th Jan[r] 1726.
John Son of Christopher and ann Rowland born 20th May 1727.
ann D of peter and alce Ragsdail born 25th May 1727.
ffrances D. of John and Mary Robinson born 3d March 1726.
Jemiah D of Wm and Mary Reed born 9th Dce[m] 1724.
John Son of Benj[a] and Martha Ragsdail Born 23d June 1728.
Deborah Son of henry and Eliz[a] Robertson Born 14th March 1727 Bap[t] 2d June.
David Son of Israil and Sarah Robertson Born 19th august 1728.
Francis Son of Tho[s] & Mary Reese born 5th of Decem[r] 1727.
John Son of Henry & Eliz Royall born 23d October 1729.
Mark Son of Jn[o] & Mary Robertson born 23d June 1729.
John Son of Jn[o] and Rebeckah Rayborn Born 30th Novm[r] 1729.
Peter Son of Roger and Sarah Ranie Born 20th March 1729 Bap[t] May 29th 1730.
Prissilla D of Hug and Sarah Riss Born 21th feb[r] 1729 Bap[t] 10th May 1730.
agnis D of Christophar and ann Roland Born 7th Jan[r] Bap[t] 22d feb[r] 1729.
Tho: Son of Thomas and Mary Rees Born 2d novm[r] Bap[t] 22d feb[r] 1729.
Benj[a] Son of John and Eliz[a] Roland Born 6th feb[r] Bap[t] 2d march 1729.
James Son of Partrick & Isabellah Royall Born 20th June 1730.
Mary D of Joseph and Sarah Reeves Born 20th Sep[r] 1730.
Baxter Son of Godfrey and Eliz[a] Ragsdail Born 16th June 1730.
Nicholas Son of Thomas and ann Rollings Born 4th octb[r] 1730.

Negro Slaves of M[r] George Robertson Minister.

Daniel male Slave Born 5th Dce[r] 1723.
Matthew male Slave Born 25th sept[r] 1725.
Harry male Slave Born 26th March 1726.
Lott male Slave Born 10th May 1726.
Sarah female slave Born 16th July 1726.
Cesar male Slave Born 4th Dce[r] 1727.
Nanny female Slave Born 4th July 1728.
Tom male Slave Born 26th Dce[r] 1728.

amy female Slave Born 25th July 1730.
Liewess male Slave Born 3d august 1730.
George male Slave Born 2d Sep[r] 1730.
Betty female Slave Born 5th Sep[r] 1730.
Jo: male Slave Born 29th March 1731.
Ned male Slave Born 15th Sep[t] 1730.

William Son of Roger & Sarȧ: Reiny Born 13th ap[r] 1731 Bap[t] 12th Sep[t]

——— Son of Shanes & mary Raines Born 12th Sep[r] 1731 Bap[t] 20th octb[r].

Nicholas Son of Israil & Sarah Robinson Born 12th sep[tr] Bap[t] novmbr 7th 1731.

Isham Son of John & anne Ratlif Born 10th octb[r] 1731.

Edward Son of John & Mary Robertson Born 22d Dce[r] 1731 Bap[t] 23d ap[r] 1732.

Winfred daughter of Benj[a] & Martha Ragsdale born ffeb[y] 17th 1731.

Martha dat[r] of Roger & Eliz[a] Reese born ffeb[y] 9th 1730 bap[t] May 21st 1732.

Jean Dat[r] Rich[d] & Jean Raybon born 28th Ap[l] 1732 bap[t] Aug[t] 13th 1732.

Martha dat[r] of Jn[o] & Sarah York born 3d June 1732 bap[t] 13 Aug[t] 1732.

Frederick son of Rich[d] & Jane Rains born 9th June 1732 bap[t] Sep[r] 14th 1732.

Alse dat[r] of Tho[s] and Eliz[a] Reams born 31st March 1732 bap[t] Sep[r] 24 1732.

Sarah dat[r] of Christ[o] & Ann Rolland born 26th Sep[r] 1732 bap[t] Dec[r] 17 1732.

Rachel D: of peter & alice Ragsdail Born 27th feb[r] 1732 Bap[t] march 15th.

William Son of James & Sarah Rutlidge Born 9th may 1732 Bap[t] ap[r] 7th 1733.

Isham Son of hugh & Sarah Reese Born 8th august 1732 Bap[t] 20th may 1733.

John Son of Thomas Reese Born 30th Sept[r] 1731 Bap[t] 20th may 1733.

Josept Son of Joseph & Sarah Reaves Born 5th Dec[r] 1732 Bap[t] 1th august 1733.

Francis son of Thos & Hanah Roberts Born 29th June 1733 Bapt 5th Augt

Charles Son of Israil & Sarah Robinson Born 24th July 1733 Bapt 28th Sepr.

——— of Roger & Sarah Rainy Born 12th octobr 1733 Bapt Dcer 10th.

Charles Son of Roger & Eliza Reese Born 3d apr 1733 Bapt 30th dcer.

Phill male Slave of Thomas Ravenscroft Born 8th June 1734.

Benjamine Son of Benjamine & Martha Ragsdail Born 28th March 1734 Bapt July 14th.

Michael Son of John & Judith Roberds Born 7th may 1734 Bapt 30th June.

Thomas Son ot Thomas & Elisabeth Reams Born 10th Janr 1733 Bapt 28th July 1734.

Robt S of John and Mary Robinson Born June 10th 1734.

Ann d of Henry & Ann Robinson Born May 8th 1734.

Mary D. of Thomas & Mary Reese Born 8th Octobr 1733.

Sarah D. of Hugh & Sarah Reese Born 10th Octobr 1735.

Isham s of Joseph & Sarah Reaves Born January ye 25 1740.

John s of Hugh & Elisabeth Ray Born June ye 14 1741.

Thomas S of Robert and Hannah Rivers B June 28th 1740.

Thomas S of John & Mary Reess B Febry 12th 1739.

George S of Martha & Sarah Robarson B Decr 6th 1740.

Mason D of Thomas & Mary Reess B July 10th 1740.

James S of Hugh & Sarah Reess Born August ye 29 1741.

Hannah female Slave of of Judath Roberts Born Decm ye 1st 1735.

Jack male Slave of Dito was Born January ye 29th 1737.

Sarah female Slave of Dito was Born July ye 15th 1741.

William S. of Samuel & Anne Rawthorns Born Novr 4th 1741 & Bapt May 2d 1742.

Peter S. of Henry & Susanna Robertsons Born Mar: 21st 1742 & Bapt July 25th 1742.

David & Lowerel twin Childn of Charles & Anne Roupers were Born June 29th 1742 & Bapt Aug. 15th 1742.

Elizabeth D. of Hugh & Elizabeth Raes born April 25th 1743 & baptd May 22d 1743.

Usiller D. of Timothy & Mary Reeves born July 7th 1743.

Sarah D. of Peter & Sarah Roshill born march 1st 1743-4 bapt[d] apr 29th 1744.

Judith D. of William & Priscilla Reeves born Aug. 10th & baptized Octob[r] 14th 1744.

John S. of Philip & Mary Rogers born Aprile 14th & bapt[d] July 21st 1745.

Elizabeth D. of Patrick & Sarah Roney was born March 5th 1745-6.

Neil S. of Hugh & Elizabeth Raes was born Feb. 19th 1745-6 bapt[d] Apr 2d 1746.

Sarah Slave to partrick & Sarah Roneys born Septem[r] 3d 1754.

William Reaves Son of John & France[s] Reves was Born July y[e] 13 1743.

Mary Reves Daughter of Ditto was Born July y[e] 17 1745.

John Reves Son of Ditto was Born Nov[r] the 15th 1747.

Richard Reves the Son of Ditto was Born Octo[r] the 5th 1750.

Thomas Reves their Son of Ditto was Born Sep[r] the 15 1753.

Thomas Roney son of Patrick and Sarah Roney was born Jan[r] 19 1756.

John Roney the son of Ditto Born October the 8th 1757.

Richard Russell Son of Wm and Rachel Russell was Born 1759 Sep[r] y[e] 10th.

Tim, Son of Nanny, a Slave belonging to William Robertson, born August 28th 1791, & baptized March 25th 1792.

Thomas, Son of Jeany, a Slave belonging to William Robertson, born January 4th & baptized March 25th 1792.

Susannah, Dau[r] of Joel Reading (of Sussex) & Martha his Wife, born Nov[r] 6th 1791, & bap. May 13th 1792.

Elizabeth Archer, D[r] of James Robertson, & Martha F, his Wife, born Nov[r] 27th 1791, & bap[d] May 30th 1792.

Robert, S, of Robert Russel and Jenny his Wife, born the 6th & baptized the 12th of August 1792.

Edmund Ryan of the Town of Petersburg died the 25th, and was buried the 26th of October 1792.

John Fetherstone, S, of Jacob Reese & Diancy, his Wife, born May 14th, & baptized December 15th 1792.

Littleberry S, of William Royal & Sarah his Wife, born Nov[r] 2nd & baptized Dec[r] 27th 1792.

Anne, Dau^r of William Robertson & Elizabeth his Wife, was born Novr 25th, 1792 & baptized January 6th 1793.

——— Reeves wife of James Reeves buried 20th Decr 1794.

Col. John Reeves (of Sussex) buried March 15th 1795.

Patrick, Son of Robert Roe & Nancy his of Albemarle Parish—Sussex County—was born April 9th 1792. & baptized May 26th 1793.

John Alexander Son of James Robertson & Martha Feild his Wife born May 29th & baptized August 7th 1793.

S

Thompson son of Thompson & Ruth Staples born 12th instant bap^t Nov: 27th 1720.

Jeny a negro girl belonging unto Ja: Sturdivant born 6th March 1720–1.

Rebecca dau of Wm & Rebecca Scoggin born 7th Jan^r last bap^t Aprill 30th 1721.

John son of Rich: & Mary Scoggin born 22th July last bap^t 17th Sep^tr 1721.

Griffin son of Drury & Eliz: Stith born 28th Nov: last bap^t July 18th 1721.

John son of Wm & Mary Spain born 22th March last bap^t octob^r 23th 1721.

Catherine dau: of John & Mary Sturdivant 16th instant bap^t 23th octobe^r 1721.

Edw: son of Eliz: Stuard born 19th August last bap^t octob^r 29th 1721.

Eliz: dau: of James & Eliz Sandert born 23th May last bap^t July 29th 1722.

Mary dau: of Tho: & Mary Stonebank born 10th Octob: last bap^t 2d decem 1722.

Phebe bast dau of Ann Shipton born 9th July 1721 bap 22th July 1722.

Agnis dau of Rich & Agnis Smith born 9th Arill last bap^t 25th July 1722.

Angelica dau of Geo & Ann Stell born 18th decem: 1718 bap^t 25th August 1722.

James son of ditto born 17th Aprill 1720 bap^t Aug: 25th 1722.

David son of Geo & Eliz: Smith bor 2d instant bap 13th Aug: 1722.

James son of John & Agnis Smith born 15th Nov last bap: 13th Aug: 1722.

Phebe dau of Wm & Mary Smith born 7th May last bap Aug: 13 1722.

Eliz dau of Ann Shipton born 26th Novem: Last bap^t 27th decem 1722.

Wm son of Wm & Mary Spain born 9th of March last bap^t May 5th 1723.

Rich son of Rich & Mary Scoggin born 15th fe^b last bap^t May 26th 1723.

Wm son of Wm & Rebecca scoggin born 18th march last bap^t May 26th 1723.

Eliz: dau of Robt & Eliz: Stoker born 14th octob^r last bap^t Nov: 7th 1723.

John son of Drury & Eliz Stith born 20th march last bap^t Aprill 10th 1724.

Wm son of John & Eliz: Sturdivant born 12th Nov: 1723 bap^t 2d feb. 1723-4.

——— a negro born belonging to ditto born 12th Sep^t 1723.

Rinnian A negro boy belonging to Dan Sturdivant born 4th May 1724.

Phillis A negro Girl belonging to ditto born May 5th 1724.

Han: d of Wm & Marg^a Stow born ——— bap^t May 24th 1724.

Sarah d of Rich & Agnis Smith born 30th Aprill last bap^t 2d July 1724.

fran d of Thompson & Ruth staples born 14th May Last bap^t June 21th 1724.

Joss s: of Geo: & Eliz: Smith born July 2d last bap^t 27th ditto 1724.

Fran: D. of Jmes & Mary Sturdivant born 25th August last bap^t decem: 31th 1724.

Catherine D. of Wm & Mary Smith born 25th octob^r last bap^t Aug: 22th 1725.

Joshua son of Wm and Mary Spain born 10th July last 1725.

David son of wm and Rebeckah Scogin born 27th nov^m 1725.

Sarah Dat of Jno and agnis Smith born 15th ap^r 1725.

Mary Dat of Robt and frances Stanfield born 6th Jan^r 1724.

francis son of Rich^{d} and mary Scogin born 22d augst 1725.

Elizab Dat of Th^{o} and mary Satterwhite born 22d Ap^{r} bap^{t} 8th may 1726.

matthew son of Jno and mary Sturdivant born Ap^{r} 29th bap^{t} 8th may 1726.

Olive Da^{t} of Jno and Jane Stroud born 17th feb^{r} bap^{t} June 6th 1726.

Mary D of Thomas and Ann Stunks born 12th Augt 1726.

Jane D of Wm and Mary Smith born 28th November 1726.

Abrattam Son of Wm and Marg^{t} Stow born 6th oct^{m} 1726.

Matthew Son of Eliz^{a} Stuard born 6th Jan^{r} 1726.

John Son of Wm and Margaret Stroud born 29th Nov^{m} 1726.

Eliz^{a} D of Th^{o} and Mary Sturdifant born 18th Nov^{m} bap^{t} 18 feb 1727.

Eliz^{a} D of Th^{o} and Ann Stunks Born 25th aprill 1728.

Jane D of George and Eliz^{a} Smith Born Jan^{r} last 1727 Bap^{t} 2d June.

Eliz^{a} D of Rich^{d} and ann Stanley Born 26th June 1727 Bap^{t} 29th July.

Priscilla D of William and Eliz^{a} Standley Born 10th august 1728.

Mary Dat^{r} of John and mary Sturdifant Born 21th Novm^{r} 1728 Bap^{t} Dec^{m} 25th.

Samson male Slave of Ditt^{o} Born 20 aprill 1728.

Robt Son of Robt and Frances Stanfield Born March 11th 1729.

Jonathan son of samuel and Mayr Sental Born 26th May Bap^{t} 6th June 1729.

Barthurst Son of Drury and Eliz^{a} stith Born 19th sep^{t} 1729.

Mary D of James and Mary Sturdivant Born 18th august 1729.

Tom Male Slave of Ditt^{o} Born 31th august 1729.

Martha & Lutia D^{rs} of Rich^{d} & Mary Scoggan Born 11th of July 1729.

William Son of William and Eliz^{a} Stanley Born 11th Jan^{ry} Bap^{t} 19th March 1729.

Matthew Son of Robert and Eliz^{a} Stoker Born august 21th Bap^{t} oct^{r} 2d 1729.

Wm son of Joseph and Mary Stroud Born 22d feb^{r} 1729 Bap^{t} 10th may 1730.

Eliz^{a} D of Lewellin and Mary Sturdvant Born 19th Novr 1729 Bap^{t} 31 may 1730.

frances D of Tho and Martha Spain Born 9th Decmr 1729 Bapt 30th march 1730.

Mary D: of Jno and Jean Stroud Born 29th aprill 1730 Bapt 12th July.

Toby Male Slave of James Sturdivant Born 1th Sepr 1730.

Eliza D of Wm & Mary Spain Born May 30th 1731 Bapt august 1th.

Mary D. of Jacob & Mary Summerell Born march 1th 1730 Bapt august 1th 1731.

amy female Slave of William & mary Spain Born 7th march 1730 Bapt 29th august 1731.

Prissilla D of Thomas & anne Stunks Born 25th august 1731 Bapt 10th octber.

Thomas william Shorie Son of William shorie Born 6th febr 1726.

Prisilla D: of Thom & martha Spain Born 7th Sepr Bapt 24th Sepr 1731.

Thomas son Drury & Eliza Stith Born 29th Dcer 1731 Bapt 24th apr 1732.

Elisabeth female Slave of Drury & Eliza stith Born 12th June 1725.

Poll female Slave of Ditto Born 20th June 1725.

Liewess male Slave of Ditto Born 3 febr 1726.

Christian female Slave of Ditto Born 5th Novr 1727.

Martha female Slave of Ditto Born 4th Novr 1728.

Hannah female Slave of Ditto Born 30th april 1730.

Ned male Slave of Ditto Born 29th Janry 1731.

Moses son of Jno & Eliza Smith born Novr 28th 1731 Bapt May 8th 1732.

Ann Datr of Robt & Eliza Stoaker born Jany 30th 1731 Bapt June 10th 1732.

Joell Son of Jno & Mary Sturdivant born May 18th 1732 Bapt June 16 1732.

Fras a girl Slave of Do born Apl 15 1730 Do.

Roben a boy Slave of Do born June 11 1732.

Eliza Datr of Biggen & Sarah Sturdivant born Apl 28th 1732 Bapt June 18th 1732.

David son of Joseph & Mary Stroud born 19th March 1731 Bapt June 18th 1732.

Mary dat^{r} of Rich^{d} & Mary Scoggan born 1st July 1732 bap^{t} 20th Augt 1732.

Mary dat^{r} of Lewellen & Mary Sturdivant born 20th Novr 1731 bap^{t} Sepr 20th 1732.

Ann Dat^{r} of Thos & Mary Savage born Decr 28 bap^{t} Decr 31. 1732.

——— Son of Jacob & Mary Summerrell Born 25th June 1727 Bap^{t} octb^{r} 15th.

Thomas Son of Partrick & Eliz^{a} Smith Born 23d octb^{r} 1731 Bap^{t} Jan^{r} 30th.

Phillis fe^{m} slave of James & mary sturdivant Born No^{r} 1731.

Ceasor male slave of ditto Born 15th feb^{r} 1732.

Mary Mullatto girl of Elizabeth stuart Born 19th Sepr 1732 Bap^{t} feb^{r} 4th.

Thomas son of Thomas & sarah suttawhite Born 15th Febuary 1732 Bap^{t} 26 march 1733.

Rebeckah D^{r} of James & Mary Sturdivant Born 22d ap^{r} 1733 Bap^{t} may 8th.

Roger male Slave of william & mary Spain Born 29th 1732 Bap^{t} 8th ap^{r} 1733.

antony male Slave of Ditto Born 7th feb^{r} 1732 Bap^{t} 8th ap^{r} 1733.

David son of Thomas & Martha Spain Born 1th march 1732 Bap^{t} 8th ap^{r} 1733.

Batt peter son of william & mary Spain Born 9th Sepr 1733 Bap^{t} 21th octb^{r}.

Bolling Son of Wm & Mary Starkes Born 21th Sepr 1733 Bap^{t} 11th nov^{r}.

Jane D: of Samuell & Mary Sentall Born 5th March 1733 Bap^{t} 20th May 1734.

Thomas Savage Decs^{d} 7th June 1734.

anne D: of John & Mary Shern Born 3d march 1733 Bap^{t} 23d June 1734.

anne D: of Richard and Mary Scogin Born 25th May 1734 Bap^{t} 11th august.

William Son of Jacob & Mary Summerell Born 29th May 1733 Bap^{t} July 2d.

Henry Fitz Son of Ann Sental Born 18th July 1734 Bap^{t} 26 day Septemb^{r}.

Isaac S of Luellin & Mary Sturdivant Born June 8. 1734.

James Son of James and Mary Sturdivant Born March 28. 1735 Bap^{t} 27 Ap^{r}.

John S. of John and Mary Stuart. Born 16 Octob^{r} 1734 Bapt 19 Ap^{l} 1735.

Margaret D of Robert and Elizabeth Stoaker Born Augt 26. 1734 Baptiz^{d} Sept 6th.

James S of William and Elizabeth Stanley Born Octob^{r} 16th 1734.

James S. of Daniel and Sarah Sturdivant Born 18th June 1735.

Henry S of James & Elisabeth Smart Born December ye 15 1740.

Martha D of Daniel & Sarah Sturdefant Born March ye 22 1740.

Abby female Slave belonging to James Sturdivant Born March ye 15th 1740.

Dennice Male Slave of James Sturdivant Born August ye 5 1741.

Thomas s of Thomas and Mary Short was Born August ye 6 1741.

Wm son of George and mary Smith Born August ye 4th 1739.

Fanney D of Ann Steward B August 1st 1740.

James S of Wm and Elizabeth Stanley B. Novem^{r} 11th 1740.

Elizabeth D of Thomas & Susannah Snipes B Novr 28th 1740.

James S. of John & Mary Still B Feb^{ry} 28th 1740–1.

Mary D. of Archiball & Mary Smith B May 11th 1741.

Susannah D of George and Mary Smith B Apr^{l} 8th 1741.

Hardship D of Clemond and ——— Stradford B Decem^{r} 2d 1740.

Frederick S. of Matthew & Sarah Smart B Feb^{ry} 8th 1740.

Wm S. of Richard Cross & Frances Still B April 13th 1740.

Benjamine Son of Richard & Agnis Smith Born June 22 1741.

Lidey female Slave of James Sturdavant B Febuary ye 25 1741.

Phebe female Slave of John Sturdavants B Febuary ye 20 1741.

Anne D of John & Mary Saunders Born Novr 9th 1741 & Bap^{t} Feb^{ry} 28th 1741–2.

Patie Tadlock D. of Mary Stephens Born Aug. 25th 1741 & Bap^{t} Feby 14th 1741–2.

Matthew S. of John & Anne Scoggins Born Decr 31st 1741 & Bap^{t} Ap^{r} 11th 1742.

John S. of Susanna Stewart Born Aug. 30th 1741 & Bap^{t} July 4th 1742.

Martha D. of Elizabeth Stewart Born Octob 3d 1741 & Bap^{t} July 4th 1742.

John a Slave of Col^{l} John Stith Born July 16th 1741 & Bap^{t} July 25th 1742.

William S. of William & Rebecca Saunders Born March 7th 1741–2 & Bap^{t} July 4th 1742.

Susanna D. of Francis Sturdivant Born Mar. 13th 1741–2 & Bap^{t} Aug. 7th 1742.

Drury S. of Patrick & Elizabeth Smiths Born Aug. 7th 1742 & Bap^{t} Sep^{t} 19th 1742.

Agge Slave of James Sturdavant was Born February 23d 1742.

Answich Female Slave of Ditto was Born April 24th 1743.

Agge D. of Mary Sauntie born Decr 25th 1731 & bapt^{d} Novr 14th 1742.

Clement S. of David & Obedience Smiths born Novr 27th 1742 & bapt^{d} May 15th 1743.

David S. of John & Priscilla Smiths born Decr 18th 1742 & bapt^{d} June 12th 1743.

Sylvana D. of James & Elizabeth Smarts born April 16th & bapt^{d} June 12th 1743.

Joshua S. of George & Mary Smiths born Septr 9th & bapt^{d} Octo^{b} 16th 1743.

Mary D. of George & Goodith Stillmans born Octob 8th & bapt^{d} Novr 13th 1743.

Martha D. of Mr Thomas & Mary Shorts born Decr 26th 1743 & bapt^{d} Jan^{ry} 22d 1743–4.

Joseph S. of Henry & Catharine Spires born Sep^{tr} 5th 1743 bap^{td} ap. 29th 1744.

Mally D of Daniel & Sarah Sturdivants born Aug 5th & bap^{d} Sep^{t} 17th 1744.

Lucy D. of Patrick & Elizabeth Smiths born Octob^{r} 12th & bapt^{d} Novr 25th 1744.

David & Elizabeth Children of David & Obedience Smiths born Decr 24th 1744 bapt^{d} Jan^{r} 7th 1744–5.

William S. of Mr John & Jemima Scotts born Sept^{r} —— 1740 baptized March 18th 1744–5.

Stephen S. of Mr John & Jemima Scotts born Aug. 31st 1742 baptized March 18th 1744–5.

Jumbo born Octobr 6th 1738 Sarah born Aprile 1739 Lucy born Novr 15th 1741 Nann born May 3d 1744 Harry born Decr 22d 1744 Doctor born Septr 14th 1745 Antony born Octobr 27th 1745	Slaves belonging to Capt Thomas Short baptized Janry 5th 1745–6.

Millinton S. of George & Mary Smiths was born Decr 7th 1745.

George S. of George & Elizabeth Scoggins was born Janry 28th 1745–6 & baptd Feb 19th 1745–6.

Daniel S of Daniel & Sarah Sturdivants was born March 29th & baptd June 1st 1746.

Cesar born March 29th 1748 Argan a female born 29th of Aprile 1748	Slaves belonging to Mr William Skipwith

Charles Son of Matt Steward and Mary Toney born Decemr 22d 1750.

Thompson son of John & Ann Sturdivant born Sepr 11th 1752.

Rachel a Negro Girl slave Belonging To Sr William Skipwith was Born May 13th 1761.

Mary Epes Stirdevent Daughter of John & Ann Stirdevent was Born Janr 18 1750.

Ann Isham Stirdevent Daughter of Ditto was Born Octor 10th 1754.

John Stirdevent son of Ditto was Born may 20th 1756.

Salley Stirdevent Daughter of Ditto was Born July 20th 1758.

Joel Stirdevent son of John & Ann Stirdevent was Born January ye 15th 1764.

Elizabeth, Daughter of William Stainback & Ann Lamboth his wife, was Born Novr ye 20th 1766.

John Sturdivant ye 3d Son of James & Mary Sturdivant was born the 22d day of September 1766. on a Monday between three & four OClk in the afternoon.

Ann Grant Spencer Daughter of Richd Spencer & Elizth his wife was Born February the 15th 1767.

Ann the daughter of William & Ann Stainback was born febr 20th 1769.

Rebecka Stainback Daughter of Wm and —— Stainback Born Feby 4. 1770.

Sally Hall, Daughter of Charles & Ellen Stimpson, was born January 24th & baptized February 26th 1792.

Elizabeth D[r] of Polly Spruce, a free Mulatto, born May 1st 1791, & baptized March 4th 1792.

Sarah Feild D[r] of Alexander Glass Strachan & Sarah his Wife, born January 22d and baptized March 18th 1792.

William Allfriend Son of Nancy a Slave belonging to Alex[r] Glass Strachan, born January 13th & baptized March 18th 1792.

William, Son of William Smith (of Petersburg) died April 8th & was buried April 9th 1792.

James, Son of William Scoggin & Selah his Wife, born April 7th 1790, & bap: May 13th 1792.

Sally Dau[r] of the same born Nov[r] 17th 1791, & baptized May 13th 1792.

Sarah Feild Dau[r] of Alexander G. Strachan died May 17th & was buried May 19th 1792.

John Taylor, Son of Judy, a Negroe Slave belonging to Anthony Sidner, was born December 18th 1791, & baptized May 27th 1792.

Letty Rays D[r] of Sally Rays, a Mulatto Slave belonging to Thomas Shore, born Aug[t] 9th 1791, & baptized June 17th 1792.

Mary Anne Thompson, D[r] of Joel Sturdivant & Frances W. his Wife, born July 9th 1789.

Sally Servant, D[r] of the same, born May 1st & baptized June 17th 1792.

Johnny S, of Jeanie, a Negroe Slave belonging to Zachariah Shackleford, born June 16th & baptized July 15th 1792.

John Benjamin, Son of Benjamin Smith, and Anne his Wife, was born September 23rd and baptized October 27th 1792.

Nathaniel Birchett, S. of James Sturdivant & Patsey his Wife, was born March 7th 1790, and baptized October 7th 1792.

Robert S. of D[o], born January 9th & baptized October 7th 1792.

Margaret Lang, Dau[r] of William Sharp, & Winnifred his Wife, born, June 5th & baptized Dec[r] 25 1792.

Sarah Howlet, Dau[r] of Launcelot Stone & Elizabeth his Wife, was born January 30th & baptized May 5th 1793.

Sarah Daughter of John Shore & Anne his wife, was born —— of —— & baptized June 28th 1793.

John Sturdevant sen^r died August 25th & was buried Septr 5th 1793.

Thompson Sturdevant died August 25 & was buried Septr 5. 1793.

—— Shore dau^r of Dr. John Shore buried 29th Novr 1794.

John Sturdevant died 18th & was buried 19th Feby 1795.

—— Sturdivant Son of Daniel Sturdivant buried 20th May 1795.

Daniel Sturdivant was buried Jany 21st 1798.

Helen Stott dau^r of Ebenezer Stott & Elizabeth his wife, born 15th Aug^t & bapt^d 18th of Septr 1796: died 5th Septr 1797.

T

Drury son of John & Cath: Tucker born 24 sep^t 1719 bap^t octob^r 24th 1720.

Anne dau: of Robt & Martha Tucker born Aug: 29th last bap^t octob^r 9th 1720.

Geo: son of Hen: & Hannah Thweat born 7th March last bap^t Aprill 18th 1720.

John son of John & Judith Thweat born 11th Jan^r last bap^t 17th Aprill 1720.

Tabitha dau of Geo: & Mary Tilman born 14th sep last bap xb^r 17th 1720.

Robt son of Joss: & Martha Tucker born 3d of Octob^r Last bap^t May 28th 1721.

Hen: son of Hen: & Mary Tatum born 28th May last bap^t 11th June 1721.

Amy dau of Francis & Anne Tucker born 12th May last bap^t July 9th 1721.

Abra: son of John & Anne Talley born 2d sep^tr last bap^t octob^r 21th 1721.

John son of John & Judith Thweat born 21th March Last Bap^t ————.

Sara dau of John & Ann Tucker born 12th Jan^r last bap^t May 13th 1722.

Micael son of James & Mary Tucker born 11th July 1721 bap 7th Octob^r 1722.

John son of Hen: & Hannah Thweat born 12 Aprill last bap^t 20th May 1722.

James son of John & Judith Thweat born 12 March last bap^t May 20th 1722.

John son of Rich & Eliz Tidmust born 28th decem 1721 bap^t 29th March 1722.

Joseph son of Robt & Martha Tucker born 22th June last bap^t 15th Aprill 1723.

Fran: son of Sam: & Mary Tatum born 17th of Aprill 1721.

susanna dau of Wm & Eliz: Tucker born 19th of Aprill 1721 bap 14th feb 1722–3.

John son of Sam: & Phebe Tatum born 7th June 1710.

Wm son of Sam: & Eliz: Tatum born 26th June 1717.

Eliz: dau of ditto born 29th of Nov: 1718.

John son of John Thweat died June 10th 1722.

Sam: son of Sam: & Eliz: Temple jun^r born 7th Jan^r 1720.

Mary dau: of ditto born 20th Sep^t 1722.

Wm son of Geo: & Mary Tilman born 21th May last bap^t Augt 22th 1723.

Nath: son of Nath: & Katheren Tucker born 20th feb^r last bap^t July 10th 1723.

Fran: son of Fran: & Anne Tucker born 1st Nov last bap^t 7th Nov 1723.

Lucy d: of Ja: & Mary Tenheart born 10th May last bap^t 15th sep^r 1723.

Tho Temple had A Child born June 4th And died 7th ditto 1724.

Frances D of Thompson & Ruth Staples born 14th May last bap^t June 21th 1724.[*]

Eliz d: of Jno & Judith Thweat born 11th March last bap^t May 24th 1724.

Mary d: of Ja: & Mary Thweat born 28th feb last bap^t May 24th 1724.

Susanna d: of Hugh & Mary Lee born 10th feb: last bap^t May 24th 1724.

Frances D of Hen: & Mary Tatun born June 6th bap^t 12th July 1724.

---

*Erased in original.—C. G. C.

Geo S: of Wm and Eliz: Tucker born 4th Sep^{tr} 1723 bap^{t} 11th octob^{r} 1724.

Ruth d of John & Anne Tally born 28 Jan^{r} last bap^{t} Novr 6th 1724.

John son of John & Anne Tucker born 9th Sep^{tr} last bap 6th Nov 1724.

Geo: Son of Wm & Eliz: Tucker born 4th sep^{t} 1723 bap^{t} 11th octob^{r} 1724.

Obedience D: of Hen: & Hannah Thweat born 15th sep^{t} last bap^{t} 1st Nov 1724.

Eliz: D: of Wm & Eliz Temple born 7th March last bap^{t} May 16th 1725.

Dan: of Robt & Martha Tucker born Jan^{r} lest bap^{t} May 10th 1725.

Geo S of Roger & Mary Tilman born 21th Jan^{r} last bap^{t} May 30th 1725.

phebe D of Edmond & Elisabeth Trayler born 2d Sepr bap^{t} 18th octob^{r} 1725.

Frances Da^{t} of Allen and mary Tye born 16th march last 1724.

Frances Da^{t} of James & Ann Thweat born Dce^{m} ye 25 bap^{t} ye 8th Aprill 1725.

Jno son of Jos and Eliz^{a} turner born 11th Dce^{m} 1725.

Jamey slave of Jo^{s} Turner born 19th Aprill 1726.

Dinah slave of D^{o} born 8th may 1726.

Wm son of Wm and Mary Totty born Dec^{m} 5th 1725 bap^{t} May 30 1726.

John son of Frances and Ann Tucker born 25th June bap^{t} 28th sep^{tr} 1726.

——— Da^{t} of Jno and Anne Tucker born ———.

Robert son of Nathaniel and Emelea Tatam born 30th Janr^{y} 1725.

John Son of Jno and Judith Thweat born 22d august 1726.

Daniel Son of William and Eliz^{a} Tucker born 29th Jan^{r} 1725.

Amy D of John and Mary tucker born 23d August 1726.

francis Son of John and Ann tucker born 3d Jan^{r} 1726.

Anne D of of James and Mary Thompson born 3 feb^{r} 1726 bap^{t} 25: 1727.

Eliz^{a} D of Roger and Mary tillman born 15th Nov^{m} 1726.

Martin Son of Rich^{d} and Mary tally born 15th July 1727.

Agnis D of henry and Mary Tatam born 14th Oct^{m} bap^{t} 26th November 1727.

Eliz^{a} D of Roger and Mary Tillmon 15th Nov^{m} 1726.

Martha D of Robt and frances Tucker born 10th July 1727.

Eliz^{a} D of Henry and Hanna Thweat born 20th august 1727 bap^{t} 1t octb^{r}.

Judith D of John and Martha Traylor Born 6th March 1727.

Wm Son of Wm and Mary Totty Born 15th March 1727 Bap^{t} 3d June.

Th^{o} Son of Th^{o} and Eliz^{a} Tucker Born 30th March 1728 Bap^{t} 28th July.

Holenberry Son of Joseph and Eliz^{a} Turner Born 14th June 1728 Bap^{t} July 28th.

archer of John and Mary Traylor Born aprill 20th 1729.

Roger Taylor Dces^{d} 7th June 1729.

Wm Son of John and Judith Thweat Born 11th Sepr Bap^{t} 4th March 1728.

ann Dau of James and Mary Thompson Born 3d feb^{r} 1726.

Elizabeth D of Henry & ——— Tucker Born 2d Sepr 1729.

Lucretia D. of James & Mary Tucker. Born. 5th June 1729.

ann D of francis and ann Tucker Born 19th feb^{r} Bap^{t} 19th March 1729.

Matthew Son of Matthew and Mary Tolbert Born 27th Novm^{r} 1729.

Christian D of James and ann Thweat Born 9th feb^{r} 1729 Bap^{t} 31th May 1730.

David Son of Joseph and Martha Tucker Born 24th Dcember 1729 Bap^{t} 31th May 1730.

William Son of allen and Mary Tye Born 10th May 1730 Bap^{t} July 12th 1730.

Thomas Son of Thomas and Eliz^{a} Totty Born 5th aprill 1730 Bap^{t} 12th July.

David Son of John and Mary Tucker Born 25th Sepr 1730.

William Son of Robert & Mary Taylor Born 22d august Bap^{t} 20th Nov^{r}.

Nevil Son of Daniel & Eliz^{a} Tucker Born 25th aprill 1730.

Kezia Dat^{r} of Jno and Judith Tally Born 23d Sepr 1730.

William Son of Jno and Phelis Thacker Born 10th Nom^{r} 1730.

Ann D: of Joseph & Eliz^{a} Turner Born 8th Nom^{r} 1730.

Hanna D: of George & frances Tucker Born 30th March 1731 Bap^{t} 29th august.

Frances D of Robert & Frances Tucker Born 11th March 1730.

——— D of Henry & ELisabeth Tucker Born 8th May 1731 Bap^{t} 29th august.

Amy D: of William & Eliz^{a} Temple Born 3d June 1731 Bap^{t} octb^{r} 17th.

Lucretia D of Joseph & Lucretia Tucker Born 15th august 1731 Bap^{t} 10th octbe^{r}.

Sarah D: of George & Mary Tillman Born 8th octb^{r} Bap^{t} novmb^{r} 6th 1731.

Martha D: of James & anne Thweatt Born 29th Sepr Bap^{t} 14th novmb^{r} 1731.

Littleberry Son of peter & mary Tatam Born 10th ap^{r} Bap^{t} 18th novm^{b} 1731.

Marth D: of John & Judith Thweat Born 21th octb^{r} 1732 Bap^{t} Dce^{r} 17th.

Littlepage of Hen^{y} & Judith Tally Born 13th Jany 1731 Bap^{t} May 7th 1732.

Warner son of James & Mary Tucker born 15th April 1732 bap^{t} 1st June 1732.

Jno son of Roger & Eliz^{a} Tayler born Novr 12th 1731 bap^{t} Decr 20th 1731.

Jane dat^{r} of Jno & Eliz^{a} Tomlinson born July 16th 1732 bap^{t} Sepr 20th 1732.

Burrell son of Miles & Sarah Thweat born 4th July 1732 bap^{t} Sepr 17th 1732.

Wilmut dat^{r} of Jno & Mary Trayler born 19th Augt 1731 bap^{t} May 22d 1732.

Rebeckah d of Thomas & Frances Temple Born 18th Novr 1732 Bap^{t} 29th Dce^{r}.

Blanch d of Edmond Eliz^{a} Traylor Born 17th Sepr 1732 Bap^{t} dce^{r} 31th.

Martha D^{r} of Francis & ann Tucker Born 21th feb^{r} 1732 Bap^{t} march 3d.

Isham Son of Jno & mary Tucker Born 1th feb^{r} 1732 Bap^{t} 3d march.

Joseph Son of John & mary Tucker Born 14th Novr 1732 Bap^{t} Jan^{r} 14th.

Joseph Son of Joseph & Eliz^a Turner Born 2d ap^r 1733 Bap^t 20th may 1733.

William Son of Robert & Frances Tucker Born 15th ap^r 1733 Bap^t 3d June 1733.

Agnis D^r of allen & mary Tye Born 9th March 1732 Bap^t 3d June 1733.

James Son of Matthew & Mary Tolbot Born 7th Novr 1732 Bap^t 7th ap^r 1733.

Frances of Henry & amy Tucker Born 25th ap^r 1733 Bap^t June 3d 1733.

Margret D: of William & Mary Totty Born 30th feb^r 1732 Bap^t octb^r 20th 1733.

William Son of Edward & Mary Traylor Born 12th June 1733 Bap^t 21th octb^r.

Robert Son of George & frances Tucker Born 3d dce^r 1733.

Judith D: of George & Eliz^a traylor Born 8th march 1733 Bap^t 7th ap^r 1734.

Martha D: of Henry & Judith Tally Born 31th Jan^r 1733 Bap^t 10th March.

John Son of John & Margret Tillman Born 20th ap^r 1734 Bap^t 26th May.

Lucia D: of William & Sarah Tate Born 19th feb^r 1733 Bap^t 20th May 1734.

William Son of Roger & Eliz^a Taylor Born 16th May 1734.

Willmoth D: of Richard & Eliz^a Thorn Born 10th June 1734 Bap^t 4th august.

Elizabeth daugh^r of James & Ann Thweatt Born Augt 5 1734.

William Son of Miles & Sarah Thweatt Born 14th Septr 1734 Bap^t ye 9 Feb^{ry} 1734-5.

Peter S. of Peter and Elizabeth Thomas Born 2d Xb^r 1734.

Lucretia D. of John and Mary Traylor Born Augt 16th 1734.

Ann D. of William & Sarah Trayler Born Augt 23d 1734.

Solomon S. of Allen and Mary Tye Born 20th March 1734.

Abraham S. of John and ——— Tucker Born 22d Jan^{ry} 1734 Bapt. 7th March.

Elizabeth D. of Joseph and Elizabeth Turner Born 6th Octob^r 1735.

Nathan S of William & Sarah Tate Born the 23 april 1736.

William S of William & Sarah Tate Born august 26 1738.

John Son of Charles & Frances Thomson B Aug[t] 28th 1740.
Rebeckah D. of Thomas & Mary Twitty B Sep[r] 5th 1740.
Mary D of Richard & Mary Thomas B March 12th 1739-40.
David S of Peter and Elisabeth Thomas B Dc[r] 24th 1740.
Thomas. S. of Thomas & Anne Tunks Born Oct. 29th 1741 & Bap[t] Nov[r] 29th 1741.
Samuel. S. of William & Sara Tates Born Nov 3d 1741 & Bap[t] Dce[r] 12th 1741.
David. S. of Drury & Elizabeth Thwets Born Oct. 27th 1741 & Bap[t] Dec[r] 25th 1741.
Anne. D. of Henry & Elizabeth Toudress Born Aug 15th 1741 & Bap[t] Jan[ry] 3d 1741-2.
David. S. of Samuell & Mary Temples Born Oct. 23d 1741 & Bap[t] Jan[ry] 24th 1741-2.
Miles. S. of Abram & Helenour Tuckers Born Feb[y] 16th 1741-2 & Bap[t] Mar. 14th 1741-2.
Alick. S. of Miles & Sara Thwets Born Jan[ry] 29th 1741-2 & Bap[t] May 9th 1742.
Catharine. D. of Richard & Mary Thomas's Born May 3d 1742 & Bap[t] July 4th 1742.
Anderson. S. of Allan & Mary Tyes Born Mar 11th 1741-2 & Bap[t] July 25th 1742.
Martha D. of William & Sara Traylors Born Oct. 18th 1741 & Bap[t] Aug 14th 1742.
Elizabeth D. of Drury & Elizabeth Thwets born Feb. 10th 1742-3 & bapt[d] March 27th 1743.
Peter S. of Peter & Mary Tatums Born Jan[ry] 27th 1742-3 & bapt[d] May 29th 1743.
Judith D. of John & Judith Thweats born June 19th 1743 & bapt[d] July 23d 1743.
Elizabeth D. of Samuel & Francis Temples born Ap[r] 1st & bapt[d] May 13th 1744.
Jacob S. of Samuel & Mary Temples born Sept[r] 24th & bapt[d] Nov[r] 11th 1744.
Lucretia D. of William & Elizabeth Temples born Sept[r] 16th & bapt[d] Nov[r] 11th 1744.
Mary D. of Joseph & Lucretia Tuckers born Aprile 3d & bapt[d] May 26th 1745.

Nathaniel S. of Rob[t] & Keziah Tatums born March 30th & bapt[d] May 12th 1745.

Edith D. of Drury & Elizabeth Thweats born Aprile 25th & bapt[d] June 30th 1745.

Mary D. of Samuel & Frances Temples was born March 26th 1745.

John S. of James & Sarah Thweats was born June 12th & bapt[d] July 28th 1745.

Mary D. of Edward & Mary Thweats was born Sep[tr] 17th 1745 & bap[td] Nov[r] 3d 1745.

Elizabeth D. of William & Anne Turners was born Sep[tr] 3d & bap[td] Nov[r] 10th 1745.

Elizabeth D of Richard and Sarah Taylors born 29th June 1736.

George S of Ditto born 23d June 1738.

Richard Son of Ditto born 26th Decem[r] 1739.

Nanney D of Ditto born 1st May 1742.

Alice Taylor departed this life 17th August 1750.

Jack Male Slave of Richard & Sarah Taylors born 14th June 1750.

Frankee Daughter of Drury & Eliz[a] Thweat born ——— bap[t] Feb 17th 1750.

Tabitha, Daughter of James & Sarah Thweats born 27th May 1749.

James Son of Ditto born April 3d 1752.

Frank Male Slave of Ditto June 15th 1748.

Feby Female Slave of ditto born Septem[r] 14th 1750.

Nan Female Slave of Ditto born March 11th 1752.

Ned Male Slave of Rich[d] & Sarah Taylors born May 12th 1753.

Thom, Son of Betty, a Slave belonging to John Thweatt, born November 25th 1791, & baptized April 9th 1792.

Charlotte, Dau[r] of Cate, a Slave belonging to the same, born April 9th 1791, & baptized April 9th 1792.

Aleck, Son of Cressy, a Slave belonging to Richard Taylor, born March 1st, & baptized April 29th 1792

Mary-Henry, D[r] of Henry Tench & Nancy his Wife, born March 12th & bap: June 21st 1792.

Notise, Dau[r] of Abby, a Negro Slave belonging to John Thweatt, was born January 25th & baptized Nov[r] 18th 1792.

William Taylor, of the Town of Petersburg, died December 30th 1792 and was buried January 1st 1793.

Candace, Dau^{r} of Peter Temple & Nanny his Wife, born July 18th 1792 & baptized January 4th 1793.

William Eppes, Son of Eppes Temple & Elizabeth his Wife, born Decr 16th 1792 & baptized March 24th 1793.

Edward, S, of Dorcas, a Mulatto slave belonging to John Thweatt, was born December 17th & baptized April 1st 1793.

U–V

Abigaell dau: of John & Elinor Vaughan departed this life feb: 23th 1720–1 in the 6th year of her Age.

James son of Rich & Alice Vaughan born Jan: 23th last bap^{t} March 4th 1721–2.

Eliz dau of Wm & Ann Vaughan born 14th Sepr last bap^{t} Novr 8th 1721.

Anne dau: of Hen: & Martha Vauden born 19th Jan^{r} last bap^{t} 21th March 1722.

Pearc son of Wm & Prissilla Vaughan born 15th March last bap^{t} 16th Sep^{t} 1722.

Luis son of Nico: & Ann Vaughn born 20th feb 1719 bap^{t} June 7th 1722.

Abra son of ditto born 16th March 1721 bap^{t} June 7th 1722.

Joss son of Dan: & Eliz: Vaughan born 14th decem last bap^{t} feb: 3d 1722–3.

Martha D of Rich & Alice Vaughan born 18th Nov: last bap^{t} Sep^{tr} 12th 1724.

Wm son of Wm & Priss Vaughan born 5th August last bap^{t} Jan 10th 1724–5.

Jane a negro belonging to Wm Vaughan Senr born 25th Novr 1724.

Williams s of Dan: & Eliz: Vaughan born 14th August last bap^{t} Jan^{r} 17th 1724–5.

Hen: s: of Hen: & Martha Vaden born 6th feb^{r} last bap^{t} March 28th 1725.

Isham Son of Daniel and Eliz Vaughan born feb^{r} ye 4th 1725.

James Son of Wm and Prissillah Vaughan born 6th March bap^{t} 18th sep^{t} 1725.

Eliz^{a} D of Jno and Catherine lee born ——.

James Thompson Son of Sarah Vaughan born 24th Sep^{t} 1726.

Henry Son of Henry and Eliz^{a} Vodin born 12 Sep^{t} 1694.

Sipio M Slave of Wm and Julia Vaughan born 31 Decemberr 1726.

Richard Son of Richard and Alce Vaughan born 16th Oce^{m} 1726.

Eliz^{a} D of Nicolas and Ann Vaughan born 18th Aprill 1727.

Ann D of Daniel and Eliz^{a} Vaughan Born 15th Dec^{m} 1727.

Susannah D of Wm and prissilla Vaughan Born 25th Decm^{r} 1727.

Frances D of William and frances Vodin Born 18th Sep^{t} 1728.

Nicolas Son of Nicolas and ann Vaughan Born 20th febr 1728.

Susannah D of Henry and Martha Vodin Born 19th Novmber Bap^{t} 26th Decm^{r} 1728.

abigal D of Wm and Mable Vaughan Born 15th 1729 Jan^{r}.

Peter Son of Daniel & Eliz^{a} Vaughan Born 28th Sepr 1730.

Caleb son of Wm & Mable Vaughan born 25th January 1731 bap^{t} Ap^{l} 30th 1732.

Mary dat^{r} of Hen^{y} & Mary Voden born 14th Jany 1731 bap^{t} May 7th 1732.

Phebœ dat^{r} of Robt & Martha Vaughan born 18th May 1732 Bap^{t} June 1st 1732.

Ann dat^{r} of Danl & Ann Vaughan born 10th of Octr 1732 bap^{t} Novr 12th 1732.

Wilmot D^{r} of Isham & Temperanc Vaughan Born 3d March 1732 Bap^{t} 3d June 1733.

Mary D^{r} of William & pricilla Vaughan Born 12th November 1732 Bap^{t} 27th May 1733.

Burrell Son of Henry & Martha Voden Born 2d Sepr 1733 Bap^{t} 21th octb^{r}.

abner Son of William & Mable Vaughan Born 25th feb^{r} 1733 Bap^{t} 28th ap^{r} 1734.

Mary daughter of Daniel & Ann Vaughan born ye 1 January 1734–5 Bap^{t} 9 Febrary.

Henry Son of Morris and Rebecca Vaughan born 14 Decr 1734 Bap^{t} 9th February.

Peter male Slave of Wm & Julia Vaughan Born 14 Feb^{ry} 1734.

Sarah D of John and Sarah York Born 17th of Feb^{ry} 1734 Bapt 4 May 1735.[*] Carry'd to Y.

James S. of Elizabeth Valentine Born August 27th 1733.

Nicholas S. of Robert. and Martha Vaughan Born the 21st Novr 1734.

Sarah D. of Samuel & Margrett Vaughan Born 29 July 1735.

Anne D of William and Mary Vaughan Born 7th Jan^{ry} 1735.

Mabel D of William & Mabel Vaughan Born January ye 12 1740.

Ruth. D. of Nathanael & Amith Vaughans Born Decr 28th 1741 & Bap^{t} Mar. 7th 1741–2.

Abram S. of Peter & Anne Vaughans Born Mar. 11th 1741–2 & Bap^{t} Apr 18th 1742.

Anne D. of William & Mary Vaughans Born Jan^{ry} 20th 1741–2 & Bap^{t} June 13th 1742.

Thomas S. of Thomas & Elizabeth Vaughans Born July 12th 1742 & bap^{t} Septr 12th 1742.

David S. of Morris & Rebecca Vaughans born Jan^{ry} 1st 1741–2.

Sylvana D. of Samuel & Margret Vaughans born Aug. 1st & bapt^{d} Novr 7th 1742.

Phebe D. of Daniel & Anne Vaughans born Novr 12th 1743 & bapt^{d} Jan^{ry} 1st 1743–4.

Phebe D. of Salathiel & Anne Vaughans born Novr 23d 1743 & bapt^{d} Jan^{ry} 8th 1743–4.

Martha D. of Maurice & Rebecca Vaughans born March 10th 1743–4 bapt^{d} May 13th 1744.

William S. of Salathiel & Anne Vaughans born Feb. 16th 1744–5 bapt^{d} Aprile 14th 1745.

Silvester S. of Samuell & Margaret Vaughans born March 14th 1744–5 & bapt^{d} May 19th 1745.

James S. of Joshua & Sarah Vaughans was born Jan^{ry} 22d, bapt^{d} Feb 23d 1745–6.

David Son of Salathiel & Anne Vaughans born ——— bap^{t} 4th March 1749–50.

Ezekiel Son of Henry and Eliz^{a} Vaughans born 29th Decem^{r} 1750.

Jessee Son of Joshua & Sarah Vaughans born ——— Bapt^{d} 28th Ap^{r} 1751.

---

* Erased in original.—C. G. C.

Jemina Daughter of Morris & Rebecka Vaughans born ——— bap^{t} 21 June 1752.

Mary D of Williams & Ellinor Vaughans born July 26th 1752.

John, Son of Howel Underhill (of Sussex County) & Nancy his Wife, born March the 3d, & baptized April 6th 1792.

Anne Unckle, Dau^{r} of Lewis Unckle, was buried September 22nd 1792.

Sally Newsum Dau^{r} of John Verell jun^{r} and Martha his Wife, born April 15th, and bap: September 23rd 1792.

Lucetta, Dau^{r} of Sarah a Negroe Slave, belonging to John Verell jun^{r} was born February 24th and baptized September 23rd 1792.

Peg, Dau^{r} of Peg, D^{o}, D^{o}, was born March 4th and baptized September 23rd 1792.

Mary-Ann-Elizabeth, Dau^{r} of Drury Vaughan & Susannah his Wife born April 21st & baptized July 14th 1793.

Robert Winn, Son of Enoch Vaughan & Mary his Wife, born April 3rd & baptized October 13th 1793.

W

Martha dau: of Cha: & Eliz: Williams born 18th octob^{r} last bap^{t} 20th Nov: 1720.

Martha dau: of Joss: & Mary Wynn born 1st May last bap^{t} 8th Jan^{r} 1720–1.

Tho: son of Tho: & Mary Webster born 20th June last bap^{t} March 5th 1720–1.

Gardner son of Geo: & Eliz: Wilson born 15th feb: last bap^{t} March 26th 1721.

Daniel son of Wm & Rosamund Worsham born last Nov: bap^{t} March 26th 1721.

Martha dau of Wm & Dorcas Worsham born 18th Nov last bap^{t} Aprill 21th 1721.

David son of Geo: & Sibbil Williams born 22th of Aprill last bap^{t} May 28th 1721.

Tho: son of Tho: & Amy Wilson born June 21th 1721 bap^{t} June 21th 1721.

Jeremiah son of Hen: & Mary Walthall born 28th Aprill lest bap^{t} June 4th 1721.

Martha dau: of Wm & Dorcas Worsham born 26th march last bap^{t} June 4th 1721.

Abraham son of Wm & Sarah Whitamore born 14th feb: last bap^{t} Octob^{r} 8th 1721.

Sarah dau: of David & Sarah Williams born 15th March last bap^{t} July 18th 1721.

Stevens son of ye decd: Hen: Wilson & Mary his relict born 15th sep^{tr} last bap^{t} octob^{r} 8th 1721.

Dan: son of John & Cath: Walker born feb^{r} 14th 1712–3 bap^{t} Novr 2d 1721.

Wm son of John & Mary West born 12th Sep^{tr} last bap^{t} Nov 8th 1721.

Ann dau of Rich & Mary Walthall born 25th octob^{r} last bap^{t} 5th March 1721–2.

Sarah dau of Rich: & Judith Wilson born 23d decem last bap^{t} March 11th 1721–2.

Eliz: dau of Robt & Mary West born 21th March last bap^{t} May 13th 1722.

Eliz: dau of Cha: & Eliz: Williams born 24th Aprill last bap^{t} May 27th 1722.

Wm son of Wm & Rose: Worsham born 27th sep^{t} last bap: Nov 25th 1722.

Rich: son of Rich: & Rebecca White born 13th Nov: 1721 bap^{t} March 27th 1722.

Cha: son of Ja: & Olive Williams born 23d feb: 1721 bap^{t} March 29th 1722.

Mary dau of Robt & Mary Wynn born 26 Nov: 1722.

Joss son of ditto born 3d August 1722.

Joss son of Joss & Mary Wynn born 24th Jan last bap^{t} Aug: 13th 1722.

Cha son of Cha & Ann Williams born 26th May last bap^{t} 13th Aug: 1722.

Eliz dau of Hen: & Phebe Walthall born 10th Jan last bap: March 10th 1722–3.

Burgess son of John & Ann Wall born 22th May 1722 bap^{t} June 20th 1723.

Joss: son of Joss & Martha Wall born 21th feb^{r} last bap^{t} June 20th 1723.

Sibilla dau of Geo & Sibilla Williams born 18th this Inst bap August 22th 1723.

Jude a negro girl belonging unto Hen: Walthall born 31th August 1723

Eliz: D: of Wm & Anne Wall born 6th last sep^{tr} bap^{t} August 6th 1723.

John son of Hen & Mary Walthall born 5th Nov: 1723.

Marg^{a} dau of Cha & Eliz: Williams born 19th of Nov: last bap^{t} 22th decem 1723.

Wm son of Wm & Martha Womack born 10th of sep^{tr} last bap^{t} Jan^{r} 19th 1723-4.

John son of Tho & Eliz: Wilkinson born 25th Nov last bap^{t} Aprill 10th 1724.

Mary d of David & Sarah Williams born 29th August last bap^{t} 10th Aprill 1724.

Wm son of Wm & Martha Womack born 10th sep^{t} last bap^{t} Jan^{r} 19th 1723-4.

Rich s of Dan & Anne Wall born 19th Aprill last bap^{t} June 21th 1724.

Anne d of Wm & Sarah Wells born 8th March last bap^{t} May 20th 1724.

Ephraim son of Fran: & Eliz: West born 2d feb^{r} last bap^{t} sep^{tr} 12th 1724.

Abra son of John & Mary West born 2d feb^{r} last bap^{t} 16th sep^{tr} 1724.

Rich son of Rich & Judith Wilson born 18th May last bap^{t} Nov 1st 1724.

Obedience D of James & Olive Williams born 10th May last bap^{t} Nov 6th 1724.

Rich son of John & Eliz: Williams born 14th Sep^{t} last bap^{t} 6th Nov 1724.

———— of Ja & Kath Wood born ye last of October bap^{t} Aprill 19th 1724.

Maball D: of Hen: & phebe Walthall born 10th of May last bap^{t} June 27th 1725.

Christopher s: of Rich: & Mary Walthall born 28th Jan: last bap^{t} feb^{r} 6th 1724-5.

Marg^{a} D. of Joss: & Mary Wynn born 25th Nov: last bap^{t} feb^{r} 8th 1724-5.

Marg^{a} D of Ditto born 31th decemb^{r} 1723.
Drury s of Wm & Ann Wall born ye last July bap^{t} Jan^{r} 12th 1724–5.
Isham s: of Joss & Martha Wall born 25th Nov last bap^{t} May 30th 1725.
Cha: s of Cha & Eliz: Williams born 11th June 1725.
susanah and francis daughters of Robt and Mary west born 2d March bap^{t} 6th March 1725.
David Son of Jno and Ann Wall born 12: June bap^{t} 21: aug 1725.
John Williams Departed this life Jan^{ry} ye 16th 1725.
Sarah Da^{t} of Charles W^{ms} And Ann born 20th Sep^{t} 1725.
henry Son George and Sybellah williams born 4th november 1725.
Daniell Son of Daniell and Amy Wall born 25th march 1726.
Ann Da^{t} of Th^{o} and mary Westmoreland born 12 ap^{r} bap^{t} June 6th 1726.
John Son of David and Sarah Williams born Jan^{r} 23d Bap^{t} June 6th 1726.
Dick Slave of henry Waltal born 15th August Last 1726.
Joseph Son of Jno and Eliz^{a} William born 15th July 1726.
Margarit D of Joseph and Margaret Wilson born 27th octm 1726.
Thomas Son of Joseph and Mary Wyn born 6th Aprill 1726.
Sarah D of henry and Martha Wilson born 9th Dece^{m} 1726.
Agnis Waller D of Charity Smithis born 30th May 1726.
francis Son of francis and Eliz^{a} West born 9th feb^{r} 1726.
Ann Daughter of Richard and Aann Westmoreland born 2d aprill 1722.
——— of Wm and Ann Wall born born 15th Dce^{mr} 1726.
henry Son of Joshua and Martha Wall born 3d Jana^{r} 1726.
Mary Daughter of John and Ann Wall born 13th Dec^{m} 1726.
Mary D of Charles and Eliz^{a} Williams born 19th aprill 1727.
Lucy D of Charles and Ann Williams born 6th May 1727.
Jane D. of John and Mary Willingham born 2d May 1727.
John Son of Jno Eliz^{a} Watts born 10th oct^{m} 1726.
Joel Son of John and Catherine Willson born 6th November 1727.
Joseph Son of Edward and Martha Willson born 1th feb^{r} 1727.
Peter Son of Jame and ann Williams born 7th Dce^{r} 1728.

Henry Son of Essex and ann Worsham Worsham Born 5th august 1727.

Marthew Son of Th^{o} and Margrat Westmoreland Born 18th March 1727.

Martha and th^{o} of Robt and Mary West Born 17th May 1728 Bap^{t} June 2d.

Micael Son of John and ann Willson Born 18th aprill 1728 Bap^{t} 2d June.

Henry Son of Henry and Phebe Wallton Born 25th June 1728 Bap^{t} 19th July.

Helen Son of Charles and Eliz^{a} W^{ms} Born 3d June 1728 Bap^{t} July 28.

Frances D of. Wm and Roson Worsham Born 8th feb^{r} 1727 Bap^{t} 28th July.

Mary D of George and Sibylla Williams Born 15th ocb^{r} 1727.

Susan D of Charles and Prissilla Williamson Born 1d march 1727.

Joel Son of Thomas and Frances Walker Born 14th June 1727.

Eliz^{a} D of Aron and Mary Wood Born 5th June 1727 Bap^{t} July 23d.

Th^{o} Son of Wm and Eliz^{a} Walter Born 16th Jan^{r} 1727.

Mary D of henry and Martha Willson Born 24th No^{m} 1728 Bap^{t} 27th Dce^{m}.

Winiford D of Joshua and Martha Wall Born Jan^{r} 20th 1728.

Wm Son of Wm and frances Wells Born 20th oct^{r} Bap^{t} 25th Dce^{r} 1728.

ann D of John and Eliz^{a} Williams Born 25th oct^{r} Bap^{t} 1 Decem^{r} 1728.

Laurana D of Eliz^{a} Womack Born 20th March 1728.

———— of George and Sibellah W^{ms} Born 12th oc^{tr} 1728 Bap^{t} 6th aprill 1729.

Robert Son of David and Mary Walker Born 10th oct^{r} 1729 Bap^{t} 26th octr.

Alexander Son of Ditto Born 3d octob^{r} 1727.

Linder female Slave of Ditt^{o} Born 2d august 1728.

Simon Male Slave of Ditto Born 20th June 1727.

Phebe female Slave of Ditto Born 12 Sep^{t} 1729.

Martha D. of Danl & Amy Wall. Born 23d June 1729 Bap^{t} 26th Oct^{r}.

John Son of Charles & Ann Williams Born 17th March. Bap^{t} Sepr 2d 1729.

Edward Son of Thos & Eliz^{a} Winingham. Born 3d May 1729.

Susannah & Abigall D^{rs} of Joseph & Isabella Westmoland born 30th Aprill 1729.

John Son of Robt & Temporance West Born 10th May 1729.

John Son of frances and Eliz^{a} West Born 2d March 1729.

ann D of Wm and Margret Whood Born 24th March Bap^{t} oct^{r} 2d 1729.

Jno Son of Charles and Eliz^{a} Williams Born 11th March 1729 Bap^{t} 10th May 1730.

Amy D of Th^{os} and francis Walthal Born 19th feb^{r} 1729 Bap^{t} 10th May 1730.

Jack Slave of Garrat Waltal born 14th March 1725.

Lusie Dater of Robt and and Mary West Born feb^{r} 4th 1729 Bap^{t} 31th May 1730.

Gerrat Son of Gerrat and Eliz^{a} Walthal Born 25th feb^{r} 1729 Bap^{t} 10th May 1730.

John Son of Charles and Prissilla Williamson Born 24th 1730 Bap^{t} 10th May 1730.

Miles Son of James and Olive Williams Born 15th Jan^{r} 1729 Bap^{t} 31th May 1730.

Richard Son of aron &: mary Wood Born 15th Sepr 1729.

John Son of francis and Eliz^{a} West Born 2d March 1729 Bap^{t} 2d May 1730.

Phebe and Mary D^{s} of Jno and Mary Willson Born 16th June 1730.

Sarah D of John & Susannah Write Born 2d august 1730 Bap^{t} 30th octb^{r}.

Precillah D of Thomas & Eliz^{a} Winingham Born 30th June 1730.

Mary D of Richard & Mary Walthal Born 15th Sepr 1730 Bap^{t} 9th Dce^{r}.

Mary D of Robert & Temporance West Born 7th Sepr 1730.

Eliz^{a} D of Henry & Martha Willson Born 28th Sepr 1730.

Francis son of Henry & Mary Wyatt Born 29th March 1731.

Zachariah Son of John and ann Wall Born 25th July 1731 Bap^{t} aug^{s} 29th.

David son of Wm & francis Wells Born 23d November 1730 Bap^{t} Jan^{r} 10th.

Anne D: of Edward Whit Born 11th Dce^r 1730 Bap^t 17 Jan^r Eliz^a his Wife.

Benjamine son of francis & martha Walthal Born 9th feb^r 1730 Bap^t 3d march 1730.

Richard Son of Henry & Phebe Walthal Born 15th June 1731 Bap^t July 27th.

Ruben Son of abraham & Sarah Wells Born 28th July 1731 Bap^t 30th august.

Henry Son of Isack & Sarah Winingham Born 16th June 1731 Bap^t 12th Sep^r.

Jones of David & Sarah Williams Born 23d ap^r 1731 Bap^t 12th august.

Martha D: of Henry & Martha Willson Born 7th sep^r 1731 Bap^t 7th octb^r.

Tabitha D: of Joshua & Mary Wynn Born 23d May 1731 Bap^t 10th octb^r.

Mary D: of Charles & anne Williams Born 5th august 1731 Bap^t 10th octbe^r.

Samuel Son of Jno & anne Willson Born 31th octb^r 1730 Bap^t 23d ap^r 1732.

David & Mary twinns of David & Mary Walker Born 6th March 1731 Bap^t 23d ap^r 1732.

Joell Son of Edward & Mary Winfield born 30th Decem^r 1731.

Christian dat^r of Robt & Mary West born Ap^l 8th 1732 bap^t May 7th 1732.

Edward son of Jerrott & Eliz^a Walthall born Mar. 17. 1731 bap^t June 4th 1732.

Wm Son of of Wm & Sarah Winingham born 16th Decr 1731 bap^t July 2d 1732.

Christian dat^r of Jno & Mary Winingham born 20th March 1731 bap^t July. 7. 1732.

Robert son of Robt & Eliz^a Williams born 17th June 1732 bap^t 13th Augt 1732.

Essex son of Essex & Ann Worsham born 11th June 1732 bap^t 20th Augt 1732.

Edward Son Cha & Eliz^a Williams born 11th June 1732 bap^t 10th Sepr 1732.

John Son of John & Mary Willson born 11th Sepr 1732 bap^t 12 Novr 1732.

Mary d of Daniel & amy Wall Born 23d august 1731 Bap^{t} 2 Jan^{r}.

James Son of Joseph & Sybilla Westmoreland Born 28th Sepr 1731 Bap^{t} 2d Jan^{r}.

Susanah D: of John & Susanah Write Born 26th Dce^{r} 1732 Bap^{t} feb^{r} 4th.

Phebe D: of Wm & frances Wells Born 31th Dceb^{r} 1732 Bap^{t} feb^{r} 4th.

Judith D^{r} of Henry & Martha Willson Born 24th feb^{r} 1732 Bap^{t} 28th march 1733.

Elisabeth D: of Francis & Eliz^{a} Wyat Born 22d Dce^{r} 1732 Bap^{t} feb^{r} 25th.

Christian D^{r} of Joseph & Sibylla Westmoreland Born 26th feb^{r} 1732 Bap^{t} 20th may 1733.

Frances of John & Eliz^{a} Williams Born 21th feb^{r} 1732 Bap^{t} 8th ap^{r} 1733.

Mark Son of John & ann Willson Born 20th Novm^{r} 1732 Bap^{t} 20th may 1733.

amy D^{r} of Robert & Temperanc West Born 24th Sepr 1732 Bap^{t} 17th June 1733.

Amy D^{r} of Francis & Eliz^{a} West Born 2d June 1733 Bap^{t} 5th August.

Peter Son of Thomas & Frances Walker Born 19th July 1733 Bap^{t} 28th Sep^{r}.

amy D: of Thomas & Mary Winingham Born 11th august 1733 Bap^{t} Novr 4th.

abram Son of abram & Sarah Wells Born 7th Sepr 1733 Bap^{t} 11 Nov^{r}.

John Son of Daniel & amy Wall Born 10th Dce^{r} 1733 Bap^{t} Jan^{r} 27th.

Elisabeth D of Thomas & Margaret Westmoreland Born 31th octb^{r} 1733.

Elisabeth D of Charles & pricilla Williamson Born Jan^{r} 1733 Bap^{t} 2d feb^{r}.

Josep^{t} Son of Charles & Elisabeth Williams Born 2d Jan^{r} 1733 Bap^{t} 2d feb^{r}.

Ann D: of Henry & phebe Walthall Born 10th March 1733 Bap^{t} 14th ap^{r} 1734.

frances D: of Joshua & Martha Wall Born 11th octb^{r} 1733 Bap^{t} 24th March 1734.

Hannah D: of John & ann Winfield Born 12th feb^r 1733 Bap^t 20th May 1734.

John Son of Charles & ann Williams Born 14th May 1734 Bap^t 4th august.

Mary D: of Adam & Elener Wells Born 18th June 1734 Bap^t 11th August.

John Son of Edward & Mary Whitt Born 10th July 1734 Bap^t 11th august.

John Son of William & Sarah Westbrook Born 4th May 1733 Bap^t July 15th.

Henry Son of Richard & Mary Walthall Born 16th May 1733 Bap^t July 13th.

Daniel Son of francis & Martha Walthall Born 8th march 1732 Bap^t July 13.

Freeman Son of David & Mary Walker Born 3d September 1734 Baptizd ye 9th.

Betty female Slave of Ditto Born ye 15th October 1734.

John Son of Robert & Eliz: Williams Born July 27th 1734.

Martha D. of David and Sarah Williams Born 22d March 1734 Bap^t 4 May 1735.

James S of Henry & Martha Willson Born 19. Decemb^r 1734 Bap^t 9 January.

Mary D. of William and Sarah Westbrook Born 3d January. 1734-5.

Ephraim S. of Robert & Temperance West Born 4th Sep^t 1734.

David S. of Thomas & Francis Walker Born Sep^t 23d 1734.

Gerrald S. of John and Mary Winingham Born ye 1st August. 1734 Baptizd 13th Octo.

Thomas S. of John & Elizabeth Whitmore Born 4th Aprill 1734.

Edward S. of Langsdown & Elizabeth. Washington Born the 18th Octob^r 1734.

Margerett D. of Barnabas and Joyce Wells Born ye 1 Decr 1734.

Jane D. of Abraham & Amy Wells Born 23d Sep^t 1735.

Anne D. of Adam and Eleanor Wells Born 6th Octob^r 1735.

Joseph Son of Susanna Wright born 3d Feb^ry 1734.

Jeremiah Son of David & Sarah Wells Born ye 16. Decr 1735.

Jonathan S of Jonathan & Elisabeth Webster Born ye 11 D November 1740.

Anne D of Henry & Martha Wilson Born ye 10 of Febuary 1740.

Francise D of William & Francise Wells Born ye 4th of April 1741.

Deury s of Adam & Elener Wells Born ye 4 May 1741.

Roland s of Thomas & Jane Williams Born July ye 19 1739.

Jane D. of Thomas & Jane Williams Born June ye 12 1741.

Thos S. of Robert & Ann Whitehall B December 17th 1738.

Robert S of Robert & Temperance West B Septem^{r} 17th 1740.

John S. of Joseph & Martha Worsham B October 3d 1740.

Robert Hicks Son of Joseph & Sib Westmorland B Sepr 16th 1740.

Joseph S of Thomas & Margaret Westmorland B Novr 16th 1740.

William S of Miles & Elisabeth Wootten B Feb^{ry} ye 14th 1740.

Mary D. of Martin & Anne Wilkisons Born Octob 28th 1741 & Bap^{t} Novr 22d 1741.

Drusilla D. of Charles & Priscilla Williamsons, Born Novr 12th 1741 & Bap^{t} Decr 27th 1741.

Margret D. of Robert & Francis Wines Born Oct. 25th 1741 & Bap^{t} Jan^{ry} 17th 1741–2.

John S. of Thomas & Francis Wilsons Born Decr 5th 1741 & Bap^{t} Decr 19th 1741.

John S. of Robert & Sara Weeds Born Decr 10th 1741 & Bap^{t} Feby 28th 1741–2.

Martha D. of Joshua & Martha Walls Born Aug. 23d 1741 & Bap^{t} Apr. 11th 1742.

Amy D. of Robert & Anne Whitehalls Born June 7th 1742 & Bap^{t} July 4th 1742.

Daniel S. of Joshua & Martha Worshams Born Apr 29th 1742 & Bap^{t} July 4th 1742.

Susanna D. of Francis & Elizabeth Wyats Born June 15th 1742 & Bap^{t} July 25th 1742.

Elimelech S. of John & Anne Wilsons Born Apr. 18th 1742 & Bap^{t} Aug. 10th 1742.

Edward S. of Edward & Mary Winfields Born July 2d 1742 & Bap^{t} Sep^{tr} 19th 1742.

Edward S. of Thomas & Elizabeth Woodliths born Novr 9th 1742 & bapt^{d} Decr 12th 1742.

Anne D. of John & Elizabeth Wests born Novr 5th & bapt^{d} Decr 19th 1742.

William S. of Edward & Mary Wheats born Aug 12th 1742 & bapt^{d} Decr 25th 1742.

Henry S. of Henry & Mary Wilkasons born Feb^{ry} 26th 1742–3 & bapt^{d} May 22 1743.

William S. of William & Mary Williams born Aug. 30th 1743 & bapt^{d} Octob^{r} 9th 1743.

Isham S. of William & Francis Wells born Aug 4th 1743 & baptd Octob 9th 1743.

Sarah D. of Adam & Helenor Wells born Feb^{ry} 18th 1742–3.

Thomas S. of Thomas & Jane Williams born Octob^{r} 24th 1743 & bapt^{d} Decr 18th 1743.

Winnifred a female slave belonging to Willm Wells born Feb 5th 1743–4 bapt^{d} May 14th 1744.

Amie a female slave belonging to Ditto born Jan^{r} 9th 1743–4 bapt^{d} May 14th 1744.

Henry S. of Adam & Eleanor Wells born Feb 5th & bapt^{d} March 15th 1744–5.

Hannah D. of Edward & Mary Winfields born Decr 12th 1744 bapt^{d} March 3d 1744–5.

Mary D. of James & Elizabeth Wortham born Decr 13th 1744.

Thomas S. of William & Mary Williams born Decr 27th 1744 bapt^{d} March 24th 1744–5.

Mason D. of Robert & Frances Wynnes was born May 29th & bapt^{d} Septr 1st 1745.

Agnes D. of Henry & Mary Wilkisons was born Sep^{tr} 8th bapt^{d} Oct 1745.

Katharine D. of Henry & Martha Wilsons born Octob^{r} 24th & bapt^{d} Novr 1745.

Millison D. of James & Jane Williams was born Decr 3d 1745 & bapt^{d} Jan^{ry} 6th 1745–6.

Mary D. of Joshua & Martha Worshams was born Novr 4th 1745 & bapt^{d} March 2d 1745–6.

Lucy D. of Thomas & Jane Williams was born Jan^{ry} 2d 1745–6 bapt^{d} March 16th 1745–6.

Sarah D. of Mr. Anthony & Anne Walke was born Feb. 16th 1744–5.

Ben Peter Mason	Negroes belonging to Ditto born	Septr 1744 Decr 6th 1745	bapt^{d} Ap. 2. 1746.

Sloman S. of Joshua & Lucretia Wynne was born Octob. 13th 1745 baptd Feb. 16 1745-6.

Mary D. of Arthur & Alice Wyatts was born Janry 24th & baptd Feb 23d 1745-6.

Pattie D. of Adam & Eleanor Wells was born Ap. 6th baptd May 19th 1746.

Thomas S of Thomas & Francis Wilson was born March 30th & baptd June 1st 1746.

Robert S of Mr. Antony & Anne Walkes was born Aug. 16th & baptized Sept 1747.

Antony S of Ditto departed this Life Septr 1747.

Neptune a negro boy born Decr 24th 1747 } belonging to Mr.
Bristol born May 1748 } Anthony Walke.

Sarah D of Arthur & Alice Watts was born Janry 24th 1748.

Richard Son of Richard & Hannah Wells born 17th February 1747-8.

Randolph Son of Adam and Elanor Wells born 15th Feby 1749.

Eliza Daughter of James & Jane Williams Born 21st April 1752.

Frederick Son of ditto Born October 24th 1749.

Joshua Son of Ditto Born ——.

Hannah Daughter of Miles & Martha Williams born June 7th 1752.

Edward Son of Arthur & Alice Watts born April 20th 1753.

Jos Walkers Register.

Gollorthun Walker son of Joseph & Penelope Walker was born Sepr ye 10th 1745.

Reubin Walker their son was Born march the 20th 1751.

Penelope their Daughter was Born August the 3d 1753.

Pattey their Daughter was Born Novemr the 19th 1755.

Lettisha their Daughter was Born Febr the 9th 1758.

Martin their son was Born Novr the 16th 1759.

Jean Woolfolk, Wife of Fracis Woolfolk, of Sussex County, died March 21st, & was buried April 6th 1792.

John, Son of Ludwell Williams (of Sussex) & Johannah his Wife, born March 25th 1792.

Sally Allen Daut of John Winn (of Sussex) & Katy his Wife, born Jany 8th & bap: May 13th 1792.

Martha, Dau^{r} of Edmund Weathers (of Sussex) & Mary his Wife, born Mar: 18th & bap. May 13th 1792.

William Baird, S, of Joseph Westmore and Elizabeth his Wife, born November 10th 1791 and baptized August 21st 1792.

Henry, S, of Wm Worsham & Clarissa his Wife, born August 17tn 1791 & baptized Decr 28th 1792.

Y

Edw: son of Edw: & Mary Yeans born 5th Jan^{r} last bap^{t} 14th Aprill 1723.

John: son of Edwd & Mary Yanes born 2d July last: bap^{t} 26 sep^{t} 1725.

Eliz^{a} D of Edward and Mary Yeans Born 6th May 1727 Bap^{t} oct^{m} 1th.

Thomas Son of Edward and Mary Yanes Born 7th feb^{r} 1728 Bap^{t} novm 23d.

Jane D of John and Sarah York Born 7th Sepr 1729.

Francis Cadet Son of Micael cadet and Temperance young Born 25th octb^{r} 1731 Bap^{t} 25th Dcer.

Martha dat^{r} of Jno & Sarah York born 3d June 1732 bap^{t} Augt 13th 1732.

Josiah Son of Edward & Mary yanes Born 17th June 1733 Bap^{t} 8th Sepr 1733.

John Son of Saml & Judith young Born 10th Sepr 1733 Bap^{t} Jan^{r} 27th.

Sarah D. of John and Sarah York born 17th Feb^{ry} 1734 Baptizd 4th May 1735.

James Smith The son of William & Dianer Yarbrough was Born Sepr ye 2d 1745.

Richard son of Ditto was Born March ye 18 1747–8.

Elizth Daughter of Ditto was Born October ye 23 1750.

William son of Ditto was Born April ye 7th 1753.

Ozwell son of Ditto was Born april 24 1756.

Joseph son of Ditto was Born November ye 4 1758.

Ruth Their Negro Girl slave was born Jan^{r} ye 15 1751.

Marsilva their Negro Girl slave was Born March 22d 1753.

Anthoney their Negro Boy was born March the 1st 1763.

Sukey their Negro Girl was Born January the 31 1766.

Dianer, Wife of William Yarbrough departed this life, may the 18th 1767 aged 42 years.

Tom a Male slave Belonging To William Yarbrough was born may the 3d 1768.

Nanny a Negro Girl belonging to William Yarbrough was Born February the 13th 1769.

Henry. S. of Henry Young & Winney his Wife, of Bath Parish, Dinwiddie, born May 3d and baptized September 17th 1792.

ERRATA, &c.

Page 9, line 16, change "(is)" to "[is]."

Page 19, line 10, erase period after "that" and insert after "Rich."

Page 56, line 16, for "Jo^{s} Thompson" read "Ja^{s}," etc.

Page 56, line 22, for "Rohowiçh" read "Rohowick."

Page 65, line 18, for "M^{e}clain" read "M^{c}clain."

Page 107, line 31, for "Ilonour Whitmore" read "Honour Whitmore."

Page 108, line 34, for "Whweet" read "Thweet."

Page 121, line 33, for "Disbute" read "Dispute."

Page 145, line 17, for "Chennlis" read "Chamlis."

Page 145, line 24, for "Jordon" read "Gordon."

Page 158, line 20, for "Cole" read "Cate."

Page 188, line 8, "Jean Jones" may be "Fran Jones" in original; probably correct, however, as here rendered.

Page 215, line 21, for "Seoggin" read "Scoggin."

Page 218, line 5, for "Hanks" read "Hauks."

Page 241, line 14, for "Wiikerson" read "Wilkerson."

Page 275–80, wherever date is shown thus "172—." it should have been printed thus "172 [ ]."

Page 281, line 29, "Nunsry" illegible in original; apparently as here rendered.

Page 282, line 36, for "Benton" read "Berton."

Page 314, line 12, for "Hankins" read "Haukins."

Page 328, line 34, for "Williaw King" read "William," etc.

INDEX.

www.ingramcontent.com/pod-product-compliance
Lightning Source LLC
Chambersburg PA
CBHW060131280326
41932CB00012B/1485
* 9 7 8 0 8 0 6 3 4 8 4 3 8 *